# THE
# UNITED ARAB EMIRATES

# The Middle East in the International System

ANOUSHIRAVAN EHTESHAMI &
RAYMOND HINNEBUSCH,
SERIES EDITORS

# THE
# UNITED ARAB EMIRATES

## A Study in Survival

Christopher M. Davidson

LYNNE
RIENNER
PUBLISHERS

BOULDER
LONDON

Published in the United States of America in 2005 by
Lynne Rienner Publishers, Inc.
1800 30th Street, Boulder, Colorado 80301
www.rienner.com

and in the United Kingdom by
Lynne Rienner Publishers, Inc.
3 Henrietta Street, Covent Garden, London WC2E 8LU

**Library of Congress Cataloging-in-Publication Data**
Davidson, Christopher M.
    The United Arab Emirates : a study in survival / Christopher M.
Davidson.
      p. cm. — (The Middle East in the international system)
    Includes bibliographical references and index.
    ISBN 1-58826-274-X (hardcover : alk. paper)
    1. United Arab Emirates—Politics and government—1972–
2. Globalization.   3. Civil society—United Arab Emirates.   I. Title.
II. Series.
DS247.T88D384    2005
953.57—dc22

                                                          2004020540


**British Cataloguing in Publication Data**
A Cataloguing in Publication record for this book
is available from the British Library.


Printed and bound in the United States of America


The paper used in this publication meets the requirements
of the American National Standard for Permanence of
Paper for Printed Library Materials Z39.48-1992.

     5   4   3   2

# Contents

v

# Tables and Figures

## Tables

## Figures

# Acknowledgments

*The United Arab Emirates: A Study in Survival* is the product of almost five years of fieldwork and archival research in both the UAE and the UK. Much of the information contained in this book was derived from personal interviews, personal correspondence, and seminars, and I am greatly indebted to a very large number of informants, facilitators, and benefactors spread across many locations. These have included university academics, professional analysts, journalists, consular staff, agency staff, veteran expatriates, local and federal government officials, and prominent members of three of the seven ruling families. While the majority of these individuals have preferred to remain anonymous given the very real sensitivities associated with many of the topics addressed in this volume, I would like to take this opportunity to thank the following people for their advice and, in some cases, their practical assistance.

In Abu Dhabi: Frauke Heard-Bey of the Centre for Documentation and Research at the Presidential Court for her factual contributions and proofreading. Peter Hellyer of the Ministry of Information and Culture for his content-based contributions. The staff members of the Department of Research Studies at the Abu Dhabi Chamber of Commerce and Industry for their supply of statistics and other materials. The staff members of the Abu Dhabi Cultural Foundation for their supply of materials. The Osman and Hinchcliffe families of Abu Dhabi for their practical assistance. Marjorie Estivill, Karen Oremus, and Christopher Brown of the College of Arts and Sciences at Zayed University in Abu Dhabi for their practical and technical assistance. The students at Zayed University in Abu Dhabi who were enrolled in my "Social and Economic Trends in the Gulf" and "Development and Underdevelopment" courses for their enormous content-based contributions, most of which were derived from unpublished oral family histories.

In Dubai, Sharjah, and the northern emirates: The staff members of the

Department of Research Studies at the Dubai Chamber of Commerce and Industry for their input, in particular Soheir El-Saba for her content-based contributions. The staff members of the Dubai government's Department of Economic Development, in particular the director of media relations, for their supply of statistics and other materials. The staff members of the Juma al-Majid Cultural Foundation in Dubai for their supply of materials. The Rodrigues, Sultan, Galadiri, and al-Ghurair families of Dubai for their practical assistance. Peter Stromberg of the College of Arts and Sciences at Zayed University in Dubai for providing me with career opportunities in the later stages of the project. The faculty members of the Department of Sociology at the University of Sharjah for their input, in particular Sulayman Khalaf.

In the United Kingdom and United States: Mehran Kamrava of the University of California in Los Angeles for his detailed correspondence and theoretical contributions. Gerd Nonneman of the Department of Politics at the University of Lancaster in England for his content-based and theoretical contributions. Michael Pinder for his detailed correspondence, content-based contributions, and practical assistance. The treasurers of the Royal Historical Society in London and the Carnegie Trust for the Universities of Scotland in Dunfermline for their practical assistance. Abd al-Fattah el-Awaisi and the faculty of the Al-Maktum Institute of Arabic and Islamic Studies at the University of Abertay in Scotland for their content-based contributions. Oliver Richmond and Joshua Stacher of the Department of International Relations at the University of St. Andrews in Scotland for their theoretical contributions. Magnus Ranstorp of the Centre for the Study of Terrorism and Political Violence at the University of St. Andrews in Scotland for his practical assistance and for providing me with career opportunities in the early and later stages of the project. The Carradice family of St. Andrews for their practical assistance. Michael Sonenscher of King's College, University of Cambridge, for providing me with career opportunities in the early stages of the project. Raymond Hinnebusch of the Institute for Middle East Studies at the University of St. Andrews in Scotland for his enormous content-based contributions, detailed correspondence, and practical assistance; for providing me with career opportunities in both the early and later stages of the project, supervising my PhD thesis, and offering advice; and for his overall professionalism and dedication to scholarship and his important contributions toward much of the theoretical framework employed in this book. Finally, James and Mary Davidson for their proofreading and of course their enduring support.

With regard to transliterations, although some of the accuracy (namely long vowel indications) has been reduced in the interests of simplification for an international audience, the majority of Arabic and Farsi words appearing in this text have been transcribed by the author according to

Modern Standard Arabic (MSA) conventions rather than having been reproduced as they appear in secondary sources. The only exceptions are those words that are popularly misspelled when converted into English.

*—Chris Davidson*

# THE
# UNITED ARAB EMIRATES

# Introduction

In one of history's great ironies, the past thirty years have witnessed the transformation of the shaikhdoms of the lower Gulf from sleepy, undeveloped backwaters of the British Empire into some of the world's wealthiest oil producers, with socioeconomic conditions comparable with—and in some cases superior to—those of many Western states. Furthermore, following the withdrawal of their superpower protector and in defiance of the critics, the federation of these shaikhdoms, the United Arab Emirates (UAE), has remained a mainstay of stability in an increasingly volatile Middle East and, crucially, has managed to maintain and even consolidate an essentially traditional polity despite rapid modernization and the often intrusive forces of globalization. Underneath these layers of success and stability, however, the UAE's development path has been far from smooth, and a number of problems, many of which appear to be deeply ingrained, continue to surface. Thus the purpose of this book is not only to consider the UAE's significant socioeconomic achievements and the survival of its seemingly anachronistic political structures, but also to provide a greater understanding of some of the key pathologies that have persistently undermined the development objectives of the nascent state.

In this volume, I seek to expand the body of empirical knowledge provided by the small number of existing works on the subject,[1] while concurrently attempting to assess the UAE's development within the context of recent research conducted on the region's other surviving traditional monarchies and oil-rich "rentier states." (Most notable in this regard are the applied core-periphery theories of Abdulkhaleq Abdulla and Jacqueline Ismael,[2] the rentier models of Jill Crystal and Gregory Gause,[3] the civil society approaches of Sheila Carapico and Mehran Kamrava,[4] and Michael Herb's investigation of the evolution of "dynastic monarchy" structures.[5]) Specifically, I draw on the two major schools of thought: dependency theories that can be used to provide an excellent starting point for explaining the remarkable stability of the many structures that remain in place and continue to shape the UAE's development; and modernization theories and their variants that provide not only a better understanding of the UAE's significant efforts to adapt within "dependent development," but also to underscore the importance of some of the development problems that are now being faced and, under the guise of benign globalization, highlight the potential for future change.

Working within a dependency framework, Chapter 1 provides a detailed overview of the UAE's inherited situation, including the early peripheralization of the region's economy and its historic reliance on foreign labor, foreign technology, and the export of a single primary product, the emergence of significant pre-oil rentier structures, and the external reinforcement of a client elite capable of blocking both participation and indigenous reform.

In an attempt to account for the inaccuracies of early modernization theory and to explain why these precapitalist traditional structures were not swept away during the oil era, in Chapter 2 I apply a combination of rentier-dependency models and "modernization revisionism" (emphasizing how certain traditional forces can be adapted and made functional[6]) to illustrate the way in which the UAE's monarchies have managed to construct multidimensional "ruling bargains" between themselves and their local populations, thereby securing both political stability and much needed sources of nondemocratic legitimacy.

Chapter 3 focuses on the efforts of these "selective modernizing" monarchies to reduce some of the most obvious weaknessess of their dependent economies and thus improve their long-term situation. While much attention is given to the significant successes in this field, primarily with respect to the UAE's recent economic diversification, I show that there have also been serious development pathologies and that in many ways these must be regarded as the hidden costs of escaping the inevitability of early modernization predictions and the demise of tradition.

In Chapters 4 and 5 I illustrate some of the ways in which the freezing and reinforcement of the structures that initially allowed for the stability can in many ways be seen to have gone too far, as allocative systems, neopatrimonial/clientalist networks, complex elite orientations, nonparticipatory structures, a lack of transparency, and retarded civil society have all made legal-rational objectives difficult to achieve.

Finally, I suggest that greater modernization, especially in the form of positive globalizing forces, may still provide solutions for these pathologies in the future. Indeed, whereas the first wave of globalization may have reinforced dependency structures and problems, and there still remains great uncertainty, there are clear indications that something of a second wave may well lead to liberalizing reforms, a more diverse economy, and a stronger civil society.

## Notes

1. See, for example, AL-ABED (2001); ABU BAKER (1995); ANTHONY (1975, 2002); FENELON (1973); HAWLEY (1970); HEARD-BEY (1996); AL-MUSFIR (1985); AL-NABEH (1984); AL-NUHAYYAN (2000a, 2000b); PECK (1986); AL-SAYEGH (1997, 1998, 1999); AL-SHAMSI (1999, 2001); and VAN DER MEULEN (1997).

2. See ABDULLA (1985); and ISMAEL (1993).

3. See CRYSTAL (1990, 1995); and GAUSE (1994, 2000).

4. See CARAPICO (1998); and KAMRAVA (2000, 2002).

5. See HERB (1999).

6. For a discussion of modernization revisionism, or "revised modernization theory," see RANDALL and THEOBALD (1998), pp. 45–48. Modernization revisionist studies have demonstrated not only that traditional institutions may adapt and coexist with modern institutions, but also that the process of modernization may actually revitalize dormant traditional institutions and practices.

# 1

# The Historical Background

In the name of God, the merciful, the compassionate. Praise be to God, who hath ordained peace to be a blessing to His creatures. There is established a lasting peace between the British Government and the Arab tribes, who are parties to this contract.[1]

Under the federal banner of the United Arab Emirates, the shaikhdoms of the lower Gulf were transformed by the massive oil booms of the 1970s. A development miracle was born, and remarkably, these once impoverished territories suddenly found themselves guardians of the modern world's richest resource. There is no doubt that this great and rapid wealth, more than any other factor, has been the driving force behind almost all aspects of change and development in the region. Certainly, as the later chapters of this book demonstrate, oil and its politics can rarely be separated from any study of the Gulf states, and the UAE is no exception. Nevertheless, it is the purpose of this chapter to establish that the oil era cannot be used as the sole starting point for any comprehensive study of the lower Gulf. Nor, for that matter, can one focus exclusively on the time of independence and the subsequent creation of the federal state. Instead, one must also consider the region's traditional structures, its preoil dynamic, and its historical relations with other powers. Indeed, while some of these features have now faded from memory, a significant number have survived and evolved; and as important antecedents of the current order, many of these have continued to form the cornerstones of the contemporary state.

## The Traditional Economic Structure

The first postage stamps to be issued in the lower Gulf depicted a string of pearls, local sailing craft, and date palms.[2] Together with animal husbandry, hunting, fishing, and of course periodic desert raiding and caravan protection,[3] these were the activities that formed the basis of the region's traditional economy for much of the nineteenth and early twentieth centuries. Although agriculture was severely constrained by the harsh climate, date farming did provide some sustenance in the vast interior, especially for those near to the many oases that stretched across the Rub' al-Khali, and for those working the *falaj*-irrigated lands in the shadow of the Hajar mountains.[4] Animal husbandry, especially of camels and sheep,[5] provided a similarly limited source of wealth and nutrition, as did the hunting of gazelles and the fishing of grounds close to the northern coastlines.[6] Pearl diving or "pearling," however, provided a much higher but more seasonal source of income for those who traveled to the seashores or to the many tiny islands of the lower Gulf, and in turn numerous other associated activities and industries such as pearl trading and boat building were also able to flourish in the small coastal towns.

Indeed, pearling soon became the region's primary economic activity during the preoil era, given the lower Gulf's abundance of oysters and the shallowness of its seas. However, it is important to note that, over time, the intensity of the activity did vary as a function of both international demand and regional security.[7] The industry reached its zenith in the late 1890s, a period when wealthy merchants from Bombay and even as far afield as East Africa would frequent the Gulf during the pearling season *(al-ghaus al-kabir)* and buy up all of the best specimens for export to their affluent foreign clients.[8] Furthermore, many of these merchants began to settle in the growing ports, and many of their descendants remain based there today, even if their present-day economic activities are very different to those of their ancestors. J. G. Lorimer provides a good insight to the scale of this boom, reporting in his *Gazetteer of the Persian Gulf* that in one year alone (1896–1897) pearls valued in excess of 100 lakhs were exported (approximately three-quarters of a million pounds sterling), this compared with just 10 lakhs per year in the 1870s.[9]

Moreover, as by-products of the pearling industry and the pearling trade, a number of other economic activities began to emerge in these towns. Indeed, while there were some small-scale cottage industries producing pottery and items of metal- and woodwork, most of the manufacturing that did exist was in direct response to the needs of the pearling community. Most obvious, pearling led to a boom in the local boat-building industry, with Umm al-Qawain and Dubai establishing themselves as the main centers for the assembly of a wide variety of craft built from imported African ropes and sails.[10] Furthermore, as pearling brought greater wealth to the region, other activities geared toward more luxury items were also able to develop, a good example being tailoring and weaving.[11] Although weaving was already a well-established activity in the region, with many traveling great distances to buy from the renowned tailors in Buraimi, the greater purchasing power during the pearling boom undoubtedly catalyzed its growth in the coastal communities. Indeed, as a testament to this period one can walk the older quarters of Ra's al-Khaimah today and still see row after row of professional tailors.

However, by the early 1930s the pearling industry and these associated coastal activities had already begun to decline due to a combination of worldwide depression and increasing competition from Japanese cultured pearls.[12] This rapid downswing illustrates how, even in preoil times, the lower Gulf's economy was already heavily reliant on the export of a single primary product and was therefore extremely vulnerable to external market forces. Indeed, as Lorimer noted: "Were the supply of pearls to fail . . . the ports of Trucial Oman, which have no other resources, would practically cease to exist; in other words, the purchasing power of the inhabitants of the eastern coast of Arabia depends very largely upon the pearl fisheries."[13] Similarly, as Abu Jaml, the son of a wealthy Dubai "pearl king," emphasizes, pearling had led to an early form of dependency in the region, thus creating many dilemmas for his father's generation:

> Pearl prices were governed by the dynamics of supply and demand, as is the case with oil today, and there were times when the catch of a whole season did not fetch enough money to cover the cost of the meals consumed by the divers and sailors. At one stage things got so bad that the British government decided to give pearl traders access to markets in Ceylon. But in return for this the traders had to forfeit two-thirds of their earnings to the British and Ceylonese governments to be shared equally between them.[14]

Clearly, as the operations of these pearl kings expanded, they became increasingly susceptible to the fluctuations of the international economy, and in some cases they even had to forego most of their profits simply to survive, as this example describes. Furthermore, and even more ruinous, many of these men were also resistant to the concept of diversifying their interests. Indeed, as Jaml explains, pearling and pearl trading had come to represent not only a source of income but also a way of life, and as such the pearlers were overly cautious when it came to considering any other activity:

> Even though some pearl merchants went bankrupt as a result of the slumps that hit the pearl markets from time to time, most of them would not explore new areas of business. I was with my father in Bombay when he sold pearls worth more than one million rupees and was advised by a Bahraini merchant to buy Madinat Hotel that was offered for sale at 70,000 rupees. My father told the man that he was out of his senses to advise him to freeze so much money. . . . [T]hat hotel is still in business in Bombay while the pearl era eclipsed more than 40 years ago![15]

This is entirely the fate that the contemporary UAE, and especially Dubai, has been trying to avoid. Hotels, commerce, light industry, and all manner of activities are being explored as part of an unceasing attempt to diversify the narrow base of the oil dependent economy.[16]

Although clearly not self-sustaining, another important aspect of the Gulf's pearling economy was that it was beginning to exhibit signs of indigenous capitalist development. Indeed, while the region has often been associated with noncapitalist relations of production in which capital and labor were rarely separated (the farmers would own their land, the Bedu would own their camels, the fishermen would own their boats, etc.), the growth of the pearling industry nevertheless led to an evolution of capitalism not too dissimilar to that found in feudalist-capitalist Europe. The key to this change was the matter of ownership of the pearling boats. In the early years of pearling, the well-practiced *ikhluwi* was a communal system in which the crew would jointly own a boat and would share all of the season's profits, distributed according to the type of work each individual performed. However, as the size of boats increased and the period of expeditions lengthened, it became more expensive to maintain and equip such boats. This was further exacerbated by the influx of expatriate pearling crewmen, who were present for only a short period and required a more tangible wage. As such, the *'amil* system became more prevalent. Under this system the boats were owned and fitted out by wealthier individuals who possessed the necessary capital outlay, and in return would receive a large part of the take at the end of the season, leaving the rest to be divided among the crew. Inevitably, this arrangement led to the emergence of two distinct groups: those who were unable to jointly equip a boat and therefore had to offer themselves as salaried crewmen, and those who were able to invest in pearling boats and thereby claim a share of the profits without even having to participate in the expedition.[17] Furthermore, this system of financial interdependence was being continually reinforced by the captains, many of whom doubled up as brokers *(musaqqam)* and were often relied on by their crewmen to obtain the necessary outlay from the entrepreneurs. These intermediaries charged high rates of interest (between 10 and 25 percent) and also claimed a further share of the profits for themselves.[18] Thus, in many ways a clearly identifiable "pearling proletariat," the *ghasa,* was beginning to emerge underneath an early form of a capitalist/entrepreneurial class.[19]

Last, alongside these pearling-related activities and their mode of organization, it is also worth noting some of the other forms of commerce that were practiced in the area, as before the nineteenth century, overseas and regional trading had provided another important means of livelihood for those in the coastal towns and for those based near the major *souqs* of the interior. Indeed, the lower Gulf maintained trade links with many foreign ports, including Manama, Basra, Muscat, and even Zanzibar. Similarly there were many well-established land routes for caravans from Oman and other parts of Arabia. Many of the old trading posts, such as the camel and fruit markets north of Buraimi oasis, still function today, and continue to help support the local economy while also boosting the tourist appeal. Simple commodities formed the bulk of the goods, but two especially lucrative activities are worthy of mention: slaves and gold. The lower Gulf has long been associated with the slave trade and, as will be discussed later, at one point its towns served as entry points for close to 12,000 African slaves a year, many of whom were then transported by land into the Arabian interior or across the Gulf to Persia.[20] The gold trade was another important component of the preoil economy, and continued to grow in volume well into the twentieth century. Indeed, it is believed that in the 1960s, on the eve of the creation of the federation, no less than one-tenth of all of the noncommunist world's gold passed through the region's ports.[21]

With the exception of Dubai, which continued to position itself as the commercial hub of the lower Gulf,[22] overseas trade nevertheless began to fall into long-term decline, with many of the towns' commercial activities only beginning to pick up in more recent times as a result of the oil boom and the resulting improvements in infrastructure and ports. Britain's controversial military actions in the early nineteenth century and its antislavery treaties, both of which will be considered later in this chapter, effectively capped the region's trading potential and in many ways terminated what used to be a prosperous Arabian monopoly. Furthermore, with the development of more advanced ships requiring deeper berths, the coastal towns found themselves unable to accommodate many of the larger European vessels. As Frauke Heard-Bey describes:

> A great number of coral reefs and sandbanks, together with the numerous low lying islands make navigation extremely difficult and hazardous. Due to the extreme difficulty of approach and the lack of any sizable natural harbours there was comparatively little long distance shipping undertaken during the last few centuries from the ports of this coast . . . and overseas trading has consequently not been a very important feature of its economy until recently.[23]

In summary, most of the lower Gulf's traditional economic activities were centered around the scant geographical resources of the desert. The camels and gazelles of the hinterland allowed for some limited animal husbandry, caravan trading, and hunting, while the oases and mountainous areas provided the opportunity for some small-scale agriculture. The exception to this scarcity was the richness of the Gulf itself, which provided both plentiful fish and, more important, an abundance of pearls. Indeed, pearling was especially significant, given that it provided a lucrative source of income capable of fueling other associated economic activities in the coastal towns. Nevertheless, pearling was unstable, being highly vulnerable to the vagaries of overseas markets, and its eventual collapse had damaging repercussions for the entire economy. Thus, given the general impoverishment of the region and its overreliance on the export of single primary product, the lower Gulf was in many ways doomed to be a periphery of the international economy long before the oil era. Finally, however, with the emerging capitalist mode of production clearly evident in the pearling industry, and with the trading links forged between the Gulf and other Asian economies, a significant level of indigenous economic organization and regional integration was taking place, developments that were to be later blocked and reversed during the years of British control.

## The Traditional Social Structure

Alongside the development of these economic activities, a distinct social structure was forming as a result of both the lower Gulf's natural resources and the circumstances surrounding their exploitation. Important social groupings and divisions have been evident in the region since nomadic times, and many of these were further stratified as a result of the shift of activity toward the coasts in pursuit of pearling. Moreover, the influx of foreigners and the described relations of production led to additional layers, as expatriate workers and pearling merchants gradually became a part of the new social fabric. Further related to these changing economic conditions, the increasing urbanization of the population became another important feature of this period as the region's communities were permanently transformed and its people began to adapt to a more sedentary life.

In the years preceding British intervention and the pearling boom, the desert and the nomadic lifestyles were still the greatest influences on society. The well-established Bedu tribes, many of which still exist today, at least in name, can be seen as having spawned the first set of distinct classes in the lower Gulf. As shown, many of these nomads survived simply by hunting or through animal husbandry. These activities afforded only a subsistence living given the meager resources, but the importance of the latter cannot be understated, as it reveals an important early difference between the region's various tribes. Animal husbandry usually took two forms: sheep herding and camel herding. Of these, camel herding was a far more mobile pursuit given the greater range and resilience of the camels, and as such the *sharif,* or camel-herding tribes, were slowly able to achieve something close to hegemony over their sheep-herding counterparts, many of whom were reduced to tending sharif flocks and maintaining sharif pastoral lands.[24] Moreover, this distinction was reinforced by means of social exclusivity and selective intermarriage, allowing the members of the sharif tribes to assume an almost aristocratic status over the less mobile tribes. Thus, in an almost tributary system, these weaker tribes were left to evolve into a dependent class of producers and forced to accept a subservient role in exchange for economic and military security from their more powerful fellow tribes.

The origins of the lower Gulf's social structure can therefore be traced back further than the relatively recent move toward the town life of the ports. Indeed, the desert hierarchy provides the first real example of social stratification in the region as well as underscoring the early significance of descent lineages, many of which are of course still carefully maintained today. Essentially, these lineages reinforced exclusivity and formed a key pillar of Bedu society, allowing tribesmen to claim authority and status based solely on their descent from esteemed ancestors, whether real or fictional. In practice, the lineages were inevitably subdivided given the large number of disparate tribes and the vast geographical area of the desert, but, as Ibn Khaldun foresaw, they continued to provide a strong sense of security and allowed for several economic advantages that were normally beyond the capabilities of individual families. Indeed, group endeavors were often only possible with the support of a tribe, given the large membership and the mutual trust resulting from their shared ancestry.[25] As such, cooperative social labor often became the norm within a greater kinship organization, or *'ashira,* as competition over herds or pasturelands could be moderated and as large-scale agricultural projects could be undertaken and shared for the benefit of the whole group.

The second major feature of the region's early social structure developed out of the need to diversify and escape from the subsistence living afforded by the desert's extremely limited wealth. Clearly, the climatic limits on all of the region's traditional pursuits, coupled with the high population density relative to the available resources, prevented not only the expansion of any one activity but also the emergence of any distinct occupational groups such as fishermen or farmers. Indeed, unlike many of the neighboring Omani and Yemeni tribes,[26] a shortage of fertile land prevented most from leading any form of settled existence (unlike the *hadhr* people), and, as the move to the coasts was a very gradual process, there was a long period in which many Bedu would engage in different activities at different times of the year. As such, a seminomadic pattern emerged, and led to a great deal of versatility among the tribes. In the winter tribesmen would tend to their herds in the desert, while in the summer they would move to the cooler coastlines to fish or, as later became the case, dive for pearls; and at various other times some would harvest dates or even harvest millet high in the Hajar mountains.[27] As one might expect, this level of versatility seems to have been particularly evident along the Indian Ocean, or

Batinah coastline (Fujairah, Khor Fakkan, Kalba, etc.), where both the sea
and the palm groves were within easy reach of the villages, therefore dis-
couraging any occupational specialization.[28] Moreover, in general very few
of the region's tribes were ever tied to one geographic location or to one
specific activity, as eventually circumstances would change and they would
be forced to either diversify or relocate. Indeed, severe droughts could push
agriculturalists out into the desert to take up animal husbandry once more,
and equally the nomadic tribes could plunder and assume control of agricultural lands, they themselves switching their primary occupation.[29]

Significantly, the pearling boom and the subsequent growth of the
ports exercised major changes on this traditional society as the growing foreign demand for Gulf pearls meant that many of the previously seminomadic Bedu who had occasionally participated in the aforementioned
ikhluwi cooperatives finally had enough money to purchase more than the
basic necessities and, crucially, were also able to build houses in the
expanding coastal towns.[30] However, despite this greater urbanization, in
many ways the existing social stratification remained in place as a number
of the sharif tribesmen, who were often the only pearlers possessing sufficient surplus capital, chose to reinvest in the pearling industry under the
new 'amil system, thereby becoming part of the new merchant/entrepre-
neurial class and effectively transferring the old hierarchy of the desert to
the pearling industry. Prominent figures in this emerging group included
Khalaf al-Otaibi and Hamid bin Buti of Abu Dhabi, Salim bin Musabbah of
Dubai, and Humayd bin Kamil of Sharjah, all of whose families remain
prominent in Emirati society today.[31] Over the years, many of these
wealthy notables came to exercise great political power behind the scenes,
and as Muhammad Abdullah has shown, in the case of Sharjah they were
even able to replace one ruler with another as they saw fit.[32] Furthermore,
given that their capitalist ventures were frequently more lucrative than the
rulers' more limited sources of income, it was often they who were the
main financiers of any local projects, or indeed any local wars.[33]

The relatively rewarding nature of the pearling industry and the ability
to make substantial profits from successful ventures also attracted many
foreigners to the lower Gulf for the first time. Many believe that it was only
when the oil boom began that large numbers of expatriates moved to the
area, but in fact this process had begun far earlier and the region was no
stranger to such a phenomenon. Although the bulk of these expatriates were
temporary crewmen, attracted by the high demand and high wages associated with pearl diving, there were a large number of merchants who also
began to arrive and take up semipermanent residence. Interestingly, in
much the same way as the skilled expatriates working in the UAE today,
these Hindu and Khojah merchants would often bring their families with
them to Dubai or Abu Dhabi and would spend most of the year living and

working in the town, but would always take their annual leave (and presumably their savings) back to India and did not consider their place of work to be their home.[34] Moreover, the interests of these foreigners soon began to expand beyond pearling, with many being equally attracted to the other economic activities to which the boom had given rise. Indeed, given that most of the local Arabs tended to limit themselves to dhow trading or pearling, which were considered to be honorable activities, this left plenty of opportunity for foreign entrepreneurs to monopolize shopkeeping and other retail activities (as Lorimer describes, by this stage only ten out of the seventy or so shops in the main Abu Dhabi souq were Arab-owned, with the remainder all being Indian-owned).[35]

As such, the region's foreign population continued to grow as new socioeconomic groups began to form around countries of origin. Certainly, in a study presented to the political resident in 1901 there were already believed to be 500 Persians and 52 Banians (British-Indian subjects) in Dubai, and 96 Persians and 39 Banians resident in Abu Dhabi.[36] Given their similar cultural and religious backgrounds, many of the expatriate Arabs and Persians were easily assimilated by the existing society, and as time passed some were even offered citizenship. The Indian Hindus, however, were less easily absorbed and remained a more distinct social group. Indeed, as Lorimer describes, the result was an almost alien cluster within society, but given their usefulness and the high demand for their labor and skills, they were tolerated and accepted—the parallels with the contemporary UAE's reliance on Indian labor being very clear. There was one complication at this time, however, that is not an issue today: during the pearling era many of the wealthier Indian merchants held British-Indian passports, which guaranteed them some degree of diplomatic immunity and, crucially, exempted them from taxation.[37] In the UAE most undesirable expatriates can simply be relieved of their visas and deported, but in earlier times the rulers did not possess the same level of control over their sizable British-Indian population.[38] A good example would be Heard-Bey's account of the Banian bin Lutah family. On leaving Dubai for 'Ajman, the family decided to take their pearl divers with them, without first settling their debts in Dubai. The ruler of 'Ajman, bound by an earlier British agreement to hand over fraudulent absconders, attempted to return these unwanted divers to Dubai, but the British political resident in Bushire intervened, sending a Royal Navy vessel to 'Ajman to enforce his decision in favor of the bin Lutahs.[39] Indeed, there were many examples where Britain ended up supporting absconding subjects, especially if they were indebted to British creditors who would stand to lose upon their death.[40]

Following the pearling booms, the aforementioned decline of the industry in the 1930s also had major ramifications for the region's social structure, as most of the more able foreigners began to drift away, leaving something of a void in local society. Indeed, many of the activities formerly run by the expatriates began to peter out, most notably the running of the schools. Furthermore, those foreigners who did remain during this time of hardship were far less easily integrated into society than during the boom time. The wealth and prosperity that had previously gelled the region's heterogeneous society together had declined and tensions began to surface, the situation almost certainly being exacerbated by the many foreign moneylenders who had begun to gain something of a stranglehold over the locals given their earlier financing of pearling expeditions. These predominantly non-Muslim brokers, many of whom had been able to practice usury,[41] were either attempting to call in their debts during a time of uncertainty or were simply capitalizing on the situation by charging high rates of interest for bridging loans.[42]

In summary, the pearling booms transformed the region's traditional social structure as large numbers of foreigners were attracted to the region for the first time, and in many ways this massive influx of expatriates can be seen as a clear antecedent to the contemporary UAE's labor market. More important, however, a number of these new foreign contingents, especially the wealthy Banian merchants, can also be seen as having further reinforced the early peripheral nature of the lower Gulf's economy, as many of these British-Indian subjects operated autonomously of the local rulers,[43] were exempt from taxation, and remained only semipermanent residents, regularly returning to India and thereby transferring the bulk of their accumulated capital from the region to a core economy. Nevertheless, alongside these foreign expropriators existed an extremely wealthy indigenous class who had emerged as the stronger sharif tribes (often possessing surplus capital from their camel-herding activities) were able to invest heavily in new pearling ventures. Moreover, many of these Arab merchants were also capable of funding local development projects and, on occasion, even checking the ruler's power. However, as the remainder of this chapter will demonstrate, by the early twentieth century indirect British intervention and new sources of wealth had effectively restrained the expansion of this entrepreneurial class, thus shifting the crucial merchant-ruler balance and thereby permanently altering the course of the region's socioeconomic development.

## The Traditional Political Structure

In much the same way as the region's traditional economic and social structures, the geographical context, the great distances, the harsh conditions, and the tribal hierarchy primarily defined the traditional political structures of the lower Gulf. As such, in terms of authority, the modern territorial concept of statehood was largely alien to the region's traditional polities, given the vagueness of the desert and the tribal way of life. Certainly, as Kevin Fenelon notes:

> The desert was like an ocean highway across which the nomadic tribes could move at will. Their organisation was tribal, and the ruler was not so much a territorial overlord as one who held the allegiance of several tribes or tribal groups. In times of emergency the tribes might rally round a shaykh of the strongest tribe, but the concept that the authority of a ruling shaykh had a territorial extent as well as a personal one was only brought in when the British gave the name of "state" to the sum of political influence that one of the undersigning shaykhs could muster among the tribes.[44]

Thus, in the period prior to British involvement, the political structure revolved primarily around the tribe and authority over people, rather than vast tracts of mostly worthless sand. Indeed, as Heard-Bey argues, even by the mid–twentieth century the establishment of a territorial state with distinct physical boundaries was still very much "out of tune with the traditional conduct of local politics given that sovereignty over people was far from permanently binding, let alone sovereignty over territory."[45]

Two clear examples of this need for authority over people would be the long-running struggles for mastery over the tribes of Buraimi and Ra's al-Jibal. Buraimi was a strategically important oasis and trading post, with many of the local rulers believing that hegemony over tribes in this area would soon lead to great power over other influential groups needing to visit the oasis. As such, control over the population of Buraimi has long been a source of conflict for the juxtaposed rulers of Abu Dhabi, Oman, and Saudi Arabia. Indeed, as will be described later in this chapter, the contest reached its most acute point only as recently as 1952, with the central argument still surrounding the allegiance of the local independent tribes. This aspect of the dispute was only resolved in 1959 when Abu Dhabi and Oman finally agreed to delineate boundaries through the area, thus dividing it into the present-day towns of Buraimi (in Oman) and Al-'Ayn (in Abu Dhabi emirate). This physical demarcation was seen as the only way of preventing the local tribes from continuously attempting to play one regional power against another. Similarly, the Ra's al-Jibal example highlights the attempts of another major power, Ra's al-Khaimah, to dominate an area in order to gain influence over local tribes. Certainly, given the Ra's al-Jibal tribesmen's preference for the distant and rather ineffective authority of the Sultan of Oman, Ra's al-Khaimah needed to demonstrate its ability to exert control over nearby populations. For many years, however, Ra's al-Jibal remained loyal to faraway Muscat, frustrating Ra's al-Khaimah and thereby illustrating how tenuous the concept of political power was at this time.

Certainly, with different tribes in close proximity to each other, and with many accepting the sovereignty of different rulers, it was exceedingly difficult for any one power to form a coherent political entity.[46] Indeed, even a close inspection of a map of the present-day UAE will reveal many pockets of territory that continue to exist many miles inside the territorial boundaries of neighboring states, obvious examples being the Omani-controlled Musandam peninsula and the village of Madha close to the Wadi al-Hatta, both of which have their own police stations and their own local government officials. This complex patchwork of enclaves serves as a reminder of the continuing relevance of tribal allegiances and the contemporary rulers' desire to maintain control over certain groups even if there are considerable logistical difficulties in enforcing such authority.

Despite this rather vague sense of political control, the region's traditional governments, or *hukumah,* did possess certain key institutions that were deemed necessary for administering the ruling shaikh's authority. Perhaps the most important of these institutions were the *diwan* and the *majlis.* The semiformal diwan consisted of the shaikh's appointed advisers, each of whom represented an important segment of society. The tribal nature of the political system was clearly present in the diwan given that the ruler's family tended to dominate, as they were always the largest tribe in the area (the one exception being the ruling tribe of Ra's al-Khaimah).[47] On a more informal level the majlis (pl. majalis) provided a forum for the people to air their grievances, often in the presence of the shaikh himself. Thus, in many ways this early form of government left room for a kind of consultation-based grassroots participation, as in theory any member of a town's population could find a channel of communication leading directly to the ruler.[48] This may seem very far from being a democratic system in the Western sense, but given the nature of the region's loosely defined constituencies the majalis nevertheless allowed for a form of "mobile democracy." Indeed, any tribesman who raised an issue with a ruler and was left unsatisfied could simply move to another village or town under a different administration, thereby "voting with his feet."[49]

Underneath the ruler and these rudimentary institutions there were of course many other manifestations of administrative authority, and as society gradually became more sedentary a greater number of institutions and official positions were required to protect, supervise, and govern the various towns and activities of the region:

• *Ruler:* The principal shaikh assumed responsibility of all institutions and made himself available to hear any grievances from his population.
• *Diwan:* The ruler's court of advisers.
• *Majalis:* Informal consultation chambers, often in the presence of the ruler or his representatives.

• *Ruler's personal secretary:* Normally an educated expatriate Arab responsible for administration and communication between the ruler and other authorities.

• *Qadi:* An important position for a religious man, responsible for dispensing justice according to Islamic law.

• *Qadi/pearling courts:* Tribunals presided over by either a *qadi* or representatives of the pearling committee to resolve disputes and dispense justice. As described, the complex system of financing employed by the pearling industry involved both creditors and debtors and as such was frequently the cause of dispute. As a result, pearling courts, or *salifa al-ghaus,* were set up by the ruler, or *wali,* and presided over by captains and other members of the pearling community who "had a reputation for fairness and good judgement."[50]

• *Wali/'amir* (in Dalma), *na'ib* (in Al-'Ayn): The ruler's representative in an outlying region.

• *Muzakki:* An official responsible for the collection of taxes and customs.

• *'Arif:* An official responsible for the maintenance of the falaj irrigation channels in agricultural towns such as Hatta and Al-'Ayn. These men collected a fixed sum of money (the *masha*) from the owners of date gardens in exchange for diverting the flow of water from one channel to another as necessary.[51]

• *Mutarizaya:* The ruler's armed retainers.

• *Haras:* Armed guards at the ruler's fort in the main town.

• *'Askars:* Armed tribesmen paid a salary to enforce the ruler's authority in outlying regions.

• *Duris:* Armed guards in the oasis towns and outlying regions responsible for protecting camels and other livestock from raiders.

• *Supervisor of the souq:* An official responsible for ensuring the smooth functioning of the town's marketplaces.[52] (See Figure 1.1.)

Of these other hukumah positions perhaps the most useful in contributing to a further understanding of the traditional political structure would be the ruler's representatives, who were usually placed in charge of outlying territories, often beyond the range of the ruler's personal authority. Broadly speaking, this system of delegation was practiced throughout the region, albeit with different titles and slightly different responsibilities. In the northern shaikhdoms, for example, the rulers appointed walis to collect taxes from their more remote towns, and also to organize the defense of any outposts against raiders or attacks from rival shaikhs. Moreover, the walis were also expected to serve as the rulers' de facto governors in these towns, holding local majalis, arbitrating disputes, and dispensing justice with the assistance of qadis and pearling courts.[53] Similarly, Abu Dhabi

**Figure 1.1 The Hukumah**

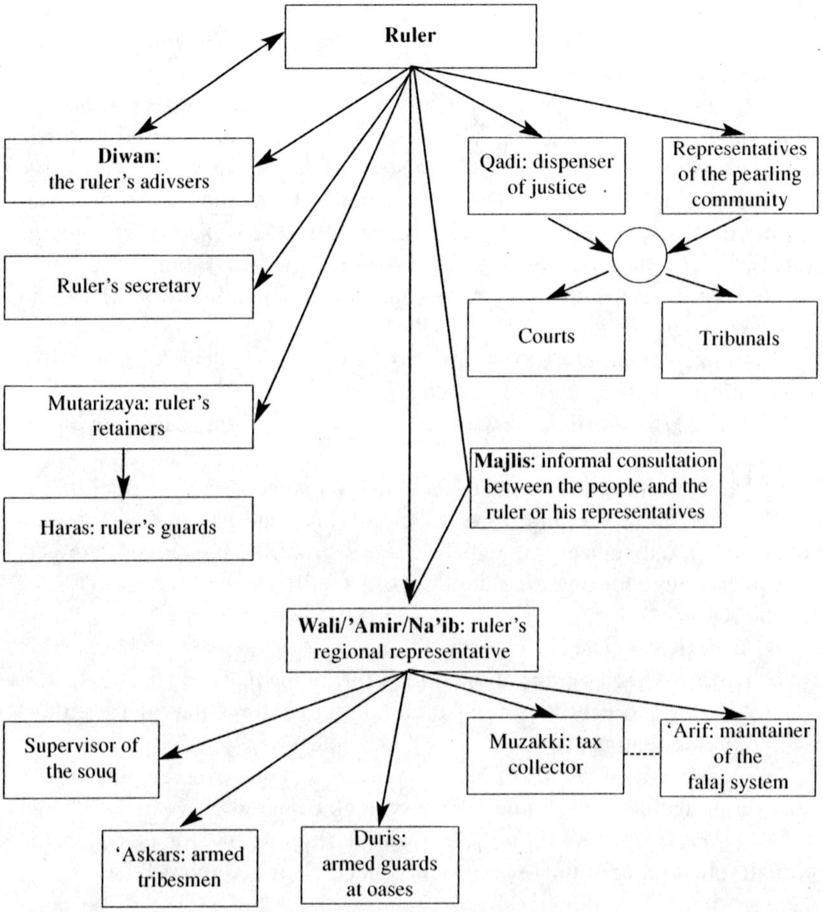

employed *'amirs,* representatives who would live and work on the many scattered islands belonging to the ruler. Their task, like that of the wali, was to collect pearling taxes and settle disputes with the assistance of the *muzakki* and various other customs officials.[54] The crucial difference being that the 'amirs received a fixed payment from the ruler rather than a share of the local taxes, thus making them the region's earliest form of salaried bureaucrat.

Significantly, and again illustrating the decentralized and fluid nature of politics during this period, in many cases these representatives grew autonomous of the ruler as their control over local taxes and populations invariably allowed them to develop personal fiefdoms. Indeed, as Heard-

Bey describes, very often the farther away a wali was from the ruler's town, the greater became his political weight.[55] Certainly, there have been many examples in the region's history of such representatives seceding and in some cases even returning to usurp the ruler's control over the main town; a good example of such a struggle being how, in 1948, the nephew of the ruler of Sharjah used his position as a wali to gain immense local popularity and power by supporting those who wanted a reduction in the pearling tax imposed by the ruler. By successfully defying his uncle he managed to build sufficient support to take over as ruler of nearby Ra's al-Khaimah.[56] Of course a more recent example would be the events surrounding the accession of Shaikh Zayed al-Nuhayyan during the 1960s. As governor, or *na'ib,* of the large agricultural town and the nearby villages of Al-'Ayn, Zayed had proved himself a capable ruler in his own right and had amassed considerable popular support. Thus, as will be discussed in the next chapter, when the time came for pressure to be placed upon his older and more conservative brother in the capital, Zayed was seen as the natural successor and, given his existing power base, the transition was both straightforward and popularly accepted.[57]

Another crucial aspect of the traditional administrative structure was its ability to subsidize the population. This was an important manifestation of the ruler's authority and in many ways a precursor to the system of wealth distribution practiced during the oil era. Indeed, during this period the rulers frequently used heavy subsidies to buy influence and protection from other tribes, thereby keeping the peace.[58] Lorimer illustrates this point showing how the rulers were able to maintain control over Bedu groups simply by giving their chiefs a steady stream of gifts.[59] Even more noteworthy than these subsidies, however, were the taxes imposed upon the population at this time. Although the taxes collected were never particularly high and never reached the same levels as those in the European states, they nevertheless required the hukumah to operate certain extractive institutions and allowed the ruler to raise funds for various projects: fiscal capabilities that have rarely been employed by the contemporary state.

By far the most important of these taxes were those levied on pearling and its associated activities, especially during the boom period. *Taraz* taxes were collected to pay guards to protect towns during the height of the pearling season, when many of the men were out at sea, and also to protect the many pearling boats that were left unattended along the coasts during the off-season.[60] The taraz was levied from each two-man pearling team (a diver and hauler partnership called a *qalta),* and the pearling crews had to pay collectively a *naub* tax on their boat in addition to royalties on any pearls valued at more than 1,000 rupees.[61] Other lucrative forms of dues included the customs duties the ruler imposed on the ports, the ruler's collection of rent from shops in the souqs, and also the ruler's ability to issue fishing licenses and charge a commensurate fee.[62] As mentioned, a number of taxes were also levied by the walis in order to raise funds for the town's administration, the payment of its guards, and the upkeep of its forts and towers. Moreover, there were specific taxes collected by *'arif* officials for the upkeep of community projects such as the operation of the falaj irrigation channels, in addition to taxes on some of the agricultural activities themselves. If a farmer produced more than the *nisab*, which was the tax-threshold quantity of dates, then it became necessary for him to pay between 5 and 10 percent of his income to the wali. In practice, however, many areas failed to meet the nisab or were simply left untaxed, and even if the wali did begin to collect, it was usually just payment in kind in order to help feed his retainers.[63] Similarly insignificant were the taxes on livestock, the *zakat* tax, which amounted to a mere 10 rupees per camel.[64] Nevertheless the zakat and nisab taxes, although small, still served as a symbol of authority over tribesmen and in some cases were the only reminder for many Bedu people of exactly who their distant overlord was, this being underscored during the aforementioned Buraimi disputes when the different sides began to claim sovereignty over the area based on a history of zakat collection among particular tribes.

In order to better understand the impact of this taxation, a brief case study of one of the many pearling/fishing islands of Abu Dhabi clearly highlights the role of the tax collector, and provides something of an insight into the early extractive process. Dalma, a small island off the coast of Abu Dhabi, is still a base for fishermen, and used to be a major center of activity during the pearling boom. In 1955 the ruler's representative, the 'amir, gave a written description of the taxation system still in use on the island:

(1) At the beginning of the pearling season a sack of rice, juniya, and four rupees tuman were collected from every boat; half of both amounts were taken from small boats. (2) A share equal to the season's income of one rope-puller, a saib, was collected as hasila. This amount was calculated. The remainder was shared between the divers and saibs at the proportion of three for the former and two for the latter, after adding an imaginary saib. The share of that saib was the tax due to the ruler of Abu Dhabi. (3) At the end of a season a tax of two rupees was levied on every qalta (pair, a diver and a hauler). (4) On every pearl valued 2000 rupees or more a tax of 200 rupees was taken by the ruler. (5) Naub was at that time the term for the tax levied on every pearl merchant or other merchant in Dalma or the islands and coastal tracts administered by the 'amir. The tax varied between 2 and 200 rupees a year for an individual, depending on the size of his business. (6) 'Azima was a voluntary contribution of the pearl merchants towards the cost of a feast traditionally given in honour of the ruler when he or a close relative came to Dalma at the end of every diving season.[65]

Thus, no fewer than six specific forms of dues existed on the island. With the island of Dalma being a typical example of a pearling community, this demonstrates the way in which taxation was very much a part of life for the coastal region during the preoil period.

In summary, the lower Gulf's traditional political structures were in many ways products of the same factors that shaped the early economic and social structures, namely the region's geography and the tribal system. Certainly, with well-spread-out and distant settlements, and with the need to control tribal populations rather than physical territory, there evolved a decentralized and extremely fluid political system in which the power of rulers and governors would vary according to their popular support, and in which the people could exercise considerable mobile democracy by moving from one constituency to another. Eventually, as society became more sedentary the traditional governments did expand, as in Weberian terms the system evolved from one of family-based patriarchal authority to one of patrimonialism,[66] requiring new positions and institutions to arbitrate, subsidize, and tax the population. While many of these features, including the hukumah's system of appointments and the early distribution of wealth, are certainly important antecedents of contemporary political structures, it is quite apparent that other equally notable characteristics of the traditional polity have either faded or in some cases disappeared. Indeed, with well-established rulers, a more centralized state, and larger populations, little of the former flexibility of political control remains, which of course has also reduced the effectiveness of the old system of mobile democracy. Furthermore, whereas in the past the traditional government was routinely able to tax its population and was therefore a relatively "strong state" with well-defined extractive capabilities,[67] much of this ability would now appear to have been lost.

## External Influences and the Trucial States

Early Portuguese interests in the lower Gulf were essentially limited to trade. Specifically, it was the empire's intention to monopolize the trade route between Europe and its colonies in the East Indies by outflanking the traditional overland routes of Persia and the Mashriq.[68] To this end, Portugal concentrated on developing the entirely maritime route around the African Cape of Good Hope, which their navigators had successfully charted in the fifteenth century. By using such a route it was critical that the periphery of the Indian Ocean was secured,[69] and many in Lisbon believed that the Straits of Hormuz were necessary for this control.[70] As such, some form of Portuguese presence was required in Oman, and naval bases were also established in nearby Khor Fakkan (a present-day container port on the UAE's Batinah coastline) and in Ra's al-Khaimah. However, unlike the

Asian Portuguese colonies of Macao and Goa, these Arab "ocean rim" ports never became major bases due to their lack of natural harbors and the few watering places along the coast of the Gulf. Consequently, no real settlement took place in the region, and as such the period of Portuguese occupation had little effect on indigenous structures. Certainly, as Heard-Bey claims, the empire's only real impact on the region was a reduction in security in the lower Gulf, as the imperial presence frequently endangered local Arab trade by bringing Ottoman, Dutch, and British rivals ever closer to the area. Furthermore, the well-documented Portuguese practice of putting to death entire communities if local harbors and fortifications were withheld may have imprinted lasting memories on the minds of the native population.[71] As such, it has been argued that the longevity of these memories created an understandable sense of distrust and unease in the Arabs' future dealings with foreigners, and may therefore have contributed, as much as any other factor, to the initial clash with Britain, the second imperial power to take an interest in the region (see Figure 1.2).

Indeed, Britain's first major contact with the lower Gulf was a trading dispute that soon escalated into warfare. In the early eighteenth century the Qawasim (adj. Qasimi) tribes of Ra's al-Khaimah and Sharjah had been growing in strength and prestige as their trading activities flourished. When Qasimi power eventually extended to the island of Qishm,[72] they began to establish a third trading base, but this new entrepôt Arab port soon began to affect adversely the customs receipts, which had previously been divided between the British and Persian Empires. This loss of revenue prompted the British East India Company, a Bombay-based trading company, to send an armed expedition to the island to claim by force the company's share of the customs from the Arab traders.[73] Thus an intense maritime struggle over local trading networks began, a struggle that was to last well into the nineteenth century, the events of which have been clouded in historical controversy, with the Qawasim being branded as fanatical pirates on the one hand, and the British as imperial aggressors on the other.

With the benefit of hindsight, though little is clear, there appear to have been a number of different issues that contributed to this protracted and bloody conflict. First, there is no doubt that, with the growth of European competition along the Indian Ocean trading routes, the decline of the narrow maritime-oriented economic base of the Qawasim was in many ways inevitable. As such, Heard-Bey argues that with so many Qasimi boats and sailors out of action due to the decline in trade, it was foreseeable that at least some would turn their hand to something more lucrative. After all, as noted, nomadic desert raiding, or *ghazu,* was not uncommon in the hinterland, and had always proved a popular alternative during times of austerity. Thus, piracy on the seas may have been viewed by some as simply an extension of such an activity, albeit with far higher rewards.[74] Moreover,

## Figure 1.2 Layers of Control and Dependency

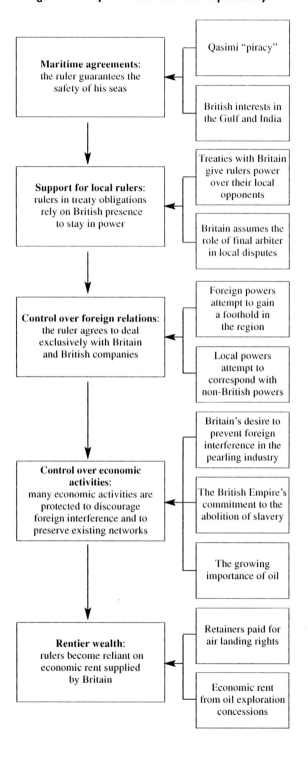

the power vacuum and the lawlessness following the concurrent decline of the Persian Empire may have compounded the economic downswing and provided even more conditions conducive to a serious conflict between the local power and the major foreign power. Indeed, Donald Hawley, a former British political agent in Dubai, supports such a view:

> While the Gulf was far from peaceful during the eighteenth century, the blame did not lie entirely with the Qawasim. Persia was in internal turmoil, and trade, which the Qawasim shared with other Gulf Arabs, was carried on against a background of strife. Piracy was also endemic in the Gulf and had broken out periodically throughout history, when no strong government controlled the area.[75]

Certainly, Hawley believes that if the region had not been so turbulent and that "if the Qawasim had not crossed swords with the rising power of British India and been branded pirates by the secure Victorians," then their fame may have rested on more peaceful foundations.[76]

Regional politics may have also played a part, with the Qawasim's traditional rivalry with neighboring Oman and the increasing influence of the Arabian Wahhabi movement both acting as catalysts. By the early 1800s the Omani fleet had grown to become a serious trading rival; in 1804 the Sultan of Oman even began to claim the exclusive right to protect navigation in the Gulf, thus making Muscat the sole distribution center for foreign goods.[77] The Omanis had therefore placed the Qawasim under considerable economic pressure; given Oman's historic alliance with Britain, a backlash may have been unavoidable. Furthermore, it is also believed that the increasingly popular Wahhabi religious reformers may have exacerbated the situation given their strengthened alliance with the Qawasim, their expansionist ambitions over Omani territory, and their hostility toward Britain and its polytheist and idolatrous Hindu Indian sailors and crewmen. Indeed, it is believed that the Wahhabism that had emerged from the heart of Arabia during the mid–eighteenth century eventually reached Buraimi and the Qawasim by around 1800. Its namesake, Muhammad bin Abdul-Wahhab, launched the movement, and after his death it was led by its first imam, the Saudi shaikh. The Wahhabis preached a more purified brand of Islam, a doctrine of pure monotheism and a return to the fundamental tenets of Islam as laid down by the Quran. As such, they were unitarians, emphasizing the "centrality of God's unqualified oneness in Sunni Islam."[78] Essentially, they sought to renew the Prophet's golden era of Islam, and all who stood in their way were to be swept aside, including other Islamic rulers who lived "impure" lives, such as the pro-British Sultan of Oman. Thus, by the time of their contact with the Qawasim, Hawley believes the movement had become something of a "religio-military confederacy under which the desert people, stirred by a great idea, embarked on a common action,"[79] and sought constant expansion in the manner of the original Islamic concept of *dar al-harb*. Indeed, in his account of the period, Charles Belgrave notes how Abdul-Wahhab "told his followers that it was their religious duty to convert their fellow men with fire and sword, and to plunder and destroy all those who professed to be Muslims but did not accept Wahhabism." He then draws the conclusion that it was this prospect of authorized and religiously sanctioned plunder that "may have attracted the desert Bedu and the pirates of the coast to align themselves under the green standard of the Wahhabis,"[80] thus adding a tinge of religious fanaticism to an already serious conflict.

Wahhabism's role as an ideological catalyst would therefore seem very clear, especially given the Qawasim's inclination to form alliances with (or swear allegiance to) any power hostile to their traditional Omani rivals. Furthermore, the clear evidence of actual physical Wahhabi control over the region during this period, underscored by the imposing Wahhabi fort constructed in Buraimi to serve as a vantage point over the oasis and to sever trade routes into Oman, may even indicate that the Wahhabis were as much to blame for the ensuing struggle as the Qawasim.[81] Indeed, it is recorded that at one point the Wahhabis were able to claim one-fifth of all Qawasim booty under something of a tributary system, and to confine the Qasimi shaikh's authority to just Ra's al-Khaimah itself.[82] Moreover, in 1809 they were even temporarily able to depose the shaikh and appoint their favored ruler, the Shaikh of Rams (a small town just north of Ra's al-Khaimah) in his place to be the Wahhabi governor and tax collector.[83] These examples of control may hint at the true extent of Wahhabi involvement, especially given that in 1809 the so-called acts of Qasimi piracy were at their peak even though Qasimi power was restricted to just one coastal town.

However, as both Lorimer and Belgrave note, the lack of an adequate British response to the initial Qasimi- and Wahhabi-inspired attacks must also be seen as a layer of explanation, at least with regard to the longevity of the conflict. Indeed, as the author of the *Gazetteer of the Persian Gulf* reported, the initial strikes on British-Indian shipping, including the assaults on the Viper cruiser and the Bassein dhow, failed to elicit any real response from Bombay.[84] With "no reparation seeming to have been exacted for this insult to the British flag,"[85] it is argued that the Qasimi-Wahhabi "alliance" was left to grow bold and overambitious. Certainly Belgrave supports Lorimer's view, believing that Bombay's lack of steps to punish those responsible led to the Arabs "finding they could attack British ships with impunity . . . with the pirates becoming more audacious."[86] Moreover, Belgrave sums up what might have been the frustration felt by the British following these attacks:

Still the Bombay government took no action. Not only was it inactive, but commanders of the Bombay Navy were ordered not on any account to attack or molest "these innocent natives of the Gulf," and were threatened with "the displeasure of the Government" if they failed to carry out their orders. This policy was due to the Government's fear of becoming involved with the Wahhabis, although it was known that they were supporting and encouraging the pirates, and receiving a portion of the spoil. The pirates, assuming that there would be no reprisals, became more daring. In 1805 they captured two brigs belonging to Mr. Manesty, the Resident at Basra. Many of the crews were murdered and the Captain of one of the brigs had his arm cut off because he was seen to fire a musket. He put his severed arm into some hot ghee, which saved his life. The two brigs were added to the pirate [Qasimi] fleet.[87]

In late 1809 an expedition was finally launched against the "pirates" of Ra's al-Khaimah but this too was seen as an inadequate response and one that failed to gain any formal submission from the Qasimi sailors, many of whom simply retreated inland. The British response in 1816 was regarded as similarly ineffective, with Belgrave describing it as having been nothing more than a "badly managed demonstration":[88]

The [British] ships then opened fire on some pirate dhows which were anchored near the shore, but the dhows were too far distant for the gunfire to be effective. Guns from the town replied with slightly more success, for one of the shots carried away part of the sail from a British ship. "At least three hundred shots were discharged from the squadron, not one of them seemed to have done any execution." The ships then set sail leaving the pirates performing jubilant war dances on the shore.[89]

Thus this second fiasco, much like the earlier mission, also portrayed the British as weak and ineffective, and was seen as prompting "the Qawasim to engage in piracy with new vigour. They had good reason to believe that the British, in spite of their superior ships and armaments, were incapable of resisting them."[90]

The final expedition did not come until 1819/1820, but this time the British response was strong, well planned, and decisive (with the British commander even reportedly rebuffing a last-minute Qasimi emissary),[91] with Ra's al-Khaimah becoming the scene of one of history's first major amphibious assaults. The Qasimi stronghold had been able to rebuild its fortifications following the 1809 attacks, with Captain Loch of the HMS *Eden* stating in his diary, "To say the least of it, Ra's al-Khaimah was no mean or insignificant work of defence."[92] Indeed, the well-defended port was seen as a very tough proposition for the Bombay landing party. The force, comprising both British officers and Indian infantry, was the largest to have ever appeared in the Gulf, with over 3,000 soldiers, three battleships, and nine cruisers. The plan was to assault simultaneously Ra's al-

Khaimah and the nearby pirate base of Zaya, and then to sail farther down the coast and crush each remaining Qasimi redoubt one at a time.[93] Loch's diary provides an understandably pro-British view of these events and although this view is unlikely to be shared by many today, Belgrave's highly controversial summary of its contents is nevertheless useful in capturing something of the British perception and mentality toward the Arabs of the lower Gulf at that time:

> Loch's diary makes the reader realise how many British lives were sacrificed in suppressing piracy. . . . Britain achieved these objectives, not with any ambitions towards territorial conquests, but in order to make the seas safe for the ships of all nations and to put an end to the people of the Gulf carrying off their fellow creatures into slavery. Unfortunately very few of the present generation of Gulf Arabs realise the part which Britain played in the past.[94]

But an account of these events would be incomplete without also considering the recent Arab revisionist history of the Qawasim. Indeed, Shaikh Sultan al-Qasimi, the current ruler of Sharjah and a descendent of the Qawasim, offers an entirely different perspective.[95] Essentially, al-Qasimi presents an alternative explanation of the events surrounding Britain's destruction of Ra's al-Khaimah, or to be precise the British East India Company's important role in the suppression of the Qawasim. Central to his claim is that Lorimer, the author of the much-celebrated *Gazetteer,* was a civil servant of the British India government and as such his views were entirely pro-British and therefore need to be treated with caution in any impartial study of the region. Furthermore, al-Qasimi emphasizes that, because Lorimer's study was the first of its kind, it was heavily relied upon by almost all subsequent scholars, including John Kelly's influential work on the Gulf.[96] Al-Qasimi has therefore sought to refute the generalizations and claims of Lorimer and these other historians that the Qawasim were simply marauders and pirates. Instead he argues that the Qawasim were simply accomplished maritime traders who were able to outcompete and undercut many of their rivals, including the British Indian merchants.

Indeed, al-Qasimi identifies the expansion of imperial trade as the key issue behind the conflict, stating that the British East India Company, a firm with vast commercial interests in the region, was "determined to increase its share of the trade in the Gulf by all possible means. Any increase in the Company's share would be at the expense of the Arab natives of the Gulf. . . . [T]he Company's government of Bombay realised that any real opposition to their plans in the Gulf would come from the Qawasim."[97] In order for the company to achieve the destruction of their enemies, it needed to be able to persuade the decisionmakers in both Bombay and London of the need to mobilize British naval forces against its principal trading rival, the Qawasim. Accordingly, as al-Qasimi describes: "A concerted campaign was mounted by Company officials to present, or rather misrepresent, the Qawasim as pirates whose depredations posed a serious threat to all maritime activities in the Indian Ocean."[98] Thus, al-Qasimi believes that any misfortune that fell upon any British ship in the area was immediately attributed to Qawasim "pirates," and as such a "big lie" was contrived, a lie so readily accepted that the coast of the lower Gulf even became known as the "Pirate Coast."[99]

As such, al-Qasimi's alternative history attempts to demonstrate how many of the accidents and unexplained incidents that occurred at sea during this period were always reported to the British political resident, and in turn to London, as being the work of dangerous pirates. His study is well researched, drawing heavily from the Bombay archives. These, unlike the India Office records held in London, house the complete files of the British East India Company and therefore contain a far more substantial quantity of the correspondence between the Gulf, Bombay, and London at that time.[100] Indeed, from this correspondence, al-Qasimi reveals how the company hoped that a sufficient body of anti-Arab evidence could be presented to the Bombay government, enough to persuade the government that the Royal Navy needed to be used to remove by force their commercial rivals. Certainly, al-Qasimi's argument would seem highly credible given that the British destruction of the "pirates," their strongholds, and their means of livelihood seemed to lead to a commensurate increase in the company's share of trade in the Gulf. With its main opponents removed by military means, al-Qasimi shows that the company's imports to Bombay rose from nearly 1.7 million lakhs in 1801 (prior to the expeditions) to over 3.3 million lakhs by 1822 (following the final expeditions). Similarly, the company's exports from Bombay rose from over 1.2 million lakhs to over 3.3 million lakhs over the same period.[101]

Finally, it is also important to consider the massive study on the subject undertaken in the mid-1990s by historian Charles Davies. Having conducted an even more detailed research of the Bombay archives and having supplemented this material with the Bushire Residency files,[102] Davies's only significant omission would appear to be an analysis of the correspondence belonging to one of the key British commanders at that time (letters that have been given a more thorough examination by Hubert Moyse-Bartlett).[103] Although reluctant to reach an overall conclusion, venturing that the Qawasim "were not pirates, though some of their activity could be classed as such,"[104] and on the one hand claiming that by 1800 the East India Company was already beginning to recommend the use of Arab shipping over European in the interests of economy, while on the other hand showing that direct imports from India on British vessels approximately doubled between 1817 and 1822,[105] Davies does strongly suggest that total

India-Gulf trade, already sizable in 1790, had increased substantially over the following three decades and that the proportional share of British shipping over the same period must have also increased.[106] As such, pirates or not, and controversy aside, it can still be understood from this most recent work that Bombay had an obvious interest in fostering the trade between its Indian territories and the Gulf in the hope of greater internal prosperity and overall increased revenues for both the British and the many private Banian merchants using the route.[107] Thus, in this light, which of course does to an extent corroborate with al-Qasimi's original arguments, the early Anglo-Arab conflict can therefore clearly be seen as being far from an accidental clash of interests and "empire by absent-mindedness," and instead as part of a long-term effort by the Bombay government and the British East India Company to suppress and displace an indigenous Arab trading network.

### Greater British Political and Economic Involvement

Regardless of these differing historical accounts surrounding the causes of the conflict, after the assault on Ra's al-Khaimah and the destruction of the other "pirate" strongholds, the immediate threat to British Indian shipping and the British East India Company's commercial interests had subsided and left many in Bombay with the dilemma of whether Britain should continue to involve herself in the region, or should simply maintain a watching brief. As Malcolm Peck describes, many believed that a permanent military establishment in the Gulf was undesirable unless the cost of the upkeep could be recovered from the Omanis or from other local sources. Furthermore, it was felt that any greater interference in internal Arab affairs would lead to unnecessary complications, especially as the Wahhabi threat had diminished and the reinstated Shaikh Saqr of Ra's al-Khaimah appeared to be a reliable and relatively pro-British ruler. However, a second, more hawkish camp intended to launch a full-scale sweep of the Gulf to destroy any remaining pirate bases and remove local rulers as they saw fit. Crucially, this interventionist camp had much support given that shortly before the 1819 expedition the Qawasim had been blamed for a number of attacks just seventy miles from Bombay itself,[108] and in 1816 had been held responsible for the plundering of three British Indian merchant ships in the Red Sea.[109]

Eventually something of a middle ground was taken, with the Bombay government deciding to follow up its expeditions by seeking to retain influence over the tribes with periodic shows of force, while at the same time preparing the ground for greater cooperation between the British and the local Arab rulers. Captain Perronet Thompson, a former governor of Sierra Leone, was brought in to supervise and, one by one, the Bombay government offered treaties to the ruling shaikhs.[110] The first of these was signed with the ruler of Sharjah in 1820, requiring him to surrender all remaining pirate vessels, fortified towers, guns, and British prisoners. In exchange he was given assurances by the British that all pearling and fishing vessels would be restored to Sharjah and, significantly, that all Sharjah trading vessels would be granted access to British ports. Thus, given the recent economic decline and war damage, both of these guarantees were major non-military incentives for the shaikh to honor the treaty.[111] Indeed, it was even reported that shortly before the treaty was drafted, Sharjah merchants had already offered to pay Britain to defend their vessels and that it was their ruler, not the British, who had initially pressed for a more permanent arrangement.[112] Although there was some initial opposition from a couple of the other rulers (especially in 'Ajman and Fujairah), a little naval shelling soon persuaded them to fall in line with their more compliant neighbors and very soon all of the signatures were in place.[113]

As a result of these early accords between Britain and the participating Trucial states, a maritime peace was finally achieved. Many among the Bombay elite were distrustful of such loose "sea borne colonialism,"[114] however, and campaigned for stricter treaties with additional provisions, such as the banning of all armed Arab vessels, the limiting of Arab commercial vessels, and the prohibition of timber exports from India to the Gulf (presumably to restrict Arab shipbuilding).[115] Although few of these draconian measures were implemented, further annually renewed maritime truces were called for, in which the rulers had to guarantee that all hostilities at sea would be outlawed. These began to be signed from 1835 onward and culminated in the 1853 Perpetual Treaty of Peace, an essentially self-enforcing truce given that the economic benefits of regional stability were still enough to ensure cooperation from most parties.[116] Indeed, following these treaties Britain was able to scale back its naval presence in the Gulf, retaining only a small squadron of six cruisers to police the region and signal the imperial presence.[117] Thus, without having to become directly involved in internal security or other expensive complications, by the mid–nineteenth century Britain had found a cost-effective means of maintaining a strong influence over the area while containing indigenous power bases and trade networks. Consistent with the overall imperial policy of extending control informally if possible and formally only when necessary,[118] the lower Gulf had therefore begun to suit ideally Lord Palmerston's famous nineteenth-century demand, "All we want is trade and land is not necessary for trade; we can carry on commerce on ground belonging to other people."[119]

Nevertheless, as an indirect result of these peace treaties Britain was drawn into a closer relationship with the rulers of the coastal towns. Indeed, as Britain's policing role inevitably expanded to include the arbitration of local disputes, many of the rulers and their courts became dependent on British support for their judgments.[120] Moreover, given that only recognized rulers were selected to be signatories of the Perpetual Treaty, some even began to draw strength from their treaty agreements, as rival shaikhs were effectively delegitimized by their nonsignatory status. After a time, Britain also began to screen potential new rulers to check if they were likely to adhere to existing as well as future treaties. If a new ruler was deemed suitable he was then sent a fresh copy of the treaties, thus formalizing his sovereignty in British eyes and often among his own people.[121] Indeed, as Rosemarie Said Zahlan has described: "One of the first concerns of a ruler after he assumed power was to obtain recognition of his status from the British government. Without it he could not survive for very long, for it was his relationship with Britain that allowed him to continue in power."[122] Thus, British influence had become paramount in approving rulers, and it often happened that if a shaikh strayed from the terms of the treaties he would lose popular support from a community that preferred to tow the line and not endanger its pearling or trading operations.[123]

As such, even though Britain was not directly involved in internal politics, its distant authority nonetheless caused a massive change to the lower Gulf's balance of power. Most obvious, the treaties and their recognition of the region's current rulers effectively froze a snapshot of local power struggles and stabilized formerly elastic territorial boundaries,[124] thus preventing any indigenous challenge to the status quo and thereby bringing to an end the previously described ebb and flow of tribal politics. Indeed, the immediate aftermath of the expedition against the Qasimi capital of Ra's al-Khaimah provides such an example. Spurred on by the Qawasim's decline in regional prestige and power, the nearby towns of Umm al-Qawain and 'Ajman seized the opportunity to claim independence, thus geographically splitting Ra's al-Khaimah from Sharjah, the other main Qasimi base. Moreover, multiple revolts in Fujairah and Hamriyyah,[125] and the family's loss of control over Lingah on the Persian coastline,[126] had also weakened Qasimi power in Ra's al-Khaimah, allowing Sharjah to emerge as the pre-eminent town of the lower Gulf.[127] When the British treaties began to be introduced, all of these newly independent towns were well placed to sign, which effectively guaranteed their future sovereignty and prevented any reprisal from their former Ra's al-Khaimah overlords.[128] Although perhaps less obvious, another important consequence of these maritime treaties for the balance of power was their effective formalization of the supremacy of the coastal tribes and towns over those of the interior, thereby allowing the maritime rulers to absorb more easily large tracts of the hinterland into their Trucial states.[129] Indeed, if one follows Jacqueline Ismael's parallel argument for Kuwait, this superiority can be seen as adding another explanatory layer for the lower Gulf's increasing peripheralization, as the coastal towns' absorption of the weakened interior further imbalanced the regional economy, thereby reducing the likelihood of future indigenous development.[130]

In addition to indirectly altering the local power structures, the presence of the British also began to have a major impact on some of the region's long-practiced economic activities, especially the slave trade, which had always been a highly profitable venture for many of the local Arabs, with even the ruler of Sharjah believed to have been levying a tax on each successfully imported slave.[131] The slaves were shipped from the east coast of Africa to the lower Gulf's ports, most notably to 'Ajman and Umm al-Qawain, and from these they would be transported by land into the Arabian interior, where they would finally be sold to wealthy patrons. Although many British individuals also prospered from slavery,[132] there was nonetheless a growing moral consensus against slavery in the empire, and by 1838 this had culminated in the outlawing of slavery in all British dominions. Given that the shaikhdoms of the lower Gulf were not actually British colonies, but simply in treaty relations with Britain, these developments did not immediately affect the region. Nevertheless, Britain did place increasing pressure on the rulers to abandon slavery voluntarily,[133] and agreements were soon drawn up that allowed British cruisers to detain and search suspected slaving vessels, and that required all Somalis (most of whom were British subjects) to be freed from slave labor in the Gulf. In 1847 a further treaty outlawed the export of slaves from Africa by Arab ships,[134] and in 1856 the restrictions were further tightened, requiring all of the rulers to embargo and hand over any suspected vessels that arrived in their ports.[135] These efforts gradually reduced slavery, but it took a long time and there were pockets of strong resistance to the policy of manumission even as late as the 1950s, especially in the interior, where tribal gangs would frequently hold up traffic and make abductions,[136] and where some slaves were even being employed by the oil exploration companies.[137]

Significantly, this persistence of slavery and Britain's continuing opposition to the lucrative activity created a window of opportunity for certain other powers, including the French and the Ottomans, to gain influence in the region. This attempted intervention, together with a number of other factors, led Britain to seek even greater control over its Trucial states in order to prevent future interference from external powers, and to discourage any "playing off" between the local powers and Britain's rivals. Thus, by the latter part of the nineteenth century, the political relationship between Britain and the Trucial states expanded even further to include control over the region's foreign affairs. This time, however, the catalyst was neither the Qawasim nor any other northern power, but instead the Bani Yas of Abu Dhabi, a powerful tribal agglomeration that controlled not only a large section of the southern coastline but also most of the slaving routes into the interior.[138] Unlike the "Qasimi pirates," the Bani Yas had been relatively untroubled by earlier British involvement given that their other economic activities were centered around the date groves of Liwa and the pearl fisheries close to Dalma island, both far away from the main trading routes of the Gulf. However, as the Bani Yas continued to prosper they also began to assume a position of supremacy over the weakened northern shaikhdoms, symbolized by their ruler's defeat of the Ra's al-Khaimah shaikh in single combat.[139] Naturally this emergence of a new indigenous power bloc became a cause of concern for the British, who were keen to maintain the detached nature of the Trucial system. Far more important, however, the British were also becoming increasingly distressed by Abu Dhabi's attempts to seek external support for their slaving activities from other regional and foreign powers. Indeed, Shaikh Zayed bin Khalifa of Abu Dhabi had begun to form a close alliance with the Sultan of Muscat, who by this stage was receiving overtures from the French. Indeed, by the 1880s the French had already given their flag and citizenship to the slave-trading sailors of the port of Sur in Oman,[140] with the clear intention of undermining the British antislavery agreements, stirring resentment among those in favor of slaving and bolstering French support in the region. Furthermore, many of the region's more enterprising slave traders were beginning to sail into the Gulf under French flags from Djibouti, thus avoiding the British restrictions.[141]

By 1890 this encroachment had become an even more serious threat, with French diplomats reportedly having begun to visit the ruler of Umm al-Qawain, who by all accounts was receptive to their advances.[142] Moreover, the ruler of Dubai was also believed to have been openly discussing the advantages of taking the French flag, thereby "escaping the malice of the English"[143] or, as one local historian has described, "courting the French in an effort to evade the British protection grip."[144] Moreover, by the end of the nineteenth century Britain had to face possible interference not only from the French but also from the Ottomans. Indeed, Ottoman influence had already begun to reach as far as Qatar, and at one point the official *Baghdad Gazette* even listed Bahrain and eight towns in the Trucial states as being part of the Turkish-controlled province of Najd.[145] Similarly disturbing for the British were the reports of Persian representatives attempting to gain a foothold in the region. These agents were thought to be stirring religious sentiments among the local Arabs and were reported to have met with the rulers of Abu Dhabi and Dubai in an effort to persuade them to denounce "Christian influences" and allow for their towns to come under the Persian sphere of influence.[146]

Inevitably, Britain regarded all such contact with foreign powers, including correspondence, as undermining both the Trucial system and imperial authority. If French, Ottoman, or Persian agents were allowed to visit and gain influence with the local rulers, the British stood to lose some or all of the control they had carefully established over the region earlier in the century. Britain's low-cost and almost self-enforcing maritime treaties would be undone, and its crucial trade routes to India and the Far East would once again face competition and possible security threats. The solution was seen as being an "exclusivity agreement" that would require all of the signatories of the earlier maritime truces to accept complete British management of their foreign policies. Consequently, in 1892 (at the height of the Bani Yas "violations") such an agreement was proposed. Although it was viewed by many of the locals as being yet another "reinforcement of the eternal subordination of the shaykhdoms,"[147] it was nevertheless accepted by the rulers, many of whom remained wary of British naval power and the economic consequences of renewed instability. Essentially, this new contract bound the rulers and their future heirs not to

> enter into any agreement or correspondence with any power other than the British Government . . . and they were not allowed to . . . cede, sell, mort- gage or otherwise give for occupation any part of their territory except to the British Government. . . . The exact international effect of these two agreements [referring to the 1892 agreement and the final maritime truce of 1853] is a matter for publicists to determine, but taken together they evidently create preferential and almost exclusive relations between the British Government and the Trucial Chiefs—relations which might be held to imply the dependency of the Shaykhs on the British Government in foreign affairs and a moral obligation on the part of the British Government to protect the Shaykhs in so far as they be endangered, or disabled from defending themselves.[148]

### Greater Peripheralization and the Emergence of Rentier Structures

Although British Indian merchants had long been involved in the lower Gulf's pearling industry on an individual level, by the turn of the twentieth century the Bombay government had also begun to take far more interest in the activity. Essentially, in much the same way as the fear of foreign inter- vention in the region's slave trade had prompted the British to assume con- trol over the lower Gulf's foreign affairs, the attempts of European mer- chants and entrepreneurs to capitalize on the region's pearling boom and to develop technologically the local industry led the British to seek greater economic protection for its Trucial states. Specifically, a number of German and French entrepreneurs had decided that by cooperating with the local Arabs and by offering them more modern equipment and access to new markets, both parties could make considerable profits.[149] Indeed, for- eigners made several requests for pearling rights in the Gulf during this period, but Bombay's policy remained unchanged and Britain began to police strictly the pearl banks against any unauthorized foreign intrusion. Furthermore, the British political resident explicitly advised against any of the Arabs accepting foreign assistance, arguing that he needed to create an Anglo-Arab monopoly in order to protect the Arabs' primary source of income,[150] because if the industry ever failed then many of the Arabs would be driven to gunrunning, piracy, and slaving.[151] Indeed, a letter from the political resident to the government made his position quite clear, warning of the danger of granting pearling concessions to Britain's rivals and forbidding the use of any modern technology in what should remain a "traditional activity."[152] Thus when this policy was eventually formalized in 1905 the following statement was issued:

> Within the three mile limit, and in any other water which might justly be considered territorial, the tribes of the Arabian Coast were entitled to the exclusive use of the pearl fisheries. As regards pearl banks outside territorial waters it was held that, as a matter of international law, such banks were capable of being the property of the tribes to the exclusion of all nations.[153]

Moreover, in 1914 this decision was reinforced by a new agreement that prevented the rulers from giving any concessions for pearling or sponge fishing without first consulting the British political resident.[154] Given that permission for such concessions was never granted,[155] the Gulf had therefore been transformed into a "British lake" under the total control of Bombay and effectively sealed off from all other economies.[156] Significantly, this protection, by inhibiting domestic and externally assisted development and by restricting access to other markets, can be seen as having limited the opportunities of the aforementioned indigenous merchant class and thereby further strengthening the already peripheralized nature of the region's economy.

As the century progressed, this economic dependency on Britain and India continued to increase, with many of the rulers beginning to receive and rely upon generous income from imperial air landing rights. During the late 1920s, refueling facilities were required for military aircraft en route from Britain to India, and, given that Persia was no longer viable, Sharjah was deemed an excellent alternative refueling point.[157] An agreement with the ruler was duly signed, dictating that he would host a British airbase and in return would receive a personal income of 500 rupees per month and a further 5 rupees for every aircraft that landed in Sharjah.[158] In 1932 another agreement was reached in which Sharjah would provide similar civilian landing facilities for Imperial Airways aircraft,[159] also in exchange for generous remuneration.[160] These air concessions were not restricted to Sharjah, and similar agreements were signed in 1937 with the ruler of Dubai, allow-ing Imperial Airways to land flying boats on the Dubai Creek.[161] Even Kalba, a small town on the Indian Ocean coastline, was temporarily granted independence from Sharjah and declared to be a Trucial state in its own right precisely so it could be used as a landing facility.[162]

Oil, or rather oil exploration concessions, added another layer of dependence and of course another source of income for the rulers. In 1922, in a further example of increasing British protection and control over the region's foreign relations, the Trucial shaikhs undertook not to consider any oil concessions that were not supported by the British government. In other words the rulers were made to refuse any offers from the rival U.S. oil com-panies that had already begun prospecting in other parts of southern Arabia. At this early stage there was no firm proof of oil in the lower Gulf but, given that Britain had already imposed similar agreements on the rulers of Kuwait and Bahrain, it seemed practical to lock the Trucial states into the same sys-tem. As such, in 1935 the London-based Iraqi Petroleum Company (IPC) formed a wholly owned subsidiary, Petroleum Concessions Ltd., which was to be the sole operator of concessions in the lower Gulf.[163] Unsurprisingly the political resident soon issued an ultimatum binding the Trucial rulers to deal only with Petroleum Concessions. Tellingly, the company had not both-ered to include distant Fujairah in this agreement, but when the Arab-American Oil Company (ARAMCO) made an approach to the Sharqiyin family, the ultimatum was immediately extended to the Batinah coastline.[164] As Peck notes, these accords, in much the same way as the 1922 agreement, should not necessarily be seen as reflections of British interest in the discov-ery of oil deposits in the region (given that Britain already had a great sup-ply at that time), but instead as expressions of the continuing British desire to exclude other foreign parties from the economic and political affairs of the Trucial states: "The oil agreements might thus be seen as symbolising the considerable degree of isolation that British protection imposed on the Trucial States."[165] Crucially, these concessions also provided another high stream of income for the rulers, which in some cases even dwarfed the gen-erous air landing fees. Indeed, the Dubai concession (signed in 1938) pro-vides such an example, as the ruler was to be given 60,000 rupees on sign-ing, a substantial annual income of 30,000 rupees, and then the oil company would pay 200,000 rupees upon the discovery of any oil.[166]

In addition to increasing the rulers' dependency on Britain as a source of easy nonearned income, the very nature of this new wealth must also be seen as an important historical antecedent of more contemporary structures. Although this subject will be discussed in greater depth in the next chapter,[167] it is nevertheless significant to note how much of the lower Gulf's preoil wealth was also derived from "economic rent" (the difference between the return made by a factor of production and the return necessary to keep the factor in its current occupation).[168] Indeed, upon closer inspection, it would appear that the region has experienced a long history of such "rentier wealth," with some of the aforementioned activities such as the booty from Bedu raids and the issuing of fishing licenses,[169] together with examples of income from guano-collecting concessions and red oxide mining authorizations, all providing early indications of rent-gathering.[170] With the generous air landing fees and oil exploration concessions, however, this rentier wealth was raised to a new level. Significantly, although now enormous, these payments continued to accrue directly to the ruler, with the bulk of the population remaining uninvolved in the wealth creation process. Indeed, Shaikh Sa'id al-Maktum, the ruler of Dubai at that time, believed, as did the other rulers receiving such vast incomes from concessions, that these guaranteed annual rents were to be his personal profit.[171] Consequently, the previously described balance of power between the wealthy indigenous merchant class and the rulers began to shift, especially as the newly rich shaikhs were able to reduce their reliance on taxation and instead distribute wealth to their people. As such, many of the traditional extractive institutions fell into decline, and eventually a new rentier relationship was born between the rulers and their populations, a relationship that is still in evidence today (see Figure 1.3).

### Local Resistance and the Suppression of the Dubai Reform Movement

Given that the early oil exploration concessions were all land-based, the IPC needed Britain to establish a more extensive security umbrella across the region, providing a secure environment for its personnel and better protection for the company's interests. These concerns, together with the rise of Ibn Saud and the perceived threat to British airbases from resurgent Wahhabism,[172] led to fresh calls for a greater British commitment to the region's internal stability. Quite simply the stakes were now higher than before. Although creating a full-blown protectorate was still deemed unnecessary,[173] many in the British Indian government, including the political resident of the Gulf, argued that these new circumstances required Britain to assume greater responsibilities in the Trucial states: to ensure more directly the orderly succession from shaikh to shaikh, to maintain the shaikhs' individual powers, and to protect the Trucial states by land as well as sea. Thus, in light of these recommendations, together with air staff memoranda along similar lines, the British prime minister and the foreign secretary responded by setting up the Gulf subcommittee of the Committee of Imperial Defence.[174]

The subcommittee's role was clarified when, in 1934, it was decided that for the first time Britain should openly intervene in a local struggle. As described earlier, Dubai had emerged as one of the region's main ports and

**Figure 1.3 A History of Economic Rent in the Lower Gulf**

> **Traditional/nomadic times**
>
> • Al-Ghanima: "booty wealth" gained from nomadic conquests was kept and later distributed by the ruler.
>
> • Fishing licenses: the ruler could issue such licenses in exchange for a fee.
>
> • Guano concessions: vast deposits of guano were sold to Gulf merchants.

↓

> **1920s to 1930s**
>
> Airways retainers: the rulers of Sharjah, Dubai, and Kalba received retainers from Imperial Airways in exchange for civilian and military air landing and refueling rights.

↓

> **1930s to 1960s**
>
> Oil concessions: exploration rights agreed between international oil companies and the local rulers, providing them with another source of revenue.
>
> Red oxide: exports of red oxide from the island of Abu Musa generated rentier wealth for the ruler of Sharjah.

↓

> **1960s to the present**
>
> Oil wealth: massive economic rent accrued from the export of oil and gas allowed the rulers to undertake comprehensive economic and social development.

by this stage had become a key distribution point for the oil companies. Thus, when the ruler narrowly escaped an assassination attempt by two of his cousins, Britain immediately responded in an effort to secure the city. British armaments were overtly delivered to the surviving shaikh, Sa'id al-Maktum. Moreover, a British message of support for the al-Maktum family was circulated throughout Dubai and backed up by a squadron of Iraqi-based British aircraft that flew over the town several times at low altitude. Following this armed response, the shaikh's cousins immediately relinquished their claims.[175]

Even more significant than this succession dispute and Britain's early show of force, however, were the events surrounding the Dubai reform movement of 1938, especially with regard to the reinforcement of the local rulers' client status and the continuing isolation and peripheralization of the lower Gulf's economy. In much the same way as Ismael's example of the Kuwaiti commercial class who had tried to reestablish trading links with other parts of Arabia during the interwar period,[176] and the Bahraini merchants who had begun to demonstrate at this time,[177] Dubai's merchants also attempted to readjust existing structures by imposing reforms on their ruler. Essentially, faced with economic decline and marginalization following the collapse of the pearling industry, they were trying to revitalize the lower Gulf's autonomous development, but as with the other Gulf merchant communities, their movement was suppressed by a ruler who had the clear support of the British.

Indeed, given that the decline in pearling was concurrent with the described rise in the rulers' rentier income, the increasing disparity prompted many of the merchants to request the rulers to share their wealth and to allow much more of it to be managed by the community in the interests of improving social conditions and boosting indigenous development.[178] Crucially, however, unlike most rulership contests, Dubai's merchants did not necessarily intend to depose their ruler. Instead the merchants and other disgruntled notables decided to set up a new consultative majlis in which the ruler would be recognized as the president of a fifteen-member chamber, but in exchange would have to share seven-eighths of Dubai's total revenue.[179] The shared revenue was to be spent in the name of the state and only with the prior approval of the members of the new majlis.

Although this merchants' majlis operated for only a very brief period, Heard-Bey nevertheless shows from the correspondence and minutes of their meetings how its members not only were concerned with practical economic reforms, but also intended to bring about key changes in the political and social structures.[180] Indeed, the majlis quickly established a number of important institutions, including a municipal council, in addition to planning for a social security system for the elderly and electing new customs officials to be employed by the state, not the ruler.[181] Moreover, Abdullah highlights the movement's considerable financial contribution to Dubai's education system and its concerted efforts to reopen Dubai's schools. Indeed, the majlis established an education department and appointed a director-general for Dubai schools; and as noted in the majlis's documents, its representatives even managed to recruit the majority of teachers from the local population (many of whom were older Dubai men who had been educated during the pearling boom when schools had flourished).[182]

Thus, in light of these efforts and their many other innovations and recommendations, the merchants believed that the presence of their majlis was welcomed by all of Dubai, and also felt that "its mandate carried a responsibility towards all groups and communities within the state, and that to reform certain aspects of government improved the lot of the common man and was therefore a national duty."[183] The ruler and those loyal to his regime, however, were far from defeated. When, in 1939, the majlis decided to add even more limitations to his income by allowing him to retain just 10,000 rupees of the state's revenue for "personal use," Shaikh Sa'id was forced to resort to military means. The majlis responded by blocking all access to Deira (the merchant-controlled eastern half of the town) from the shaikh's armed supporters in Bur Dubai, but a plan was drawn up when, in an apparent peace offering, the ruler's younger brother Rashid proposed to marry into a prominent Deira family. The merchants made the mistake of relaxing their control to allow Rashid's men to cross the creek to participate in a gun salute at the wedding.[184] When this loyal contingent of Bedu was unleashed, the majlis and its members were attacked and quickly dispersed, thereby allowing Shaikh Sa'id to regain control over all of Dubai.[185]

Crucially, this collapse of the majlis would have been inevitable in any event, given Britain's continuing support for the al-Maktum family. Given that Shaikh Sa'id and the other Trucial rulers remained the preferred clients of the Bombay government, the prospect of any potentially autonomous political movement was unacceptable to British interests.[186] Certainly, although the British publicly viewed the merchants' majlis and their reform attempts with indifference, British misgivings over the movement were nevertheless clearly in evidence. Indeed, in a revealing effort to bolster indigenous support for the beleaguered ruler following the dispersal of his opponents, the British political resident's statement erroneously claimed that the majlis had collapsed due to mismanagement and a lack of popular support:

> Recently there has been democratic movement in the State of Dubai which is in special treaty relations with His Majesty's Government. This was an internal matter and HMG however advised the Shaykh to associate

his people with himself in his government according to immemorial Arab custom by formation of a Council. The Shaykh did not take this advice and a Council was forced on him by the people which owing to maladministration later grew unpopular. At the end of March Shaykh Sa'id with his supporters dissolved the Council.[187]

Finally, despite the movement's collapse, it must also be noted how many of its actions and suggestions were not without some long-term achievement, with many of them forming the blueprints for later initiatives undertaken by the rulers themselves. Indeed, in the 1940s and 1950s, Shaikh Sa'id and his new *majlis al-tujjar* attempted to rejuvenate many of the merchants' planned improvements in an effort to boost the emirate's commercial prosperity.[188] Furthermore, upon his succession in 1958, one of Shaikh Rashid's very first acts was to reestablish the Dubai municipal council, despite having championed his brother's cause against it just twenty years previously. The municipal council, when founded, appointed councilors to represent different sections of the community for periods of two years. It was empowered to make the necessary orders for the administration of the town and to administer Dubai's first official development plans, all of which were commissioned by the ruler and prepared by British experts.[189] The key difference between this council and the merchants' majlis was of course that it had to subject all of its decisions to the ruler's confirmation and had to seek its financial support from the ruler's office. Thus the rulers of Dubai chose reform only when they had complete control and the approval of British advisers, and when the previously powerful merchant elites had completely lost their ability to operate autonomously of the core-periphery relationship.

## Britain and the Path to Federation

Shortly after the suppression of the merchants' movement, another important step took place. In 1948, Britain decided to deploy troops in the region for the first time since the 1820 landings in order to enforce peace attempts between the squabbling emirates of Dubai and Sharjah.[190] As before, a visible and direct response was effective, with the conflict soon subsiding and the security of the British airbases being maintained.[191] The most extensive British intervention, however, did not take place until the 1950s. As described earlier, the Buraimi Oasis and its surrounding villages had been a bone of contention between many of the local powers for hundreds of years, and once again the dispute had come to the fore, this time becoming international news. Increasing friction between Britain and the United States had manifested itself in a major struggle between their respective oil companies. Thus, when ARAMCO, the U.S. concession holder for Saudi

Arabia, pressed its host country to stake a fresh claim on the area, conflict was inevitable. The aforementioned zakat tax was used as a lever in the struggle and ARAMCO devoted all of its scholarly resources to proving the legitimacy of the Saudis' claim.[192] In 1952, when a Saudi force was finally sent to secure the area, Britain responded by backing an armed Omani contingent and demanding the surrender of the ARAMCO/Saudi troops. This British force temporarily secured the area, but as a side note this dispute was so difficult to resolve that it lingered until 1974, when Shaikh Zayed, the president of the UAE, reportedly had to offer Saudi Arabia the Zarara oil fields and a strategic corridor of land to the Gulf in exchange for Saudi recognition of UAE sovereignty.[193] Even then, this agreement remained informal until 1992,[194] and still today certain powerful elements in Abu Dhabi continue to dispute its validity.[195]

The severity of the Buraimi crisis therefore highlighted the need for the region's improved collective security, as the British had little desire to make repeated and expensive deployments. As such, believing that greater regional unity would better guarantee such security, by the mid-1950s Britain began to become more directly involved in the region's institutional development. Thus, in addition to providing limited military and financial support as and when required, Britain also started setting up a Trucial council with the aim of bringing the various rulers of the Trucial states together. Although this early council was merely an advisory body and had no formal constitution, it nevertheless did engender some degree of unity and "corporate sense" between the previously disparate shaikhdoms,[196] and as all decisions that were reached had to be implemented by the rulers themselves,[197] it provided valuable experience for those involved. The British political agent in Sharjah presided over the council until 1965, when it was decided that the chairmanship should be rotated among the seven rulers, and that the task of examining and preparing proposals for the council should be given to a deliberative committee comprising two delegates from each emirate.[198]

Even so, the British agent remained involved in the council's affairs and sat in on all of its subsequent meetings. He also remained active in trying to put forward Britain's views on what should be the region's key development priorities.[199] Indeed, as Heard-Bey describes, the agent or his deputy continued to preside over many board meetings ranging from hospitals to trade schools, and over many other committees engaged in local development projects.[200] The representatives of the British oil companies were also involved, and it became increasingly common for them to sit with their Arabic interpreters at the rulers' majalis and discuss matters of mutual interest, such as local employment, training, and healthcare.[201] Initially the budget for the council was provided from a British-administered Trucial development fund that, as an earlier version of the federal budget, allowed for a Trucial development office to assume responsibility for the implementation of various regionwide five-year plans.[202] Initially, Britain's contributions formed the bulk of the budget, but as the region's oil revenues began to increase, so too did the indigenous contributions, and by the time the office was transferred to a federal ministry Abu Dhabi was already contributing several million pounds sterling per annum and over 80 percent of the total fund.[203] However, this greater financial independence in no way reduced the rulers' reliance on British tutelage and support.

As Britain had anticipated, the council's first priority was to secure the hinterland and to allow for safe transport and communications between the shaikhdoms without the fear of raiders.[204] To this end the Trucial Oman Levies (renamed the Trucial Oman Scouts in 1956) was formed as a British-officered standing army and was placed under the command of the political resident in Bahrain so as "to give more weight to decisions taken by the British in internal matters."[205] As the first visible reflection of Britain's greater institutional involvement, the force was regarded as a great success given its important role in policing the Buraimi area, in mopping up the remnants of the slave trade, and in assisting the oil companies in their exploration of the desert.[206] Certainly, with a more secure environment and a greater degree of regional cooperation, the Levies provided the necessary foundation for the council to press ahead with its other objectives. Notably, by the mid-1960s, many other institutions had already been established, and many other services were being provided under the auspices of the Trucial States Development Office, including:

- The provision of agricultural services.[207]
- The operation of trade and technical schools in Sharjah and Dubai.
- The provision of scholarships abroad for talented subjects of the Trucial states.
- The provision of courses of instruction for the administrative staff of the Trucial State Council.
- The provision of health services (centered in Dubai's Al-Maktum Hospital), in addition to a touring doctor service, several rural clinics, and another hospital in Ra's al-Khaimah.
- The creation of a department to survey and develop fishery resources.
- The creation of a public works department to execute the capital works program with overall responsibility for the development of water resources, buildings, road maintenance, and the supervision of public utilities.[208]
- The establishment of a court of first appeal and a criminal assize court.
- The establishment of police forces in Dubai and Abu Dhabi.[209]

Moreover, in addition to the development office's efforts, considerable aid and assistance began to flow into the region from some of the other British-backed Gulf states. By far the most significant of these benefactors was Kuwait, which after attaining formal independence in 1961 chose to establish a Gulf Permanent Assistance Committee (GUPAC) to recommend and administer economic aid to the less developed areas of the Gulf. Soon after, a GUPAC office was set up in Dubai to coordinate Kuwaiti aid to the Trucial states, the bulk of which was concentrated in the education sector. Kuwait financed the salaries of most of the expatriate teachers, helped to train local teachers, helped to construct schools, and contributed to the development office's overseas scholarships.[210] On a smaller but still notable scale, Qatar and Bahrain also contributed, not only to the development fund but also by assisting in the construction of highways and the provision of fresh water supplies.[211] Similarly, but quite bizarrely given the kingdom's humiliation over the Buraimi step-down, there is also evidence to suggest that elements in Saudi Arabia may have made modest donations to GUPAC and these other projects. Indeed, it would seem that a friendly Saudi minority sought to quickly strengthen the lower Gulf in order to boost the potential number of fellow conservative monarchies in the Arab League.[212]

However, despite these primarily British- and British-Gulf-administered developments, many believed that London's long-term postwar retrenchment (since 1931 Britain had been running a persistent balance of payments deficit, reflecting both its weakening competitive position industrially and the reduction of its invisible earnings)[213] would soon lead to a withdrawal from the region, and that the Trucial states were still inadequately prepared for such an eventuality.[214] Without more improvements, new institutions, and new legislation, it was thought unlikely that the regional administration would be able to function smoothly; given the expansionary ambitions of neighboring Saudi Arabia and nearby Iran, it was feared that the area would quickly be absorbed by a foreign power. As such, the late 1960s witnessed even more rapid development, especially in the coordination of actions between the various Trucial states, with many of what were soon to become the UAE's federal institutions being set up. The announcement, however, came sooner than expected when in December 1967 a Westminster white paper was published calling for the termination of Britain's bases east of Suez and a proposed withdrawal by 1971.[215] Although there was a brief period of uncertainty following a surprise Conservative election victory in 1970,[216] no reversal of the Labour Party's policies took place, and all that happened was a long-drawn-out delay before Edward Heath's government finally reaffirmed its predecessor's original departure date.[217]

The local reaction, at least from the ruling elite, was one of intense disappointment, as many felt that much of the recent development work would stall or be undone without further British support. Similarly, those Britons working in the Gulf believed that the couple of million pounds sterling that London spent maintaining British forces and the administration in the Trucial states was a more than worthwhile insurance for the £2 billion in annual revenues generated by the oil companies operating there.[218] Indeed, it is believed that Shaikh Zayed al-Nuhayyan and the rulers of the other oil-producing sheikdoms were so reluctant to lose British protection that they even offered to pay toward maintaining an imperial presence in the lower Gulf. As a report to the British cabinet described:

> [Zayed] would be happy to contribute the funds himself from his oil revenues to secure the continuance of the benefits he and his fellow rulers derived from the British presence in the Gulf. His neighbour, Shaykh Rashid of Dubai, made a like proposal a fortnight later. The four oil-producing Shaykhdoms under British protection—Dubai, Abu Dhabi, Bahrain and Qatar—would be perfectly willing, Rashid said, to meet, in proportion to their respective means, the annual cost of retaining the British forces in the Gulf.[219]

This willingness, more than anything else, points to the closeness of the relationship that Britain had built with its clients by the eve of the withdrawal. New wealth was on the horizon and, without British support, the rulers were actually disinclined to accept their "independence."

## The Federation of Emirates

Although scaling back her military presence in the Gulf in the late 1960s, Britain did remain closely involved in the region. Besides continuing to help create many of the institutions that any new independent state would need to inherit, British advisers also continued to encourage plans for even greater unity and for some kind of federal framework of collective security between the various shaikhdoms, or "emirates" as they were becoming known.[220] Indeed, as both Fenelon and Zahlan contend, the British had long been aware of the possibility of such a union given that the political residency in Bahrain had been imposing some degree of uniformity on the seven emirates for over a century.[221] Furthermore, as Hawley explains, the British were also conscious of the historical effectiveness of interemirate cooperation, with the residency having recorded examples of successful meetings between the Trucial shaikhs as far back as 1905.[222] More significant, in the 1930s there had also been a British-forwarded proposal for a ten-member association comprising Bahrain, Qatar, Kuwait, and the Trucial states. Among other things, this proposal had called for:

- The establishment of a council in which each emirate would field a representative.
- The establishment of an assembly to propose regulations and ratify draft legislation.
- The unification of the judiciary and legislative systems.
- The creation of a common nationality, with the abolition of the necessity of passports for travel between the member emirates.
- The establishment of a unified education system, with a central administrative headquarters in Bahrain.
- The creation of a unified postal service.[223]

Although the outbreak of World War II had temporarily distracted Britain from the Gulf and little further energy was given to implementing the proposal, its contents nevertheless became widely known throughout the region, with the subject sparking much discussion in educated circles, especially from the Manama-based magazine *Al-Bahrain,*[224] and with many of the proposal's elements later being incorporated into the Trucial institutions of the 1950s and 1960s. Last, even if ignored by most texts, it is perhaps also useful to note the co-British/co-Arab attempts between 1959 and 1962 to create a "Federation of Emirates of the Arab South," which was to comprise the various Aden protectorates (five shaikhdoms and one sultanate in the far southwest of the Arabian peninsula). Although ultimately unsuccessful (eventually succumbing to external penetration), the experiment provided the political residency and local rulers with at least some idea of the potential advantages of such a venture in the lower Gulf.[225]

Thus, many administrators, both British and Arab, viewed federation as a natural progression for the region (provided that there was a relatively secure environment), especially as the Trucial States Council and the Trucial States Development Office had already allowed the rulers to perform jointly many of the functions that had previously been Britain's responsibility.[226] Certainly, as a former political agent in Dubai has noted, while it remained Britain's policy to protect the Trucial states right up until its departure, in these final years Britain did become far more open to granting the rulers freedom to make collective decisions of their own.[227] In fact, by this stage Britain was actively encouraging the rulers to gain as much administrative experience as possible, even in the previously restricted field of foreign relations. As such, the rulers were invited to attend international conferences, were allowed to establish foreign trade offices in their towns, and were even authorized to participate in a number of the Arab League's committees.[228] Moreover, during this ambiguous period of transition between British rule and full independence, Abu Dhabi was also permitted to join the Organization of Petroleum Exporting Countries (OPEC), the first of the Trucial states to do so, and in 1968 Shaikh Zayed al-

Nuhayyan was even allowed to visit Jordan and establish relations with Palestinian leader Yasser Arafat on behalf of Abu Dhabi and the other Trucial states.[229]

The first clear step toward a federation came in February 1969, when Shaikh Zayed met with Shaikh Rashid al-Maktum, the ruler of Dubai, and formally agreed to merge the two emirates into Al-Ittihad al-Thuna'i: a union capable of jointly conducting foreign affairs, defense, security, social services, and a common immigration policy.[230] Shortly afterward, with the added support of the British, the rulers of the five other Trucial states, in addition to the rulers of Bahrain and Qatar, met together in Dubai. These nine rulers held a constitutional conference to discuss the future of their states. The initial plan, as proposed by Qatar, called for the amalgamation of the five smallest Trucial states (Sharjah, Ra's al-Khaimah, 'Ajman, Fujairah, and Umm al-Qawain), which was to be known as the "United Arab Coastal Emirates." This union would allow these emirates to be considered as one state, thereby guaranteeing them a collective voice and easing future federal negotiations with the larger emirates of Abu Dhabi, Dubai, Bahrain, and Qatar.[231] Later that same year, a second meeting was convened, this time in Abu Dhabi, where once again the nine rulers and their advisers met to discuss the region's post-British future. Most important, all were agreed on the pressing need for some kind of federation, but already, even at this early stage, deep divides were beginning to emerge over the exact nature of the association. Bahrain and Ra's al-Khaimah demanded a popular referendum to decide upon the presidency, and some even saw the federation as a vehicle for evolving toward some form of democratic governance. The most important division, however, was the one emerging between the two principal Trucial states of Abu Dhabi and Dubai. Dubai wished for a president and a capital city to be decided upon as soon as possible, whereas Abu Dhabi and some of the smaller emirates advocated proceeding more slowly to allow everyone to adjust to the new situation.[232]

Nevertheless, despite these disagreements, the meetings continued, and in late 1969 a conference was held in which Shaikh Zayed was to be elected as president of the new federation, Al-Ittihad al-Tusa'i, with Shaikh Rashid as his vice president and Shaikh Khalifa bin Hamad al-Thani (the Crown Prince of Qatar) serving as the first prime minister. It was also hoped that the fast-growing city, Abu Dhabi, would be accepted as the federation's temporary capital until a new, permanent capital city could be built along the border of Abu Dhabi and Dubai. The name of the proposed site was Wadi al-Mawt, or "Valley of Death": not exactly an encouraging omen, and for a multitude of reasons and differences of opinion the conference collapsed and the nine shaikhs never again met as a council.[233] By this stage, Shaikh Zayed had come to terms with the fact that any proposed federation would be smaller than originally anticipated, as it was becoming increasingly unlikely that the wishes of Bahrain and Qatar could be fully accommodated. One factor was their determination that the federation's parliament or governing council needed to be based on a system of proportional representation. Given that they possessed the largest populations, however, this proposal was strongly rejected by the less populous Trucial states. Later, Bahrain did briefly agree to a system of equal representation in which each member state would supply four members, but by 1970 it had renewed its demands for representation based on population size.[234] Also, as the British ambassador to Bahrain explained, the emirate and its close neighbor were also becoming reluctant to join any kind of union that the increasingly wealthy Abu Dhabi could come to dominate. Another factor was the fear of the reaction of other regional powers to such a federation. In particular, Bahrain and Qatar did not want to be caught up in Abu Dhabi's continuing dispute with Saudi Arabia (as Saudi Arabia continued to claim nearly four-fifths of Abu Dhabian territory), and equally Abu Dhabi and the other Trucial states did not wish to be involved with Iran, which had laid claim to Bahrain.[235] Furthermore, as John Duke Anthony claims, the Trucial states collectively viewed Bahrain's population as being more politically advanced at that time and therefore potentially more radical. Indeed, following the Suez crisis in 1956 the emirate had already been obliged to exile three "reactionaries" and the British had been required periodically to impose martial law on the capital city of Manama throughout the 1960s.[236] For this combination of reasons, Bahrain and Qatar opted for complete independence, thus reducing the proposed federation to just seven potential members. However, as Zaki Nusseibeh, Shaikh Zayed's press secretary in the mid-1970s explained, this withdrawal should never have been any great concern for the Trucial states, and in many ways Abu Dhabi should have viewed Bahrain and Qatar as the real losers: "Bahrain was the real loser because she had so much to gain because she is not a wealthy country and by joining she would have shared the UAE's wealth. The sophistication of her people and their educational level would have given Bahrain a natural leadership role in the federation."[237]

As the date for British withdrawal drew closer, there was a great feeling of uncertainty and, for many, a feeling of negativity given the troubled negotiations, the absence of the two most developed emirates, and the Trucial states' uneasy relations with the other regional powers. Even many of the British were pessimistic, with a number of commentators describing the lack of confidence felt at that time. In 1966 David Holden described a distinguished journalist of the Middle East as having declared: "There is no realistic possibility of the present Gulf rulers coming together of their own accord in any political grouping worth mentioning . . . and the prospects of the British pushing them into doing so are equally weak."[238] Writing later, just a few months before the federation in 1971, Holden also reports it having been said that, "whatever happens, the Gulf has already entered a period of flux in which neither existing boundaries nor traditional regimes can be expected to prevail."[239] Even the British political resident of the Gulf at that time, Geoffrey Arthur, reflected on the negativity of the period:

> The UAE looked loose and ramshackle, and it was born, so said the facile commentator of the day, under the ill star of British patronage. . . . [The UAE] has since acquired a host of fair weather friends, but I do not recollect that a single special correspondent of a major western newspaper, let alone a politician or a statesman, took the trouble to attend the ceremony of its formation.[240]

Similarly, as Joseph Sisco, U.S. undersecretary for political affairs, retrospectively announced to Congress in 1975, the United States had also expressed grave doubts about the UAE holding together back in 1971.[241] Thus, both the old and the new superpowers in the Gulf had little confidence that the UAE would survive its infancy, with many believing it would soon succumb to either internal fragmentation or external threats.

The worst fears of many were confirmed when the British forces finally left. Although recently declassified secret documents have now shown that London spent fourteen months in 1970 and 1971 negotiating with Tehran on the Trucial states' behalf,[242] on the eve of departure Iran nevertheless immediately established a base on the island of Abu Musa, belonging to Sharjah (with the ruler's extreme reluctance),[243] and forcibly occupied two smaller islands belonging to Ra's al-Khaimah.[244] Second, Saudi Arabia's territorial dispute with Abu Dhabi remained unresolved, with the former deciding to withhold diplomatic recognition of any newly unified state and instead preferring to maintain bilateral relations with only Dubai and Ra's al-Khaimah.[245] Third, a Marxist-led rebellion was taking place in neighboring Oman.[246] Even so, despite this unpleasant cloud of doubt, a federation was officially proclaimed on 2 December 1971, and the United Arab Emirates came into being with Shaikh Zayed as its president and Abu Dhabi as its temporary capital. Soon after, a council of ministers was formed, as was a federal government in which each emirate was given a number of portfolios proportionate to its wealth;[247] within a few more days the UAE had joined both the Arab League and the United Nations as a full member. As had been expected, the transition was not entirely smooth given that certain institutions did not yet exist to take over all of the responsibilities previously fulfilled by the British; also, the Trucial Oman Scouts (renamed the Union Defence Force) continued to depend on many British officers and advisers,[248] and the judicial system still relied on British arbitration, but after a series of federal laws and with some further help from the British the takeover was finally complete.[249]

There was one internal security flaw that remained unresolved, however, and that was the absence of Ra's al-Khaimah from the federation. In much the same way as the early disputes between Abu Dhabi and Dubai, Ra's al-Khaimah's early stance is also worthy of attention, as its relative independence also had an effect on the later evolution of federal politics. The emirate had initially refused to join the UAE given that it was not accorded equal status with the other large emirates of Abu Dhabi, Dubai, and Sharjah, despite being the most populous of the former Trucial states.[250] Indeed, as this chapter has shown, Ra's al-Khaimah had enjoyed a long history of regional dominance, at one point being the main stronghold of the Qasimi traders, and as such felt that its proud past should have been better taken into account.[251] Second, the emirate had strong expectations for oil strikes of its own, which, if well-founded, would have transformed the emirate's economy and would have given it a far better bargaining position. Third, the emirate refused to sign an agreement with Iran over its two occupied islands in the same way that Sharjah had submitted to Iran over the loss of Abu Musa.[252] Fourth, Ra's al-Khaimah believed that the recent migration of two of its principal tribes (the Al-Khawatir to Al-'Ayn, and the Al-Za'ab to Abu Dhabi) had been not only encouraged but also financed by the al-Nuhayyan family, and was therefore a portent of increasing marginalization under an Abu Dhabi–dominated union.[253] Fifth, and perhaps most significant, it is believed that the ruler was still hoping that a high-level envoy he had recently dispatched to the United States would return with news that the Americans might support an independent Ra's al-Khaimah in exchange for the use of exclusive naval facilities.[254] Three months later, however, Ra's al-Khaimah did appear to accept the reality of its situation by finally agreeing to join the UAE, but only after the other emirates conceded to a number of its conditions.[255] They had to adopt the question of Iranian occupation as the main thrust of their foreign policy objectives, Ra's al-Khaimah was to receive generous federal aid for its development projects, and the emirate was to receive the same number of seats in the government as had Sharjah.[256]

Last, as another important product of these early federal negotiations, it is worth noting the rulers' careful creation of a provisional federal constitution. Although the main body of the constitution was nothing remarkable, what did make it unusual was the large number of emirate-specific clauses, including articles that permitted the individual emirates to retain control over their own oil revenues and local political institutions. Many of these were the result of long and complex debates, and were seen as necessary if a balanced compromise was to be reached. Indeed, as Heard-Bey notes: "The realities of political life in the UAE did not encourage rapid unification in every aspect, and this helped to maintain the integrity of the various local systems. It was eventually realised that these systems still had a very valuable role to play because of their immediate proximity to the citizen."[257] This attitude may explain why the constitution remained temporary for so long (until 1996) and is also perhaps one of the reasons behind the federation's initial stability. Indeed, as Ali Muhammad Khalifa has indicated, the intention to preserve certain existing laws and traditional institutions may well have eased the transition and kept the channels of access open to the people, thus allowing a more gradual shift of power between local and central administration.[258] Certainly, as will be explained in greater detail in Chapter 4, a more rigid and uncompromising constitution at this early stage would have probably unraveled within a few years, with each emirate seeking to reassert its independence and quickly falling back on more parochial forms of government.[259]

## Conclusion

In many ways the lower Gulf was doomed to a future of peripheralization given the region's scant geographical resources and the local economy's early reliance on both foreign labor and the export of a single primary product. Despite these conditions there were important signs of indigenous socioeconomic development. Indeed, with the pearling booms there began to evolve something of a capitalist mode of production and, significantly, a domestic merchant/entrepreneurial class began to emerge from the wealthier strata of the old desert hierarchy. Capable of funding local development projects and even checking the power of their rulers, these merchants were powerful players in lucrative economic networks stretching from South Asia to East Africa. Moreover, alongside these formations there also existed remarkably flexible and relatively decentralized political structures that allowed for direct channels of access to the rulers and highly effective systems of mobile and consultative democracy. Crucially, these traditional polities were also comparatively strong given that they possessed efficient extractive institutions that were capable of both collecting taxes and financing a range of rudimentary government services.

This inherited situation was fundamentally altered as the lower Gulf's increasing contact with the core economy and imperial power of Britain led to the elimination of certain traditional structures and the reinforcement of others. In particular, Britain's initial conflict with the Qawasim traders of Ra's al-Khaimah not only secured the British East India Company's trade routes but also displaced a major indigenous economic network and, through a system of maritime treaties, effectively transformed the remaining local rulers into a British client elite (see Figure 1.4). Indeed, by guaranteeing lasting peace in exchange for recognition of their sovereignty,

**Figure 1.4 The UAE: A Historical Background**

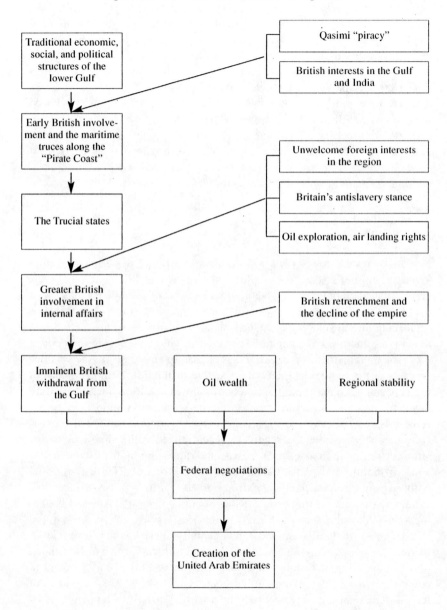

these externally strengthened Trucial rulers, many of whom would have otherwise held only precarious control over their rivals, effectively formalized their dependence on British support and thereby brought to an end the fluidity of the traditional tribal political structure. Moreover, as the region's strategic worth and the value of its resources increased, these clients were gradually persuaded by a combination of economic benefits and the implicit threat of renewed conflict to allow almost total British control over their foreign affairs and their local industries. Thus, by excluding all forms of outside intervention, Britain had for all intents and purposes turned the Gulf into a "British lake" isolated from other economic and political powers. Certainly, without such control and the detachment of the lower Gulf from the wider region, it is highly likely that the Trucial states would have either fallen under French influence or been absorbed into a Persian, Ottoman, or other indigenous economic bloc.

By the 1920s the dependency and responsiveness of these clients to their core patron was further reinforced as the rulers began to receive substantial and often personal incomes from British air companies and British oil exploration firms. Although the lower Gulf has experienced a long history of rent-gathering, these new sources of unearned rentier wealth were on a much greater scale and can be seen to have laid the foundations for many of the region's contemporary structures long before the first oil exports. Indeed, with access to such revenues the rulers were able not only to discontinue most of the existing extractive institutions and instead distribute wealth to their populations, but also to shift the traditional ruler-merchant balance of power. Certainly, with the rulers no longer reliant on their merchants for taxation, they were able to assume a new degree of autonomy over their people and, although there were attempts to reinvigorate indigenous development and share the rentier wealth (most notably the Dubai reform movement), these were easily suppressed by the British-backed clients.

Finally, even as the empire began to withdraw in the late 1960s, the British went to great lengths to ensure the survival of their former clients and their future oil suppliers by helping to build up regionwide institutions such as the Trucial States Council and the Trucial States Development Office. Indeed, by encouraging greater regional unity and a federal framework, it was hoped that the newly independent state could be guaranteed at least some measure of security from nearby powers and the threat of internal fragmentation. Significantly, many of the region's existing local systems and preferences, such as the emphasis on consultation and the direct channels of communication, were incorporated alongside these seemingly more central institutions, and as such the new state was able to ensure a relatively smooth transition without any significant break with the past. Thus, through careful negotiation and compromise the federation was able to steer its way through the initial complications and, in its early years, against the expectations of many, become one of the most stable and successful examples of Arab political union.

## Notes

1. FOREIGN OFFICE HISTORICAL SECTION (1920), p. 78; this extract is taken from the preamble to the "General Treaty Between Great Britain and the Arab Tribes of the Persian Gulf, 1820."
2. HAWLEY (1970), p. 195.
3. For an account of the lawlessness of the region and the impact of desert raiding, or ghazu, see "External Influences and the Trucial States," p. 21 in this volume. Also see "Greater Peripheralization and the Emergence of Rentier Structures," p. 34 in this volume, with regard to the division of the booty from such raids.
4. LORIMER (1915c) p. 2296. This falaj system (pl. aflaj) comprised subterranean stone tunnels that were designed to bring water down to the level of the towns from the high water tables of the nearby mountains. When the tunnels reached the agricultural gardens they would become surface channels, allowing the water to be regulated and redirected to wherever it was most needed.
5. HEARD-BEY (1982), pp. 168–169.
6. Ibid., pp. 171–172. Indeed, the name *Abu Dhabi* translates as "father of the white gazelle," the story being that hunters chased a lone gazelle onto what is now Abu Dhabi island and there encountered an abundance of such game.
7. HEARD-BEY (1982), p. 11.
8. FENELON (1973), p. 56.
9. LORIMER (1915c), p. 2252.
10. HEARD-BEY (1982), pp. 192–193.
11. Ibid., p. 195.
12. FENELON (1973), p. 56; and HAWLEY (1970), p. 197. Cultured pearls could be acquired at far less expense than the natural pearls of the Gulf.
13. LORIMER (1915c), p. 2220. Also see AL-SAYEGH (1998), p. 89.
14. JAML (1985), p. 56.
15. Ibid.
16. See, in this volume, "Diversification Through Industrialization," p. 123, "Diversification Through Agriculture," p. 128, "Diversification Through Commerce and Tourism," p. 131, and "The Physical Infrastructure for Diversification," p. 137.
17. HEARD-BEY (1982), pp. 208–209.
18. LORIMER (1915c), p. 2227. Strictly speaking, the captains were obliged to sell their boat's take to the financier at a rate of 75–90 percent of the market value, thereby avoiding any charge of usury. See LORIMER (1915c), p. 2233; and ABU BAKER (1995), pp. 94–95.
19. LORIMER (1915c), p. 2228. A great deal of information about the pearling proletariat and their treatment by the captains and financiers is contained in the interviews recorded in Abdullah Abd Al-Rahman's substantive work; see AL-RAHMAN (1990), pp. 90–91.
20. GRAHAM (1967), p. 147. For a discussion of Britain's impact on the region's slave trade, see "Greater British Political and Economic Involvement," p. 29 in this volume.
21. GREEN (1968), p. 171; and HAWLEY (1970), p. 205. Also see OXFORD

BUSINESS GROUP (2000), p. 45. Following India's independence, the New Delhi government chose to levy duties on gold, thereby boosting Dubai's attractiveness as a gold market and establishing the emirate as a base for "informal gold trading" with the subcontinent.

22. For a discussion of Dubai's commercial development strategy, see "Substrategies: Abu Dhabi and Dubai—A Comparative Analysis," p. 154 in this volume.

23. HEARD-BEY (1982), pp. 10–11.

24. Personal interviews, Abu Dhabi, March 2001. Also see ISMAEL (1993), pp. 17–18. Ismael provides a similar account of this hierarchy with reference to Kuwait.

25. KHALDUN (1377), p. 102.

26. Those tribes able to enjoy more fertile conditions in neighboring Oman were quicker to settle, and as such their communities gradually began to be organized along the lines of village neighborhood or in the form of occupational communities. See HEARD-BEY (1982), p. 24.

27. HEARD-BEY (1982), pp. 25–26.

28. Ibid., pp. 173–174.

29. KHALDUN (1377), pp. 141–142.

30. HEARD-BEY (1982), p. 200, with specific reference to Abu Dhabi.

31. For a list of other prominent merchant families (including notables in Sharjah, 'Ajman, and Umm al-Qawain), see AL-OTAIBI (1977). Also see ABDUL-LAH (1978), p. 104. In his study of the region Muhammad Mutawa' also refers to the al-Otaibi merchant family, claiming that at one point they owned many boats and employed more than 100 pearl divers; see MUTAWA' (1991), p. 31.

32. ABDULLAH (1978), p. 104. This refers to 1884, when Shaikh Saqr bin Khalid al-Qasimi was replaced by Shaikh Salim.

33. Ibid. Muhammad al-Rumaithi presents a similar view of the social and political implications of the pearling mode of production; see AL-RUMAITHI (1980), p. 49.

34. HEARD-BEY (1982), pp. 189–190.

35. LORIMER (1915d), p. 411.

36. ABDULLAH (1978), p. 105.

37. LORIMER (1915d), p. 1451.

38. With regard to British-Indian merchants and British-Indian agents (especially in Bahrain), see, for example, ONLEY (2003a).

39. HEARD-BEY (1982), pp. 212–213.

40. Ibid., pp. 214–215.

41. AL-SAYEGH (1998), p. 88.

42. ABDULLAH (1978), p. 105.

43. For further information on British Indians during this period, see ONLEY (2003a). Also see ONLEY (2003b).

44. FENELON (1973), p. 19.

45. HEARD-BEY (1982), pp. 56–57.

46. Ibid., p. 80. Other examples included Abu Dhabi's authority over the Batinah tribes in Oman, and Ra's al-Khaimah's control over areas of the Iranian coastline, notably Lingah. Personal interviews with Peter Hellyer, Abu Dhabi, October 2003.

47. PECK (1986), p. 125.

48. HEARD-BEY (1982), p. 100.

49. Ibid., p. 101.

50. Ibid., p. 217.

51. Ibid., pp. 179–180.

52. Ibid., pp. 124–125.

53. Ibid., pp. 85–86.

54. Ibid., p. 111.

55. Ibid., p. 81.

56. Personal interviews, Sharjah, October 2002.

57. HERB (1999), pp. 136–137. Also see "Dynastic Monarchy and the Evolution of the Traditional Polity," p. 97 in this volume.

58. HEARD-BEY (1982), pp. 120–121.

59. LORIMER (1915d), p. 409.

60. LORIMER (1915c), pp. 2284–2287; and HEARD-BEY (1982), p. 113.

61. HEARD-BEY (1982), p. 114.

62. Ibid., pp. 118–119.

63. Ibid., pp. 115–117.

64. Ibid., p. 117.

65. Ibid., p. 115.

66. For a discussion of patrimonial authority and Weberian groupings, see HUDSON (1977).

67. Tilly argues that the origins of a strong state must lie in its fiscal ability and tax-gathering structures; for a good discussion of Tilly's views, see CRYSTAL (1990, 1995), p. 194. Similarly, Chaudhry argues that extractive structures are a crucial sign of state strength; see CHAUDHRY (1997).

68. As described in earlier discussion of the traditional economic structure, Al-Mashriq (the eastern Arab world) was a major overland trading route, with many of the lower-Gulf's towns and ports serving as distribution points.

69. The most notable threat were the imams of Ya'aribah of East Africa, who were accused of attacking Portuguese shipping in the Indian Ocean. See ABDUL-LAH (1978), p. 81.

70. PECK (1986), p. 27.

71. HEARD-BEY (1982), p. 282.

72. Qishm being a large island close to the Straits of Hormuz and the present-day Iranian port of Bandar 'Abbas.

73. HEARD-BEY (1982), p. 280.

74. Ibid., pp. 229–230.

75. HAWLEY (1970), p. 90.

76. Ibid.

77. LORIMER (1915a), p. 436.

78. PECK (1986), pp. 29–30.

79. HAWLEY (1970), pp. 96–97.

80. BELGRAVE (1966), p. 25.

81. PECK (1986), pp. 29–30.

82. LORIMER (1915a), pp. 635–636. With regard to tributary systems, see DAVIES (1997), p. 181. Davies also suggests that the Qawasim initially tried to resist but then capitulated in the interests of self-preservation.

83. HAWLEY (1970), p. 101.

84. LORIMER (1915a), pp. 634–636. These two attacks took place in the 1790s, before the Wahhabis arrived in Buraimi, indicating an early pre-Wahhabi conflict between the Qawasim and the British.

85. Ibid., p. 634.

86. BELGRAVE (1966), p. 29.

87. Ibid., p. 30.

88. Ibid., p. 36.

89. Ibid., p. 37.

90. Ibid.

91. As Davies describes, shortly before the second decisive attack an emissary was sent from Ra's al-Khaimah "who seemed only to be in a quest of intelligence. . . . Bruce (the British Commander) dealt him a contemptuous rebuff." See DAVIES (1997), p. 295.

92. BELGRAVE (1966), pp. 135–143. Captain Loch's diaries are held in the Scottish Records Office.

93. Ibid.

94. Ibid., p. 192.

95. See AL-QASIMI (1986). Also see IBRAHIM (1978), p. 117.

96. See KELLY (1968, 1986).

97. AL-QASIMI (1986), pp. xiii–xv.

98. Ibid.

99. Ibid.

100. Ibid., p. xvii.

101. Ibid., p. 231.

102. Copies of the Bombay archives are now held at the University of Exeter. See DAVIES (1997), p. xiii.

103. The commander in question being Captain Perronet Thompson, whose letters are now held at the University of Hull and which have been more thoroughly investigated by Hubert Moyse-Bartlett; see MOYSE-BARTLETT (1966).

104. DAVIES (1997), p. 276.

105. Ibid., p. 283. Davies shows that direct imports from India on British vessels totaled 3 million rupees in 1817, and that this had roughly doubled by 1822.

106. DAVIES (1997), p. 283.

107. Ibid., p. 280.

108. PECK (1986), p. 31.

109. HAWLEY (1970), p. 107.

110. Ibid., pp. 126–127.

111. HEARD-BEY (1982), pp. 284–285.

112. LORIMER (1915a), pp. 695–696.

113. In 1821 'Ajman's fort was shelled after the ruler refused to board a British ship. The British dispatched the following message: "So my friend, be warned that your town is near the sea and therefore accessible. . . . I trust that you will have learned your lesson and that we shall have no more unpleasantness in the future." In 1825 Fujairah's fort was shelled after the ruler refused to hand over a Baluchi girl who was believed to have been abducted from Oman. The British explained that the matter could not be overlooked as it would have undermined the imperial authority. See ABU BAKER (1995), pp. 34–36.

114. ABU BAKER (1995), pp. 24–25.

115. LORIMER (1915a), p. 673.

116. PECK (1986), p. 32.

117. The squadron consisted of six Royal Navy cruisers, four of which patrolled the lower Gulf continuously. See ABU BAKER (1995), pp. 31–32.

118. See GALLAGHER and ROBINSON (1953), p. 13.

119. See HYAM (1976), p. 54.

120. Abdulkhaleq Abdulla provides excellent examples of such dependent rulers in the period following the initial treaties: the reinstated ruler of Ra's al-Khaimah, and Abu Dhabi's Shaikh Tahnun. See ABDULLA (1985), pp. 81–82.

121. Personal interviews, Abu Dhabi, March 2001. For a discussion of the "per-manent upgrading" of tribal leaders into ruling shaikhs, see HEARD-BEY (1972), pp. 15–16.

122. ZAHLAN (1978), p. 65.

123. Personal interviews, Abu Dhabi, March 2001, with reference to the Trucial system and the reliance on British support.

124. PECK (1986), p. 62. Peck argues that the British treaties, as much as any other factor, led to the replacement of the traditional *dirah,* the elastic concept of an area in which a tribe exercised sway, with something more akin to a territorially defined modern state.

125. ABDULLAH (1978), p. 90; and ABU BAKER (1995), pp. 67–68.

126. DAVIES (1997), p. 272. The branch of the Qasimi family who had con-trolled Lingah (the ruler of Lingah was the cousin of the ruler of Ra's al-Khaimah) lost authority after Tehran sent a Persian satrap to take charge of the territory.

127. ABDULLAH (1978), p. 90.

128. See PECK (1986), p. 34. Qasimi power never recovered and continued to decline throughout the nineteenth century. Added to this and the loss of Lingah, Ra's al-Khaimah had also lost its greatest patriarch, Shaikh Saqr. Upon Saqr's bequest, what remained of the once great Qasimi federation was to be partitioned among his sons (with the senior ruling Sharjah, and the others ruling Ra's al-Khaimah, Dibba, and Kalba), thus formalizing the geographical split between Ra's al-Khaimah and Sharjah.

129. HEARD-BEY (1982), pp. 290–291.

130. ISMAEL (1993), p. 152.

131. LORIMER (1915a), p. 725. Lorimer alleges that the ruler of Sharjah levied a tax on each imported slave during the 1850s.

132. LORIMER (1915c), p. 2475.

133. HEARD-BEY (1982), pp. 288–289.

134. Ibid., pp. 289–290.

135. LORIMER (1915a), p. 725.

136. See HAWLEY (1970), p. 173. Also see THESIGER (1991), p. 284. Describing his visit to Buraimi in 1950, Thesiger remarks on the continuing demand for slaves, "At Lahamma Well we found many day-old tracks of men and camels. My companions said that they were made by Ali Al-Murri and the caravan of forty-eight slaves which he was taking to Hasa. It seemed that the enormous wealth which was pouring into Saudi Arabia from the American oil companies had greatly increased both the demand for slaves and the price paid for them. They said Ali made a large profit not only from the slaves, but also from the camels which he bought in Buraimi." Also see p. 272, where Thesiger describes the flourishing slave trade practiced by Saudi merchants in the two Buraimi villages not controlled by Shaikh Zayed.

137. HAWLEY (1970), p. 136.

138. The Bani Yas was a tribal agglomeration including the Al-Bu Falah (today's Al-Nuhayyan of Abu Dhabi), the Al-Bu Falasah (today's Al-Maktum of Dubai), and thirteen other tribes of Bedu origin. For a good discussion, see AL-MUSFIR (1985).

139. HAWLEY (1970), p. 146.

140. ABDULLAH (1978), p. 25.

141. HAWLEY (1970), p. 136.

142. ABDULLAH (1978), p. 25.

143. Ibid., p. 38, in describing the letter written from the political agent in Sharjah to the political resident in Bahrain.

144. RASHID (1989), p. 129.

145. KELLY (1968), p. 729.

146. ABDULLAH (1978), p. 24–25.

147. AL-NUHAYYAN (2000a), p. 11. Also see RASHID (1989), pp. 131–132.

148. LORIMER (1915d), pp. 1450–1451.

149. At this time British Indian merchants not only provided the financing and management of the pearling industry, but also acted as conduits for local and international markets. In addition, they also controlled the technological aspects of the industry, such as drilling and bleaching. See ABDULLA (1985), p. 78. Also see HEARD-BEY (1982), p. 221.

150. HEARD-BEY (1982), p. 187.

151. ABDULLAH (1978), pp. 103–104.

152. Ibid., p. 104.

153. LORIMER (1915c), p. 2248.

154. HAWLEY (1970), p. 140.

155. Personal interviews, Dubai, March 2001.

156. For a British view of these exclusivity agreements, see ROBERTS (1985). For an Arab view, see AL-BAHARNA (1985).

157. ABU BAKER (1995), p. 43.

158. ABDULLAH (1978), p. 56.

159. Imperial Airways later became the British Overseas Airways Corporation and is now British Airways. Footage of the first British landings in Sharjah can be seen in the ruler's old fort in Al-Hosn square, Rolla.

160. ABDULLAH (1978), p. 56.

161. FENELON (1973), p. 86.

162. HEARD-BEY (1982), pp. 298–299.

163. Ibid., p. 295. This later became Petroleum Development Trucial Coast Ltd., of which British Petroleum, Campagnie Française des Petroles, and Royal Dutch Shell were the majority shareholders (with 23.75 percent apiece), with Standard Oil of New Jersey (Exxon) and Mobil also holding shares (23.75 percent combined), and with the remainder owned by Partex (Gulbenkian Interests). See AL-OTAIBI (1977), p. 45.

164. This took place in 1951. See ABU BAKER (1995), p. 70.

165. PECK (1986), p. 37.

166. ABDULLAH (1978), p. 70.

167. See "Rentierism," p. 87 in this volume.

168. BANNOCK, BAXTER, and DAVIS (1992), p. 129.

169. Four-fifths of this booty, or *al-ghanima,* would be divided among the tribesmen and one-fifth retained by the leader. Personal interviews, Abu Dhabi, March 2001. Also see HITTI (1964), p. 25; and ISMAEL (1993), p. 19, with reference to Kuwait.

170. HEARD-BEY (1982), pp. 175–176. Although seemingly an unpleasant and meager existence, there were considerable guano deposits to be found on many of Abu Dhabi's islands, such as Das and Dalma. Indeed, at one time these deposits were believed so lucrative that concessions for their collection were signed between the ruler of Abu Dhabi and prominent merchants from both Dubai and Kuwait; HAWLEY (1970), p. 203. Red oxide was mined on the island of Abu Musa.

171. HEARD-BEY (1982), p. 253.

172. ABDULLAH (1978), p. 41. In 1927 the political resident of the Gulf, Colonel Haworth, argued, "The rise of Ibn Saud and the security to which a chain of air stations along the Arab coast might be exposed by internal dissensions and the

danger of Saudi interference in the petty shaykhdoms of the Trucial Coast."

173. ABDULLAH (1978), pp. 41–43. The idea of a protectorate was rejected on the grounds that such a move would needlessly antagonize the ruler of Saudi Arabia, Ibn Saud, and indeed the Trucial shaikhs themselves, in addition to over-stretching British military resources.

174. Ibid.

175. Ibid., pp. 46–47. Also see ZAHLAN (1978), p. 151, the principal trouble-maker being Sa'id's cousin Mani'.

176. ISMAEL (1993), pp. 152–153.

177. HEARD-BEY (1982), p. 255.

178. ABDULLAH (1978), p. 126.

179. "Total revenue" included all income derived from oil concessions and air agreements. See ABU BAKER (1995), p. 107.

180. HEARD-BEY (1982), p. 256.

181. ABDULLAH (1978), p. 131.

182. Ibid., p. 109.

183. HEARD-BEY (1982), p. 256. Indeed, as a side note, the movement's sense of national duty can also be seen as a reflection of the changing political attitudes at this time, with terms such as "country" and "state" being reportedly used during the majlis' brief tenure. Also see ABDULLAH (1978), p. 131.

184. ABDULLAH (1978), p. 132.

185. HEARD-BEY (1982), p. 256.

186. Ibid., pp. 254–255.

187. ABDULLAH (1978), pp. 132–133. This was part of a broadcast made by the political resident on 28 April 1940 on the BBC.

188. AL-SAYEGH (1998), p. 96.

189. ABDULLAH (1978), pp. 134–136. The first development plan was commissioned in 1960.

190. Following the signing of oil concession agreements, in 1945 Abu Dhabi and Dubai began to dispute the ownership of a forty-kilometer tract of land south of Jebel Ali. See OXFORD BUSINESS GROUP (2000), p. 51.

191. HAWLEY (1970), p. 171.

192. Ibid., p. 188.

193. ANTHONY (1975), pp. 148–149. Abu Dhabi also had to offer the islands of Khor Duwayham and Huwaisat; see AL-NABEH (1984), p. 91.

194. FOLEY (1998), p. 10.

195. The Emirates Centre for Strategic Studies in Research, based in Abu Dhabi and backed by Shaikh Muhammad al-Nuhayyan (the deputy crown prince and the UAE's army chief of staff), still illustrates its maps of the UAE's border with Qatar, thereby denying Saudi access to the lower Gulf. See OXFORD BUSINESS GROUP (2000), p. 20.

196. As the political agent described to Anthony Eden, the British foreign secretary, "[The Council] instils in them [the Trucial rulers] a corporate sense which, owing to the distances between them, the lack of communications and their natural jealousy, has in the past been notably lacking." See ABU BAKER (1995), p. 48.

197. PECK (1986), p. 45.

198. HAWLEY (1970), p. 177.

199. HEARD-BEY (1982), p. 324.

200. Ibid., pp. 310–311.

201. Ibid., pp. 306–307.

202. FENELON (1973), pp. 25–26. Two of these five-year development plans

were drawn up, one in 1955 and one in 1960.

203. See SHARABAH (1980). Initially the budget was shared as follows: 92 percent from the British, 4 percent from Abu Dhabi, and 4 percent from Dubai. By 1970 Abu Dhabi was contributing 7 million pounds sterling per annum, 80 percent of the budget.

204. HEARD-BEY (1982), p. 312.

205. KHALIFA (1979), p. 25. There were around 30 British officers and about 1,600 soldiers of mostly Pakistani and Omani origin. See NYROP (1977), p. 324.

206. HEARD-BEY (1982), p. 312.

207. FENELON (1973), pp. 46–47, 49–50.

208. HEARD-BEY (1982), p. 321.

209. ABU BAKER (1995), p. 49. The court system was introduced in 1964, the Dubai police force was established in 1956, and the Abu Dhabi force was established in 1957.

210. FENELON (1973), pp. 26–27. Also see AL-MUSFIR (1985), pp. 92–93. Kuwait was keen to develop the lower Gulf in order to provide a lucrative new market for its merchants; in addition Kuwait hoped that a stable entity in the lower Gulf would be a more effective counterweight to increasing Iranian, Saudi, and Iraqi influences in the region.

211. FENELON (1973), pp. 26–27.

212. ANTHONY (2002), pp. 36–37. This was especially the case following the overthrow of the Yemeni monarchy in 1962 and the ensuing civil war on Saudi Arabia's southern border.

213. REYNOLDS (1991), p. 17.

214. HEARD-BEY (1982), p. 317. In addition, following India's independence in 1947 Britain had steadily been losing much of its earlier raison d'être in the Gulf. See OXFORD BUSINESS GROUP (2000), p. 129.

215. Although most texts report this withdrawal announcement as being made in 1968, it was actually made in late December 1967. See ANTHONY (2002), p. 25.

216. In opposition, Edward Heath's Conservative Party had been critical of Harold Wilson's retrenchment policies. As such, when the Conservatives came to power, many in the Gulf expected a reversal of Labour's policy, or at the very least a delay. See PECK (1986), p. 48.

217. See HEARD-BEY (1982), pp. 336–340; and PECK (1986), p. 48.

218. PECK (1986), p. 48.

219. KELLY (1986), p. 49. This quote is from Goronwy Roberts's report to the British cabinet in 1968.

220. See BECK (1978). Beck describes how Britain encouraged the UAE as a means of collective survival following the withdrawal of British military protection.

221. FENELON (1973), p. 21; and ZAHLAN (1989).

222. HAWLEY (1970), p. 148. The 1905 meeting took place in Abu Dhabi, with the ruler of Abu Dhabi acting as president and chairing a committee to discuss a border dispute concerning the villages of Masfut and Hajarain in the Hatta enclave. Also see AL-QADIR (1978), p. 61.

223. See AL-ABED (2001); and TABATABAI (1978), p. 30.

224. Ibid.

225. This union changed its name to the "South Arab Federation" following the inclusion of additional members. In 1962, following Egyptian penetration, it was replaced by the equally short-lived "Union of Arab States of Egypt and the Yemen." See ANTHONY (2002), p. 19.

226. For a general discussion of this period of transition, see KHALIFA (1979).

227. HAWLEY (1970), pp. 182–184.

228. Ibid. These committees involved representatives of the Arab League pressing for increased aid to the poorer shaikhdoms in order to thwart any Iranian expansion; also, the committees were concerned with the number of foreigners entering the Trucial states and recommended the limiting of immigration visas. See AL-MUSFIR (1985), p. 67.

229. HELLYER (2001), p. 166.

230. The majority of surveys misreport this bipartite federation as having been declared in 1968. For an independent confirmation, see ANTHONY (2002), p. 15.

231. HEARD-BEY (1982), pp. 343–344.

232. Ibid., pp. 345–347.

233. PECK (1986), p. 50; and AL-MUSFIR (1985), p. 74.

234. HEARD-BEY (1982), pp. 351, 357.

235. For decades the Iranian majlis had been allocating two seats to Bahraini representatives, even though none were ever forthcoming. See ANTHONY (2002), p. 52; and OVERTON (1983), p. 173, taken from Overton's interview with E. F. Given, British ambassador to Bahrain, in Manama, Bahrain, on 3 June 1976.

236. ANTHONY (2002), pp. 58–59.

237. OVERTON (1983), p. 173, taken from Overton's interview with Zaki Nusseibeh, press secretary to Shaikh Zayed, in Abu Dhabi on 24 May 1976.

238. HOLDEN (1966), p. 159.

239. HOLDEN (1971), p. 729.

240. HEARD-BEY (1982), p. xxiv, Geoffrey Arthur, former British political resident in the Gulf, writing the foreword to Heard-Bey's study.

241. U.S. DEPARTMENT OF STATE (1975), p. 74.

242. See MOBLEY (2003), pp. 628–644. Using recently declassified documents, Mobley has demonstrated how London attempted to solve the islands issue in the years preceding British withdrawal. Acutely aware of the importance of placating Tehran, it is shown how Britain (under the direction of William Luce) spent fourteen months testing various compromise agreements between Ra's al-Khaimah, Sharjah, and Iran. These included compensation schemes (at one point £14 million was offered!), oil rights agreements, and even a proposal for rental. Ultimately, however, London wrote off the Tunbs as Shaikh Saqr al-Qasimi refused to compromise over any aspect of sovereignty.

243. Sharjah reluctantly agreed to allow Iran to establish bases in certain agreed-upon areas of Abu Musa, in exchange for a financial aid package of around $2 million annually for nine years (or up until the time that Sharjah's oil revenues exceeded $4 million). See NIBLOCK (1980), pp. 205–215.

244. The two smaller islands were the Greater and Lesser Tunbs, or rather Tunb al-Kubra and Tunb al-Sughra; see AL-AYDERUS (1983), p. 164–165. It is reported that there were a number of fatalities involved in Iran's occupation; see NIBLOCK (1980), pp. 205–215.

245. This was a result of the aforementioned Buraimi dispute. See "Britain and the Path to Federation," p. 41 in this volume. Also see OXFORD BUSINESS GROUP (2000), p. 20; and MELAMID (1956), p. 65.

246. PECK (1986), p. 120.

247. The federal government and its various institutions are considered in detail in this volume under "The Federal Decisionmaking Structure," p. 188, and "The Emirate-Level Decisionmaking Structure," p. 197.

248. Throughout the 1970s the Union Defence Force relied heavily on British officers, British equipment, British uniforms, and a British ranking system. See

ABDULLA (1985), p. 202.

249. HEARD-BEY (1982), p. 368.

250. ANTHONY (2002), p. 72. Even today, Ra's al-Khaimah's UAE national population of around 88,000 is much higher than Abu Dhabi's 60,000, Dubai's 41,000, and Sharjah's 67,000. See VAN DER MEULEN (1997), p. 202.

251. HEARD-BEY (1982), pp. 369–370. Also see ANTHONY (1975), p. 24: "Indeed, the branch of the Qawasim family ruling Ra's al-Khaimah even considered themselves to be of nobler descent than their counterparts in the other six shaykhdoms."

252. HEARD-BEY (1982), pp. 369–370.

253. Personal interviews, Ra's al-Khaimah, January 2004. With regard to the Al-Khawatir, see AL-MUSFIR (1985), p. 76. Around 50 percent of the Al-Za'ab migrated to Abu Dhabi in 1968 following an invitation extended to them by Shaikh Zayed; see VAN DER MEULEN (1997), pp. 163–164.

254. ANTHONY (2002), p. 74. Ra's al-Khaimah's envoy to the United States in autumn 1971 hinted that the emirate would be able to provide naval facilities in the Gulf that would effectively counter the Soviet Union's attempts to construct a warm-water port at Umm Qasr in Iraq.

255. ANTHONY (2002), pp. 66. In most texts it is inaccurately reported that Ra's al-Khaimah delayed joining the UAE for a full year.

256. MANN (1969), pp. 33–50. Also, for a discussion of interemirate rivalry during this early period, see HEARD-BEY (1982), pp. 369–370.

257. HEARD-BEY (1982), p. 372.

258. See KHALIFA (1979) for an overview of this period of transition.

259. OVERTON (1983), p. 173. In his study of political stability in the Gulf in the early 1970s Overton singles out the UAE as the most impressive example of political union: "If one were to do a micro-analytical study of the Gulf region with the hope of projecting the chances for stability and growth in the future, the UAE would provide the perfect case study. . . . [I]t has not only survived but has grown stronger. If the UAE model continues to be successful, there is every reason to assume that a broader system of regionalism among the Arab states of the Arabian Peninsula is a practical goal for the future."

# 2

# The Survival of Monarchy: An Overview

As the historical background has shown, following the British withdrawal in 1971 the newly independent United Arab Emirates had little more to rely upon than its traditional political structures and a few hastily established federal institutions. Although careful negotiations and a spirit of compromise did allow the fledging state to survive its troubled inception, many observers believed that the lower Gulf's traditional monarchies and rudimentary institutions could never represent anything more than a transitional phase. Indeed, given the region's massive oil wealth and accelerating socioeconomic development, such polities were seen as being both anachronistic and irreconcilable with any modernization process. More than thirty years later the UAE continues to experience such rapid development and now boasts one of the highest gross domestic products (GDPs) per capita in the world,[1] comparable with and in some cases higher than many of the Western industrialized economies.[2] At the same time, however, despite these massive changes, the seven ruling families are still very much in place, and have retained, or at least appear to have retained, much of their traditional authority. Indeed, of the world's eight remaining absolute monarchies, in terms of autocratic structures and lack of political freedom, the UAE is consistently ranked second only to Saudi Arabia.[3]

The purpose of this chapter, therefore, is to provide an explanatory overview of the survival and continuing relevance of what were in effect the end-products of the region's history of dependent relations and its reinforced client elite formations. Essentially, by combining the tools of modernization revisionism and rentier-dependency theories, I demonstrate how there has been a subtle evolution of these primarily traditional structures and the creation of a carefully managed "ruling bargain" between the rulers and their population, a bargain that relies heavily on a number of key criteria.

## The Shaikh's Dilemma

At the time of the Trucial states' independence, many political scientists maintained that most of the world's remaining traditional monarchies would soon collapse, as pressures for political reform would inevitably overload their "weak" traditional polities. Early examples of such hypotheses included Daniel Lerner's "passing of traditional society" theory and Karl Deutsch's "social mobilization" theory, both of which asserted that modernizing forces and their consequences for society would soon render traditional monarchies anachronistic. Writing in the late 1950s, Lerner demonstrated in his studies that in every country where individuals could be classed as experiencing the effects of modernization, they would be considerably "happier" than those still living by traditional means. From his socioscientific analysis he therefore drew the conclusion that traditional society was passing from the Middle East simply because "relatively few Arabs still wanted to live by its rules."[4] In much the same way, Deutsch argued that modernizing forces in such states would invariably expand the size of the educated and literary middle classes, thereby leading to increased social mobilization, which would in turn outweigh the capabilities of the traditional polity and would eventually catalyze some kind of political development.[5] Indeed, in many ways the newly rich oil monarchies of the Gulf region were seen by such theorists as providing perfect examples of future change given that their ambitious development programs and their inevitably fast-paced modernization were predicted to engender increasing levels of political consciousness and greater demands on the state.

Published just three years before the United Arab Emirates came into being, Samuel Huntington's influential *Political Change in Traditional Polities* was similarly pessimistic with regard to the survival of traditional monarchies. Indeed, central to one chapter's framework was the assumption that in order to cope successfully with modernizing forces, traditional rulers would eventually be faced with an inescapable "king's dilemma," or in the case of Arabia a "shaikh's dilemma." Essentially, in much the same way as Deutsch and the other early modernization theorists, it was reasoned that the modernization process and the necessary innovation of economic and social development policies would invariably create new groups that the polity would have difficulty assimilating alongside existing traditional groups.[6] As such, the traditional monarch would either have to resist modernization in some way or instead have to accommodate the new groups, a route that would invariably lead to the ceding of former powers.[7] Thus, believing there was no adequate long-term solution to such a quandary, Huntington predicted the eventual demise of those traditional polities presiding over rapid modernization by arguing that "a gap opens between the increasingly modern society and the traditional polity which gave it birth; able to transform the society, but unable to transform itself, the monarchical parent is eventually devoured by its modern progeny."8

Although Huntington claimed the key question for these monarchies would ultimately "concern simply the scope of the violence of their demise and who will wield the violence,"9 he nevertheless accepted that certain short-term strategies could temporarily postpone such a fate. Indeed, it was believed that under certain circumstances a traditional monarch could provisionally circumvent the assimilation predicament by either seizing the initiative and allowing for some degree of voluntary transformation of the polity (while still retaining some traditional power), by institutionalizing coexistence within the polity, or by carefully maintaining the polity (resisting reform), and thereby limiting the effects of modernization.10 To varying extents all of these strategies have been in evidence in the remaining Middle Eastern monarchies and, although only deemed to be temporary measures by Western political scientists, they have nevertheless been recognized by the rulers as important ways in which to prolong traditional authority and sidestep the shaikh's dilemma. Although the UAE has at times made limited attempts to follow such strategies, its survival and legitimacy have never been heavily reliant on such methods; therefore the remarkable longevity and resilience of traditional polity in the UAE must be seen as being distinct from the less assured survival of some of the other Middle Eastern monarchies, including even the neighboring Gulf emirates of Bahrain and Kuwait.

## Voluntary Transformation

Both Huntington and Manfred Halpern suggested that some kind of voluntary transformation of the polity might extend monarchical rule. Essentially the ruler himself could become the main modernizing force by preempting demands for political reform and by instituting constitutional reforms on his own terms. In such a scenario it was felt that "the King may be able to reserve his power as a symbol of unity above particular parties by acting as a moderator, but never engaging himself as a final authority except in crises that party politicians cannot remedy."11 Certainly, as early as the 1930s there was evidence of such a strategy having been suggested to the rulers of the Trucial states, when during a brief period of instability the British political resident in the Gulf actively encouraged the ruler of Dubai to voluntarily yield a portion of his authority:

> You are a wise man, O Shaykh! And must be aware that all over the world cases have occurred of demands which have been made on their Rulers by their people for reforms, and which demands have been refused. The

result has often been that in the end the Rulers have had to give much more than if they had given a little in the beginning, and in some cases the Rulers have even lost their thrones. Briefly then, O Shaykh! . . . I can as your friend advise you to look carefully to the future, and to profit by the experience of other countries where early and generous reforms have deprived those who wished to oppose the Rulers of the popular support on which they relied.[12]

Although no such development took place in Dubai or indeed in any of the other Trucial states at this time, Shaikh 'Ahmad al-Sabah of Kuwait was nevertheless coaxed by the British into devolving some of his powers to restless merchants.[13] Moreover, when the subject of preemptive political reform was revived during the federal negotiations of the late 1960s,[14] the Trucial rulers again shied away from such suggestions, whereas Bahrain chose to "modify its position in the light of the recent survey of public opinion conducted by the UN emissary and in response to the popular requests for more democratic institutions."[15] Of course the more recent developments in Bahrain can also be seen as evidence of such willing-ness.[16] Indeed, while the Bahraini emir's encouragement of democratic elections and his creation of a national charter, or *al-mithaq,* may still rep-resent little more than political window-dressing,[17] such a move neverthe-less underscores how the strategy of voluntary transformation continues to be recognized, at least in the background, by the other Gulf monarchies.

### Institutionalizing Coexistence

An alternative strategy for a ruler attempting to escape the shaikh's dilem-ma would be to try to combine his traditional rule with some form of repre-sentative government. In other words the ruler could choose to institution-alize coexistence within the polity. In the UAE this strategy has also remained extremely limited. Although during the preoil and preurbanized era the traditional majalis and the easy access to the rulers' representatives did allow for a certain degree of consultative democracy and an opportunity for the people to air their grievances at the highest levels,[18] no such direct representation really takes place in the contemporary UAE. Indeed, with rapidly expanding populations and a plethora of ministries and bureaucra-cies, the only representative government bodies are the Federal National Council and, at the emirate level, the Abu Dhabi National Consultative Council. Moreover, as will be described in greater depth later in this book, even these are extremely inadequate institutions,[19] and in many ways it would appear that in real terms there has actually been a contraction of access in the UAE. Conversely, though, in many of the other Middle Eastern monarchies there have been highly visible *attempts* to institutional-ize at least some form of coexistence, although it remains important to note that in most cases these have lacked any genuine commitment. In Jordan, for example, latent pressures for political participation from underrepresented groups including the Palestinians led to national elections and the creation of a national assembly comprising a senate appointed by the king and a popularly elected house of representatives.[20] Similarly in Morocco, a bicameral parliament exists, comprising an appointed chamber of counselors and a popularly elected chamber of representatives.[21] However, this multipartyism, or *ta'addudiyya,* has had little structural impact, with parliamentary discussion often limited to local and procedural issues, with the political parties functioning as little more than "loyal opposition," and with the more radical parties being marginalized.[22] Moreover, with the case of the Shah's Iran, while coexistence was certainly institutionalized, the strategy's inherent weaknesses soon became apparent as the government was fragmented by dual responsibilities to both the monarch (royal sovereignty) and the elected assembly (popular sovereignty).[23] As such the traditional polity was seen to have provided insufficient structural space for adequate maneuver. This led to mutual frustration and repeated attempts by the monarch to limit the new authorities, most notably by suppressing the prime minister, Mussadiq. Indeed, as Dilip Hiro describes, Mussadiq's clash with the Shah over the subject of oil nationalization led to the elected premier's dismissal, and when Mussadiq returned to power on a wave of popular support, the Shah had no option but to reassert his authority with what was essentially a military operation.[24] The Kuwaiti example is also important to note, not least due to its close proximity and its seemingly similar socioeconomic structures to the UAE. In much the same way as these other monarchies, Kuwait's national assembly was seen by the al-Sabah rulers as providing a necessary degree of coexistence within the polity in order to preserve stability and control the assimilation of new groups. In reality, however, the level of representation was minimal, with all candidates being restricted to individual platforms and with all political parties being banned.[25] Moreover, when electoral platforms finally did begin to emerge around blocs and groups in the 1970s, the Kuwaiti executive felt compelled to dissolve the assembly and place restrictions on the press.[26] Only in the 1990s, following the country's liberation from Iraq, was a return finally made to the original constitution and the limited coexistence of the 1960s.[27]

### Maintaining the Polity and Resisting Reform

Third, a traditional monarch can attempt to circumvent the shaikh's dilemma and seek to maintain his traditional authority simply by resisting reform and avoiding the assimilation of new groups, often by balancing modernization alongside repression.[28] To some extent, such maintenance has been evident in the UAE, but although there has undoubtedly been an appreciable increase in internal security,[29] there has never been a heavy reliance on coercion, and at no stage has the country suffered from a particularly repressive atmosphere.[30] Instead, there have been subtle controls placed on almost all civil society organizations, religious groups, media organizations, and workers' associations. Although these restrictions will be analyzed in more detail later in this volume,[31] it is worth noting that these controls have usually been limited to financial co-option,[32] government licensing,[33] self-enforcing censorship,[34] and in the case of the UAE's mosques the supervision and approval of practicing *ulama'*.[35] As with the two other monarchical survival strategies, there has been far more evidence of strict maintenance in other Middle Eastern monarchies and potentates than in the UAE, including even Bahrain, where, as described in Chapter 1, the ruler was forced to exile three opponents and impose a state of martial law following demonstrations in the wake of the Suez crisis.[36] Perhaps the most illuminating example, however, is that of Imam Badr's Yemen. Indeed, as Muhammad Zabarah notes in his study of Yemeni state formation, although a maintenance strategy may have temporarily delayed the collapse of the traditional polity, the imam's lack of responsiveness to demand for political and socioeconomic reforms eventually reached such a level that the country became openly divided between traditionalists and modernists.[37] This struggle soon extended to the army when, wary of the new officer class, whose political notions were seen as running contrary to his own, the imam chose to inhibit the development of a strong Yemeni army.[38] Thus, driven by the need to keep modern ideas away from his domain, the ruler attempted to undermine his armed forces and instead began to rely upon the tribes in an effort to preserve traditional values, thereby irrecoverably compromising Yemeni national security and leading to a coup.

## The Legitimacy Formula

While voluntary transformation, the institutionalization of coexistence, and (often) maintenance strategies were used to varying degrees of success in many other Middle Eastern monarchies throughout the twentieth century (and even in some of the other Gulf monarchies), the UAE's reliance on such methods clearly remained limited. Moreover, the shaikh's dilemma and the problems of balancing traditional and modern forces appear to have been largely avoided without resorting to these temporary measures. Indeed, as political scientists began to argue in the late 1970s, certain monarchies were, if anything, more stable than ever before, even after experiencing great wealth and extensive socioeconomic development programs. Thus, given that these traditional monarchies were surviving despite considerable evidence of modernizing forces in their countries, there was clearly a need to reexamine the belief in the inevitability of the passing of traditional political systems. Among these modernization revisionists, Michael Hudson effectively began to contest the early assumption that monarchical legitimacy was necessarily anachronistic and reasoned that, in certain circumstances, a traditional polity could evolve toward more long-term legitimacy and stability. More specifically, it was argued that, within a Weberian framework, certain traditional sources of legitimacy could be utilized and adapted by monarchies as part of a more comprehensive survival strategy.[39] The UAE's legitimacy has evolved over the past thirty years, and its traditional polity is now beginning to survive within a much broader "neopatrimonial" network.[40]

### Personal Resources

Personal resources have always been a cornerstone of the traditional polity's legitimacy. For centuries the lower Gulf's political structures were dominated by personalities and the need for personal authority over populations, even more so than over territorial or geographical resources.[41] Central to such authority was the principle of *bay'a:* "the act by which a certain number of persons acting individually or collectively recognise the authority of another person. Thus, the bay'a of an emir/king/caliph is the act by which one person is proclaimed and recognised as the head of the Muslim state."[42] Certainly, prior to the oil era, many of the region's rulers drew considerable legitimacy from their citizens' public endorsement of their personal ability. Without the bay'a these rulers would have been unable to command sufficient respect for their traditional patriarchal governments, or hukumah. Similarly today, contemporary rulers continue to rely on the bay'a to shore up old notions of Bedu citizenship.[43] Indeed, although family and polity may no longer reach the point of absolute congruence,[44] and although the personal competence of Emirati rulers may no longer be judged in terms of their ability to fight, ride camels, or arbitrate tribal disputes, there is little doubt that personal authority remains most significant. Rulers must possess sufficient charisma, or *baraka,* together with an ability to personally mediate and supervise—these are still regarded as essential characteristics of successful rulers, and as such it is widely believed among the local Emirati populations that new rulers must still be seen to have informally earned the bay'a from respected members of the community.[45]

Among the present-day rulers the clearest example of such personal authority has of course been that of Shaikh Zayed al-Nuhayyan, the ruler of Abu Dhabi and the UAE's long-serving president. Having secured considerable popular support throughout the emirate during his time in Al-'Ayn and Buraimi, Zayed is widely credited as being the "Father of Abu Dhabi" and, in Enver Khoury's terms, "Zayedism" has been recognized as the driving force behind much of the UAE's success.[46] Indeed, as an Emirati minister claimed in a recent international conference, a significant portion of the UAE's ongoing political stability must still be attributed to Zayed's consensus rule and the enormous personal respect he continues to command from the people of all seven emirates:

> Fortunately for us and our neighbours, we have developed without undermining the social, cultural and political fabric of our society. This has been due in large part to leadership. Shaykh Zayed has served as president of the UAE since its inception in 1971. And his leadership is based on consensus among the seven emirates. In keeping with Islamic tradition, he is seen as first among equals, continuing to serve as president because he commands the respect of the nation's other leaders and the reverence of the people.[47]

Similarly at the emirate level, another good example of strong leadership would be the highly personal and very popular rule of Shaikh Rashid al-Maktum, the "Father of Dubai," who closely presided over an era of rapid socioeconomic development in the emirate until his death in 1990.[48] Indeed, in Hudson's study of monarchical legitimacy, Shaikh Rashid was singled out for his considerable input into the running of Dubai, his intensiveness, and his extraordinary level of individual commitment:

> In the early period Shaykh Rashid's personal involvement in the day-to-day running of Dubai Emirate was extremely intense: he rises every morning at 6am, before anybody else is up, and after prayers takes an inspection drive around the town. Then, after coffee he is off to the office for a morning of routine royal duties: receiving distinguished visitors and petitioners, checking the status of various projects and signing cheques. After lunch he turns his attention to new projects and planning.[49]

Thus, in these cases—and in Sharjah and the other smaller emirates where from informal research it would appear that the Qawasim, the Sharqiyin, and the other ruling families also continue to command considerable support from their local populations—there are still strong indications of personal resources playing a key role in the rulers' legitimacy formulae. Indeed, spontaneous rallies and public displays of agreement with a ruler's decisions are a frequent spectacle in almost all of the emirates.[50] This of course contrasts markedly with the former monarchs of Iraq, Afghanistan, and Libya, where, for a multitude of reasons including their lack of public accessibility and their unpopular foreign relations, it would seem that the ruling families failed to foster any real admiration or respect in their subjects.[51]

## Patrimonial Networks

However, even in the preoil era the region's political structures were already beginning to evolve from a total reliance on personal authority following the growth of the coastal towns, the increasing urbanization, and the greater administrative demands being placed on the state.[52] In more recent years, with rapidly expanding populations and a plethora of new bureaucracies, the distance between the ruler and his people has continued to grow, and although personal resources have certainly remained an important legitimacy component, these have now been augmented by the development of extensive intermediary networks. Indeed, the rulers have actively encouraged and nurtured new and extended patterns of authority based on informal relations, kinship groups, and long-standing traditional loyalties. The result has been an extension of the ruler's personal network to a much greater patrimonial network—one that filters down through all sections of society, with the ruler at the very top of the pyramid and all other echelons tied into the system at various strata beneath him.[53] Patrimonialism therefore provides additional layers of legitimacy by reducing the traditional polity's total reliance on personalism and potentially unpredictable resources such as charisma and popular veneration, and in addition has created important vertical linkages between the ruler and his people that have helped to provide individual mobility within the polity while at the same time fostering some degree of loyalty at all levels.

Indeed, with regard to reducing the reliance on personal authority, patrimonial networks have been seen as an increasingly important method of ensuring ongoing support for the various ruling families. Shaikh Rashid has now been succeeded by his sons, and Shaikh Zayed, as a great-grandfather, will soon be approaching the end of his long and illustrious reign. Despite having considerable administrative experience, few would doubt that Shaikh Khalifa al-Nuhayyan, Zayed's eldest son and Abu Dhabi's crown prince, could ever hope to draw upon the same level of personal legitimacy from his subjects as his distinguished father. As such, for the long-term survival of the traditional polity it has become essential that the UAE's elites, both inside and outside of politics, are all in some way vertically connected to the ruler and therefore are "clients" dependent on the ongoing stability of the polity for the preservation of their social status, economic advantages, and whatever other privileges they have been accorded within the patrimonial-clientalist network.

At the political level, this incorporation has been largely based on "consolation prizes" for powerful elites outside of the ruling family and for other aspiring individuals—an important feature of Emirati politics that will be returned to later in this chapter and throughout the remainder of this book.[54] Indeed, evidence of this strategy was readily apparent even at the

time of Shaikh Zayed's succession as ruler of Abu Dhabi. As Muhammad
Abdullah describes:

> From 1966 onwards, Shaykh Zayed adopted the wise policy of sharing
> the responsibilities of his new government between members of the rul-
> ing family, notable local figures and certain graduates from the more
> prominent families. . . . This was an example that was quickly followed
> in the other emirates. The trust the Shaykh showed in the young educated
> generation won him their affection and in due course they proved their
> reliability.[55]

Similarly in Sharjah, when Shaikh Khalid al-Qasimi succeeded as ruler in
1965, one of his first actions was to give young Sharjah graduates a share
in the local administration.[56] Of course, the obvious weakness of such individual incorporation into the patrimonial network is that in future years the
size of the UAE's graduate and educated "technocratic" population may
begin to exceed the polity's capacity for providing them with meaningful
public sector jobs.[57] Indeed, the UAE's bloated bureaucracies are already
routinely criticized for their "disguised unemployment," as a large number
of sinecured officials are thought to be sitting idle with no work to do.[58]
Thus the patrimonial network must also be much broader, providing other
rewards and incentives to the Emirati elite.

Perhaps the strongest example of such rewards has been the polity's
overt attempts to encourage and foster the emergence of a privileged
"local" class comprising the UAE's entire indigenous population, which of
course has now become dwarfed by the UAE's massive expatriate populations.[59] Given the small size of this national population, the "locals" form a
natural elite group (easily identifiable by their adherence to traditional
dress codes),[60] and the majority openly receive a number of generous
socioeconomic benefits from the state, thus making them reliant on the
rulers' munificence and therefore more favorably disposed toward the survival of the traditional polity.[61] Indeed, as Frauke Heard-Bey noted in her
updated study of the UAE:

> Every UAE national, however humble his or her material and educational
> circumstances and status within this society, by virtue of not being part of
> the non-national majority, has a vested interest in the continued integrity
> of the traditional society with tribal shaykhs and rulers at its apex. Being
> part of this structure is the basic reason why a national family is able
> today to lead a life in which poverty has been left behind.[62]

In recent years one of the clearest examples of such largesse has been
Shaikh Zayed's scheme to provide substantial "marriage funds" for young
locals. Ostensibly these funds were designed to tackle the problem of large

dowries and extravagant weddings, but more important they are a means of ensuring the preservation of the local population by ensuring Emirati intermarriage,[63] and of course a means of providing large state-sponsored subsidies to young Emirati men. As one spokesman described:

> [Zayed] has been particularly critical of the growing habit of extravagant weddings and of the reluctance of some young people to contribute in a positive way towards society. "Extremely high dowries, extravagance at wedding parties and everything else which burdens young people with debt when they are on the threshold of their lives as a family are matters for which there can be no justification," he said. . . . To counteract this trend, Shaykh Zayed ordered the creation of a special Marriage Fund to offer grants to young men wishing to marry, and also urged the country's tribes to take action to discourage expensive parties and large dowries. The response was immediate, both from tribal elders throughout the UAE, and from young nationals, who flocked to apply for help from the Marriage Fund. Unique of its kind in Arabia, the Fund seems set to make a major contribution to the stability of society and the preservation of local culture.[64]

Other important examples of such privileges would include the considerable business advantages conferred on the local population. Indeed, with reference to Abu Dhabi, an identifiable government aim has been to

> institutionalise a number of privileges for nationals so that they can earn income, for instance from trade agencies, renting property built with government provided loans on freely distributed land, renting vehicles to companies operating in the desert or competing on favourable terms for projects. Thus, the illiterate Bedu as well as the urbane chairmen of trading empires are well aware of the benefits of being one of the small number of Abu Dhabi nationals.[65]

Chiefly, this financial assistance is provided by the Social Services and Commercial Buildings Committee, otherwise known as the Khalifa Committee, which ensures that loans are available at low interest rates to all Abu Dhabian nationals.[66] Furthermore, as figures from Citibank UAE indicate, these considerable advantages also extend to the private sector, with different loans and terms being made available to different groups clearly indicating those favored by the broader patrimonial-clientalist network (see Table 2.1).

Evidently, non-nationals, regardless of the strength of their connections with the UAE, do not have access to the same business benefits as the nationals. Moreover, in some cases these differences in privileges have even been formalized in UAE legislation, as indicated by the Federal Commercial Companies Law, which states: "Each company incorporated in the State shall hold its nationality but it shall not necessarily be entitled to

**Table 2.1  Loan Discrepancies**

| Category of Loan | UAE Nationals | Non-Nationals |
|---|---|---|
| Start-up loans available on first day of job | 100,000 dirhams | 60,000 dirhams |
| Loans available on completion of six months employment | 250,000 dirhams | 120,000 dirhams |
| Maximum repayment period allowed | 84 months | 48 months |

*Source:* Citibank UAE (2002), "Annual Report," Dubai, Citibank.

privileges reserved only to U.A.E nationals."[67] More specifically, Article 22 provides an important advantage for UAE nationals. Certain commercial activities are restricted to UAE nationals, and in those areas that are not restricted all companies must be "sponsored" by one or more UAE nationals "whose share shall not be less than 51% of the company's capital. Therefore, any company's contract that does not incorporate such a provision shall be considered to be null and void."[68]

Last, it is important to emphasize the extent to which such rewards and advantages have also been extended to the very poorest UAE nationals, with many houses and other amenities being provided free of charge to those in the lowest income brackets and with many fully equipped farms being provided for those closer to the main agricultural areas.[69] Indeed, upon being installed as crown prince of Abu Dhabi in 1968, Shaikh Khalifa's very first act was to distribute the keys to over 150 low-cost houses to needy citizens,[70] and as Kevin Fenelon observed in his survey of the region throughout the early 1970s the lives of many other impoverished Emiratis also dramatically improved as the various local governments began to construct thousands of new free homes and public facilities:

> For lower income families, a considerable number of one-storey low cost houses were erected by the governments, including those of 'Ajman and Umm al-Qawain. These two towns in consequence began to look far less picturesque, but in compensation, the inhabitants were far better housed and were better provided for by modern amenities such as piped water and electricity. In Abu Dhabi more than 3000 low cost homes were erected and were freely distributed to Abu Dhabi nationals with limited incomes. Other Abu Dhabi nationals were given building plots on which to build houses of their own.[71]

Similarly, through the 1980s and 1990s the Zayed Housing Program, with an annual budget of over $170 million, continued to provide such homes for all nationals with a monthly salary below 10,000 dirhams.[72]

Such homes can be seen in many of the new towns (including Shahama and Khalifa City) that line the roads leading out of Abu Dhabi. Now, over a decade later, such assistance and benevolence toward more indigent nationals remains as great as ever across the UAE. Indeed, the ruler of Sharjah's February 2004 decision to distribute 100 million dirhams to his population is merely the latest of a string of such examples. As Ibrahim al-Nabuda, director-general of Sharjah's finance department, explains:

> The ruler's generous donation will be disbursed as grants for construction and other purposes, and will considerably help eligible recipients lead a stable life. The grants will be disbursed in instalments as per the rules in force. Prospective recipients may report to the section concerned in the Finance Department to fill in information required and finalise other paperwork. . . . [T]he grants are in addition to the Sharjah Government's plans to build and provide modern housing units to all citizens.[73]

### Cultural and Religious Resources

Alongside the continuing use of personal legitimacy resources and the development of a patrimonial network of socioeconomic privileges and loyalties, it is important to note how the role, or rather the revitalized role, of cultural resources *(turath)* has also formed a key component of the traditional polity's legitimacy formula. Essentially, by preserving and restoring memories of the region's rich history of traditional activities, the ruler's position at the head of a contemporary patriarchal and patrimonial society can be further reinforced. Indeed, as Eric Davis explains in his study of oil and historical memory, a state's ability to draw upon cultural resources and revive traditional experiences can in many cases greatly enhance the legitimacy of its polity: "[The state has] an ability to reconstruct, synthesise and even invent symbols that will touch a psychological nerve in the populace at large. A strong state is one that can exercise this craft and that continues to forge emotive links with the populace over which it rules."[74] Certainly, many of the lower Gulf's traditional customs and practices are still in evidence today, and in some cases these are now being reintroduced and formalized as "living memories" for the increasingly urbanized and modern population. Indeed, in her recent study of Emirati society, Sally Findlow supported this view by concluding that "this modern Muslim Gulf Arab nation-state retains strong elements of traditional conservatism while endeavouring simultaneously to preserve indigenous cultural authenticity."[75] Although the UAE's cultural revival and the state's massive investment in new museums, cultural foundations, and various other heritage centers will be discussed in greater detail later in this volume,[76] it is worth noting here how certain cultural symbols have been used (or in some cases

even invented) with the specific intention of augmenting the ruler's traditional legitimacy.

A good example of such symbolism is camel racing in the UAE,
which in recent years has evolved into a highly lucrative and widely televised sport. In an attempt to preserve a part of their Bedu heritage, the
UAE's rulers have spent millions of dirhams on racing circuits, prize
money, and thoroughbred racing camels. However, as Sulayman Khalaf
has recently demonstrated, the competitive racing of camels was rarely a
popular pursuit in traditional times, with most camel races being more of a
show *(ardha)* reserved for special occasions. Thus, in the contemporary
UAE the status of these races has been greatly elevated.[77] Indeed, as
Jordanian traveler Sa'id Abu 'Athira (who once famously journeyed by
camel from Amman to Abu Dhabi)[78] has explained: "Camel races used to
be run [only] on special occasions such as weddings. Now they are sponsored by governments to help people keep their camels and not lose their
traditional way of life."[79]

Other important and almost mythological symbols would include the
many monuments and displays dedicated to the memory of the pearling
industry; the many preserved examples of *jalbuts, baggalas,* and other traditional Arab vessels; and of course the region's numerous forts and towers,
almost all of which have now been restored or even prefabricated where
formerly nonexistent. A prime example is the "traditional fort" on Futaisi
island off the coast of Abu Dhabi. From a distance it would appear genuine,
but on closer inspection one discovers that it consists of dirt-covered
cement blocks. Somewhere in the UAE there must be a factory producing
authentic replica Arab forts.

In a similar fashion to these cultural resources, the region's long history of Islamic tradition must also be seen as an important legitimizing bridge
between the traditional polity and contemporary Emirati society, as religious association has united both modern and traditional groups behind a
common cause.[80] Certainly, Islam has continued to be an integral part of
the UAE's legitimacy formula, not only serving as the official state religion, but with Islamic *shari'a* law and the traditional qadi system still providing many of the principles upon which the state's constitution and judicial system are based.[81] Although Chapter 5 will further expand upon the
state's relationship with Islam and Islamic groups,[82] it is important here to
underscore the polity's clear commitment to bolstering its religious
resources. Unless preserved and well maintained it is undoubtedly feared
that any future erosion of Islamic standards and criteria will reduce the
importance of an Islamic variant of Weber's "natural law" as an additional
basis for legitimacy and survival.[83] To this end many of the UAE's constituent emirates and their rulers have embarked on massive Islamic-orient-
ed projects, including the building of new mosques and Islamic centers, the

funding of Islamic charities, and in some cases the introduction of new local legislation to combat declining moral standards.

As a result, in much the same way as in Saudi Arabia, where it is estimated that there are just 100 male citizens for every mosque,[84] any visitor to Abu Dhabi would be overwhelmed by the incredibly high density of mosques,[85] a number that grows every year, with some of the largest and grandest mosques in the world now being built on the outskirts of the city.[86] Furthermore, in Sharjah, the Saudi insistence on maintaining the outward appearance of Islamic propriety is also very much in evidence. Indeed, the emirate is now entirely alcohol free (even in hotels and private residences), and only lately a number of stringent "decency laws" have been declared (and enforced) in an effort to preserve and improve the Islamic nature of the community. These have covered matters such as dress codes, public conduct, gender separation, and promiscuity.[87] At one point Sharjah even attempted to encourage federal immigration officials to deny residence visas to single women under the age of thirty in an effort to curb the enormous number of prostitutes who enter the UAE every year.[88] While some have privately voiced their disapproval of Sharjah's seemingly overaustere actions (with many believing there to be a strong and ongoing financial link between the emirate and Saudi Arabia),[89] it is important to appreciate that the majority do seem to accept the necessity of such measures and the legitimacy of their ruler's actions.[90]

Moreover, given that in recent years Islamic fundamentalism has emerged as one of the greatest political opponents and internal security threats to the surviving traditional polities in the other Gulf states,[91] the need for the continued incorporation of mainstream Islamic resources into the UAE's legitimacy formula remains as crucial as ever. While there has never been an organized Islamic opposition group in the UAE (with perhaps the exception of the superficially apolitical Jamyat al-Islah, or "Reformation Association"),[92] and although the UAE survived the aftershock of the Iranian revolution and has not yet suffered from car bombings, ambushes, or assassination attempts as have Saudi Arabia and Kuwait, there has nevertheless been an appreciable rise in the number of Islamic-related terrorist incidents. Early examples would include the 1981 bomb attack on the Hyatt Regency in Dubai following the hotel's serving of alcohol to nationals in traditional dress, thereby violating an unwritten code of conduct for UAE bars.[93] Other examples would include the discovery of explosives in Dubai City Center, an upmarket shopping mall hosting a number of Western outlets, popular with both expatriates and Dubai nationals.[94] Most significant, however, has been the growing evidence linking Al-Qaida activity to the UAE in the wake of the September 11, 2001, terrorist attacks on the United States. Recent indications are that a number of the conspirators received their initial funding in the UAE, with U.S. intelligence tracing back to Abu Dhabi $500,000 used to pay for flight training, airplane tickets, and other logistics; with Muhammad Atta, the ringleader, believed to have received $100,000 dollars into his bank account via moneychangers in Sharjah; and with Marawan al-Shehhi, born in Ra's al-Khaimah and educated in Al-'Ayn, believed to have benefited from generous, federally financed overseas studies scholarships.[95] Crucially, in October 2002 the link with the UAE was further corroborated following the discreet arrest of Abdel al-Nashri in Abu Dhabi (the press release was deliberately delayed until Christmas Eve, traditionally a low-impact news day in the West).[96] As Al-Qaida's head of Gulf operations, al-Nashri was thought to have masterminded the 2000 attack on the USS *Cole,* and more recently was alleged to have been planning suicide attacks using oil tankers as weapons. Of greatest concern to Emirati internal security, he was reportedly captured as "he prepared to blow up economic installations in the country . . . aimed at causing the highest numbers of casualties among nationals and foreigners."[97]

## Ideological Resources

In addition to these cultural and religious resources, ideology can also form an important component of the legitimacy formula.[98] While secular nationalism has had relatively little impact on Emirati politics, there have nevertheless been certain key issues, especially the Palestinian question, that have undoubtedly formed important ideological symbols and, when harnessed by the state, have provided additional layers of legitimacy for the UAE's polity.

Perhaps the first example of organized secular nationalism in the region took place in the 1930s, when a group was set up in the Falah School in Dubai. Many of the expatriate Arab teachers had begun to spread the nationalist sentiments existing in Iraq at that time. As Abdullah describes, they encouraged many of their pupils to "parade through the narrow streets of the town, carrying flags and chanting Arab nationalist songs, applauded by their parents and citizens."[99] More significant, in 1953 a number of Dubai merchants formed a loose organization called the National Front. Although few in members, the front attempted to voice its concern over the growing influence of Persian and Indian merchants, and called for greater privileges and protection for local Arab merchants.[100] Later, at the time of the Suez crisis, there were again demonstrations, this time by a number of locals wishing to express their sympathy with Egypt in the fight against Israeli invasion and what was perceived to be an anti-Arab Anglo-French collaboration.[101] Moreover, it is possible that some of these demonstrators chose to join the Front for the Liberation of Occupied Eastern Arabia (FLOEA), an underground nationalist group that advocated violent action to "end British colonialism and overthrow the ruling oligarchy."[102] Indeed, a group of students were caught trying to set fire to the British air base in Sharjah as an act of protest,[103] and they may well have been FLOEA members. In 1965, again in Sharjah, then-ruler Shaikh Saqr al-Qasimi had granted an audience to Ali Naswal, the assistant secretary-general of the Cairo-based Arab League, who was intent on establishing a League-funded development office in the Trucial states.[104] This blatant attempt to undermine British authority was also deeply unpopular with the other Trucial rulers and was believed to be the causal factor in Saqr's subsequent deposition and replacement with Khalid al-Qasimi.[105] More recently, in the 1970s, the Arabic-language newspaper *Al-Azmina al-Arabiyya* kept pressing the UAE government to assume stronger Arab nationalist positions and to oppose more firmly an expanded U.S. presence in the Gulf.[106] Although on certain occasions the government did seek to acknowledge such sentiments, most notably the Dubai municipality's naming of a new city square after Nasser and a new city quarter after Port Sa'id,[107] secular Arab nationalism has nevertheless remained firmly in the background of Emirati politics, perhaps due to the aforementioned persistence of kinship loyalties,[108] and of course also due to the contrary demonstration effect of failing pan-Arab republics,[109] their military defeats, and their economic collapse.[110]

A far greater concern, however, has been the plight of the Palestinians, and predictably, given the issue's unifying popularity and its much closer association with Islamic brotherhood, this has been one of the chief ideological symbols to be adopted by the polity, both publicly and constitutionally.[111] Indeed, the rulers' support for the Palestinian people has a long history in the region. In response to the Palestinian Islamic Congress in Jerusalem of 1930, a meeting was held in the chief mosque in Sharjah during which young educated locals were encouraged to give enthusiastic speeches and to help collect money for the cause. Moreover, during the interwar period, a number of articles published in pro-Palestinian Cairo magazines were believed to have been sent anonymously from various locals in the Trucial states.[112] In more recent years there have of course been a multitude of carefully organized state-sanctioned anti-Israeli demonstrations, many of which are televised and some of which are attended by the rulers and other notables.[113] In addition, generous government-sponsored aid packages are supplied to Palestine via the UAE's Red Crescent Society or through agencies such as the Abu Dhabi Fund for Arab Economic Development (which is currently constructing the "Shaikh Zayed Residential City" in the Gaza Strip).[114] Finally, again underscoring the polity's commitment to the cause, the federal government has even sought to formalize its total boycott of all things Israeli by introducing prohibitive legislation:

Articles 1 & 2 of this law [Federal Law no. 15] stipulate that "any natural or legal person shall be prohibited from directly or indirectly concluding an agreement with organisations or persons either resident in Israel, connected therewith by virtue of their nationality or working on its behalf. . . ." Also the entry, exchange or possession of all types of Israeli merchandise, commodities or products, or any form of trading in them, is forbidden and the embargo shall apply to monetary papers and other Israeli movable amounts in the UAE.[115]

### The Two-Level Emirati Identity

Closely related to these ideological resources is the role of identity in the UAE's legitimacy formula. Although the UAE is in many ways more a loose confederation than a true federation and on one level retains many emirate-level identities and loyalties,[116] the greater awareness of communal solidarity arising from the union of the seven emirates should not be underestimated. Certainly, a sense of identity and membership of a distinct political community that does not conflict with other subnational or supranational identifications may be crucial in a heterogeneous population comprising differing tribal affiliations, different emirate loyalties, and different ethnic populations. Indeed, it has been claimed that such an identity can serve as a necessary horizontal axis in the state-building process, an axis that can actually complement the vertical patrimonial axis between the ruler and the ruled.[117]

Even before the creation of the UAE, the need for some kind of greater "Emirati" identity was already beginning to be recognized by the various Trucial rulers. A broader identity was seen as providing a stronger platform upon which to build future legitimacy without necessarily weakening other personal, cultural, and religious legitimacy resources. Indeed, even in 1966, upon his accession in Abu Dhabi, Shaikh Zayed underlined his commitment to the building of such an identity: "It is the way to power, the way to strength, the way to well-being, a high reputation. . . . Lesser entities have no standing in the world today, and so it has ever been in history."[118] Throughout the 1970s, identity building continued unabated, with the introduction of a new national flag, a new national anthem, national holidays, a "national university," and many other highly visible symbols of the new UAE/Emirati identity. At the time, most observers viewed this overt process within the context of nationalism and as part of the Gulf's commitment to "Arabism,"[119] but as Findlow has demonstrated in her recent study of contemporary Emirati identity, these were not the true foundations of the new identity.[120] Secular nationalism had only a limited impact on the region, and although Article 6 of the UAE's provisional constitution and various other official documents in the 1970s did emphasize the need for a broader Arab identity,[121] Muhammad al-Musfir convincingly argues that because the majority of these were constructed during the Nasserite era of pan-Arabism, they were merely historical by-products.[122] Certainly, as a wealthy oil-producing Arab state, the UAE and its population did provide considerable economic aid and moral support to the Arab republics during this period,[123] but this assistance should perhaps be viewed as more of a commitment to Arab brotherhood than Arab nationalism. The UAE/Emirati identity should not therefore be regarded as simply another derivative of pan-Arab nationalism but instead as part of a distinct identity fostered by the traditional polity, an identity that serves as another key layer in the UAE's legitimacy formula.

In an effort to determine the success of the identity-building process in the UAE, Findlow's 1999 survey attempted to demonstrate how UAE citizens possessed not only an Arab identity but also a strong UAE/Emirati identity (see Figure 2.1). Her results were rather disappointing, given that only 30 percent of respondents claimed to be "UAE/Emirati," with the remainder claiming either a more general Arab identity, an emirate-level identity, or in some cases even an identity linked to their home town or village. [124] However, it is important to note that this low Emirati response may have been due to the noncontextualized and geographic nature of the survey question ("Where are you from?"), the single location of the survey (Al-'Ayn), and the lack of a broad demographic cross section.

My own survey, conducted in 2002, canvassed a similar number of citizens (250 male UAE nationals), but applied a more specific identity-related question ("Which of the following best describes your identity?"), and provided three possible choices: "UAE/Emirati," an emirate-specific response (e.g., Abu Dhabi for those surveyed in Abu Dhabi), and a more general

**Figure 2.1 Findlow Identity Survey Response, 1999**

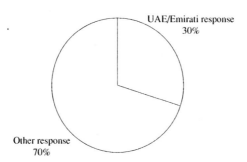

*Source:* Sally Findlow (2000), "The UAE: Nationalism and Arab-Islamic Identity," Abu Dhabi, Emirates Centre for Strategic Studies and Research (ECSSR), ECSSR Occasional Paper no. 39, pp. 29–30.

"Arab" response. Furthermore, the survey was conducted in five separate locations across the UAE, and aimed to question a variety of age groups (see Table 2.2).

**Table 2.2  Identity Survey**

| Location | UAE/Emirati Response (%) | Emirate-Specific Response (%) | Arab Response (%) |
|---|---|---|---|
| Abu Dhabi | 86 | 8 | 6 |
| Dubai | 36 | 60 | 4 |
| Sharjah | 76 | 16 | 8 |
| 'Ajman | 98 | 0 | 2 |
| Al-'Ayn | 100 | 0 | 0 |
| Overall | 79 | 17 | 4 |

*Source:* Davidson identity survey (2002).

Unsurprisingly, the "UAE/Emirati" results from Abu Dhabi, the federation's capital, and Al-'Ayn, also part of Abu Dhabi emirate, were very high. Similarly in 'Ajman the "UAE/Emirati" response was also very high, perhaps due to the emirate's small size, its non-oil-producing status, and its dependence on federal aid for much of its economic and social development. Conversely, in Sharjah, and far more notably in Dubai, the "UAE/Emirati" response was much lower, with many more respondents giving emirate-specific answers, clearly reflecting the relative economic power and the proud independent histories of these emirates.[125] Nevertheless, despite such important regional variations, it is clear from the overall results of the survey that a sense of a UAE/Emirati identity is emerging, with a significant number of UAE citizens now regarding themselves primarily as Emirati rather than "Arab" or some other, more localized identity. Indeed, a substantial 79 percent gave a "UAE/Emirati" response to the survey question, with 17 percent giving an emirate-specific answer such as "Abu Dhabi" or "Dubai," and only 4 percent giving a more general answer such as "Arab" or "Middle Eastern."

### Structural Resources and Neopatrimonialism

Alongside these essentially traditional resources, it is also imperative to consider the increasing importance of structural resources and their role in the UAE's evolving legitimacy formula. As explained in the discussion of patrimonialism, the increasing needs of the region's expanding and rapidly urbanizing population required the polity to create many new intermediaries and bureaucracies. Although the resulting institutions have remained extremely limited and are still very far from the Weberian legal-rational ideal (see Chapter 4),[126] they have nevertheless appreciably enhanced the traditional polity's legitimacy and to some extent have countered the UAE's long-standing reputation as being nothing more than a despotic *hakim* regime.[127] Indeed, if well balanced, it would seem that "neopatrimonial" networks can provide some degree of durable legitimacy without necessarily short-circuiting the polity's more traditional structures. By openly institutionalizing processes and introducing accepted regulations, both new and existing organizations and procedures can acquire much greater value and stability,[128] even if the seemingly modern institutions are still controlled by older personal and patrimonial networks.

Writing in the early 1960s, Halpern argued that any political system that still relied upon "face-to-face relationships," monarchy or otherwise, could never hope to establish any lasting authority or any firm consensus on public purpose, public interest, or public duty.[129] Although the UAE's oil wealth certainly removed some of the urgency for institutional development, at least by allowing the polity to avoid the need for the kind of penetrative extractive structures championed by Tilly and Kiren Aziz Chaudhry,[130] Shaikh Zayed and his fellow Trucial rulers were nonetheless keenly aware of the need to supplement their personal and patrimonial networks with more elaborate structures. Indeed, the need for institutional development was a key issue in federal negotiations and, following the creation of the UAE in 1971, a number of federal laws immediately sought to streamline the new government by creating a ruling council, a ministerial cabinet, and a national consultative council.[131] Given that these new structures effectively institutionalized the authority of the traditional rulers and their patrimonial subordinates, their position and legitimacy at the apex of all networks were undoubtedly strengthened. Certainly at this time, both indigenous popular opinion and foreign observers held that such structures were most definitely worthwhile,[132] adding an air of legitimacy to what were previously very simple traditional governments and, as Hudson noted with specific reference to the UAE, clearly reflecting the way in which "both the royal and the technocratic sectors of the elite seemed convinced that future legitimacy would depend upon the building of a modern government apparatus."[133]

The functioning of these institutions, together with the plethora of other structures and establishments, including the chambers of commerce, the industrial parastatals, and the various supreme councils,[134] will be explored more thoroughly in Chapter 4.[135] It is important to note, however, that the rulers' views regarding structural legitimacy from the early 1970s have remained relatively unchanged, with the present (and next) generation of Emirati rulers continuing to stress not only the need for strong personal leadership and innovation, but also the need for greater institutionalization.

Indeed, speaking at a recent conference, Shaikh Muhammad al-Maktum, the Crown Prince of Dubai and one of the leading political personalities in the Gulf, effectively summed up these notions:

> We [Gulf leaders] realise that the challenges we face are crucial and difficult . . . naturally, new realities create new challenges and responsibilities for Arab leadership. . . . The modern leader lays the cultural basis of questioning and accountability, as well as forges ahead and cares for others. In addition, the leader needs to crystallise an innovative vision that provides the platform for the takeoff for humane resource capabilities, and realise the projected targets endeavoured. It is therefore imperative that we increase the participation of people by developing institutions, while emphasising transparency and fighting corruption.[136]

Similarly, presenting at a recent symposium, Shaikh Fahim al-Qasimi, the UAE's minister of economy and commerce, described the continuing need for neopatrimonialism and the balancing of the "best of the old with the best of the new":

> Our system, like the American, is based on a living constitution. Our system combines the best of the old with the best of the new. We have retained democratic Islamic traditions, foremost amongst which are the majlis, the open council in which national and local leaders meet regularly with citizens to discuss issues of concern. Another pillar of our constitutional system is the national assembly, our parliament, which serves as a forum for debating government policies and legislation.[137]

Finally, with reference to the actual mechanisms used for promoting such institutionalization and structural legitimacy, the UAE's efforts, like those of many other developing states, can be seen as falling into two main categories: those of bureaucratic development and those of "constitutional engineering." Certainly, most of the institutionalization that has taken place in the UAE has been through the development of a large number of bureaucracies. While these are used primarily for administrative purposes, with innovation and policymaking remaining within the rulers' domain, the new bureaucracies nevertheless provide an important link and often represent the sole means of contact between the government and the population.[138] Alongside these, constitutional engineering can be used to establish the prevalence of certain principles and the routinization of seemingly modern political procedures, and in some cases can be used to guarantee certain civil liberties and democratic rights. In more authoritarian regimes, the mechanism can of course also be used to fulfill specific political purposes and to provide "window-dressing" legitimacy to cover up abuses of power and any norms or practices usually considered unpopular.[139] The UAE's constitutional engineering would seem to fall somewhere in between the two extremes. On the one hand, certain articles of the federal constitution do claim to guarantee certain basic rights, including equality before the law, the abolition of torture, the freedom of worship, and the right of assembly:

> Article 14 guarantees equality for all before the law, without distinctions between citizens on the basis of race, nationality, religion or social status. A person's liberty is also protected, and no individual may be arrested or detained except in accordance with provisions of the law. Torture and degrading treatment are forbidden.
>
> Articles 29–34 guarantee freedom of movement and residence, freedom to hold opinions and expression of the same, freedom of communication, the freedom to exercise religious worship, right to assembly and the right to choose one's occupation, trade or profession.
>
> Article 40 describes how foreigners shall enjoy, within the Union, the rights and freedom stipulated in international charters which are in force or in treaties and agreements to which the Union is party.
>
> Article 41 details how every person shall have the right to submit complaints to the competent authorities, including the judicial authorities, concerning the abuse or infringement of the rights and freedoms.[140]

Indeed, in some respects the actual existence of such articles has provided the polity with a degree of structural legitimacy, given that they are components of a national constitution seemingly predicated on internationally accepted standards.[141] However, not only has the constitution remained in a provisional state for much of the past thirty years,[142] but in many cases these original constitutional guarantees have now been clearly contradicted and undermined by numerous other official documents and revisions, many of which seem more concerned with masking potentially unacceptable controlling practices, including the limitation and co-option of civil society organizations, the restrictions on clergy, and even the enforcement of press censorship.[143]

## Rentierism

Building upon this neopatrimonial network of old and new legitimacy resources, the region's vast oil wealth has of course also reinforced the polity's legitimacy, and indeed has enhanced its prospects for survival in almost every way. Material resources have been enormously significant, and the rulers' newfound wealth has been carefully used and distributed as part of a new "rentier network." Such wealth and its associated structures and relations have formed another key component of the "ruling bargain" between the polity and the population.

Even as late as the 1960s, Halpern felt it "doubtful that most Middle Eastern countries would be able to muster such savings from domestic sources during the next decade so as to enable them to invest a sufficient proportion of national income to keep up with population growth and to create a modern society capable of self-sustaining growth."[144] By this stage, however, the Trucial states and the other Gulf monarchies, while still comparatively poor, were already beginning to emerge as important regional exceptions. With relatively small populations and, especially in the case of Abu Dhabi, easily exploitable oil reserves, these new Arab states were seemingly on the cusp of great prosperity. Thus, as a model for the early modernization theories, the UAE in the 1970s should have been perfect, as Abu Dhabian oil wealth and the resulting abundance of capital should have facilitated extensive socioeconomic development programs, which in turn should have engendered greater political mobilization and the rapid disintegration of the traditional polity. While socioeconomic development has indeed taken place, such political development has clearly not happened. To the contrary, oil wealth and selective oil-financed modernization can instead be seen as having greatly strengthened the traditional polity's legitimacy.

Central to explaining this crucial relationship between oil wealth and the monarchy is the concept of the rentier state—a state that can rely on very high levels of unearned economic rent that, in some circumstances, can often sustain the economy without any real need for a strong productive domestic sector.[145] While the concept was originally applied to the Latin American "cash crop" states, there has also been a long history of rentier activity in the lower Gulf. Indeed, since the beginning of the twentieth century the Trucial rulers were able to gather economic rent from a number of important natural and geographical resources, including Abu Dhabi's guano deposits, Abu Musa's red oxide deposits, the air bases in Sharjah and Dubai, and of course the exploration concessions granted to the Iraqi Petroleum Company.[146] The oil exports of the late 1960s were, of course, on a much larger scale and by the early 1970s, following a fourfold price increase, oil began to provide the region with enormous levels of economic rent[147] (due to relatively low production costs it is believed that over 85 percent of this inflated price was rentier income).[148] Indeed, toward the end of this period the extent of this new wealth was such that the oil-producing Gulf states, particularly Qatar, Kuwait, and Abu Dhabi, came to be seen as the purest examples of rentierism.[149] After all, given the rather minimal labor requirements of their oil industries (accounting for less than 2 percent of the total work force),[150] these Gulf states seemed much closer to the rentier model than any of the agrarian developing states, which always required the involvement of at least some of their domestic work force in the wealth creation process.[151] Thus, as Hazem Beblawi described of these oil monarchies in his study of rentier wealth in the Arab world:

Their promotion to the forefront of world trade and finance resuscitated the concept of rentier economies. A windfall wealth of unprecedented magnitude in such short time revived the idea of unearned income, hence the epithet of rentier economies. The impact of the oil phenomenon on the role of the state and on economic behaviour in general has been so profound in the Arab world during the seventies as to justify special treatment.[152]

Given that this vast unearned wealth accrued directly to the rulers and their offices, the new opportunities for state-sponsored largesse soon became boundless. Indeed, although subsidies had always played a key role in traditional politics,[153] the oil revenues of the 1970s allowed for far greater wealth distribution and the creation of a new allocative state.[154] By providing schools, hospitals, jobs, housing, and in some cases even direct payments such as the aforementioned "marriage funds," rentier wealth enabled the state to become the principal economic actor,[155] and consequently created a new material link between the polity and the population. Thus, in the context of legitimacy and monarchical survival, this "rentier package" has served to consolidate and boost the existing patrimonial network of vertical linkages and socioeconomic privileges. Certainly, UAE nationals are clearly the primary recipients of the bulk of the distributed wealth (recent surveys indicate that nearly 11 percent of per capita income for UAE nationals is now made up of government transfers),[156] with most fitting into a well-defined hierarchy of rentiers with the rulers at the top and with other locals linked into the material network at different layers beneath. Indeed, it has been claimed of "rentier" Gulf citizens: "A rentier is more of a social function than an economic category, and is perceived as a member of a special group who, though he does not participate actively in the economic production, receives nevertheless a share in the produce and at times a handsome share."[157]

Moreover, it is important to note that the rentier network also has the flexibility to tie in virtually all other members of the community, including the UAE's many expatriate workers. Although undeniably more closely involved with the wealth creation process and of course not in receipt of explicit government transfers,[158] expatriates are nevertheless a part of this rentier network, as the majority reap the rewards of the generous (and tax-free) salaries afforded by the oil-rich state. Broadly speaking, the UAE's many foreign rentiers fit into the system at fairly rigid and easily identifiable tiers depending on both their nationality and their occupation and qualification levels. These range from Western high-end professionals who can expect very large earnings, extensive medical benefits, free air travel, and completely free luxury accommodation, to Pakistani and Keralite Indian laborers who are housed in temporary camps outside of the city limits and who are bussed to work every day. Although for this latter category of expatriates the monthly wages are seemingly extremely low (around 400 dirhams) and the benefits virtually nonexistent, such employment nevertheless offers an escape from the South Asian poverty trap and an opportunity to send remittances back to their families.[159] Thus, although few foreigners may be accorded the same privileges as the local rentiers, their overall access to wealth is nonetheless comparatively good, and likely to be much higher than in their country of origin.[160] As such, it would seem that something of a material pact has emerged throughout the UAE, an unwritten and unspoken contract in which almost all of the population accept the legitimacy of the polity in exchange for the constancy and rewards of their well-paid employment (see Table 2.3).

### Rentier Wealth and Ruling Coalitions

Expanding upon the concept of rentier networks, it is also important to consider the manner in which rentier wealth has allowed the traditional rulers

**Table 2.3 The Rentier Network**

| Local Rentiers | UAE Nationals | In Receipt of Explicit Government Transfers |
| --- | --- | --- |
| High-end professionals and executives | Westerners and nonlocal Arabs (mainly Egyptian, Lebanese, Iraqi, and Palestinian) | Large salaries, medical benefits, free flights, free luxury accommodation |
| Low-end professionals, civil servants, and high-end IT professionals | Nonlocal Arabs, educated Indians (from Bombay and Delhi), Muslim Africans (often from Sudan), and some Westerners | Generous salaries, medical benefits, free accommodation (although often shared with one or two other people) |
| Other white-collar workers, including high-end retail occupations, hotel and leisure industry staff, and low-end IT staff | Nonlocal Arabs, educated Indians, Filipinos, and Eastern Europeans | Modest salaries with some medical benefits, but no housing allowance |
| Low-end retail occupations, taxi drivers, and other transport workers | Southern Indians (mainly from Kerala), Filipinos, and Pakistanis (mainly from Peshawar) | Sufficient wages to allow for monthly remittances, occasionally free accommodation, but between ten and twenty per small apartment |
| Laborers | Southern Indians and Pakistanis | Sufficient wages to allow for monthly remittances, forced to live in "labor collectives" (camps outside the city often lacking in basic amenities and requiring men to "shift-sleep" two to a bed) |

to break down old and well-established ruling coalitions and replace them with newer, materially based arrangements with segments of the Emirati population more likely to support the longevity of their traditional polities. As described in Chapter 1, direct and often personal access to the early sources of rentier wealth had already allowed the rulers to gain some degree of structural space and political distance from the merchant elite.[161] However, with the massive economic rent from oil exports this structural space widened to such an extent that the historical ruler-merchant relationship soon became irrelevant, and was eventually replaced by a much broader ruler-citizen coalition in which all members of the national population, including those of the hinterland and the recently urbanized Bedu, became materially bound to the ruler and the traditional polity. Thus, with a well-financed distributive state in place, the formerly politically active merchant elites were essentially marginalized:[162] the rulers were no longer reliant on their support and taxes and, by generously allocating the new wealth,[163] could instead forge a more one-sided political relationship with the remaining bulk of the population.

Moreover, in most cases these sidelined merchants were themselves incorporated into the new rentier coalition, effectively trading in their former political clout for a share of the new wealth.[164] Indeed, using the example of Kuwait, Jill Crystal illustrates this important political adjustment by showing how the merchants "renounced their historical claim to participate in the decision-making process, and in exchange the rulers guaranteed them a large share of the oil revenues. . . . [W]here economic elites once entered politics to protect their economic interests, after oil, merchants left the realm of formal politics to preserve those [same] interests."[165] However, as shown in earlier discussion of the shaikh's dilemma and the various short-term strategies available to traditional rulers, even in Kuwait there have been a series of parliament-related political concessions made to the nonruling elites. Similarly in Bahrain there are constitutional developments under way that appear to point to the reentry of nonruling elites into the emirate's formal political structure. Once again, the UAE appears to be distinct from its oil-producing neighbors in the Gulf, given that the rentier ruling coalition and the pattern of political control remain relatively unchanged, and that the nonruling elite remain firmly outside the highest levels of the decisionmaking process. Thus, while one might expect that oil wealth should lead to a patterned response in state building, the variation between these nearby states clearly indicates this may not always be the case.[166] Obviously, on one level this discrepancy can be explained by the comparative oil wealth and the corresponding rentier packages of these Gulf states, especially given that the Abu Dhabi–backed UAE controls nearly 10 percent of the world's proven oil reserves and its exports now rival those of Iran and Russia,[167] whereas the oil wealth of emirates such as

Bahrain and Qatar is considerably more finite.[168] This in itself, however, cannot be a sufficient explanation given that Kuwait, like the UAE, still commands considerable per capita material resources.[169]

Instead, as Crystal has convincingly argued in her comparative study of rulers and merchants in Kuwait and Qatar, the answer may lie in the historical foundations of the Gulf's rentier ruling coalitions. In Kuwait, for example, oil production began far earlier than in the other Gulf states, and at that time the merchant classes and other economic elites remained strong and powerful. They had not yet been weakened by economic depression, the collapse of the Gulf's pearling industry, and the aftermath of World War II. Instead they were able to bargain from a position of strength when the ruler first began to receive oil revenues, and as such the new Kuwaiti ruling coalition had to make at least some attempt to incorporate rather than sideline the nonruling economic elite.[170] In complete contrast, the Trucial states did not begin to receive significant oil revenues until the late 1960s and even then only Abu Dhabi and Dubai were in any way affected. By this stage the old merchant elites who had previously held the rulers' powers in check were already considerably undermined, with their main sources of livelihood having long been in decline. As such, they had little option but to accept the rulers' new coalitions, and thus began to receive distributed wealth and many of the described financial patrimonial-clientalist favors in exchange for their complete political acquiescence.[171]

Indeed, as the example of the Dubai reform movement demonstrated in the previous chapter, by the 1940s the merchant elites had already lost much of their former bargaining power.[172] Similarly in Abu Dhabi and the other Trucial states, with little hope of reestablishing the old and more equitable ruler-merchant ruling coalition, the merchants became relatively easy targets for absorption into a new ruling coalition that offered them tempting distributed wealth for the mere price of political compliance. Essentially, the historical foundations of the UAE's rentier coalition can be seen as being far stronger than those in the other Gulf states, primarily due to the rulers' almost complete co-option of the economic elites by the beginning of the oil era. Although there have certainly been occasions in which former merchant elites have attempted to challenge the UAE's political system,[173] the severity and frequency of these demands have clearly been far less than in the UAE's neighboring states, again pointing to the legitimacy and stability that a traditional polity can derive from a well-established rentier ruling coalition.

## Rentier Wealth and Favorable International Relations

Further related to rentier wealth, the region's favorable international relations with its oil-purchasing customers and oil-investing partners must be seen as adding another materially based layer to the traditional polity's survival formula.[174] While a full discussion of UAE foreign policy remains beyond the scope of this book, it is nevertheless crucial to consider the key role of external support in ensuring the ongoing survival of the monarchy. Indeed, without oil and the continuing military backing of its former patron, Britain, and the new superpower, the United States, it would seem unlikely that the UAE would have been able to secure itself from foreign aggression in an increasingly volatile region. As demonstrated in the discussion of the federal negotiations, on the eve of independence Iran had already occupied three strategic Emirati islands (two of them by force).[175] Moreover, with the fresh memories of Iraqi annexation threats on Kuwait in the 1960s,[176] and with increasing Marxist activity in neighboring Oman and southern Arabia,[177] powerful Western backing became seen as more necessary than ever before. More recently, the continuing territorial disputes with Saudi Arabia, the increased Iranian subjugation of Abu Musa in 1992[178] (reneging on the original 1971 deal, in which Sharjah would maintain sovereignty in exchange for allowing an Iranian base),[179] and of course the clear ambitions of Ba'thist Iraq to assume greater control over Gulf oil, have also constituted considerable threats to UAE security and, with the exception of Iraq, have continued to underscore the need for future external military support.[180]

One vital way of ensuring such foreign backing has been the UAE's skillful sharing of its oil and gas industries over the past three and a half decades. Although commonly believed to have been nationalized following the establishment of the federal oil ministry and the Algerian-managed Abu Dhabi National Oil Company (ADNOC) in 1971,[181] the closely guarded reality is that Abu Dhabi's various oil companies, especially the major operators, are all 40–49 percent owned by British, French, Dutch, U.S., or Japanese oil giants (see Figures 2.2 and 2.3).

For example, the Abu Dhabi Company for Onshore Oil Investments (ADCO) is 60 percent owned by ADNOC, 10 percent owned by British Petroleum (BP), 10 percent owned by Campagnie Française des Petroles (CFP), 10 percent owned by Royal Dutch Shell, 5 percent owned by Exxon (Standard Oil of New Jersey), 5 percent owned by Mobil, and 2 percent owned by Partex (Gulbenkian Interests). The Abu Dhabi Marine Areas company (ADMA), responsible for operating the bulk of Abu Dhabi's vast reserves in the Persian Gulf, is 60 percent owned by ADNOC, 15 percent owned by BP, 13 percent owned by Total, and 12 percent owned by Japan Oil Development Company (JODCO). The Zakum Development Company (ZADCO), responsible for the remainder of offshore operations, is similarly shared, with 51 percent owned by ADNOC and 49 percent owned by JODCO. Likewise, Abu Dhabi's principal gas company (ADGAS) is 51 percent owned by ADNOC with the remainder shared between BP, Mitsu,

**Figure 2.2 ADCO Ownership**

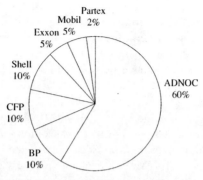

*Sources:* Abdulkhaleq Abdulla (1985), "Political Dependency: The Case of the United Arab Emirates," PhD thesis, University of Georgetown, pp. 107–114; Manna Sa'id Al-Otaibi (1982), *The Petroleum Concession Agreements of the United Arab Emirates,* vols. 1–2, London, Croom Helm; Albadr Abu Baker (1995), "Political Economy of State Formation: The United Arab Emirates in Comparative Perspective," PhD thesis, University of Michigan, pp. 15–151; Oxford Business Group (2000), *Emerging Emirates 2000: The Annual Business, Economic, and Political Review,* London, p. 48; and personal interviews in Abu Dhabi in 2003.

**Figure 2.3 ADMA Ownership**

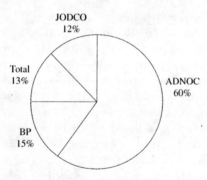

*Source:* See Figure 2.2.

CFP, and Bridgeston[182] (see Figures 2.4 and 2.5).

In Sharjah, the sole oil operator, Saja, is believed to be 100 percent foreign owned (by Amoco, a subsidiary of the Standard Oil Company of Indiana). In Dubai, although shrouded in secrecy (with oil revenue having always accrued directly to the ruling family rather than to the government),[183] it is also believed that the primary operator, the Dubai Petroleum Company (DUPETCO), is 100 percent foreign owned (50 percent by the Continental Oil Company, 25 percent by CFP, and 25 percent by Hispanoil).[184] Crucially, the majority of these oil and gas concessions are up for renewal in 2005, and if one ignores the token public pretense that they were signed under conditions of "colonial duress and monopoly,"[185] there are strong indications that they will be extended for an additional twenty-five-year period. Indeed, in elite circles, the decision to allow such large Western stakes in the UAE's key economic sector is now generally thought to have paid for itself many times over not only by providing the industry with the latest technology and skills, but also by guaranteeing relatively stable foreign relations with the first world economies and by emphasizing the need for decisive external action in the event of regional instability or any other potential threat to mutual hydrocarbon investments.[186]

Although sizable Western forces have rarely been based on Emirati soil since British withdrawal in 1971, the perceived support and belief in the rapid reaction of a military superpower to a local conflict has nonetheless been of equal significance. Like the populations of Kuwait, Bahrain, and

**Figure 2.4 ZADCO Ownership**

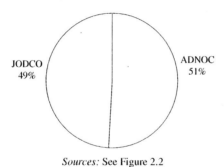

*Sources:* See Figure 2.2

**Figure 2.5 DUPETCO Ownership, Dubai**

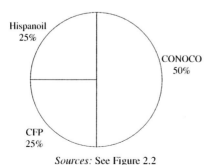

*Sources:* See Figure 2.2

Qatar, many UAE nationals accept that their own armed forces, albeit modern and well-equipped (the Union Defence Force is one of the few non-Western militaries eligible to receive sophisticated items from superpower inventories),[187] cannot realistically expect to expel any determined foreign invader,[188] but do believe that these forces can still serve as a vital "tripwire," buying enough time for Western military support to arrive and reinforce their country's defenses.[189] Indeed, the UAE's biggest arms supplier, France, has agreed to deploy 75,000 troops to the UAE "in the event of an emergency," and it is believed that Britain signed a similar defense treaty in 1996, albeit without specifying exact troop numbers.[190] The rulers' close military relations with the Western powers are therefore generally viewed as necessary and legitimate measures in safeguarding national security and preserving the Emirati way of life.[191] Indeed, symbolized by Abu Dhabi's biannual Triple International Defense Exhibition (TRIDEX) and International Defence Exhibition (IDEX) events, which attract over 800 leading arms manufacturers, and by Dubai's air show, which attracts over 500 exhibitors,[192] the UAE's defense minister recently claimed of this international presence: "The fact that many renowned defence manufacturers from around the world are showcasing their products here is a proof of the success of this year's show. It is also a message that the UAE, under the leadership of the President, His Highness Shaykh Zayed Al-Nuhayyan, is a stable and secure country."[193]

Of course, this continuing Western military support may prove something of a double-edged sword for the rulers unless a necessary balance is reached. Indeed, there are many instances where a ruler's other legitimacy resources, namely the commitment to Islamic and Arab brotherhood, have been seriously compromised by an all too public presence of foreign and non-Muslim support. Particularly strong examples would include the Iranian Shah's very open backing from the United States, and of course the Iraqi monarchy, which almost certainly suffered from its overly close relationship with Britain, eventually alienating most segments of its largely anti-Western population.[194] Indeed, Elie Kedourie argues that the rapid decline in the Iraqi polity's legitimacy stemmed primarily from "a nagging feeling that it was a make-believe kingdom built on false pretenses and kept going by a British design for a British purpose."[195] Thus, in the case of the UAE, the rulers have had to ensure that they carefully weigh up their country's immediate security needs against a potential backlash caused by any overt non-Muslim or non-Arab alliance. In 1990 and 1991, in the months preceding Operation Desert Storm and the liberation of Kuwait, this legitimacy balance was particularly keen given that the proposed target of the Western troops was a fellow Arab state.[196] In retrospect, the carefully managed Damascus Declaration "coalition," which included many other Arab nations,[197] together with the relative invisibility of Western forces in the

UAE (the majority of personnel were stationed outside of the cities and restricted in their "downtown" activities),[198] circumvented this problem, allowing the UAE's rulers to be seen as supporting a joint Arab military initiative while playing host to a discreet and essential foreign force.[199] The military buildup of late 2002 and 2003 was far more difficult to contain within the legitimacy formula, however, given that no Arab coalition emerged to enforce the disarmament of Iraq, given that many of the UAE's neighbors remained reluctant in supporting the deployment of Western forces,[200] and given that a number of anti-U.S. grassroots movements were already beginning to emerge in the UAE with the dual aims of boycotting U.S. goods and promoting solidarity with the Iraqi people.[201] Thus, although the UAE quietly permitted the use of its Dhafrah base in 2003 and covertly billets U.S. soldiers on short-term leave from Iraq,[202] if future situations are not adequately addressed then any further non-UN and non–Arab League sanctioned attacks in and around the Gulf that are launched from UAE territory may considerably delegitimize the rulers' positions by weakening their religious and ideological unifying resources.

## Dynastic Monarchy and the Evolution of the Traditional Polity

Rentier coalitions and materially based legitimacy resources may still be unable to guarantee the long-term survival of the neopatrimonial polity. Most obvious, hydrocarbon reserves are finite, and although Abu Dhabi's oil will last for at least another generation, the other oil-producing emirates of Dubai and Sharjah will not be so fortunate.[203] If economic austerity measures are ever required due to declining revenues, it may become difficult to impose extractive measures and placate a once privileged population.[204] Furthermore, no matter how historically well founded the UAE's ruling rentier coalition is, new and younger generations of Emiratis unfamiliar with the region's early state formation may begin to assume the distributive economy as an irreversible birthright,[205] and may therefore begin to regard rentier pacts of political acquiescence as being both illegitimate and anachronistic. Added to this, it still remains possible that the formerly weakened merchant elites, or rather their sons, may be able to reenter politics via the back door: the described plethora of new institutions and bureaucracies required by the neopatrimonial state and its extensive distributive economy may provide future opportunities for parallel power bases[206] and, in much the same way as the walis of the preoil era, may allow for personal fiefdoms to develop outside the patrimonial and rentier networks.

Although the UAE's development planners and "modernizing monarchs" are acutely aware of the need for economic diversification in order to supplement and reduce the reliance on rentier wealth and rentier derived legitimacy, the ruling families themselves have actually evolved in an effort to better ensure their stability and longevity, and to bolster their polity's material resources. As of yet, parallel power bases have largely been prevented by the rise of a more unitary and more extensive state, which has allowed for greater power-sharing opportunities for royals and notables within the patrimonial network. In addition, alongside the maintenance of the described bay'a mechanism has been the institutionalization of a dynamic crown prince mechanism that has practically put an end to damaging succession struggles. Third, the evolution of collective action mechanisms and bandwagoning have served to reduce the divisiveness and factionalism that have historically plagued and delegitimized the Gulf's monarchies for much of the past century. The result of these mechanisms has been, in Michael Herb's terms, the emergence of "dynastic monarchy" in the lower Gulf: with greatly expanded membership these extensive ruling families can be seen as having become self-regulating proto-institutions,[207] perhaps providing the strength and stability normally associated with large-scale single-party political systems.

As demonstrated in Chapter 1, the Trucial states were originally rather segmented, as the rulers often had to delegate control over their more far-flung provinces to local representatives; the walis, 'amirs, and na'ibs.[208] Furthermore, before oil wealth, the state was simply too small to accommodate any real power-sharing mechanisms. Consequently, any attempts to allow powerful relatives key positions tended to lead to the creation of parallel states, or in some circumstances even resulted in the wali returning to the main town and usurping the ruler. Indeed, as mentioned, Shaikh Saqr's takeover of Ra's al-Khaimah in the 1940s, and of course Shaikh Zayed's succession in Abu Dhabi in the 1960s, were both facilitated by their relative autonomy and their development of independent power bases in somewhat remote regions.[209] With the beginning of the oil era, however, the region's segmentary politics were considerably reduced: the explorations and advanced communications required by the new industry brought the region's many outlying regions within much closer range of the rulers' influence, but (far more important) the increasing size of the distributive rentier state began to provide the rulers with many more "safe" consolation prizes. Indeed, the many new posts created by the new government ministries, the bureaucracies, the oil companies, and the armed forces, could be distributed to powerful and potentially influential members of the ruling families and their associates. In this more unitary state, the ruler could therefore share power within a more closely supervised patrimonial hierarchy without fearing autonomy or any loss of personal authority.

Abu Dhabi provides a very strong example of this power-sharing mechanism, with Shaikh Zayed having made great effort to create and fill executive positions in the expanding rentier state with other influential members of the al-Nuhayyan family who fell just outside his inner sanctum of immediate relatives. Indeed, of particular interest during this period was the seemingly successful accommodation of an almost parallel branch of the al-Nuhayyan family who had emerged earlier in the century following a series of bloody fratricides and internecine conspiracies.[210] Whereas both Shaikh Zayed and his brother, the former ruler Shaikh Shakhbut, were both from the Sultan family line, a number of other Abu Dhabi shaikhs were of the nonruling yet still powerful Khalifa line.[211] Given that this distaff line had avenged the death of Shaikh Zayed's father, had supported Zayed's succession, and were at the time older and more experienced than Zayed's sons,[212] the Bani (sons of) Khalifa al-Nuhayyan were all accorded with an appropriate share of power in the early years of the new administration. Indeed, this astute dynastic balancing act involved appointing Shaikh Mubarak al-Nuhayyan as the UAE's first interior minister, while his brother, Shaikh Surur al-Nuhayyan, was elevated to serving as one of Zayed's closest advisers.[213] Even today, Mubarak's son, Shaikh Nuhayyan al-Nuhayyan, continues to represent the collateral Bani Khalifa, in his role as both UAE minister of higher education and scientific research and president of Zayed University, while other members of the family dominate Gulf Air, the Abu Dhabi civil aviation department, Abu Dhabi's town planning department, and governmental affairs in Abu Dhabi's western province (the location of the emirate's major onshore oil fields).[214] Although the al-Maktum family of Dubai remained segmented and quarrelous for a longer period of time, the emirate's ruling family, following British intervention against the troublemaking Shaikh Juma' and his sons,[215] was also able to consolidate itself in the same fashion as the al-Nuhayyan family by using the new positions and opportunities created by the rentier state to share power and to accommodate potentially divisive members of the family and the ruling elite.[216] In particular Shaikhs Marwan, Butti, and Muhammad of the contemporary Bani Juma' were given key posts in the politically significant Dubai Defence Force, while one of Shaikh Rashid's more ambitious cousins, Shaikh Mani', was elevated to the directorship of the Diwan.[217] Similarly in Fujairah, one can see clear evidence of such arrangements, with the ruler having carefully distributed the command of the local Emiri guard, the chairmanship of the Fujairah port authority, and the directorship of the Fujairah national bank to his sole brother, and having granted the deputy rulership to an influential cousin who continues to represent a separate but historically significant branch of the Sharqiyin family.[218] More recently in Sharjah, which has remained the least stable of the seven emirates,[219] following a failed coup attempt in 1987 the reinstated Shaikh Sultan al-Qasimi immediately ensured accommodation of the main protagonists in his new administration and provided them with significant consolation prizes. Most notable, Shaikh Abdul-Aziz al-Qasimi, the ruler's elder brother and the leader of the coup, was appointed crown prince and deputy chairman of the new Sharjah Executive Council. Although these appointments were only temporary, with the ruler eventually dismissing Shaikh Abdul-Aziz from his deputy chairmanship in favor of one of his first cousins and preferring to leave the crown prince position vacant,[220] high-level power sharing was nevertheless a useful stopgap measure until the ruler was able to reaffirm his position.[221]

Conversely, it can be demonstrated that those traditional monarchies that have not allowed for greater power sharing and accommodation of other members of the ruling family have often suffered from considerable internal instability and, as a result, have been more vulnerable to divisive and revolutionary forces. The example of Libya is especially appropriate here, as in many ways it used to resemble the Gulf states, having a small population, a tribal structure, and oil wealth. However, unlike the dynastic monarchs of the Gulf, King Idris of Libya effectively blocked all of his relatives and their key associates from gaining any positions of power. Thus when revolution came in 1969, the monarchy quickly collapsed as all stood to gain—those inside as well as those outside of the ruling family.[222] Similarly in Afghanistan, the traditional monarch Shah Zahir forced through a new constitution that barred all other members of the ruling family from occupying significant posts. Once again, when the inevitable struggle for power occurred, the monarchy soon disintegrated and a republic was duly formed.[223] Thus, in states that fail to develop additional patrimonial mechanisms within the ruling families, their nondynastic monarchies are more prone to failure as the ruler has to balance all forces of opposition on his own, and when he falls the monarchy will fall with him. Indeed, the crucial difference between these "one-bullet regimes" and the power-sharing dynastic monarchies of the Gulf (and to a lesser extent Oman and Morocco)[224] is that, quite apart from increasing the polity's vulnerability to assassinations,[225] these more rigid regimes are far more likely to succumb to internal challenges from disgruntled rival claimants, many of whom will have nothing to lose given their existing exclusion from power.

A second identifiable priority of these dynastic monarchies has been to safeguard the succession process from divisive and weakening forces. By maintaining the traditional bay'a mechanism and by institutionalizing a crown prince mechanism, instability arising from succession disputes has now largely been eliminated in the Gulf states, and especially in the UAE. Indeed, many of the weaknesses normally associated with primogeniture have been avoided by requiring potential successors to have wide political support within the family in order to receive the necessary bay'a and approval from their elders. Thus, instead of following a clear succession pattern from father to eldest son, the strongest member of the family is able to succeed, thus preventing any unworthy or potentially discordant rulers from coming to power.[226] Although technically a contradiction to the bay'a mechanism, the practice of appointing crown princes has further strengthened the succession process by formalizing the inheritance of power and delegitimizing rival claims. Crucially, however, crown princes do not necessarily follow the primogeniture system and can therefore be used to complement bay'a approval by guaranteeing the succession of the most popular and able future ruler.[227]

Dubai provides a particularly strong example of such succession arrangements. When Shaikh Rashid al-Maktum, the aforementioned "Father of Dubai," died in 1991, he was left with four principal sons. As would be expected, his eldest son, Shaikh Maktum al-Maktum, immediately succeeded his father and became the new emir, while the second eldest son, Shaikh Hamdan al-Maktum, predictably became the deputy ruler. However, in January 1995 the late ruler's third son, Shaikh Muhammad al-Maktum, was proclaimed crown prince.[228] To most observers accustomed to primogeniture this would seem an unusual development given that in most monarchies the eldest son (or at least one of the sons) of the new ruler, in this case Shaikh Maktum al-Maktum, would have automatically become the crown prince, certainly not one of his younger brothers. This awkward arrangement serves to indicate the internal bargaining that must have taken place within the dynasty shortly after their father's death. The highly motivated and ambitious Muhammad could only be satisfied with crown prince status and therefore the promise of future rulership.[229] Moreover, a decade later the internal dynamics of Dubai's dynastic monarchy seem to be working given that the status quo is being maintained, there exists a formal division of powers, and Muhammad is effectively able to run the day-to-day affairs of the emirate with the approval of his older brothers.[230]

In the near future Abu Dhabi will also be faced with the need for careful succession compromises. Although, thus far, the crown prince appointment remains in accordance with the customs of primogeniture, it is important to note how Shaikh Zayed has attempted to balance the ambitions of the numerous other al-Nuhayyan princes in an effort to safeguard his eldest son's succession. Essentially, the problem stems from the perceived division between the crown prince, Shaikh Khalifa, and Shaikh Zayed's other prominent sons, including the second eldest son, Shaikh Sultan al-Nuhayyan, and a powerful progeny of six full brothers from the "Bani Fatima bloc": the sons of Shaikh Zayed's favored wife, Shaikha Fatima bint Mubarak al-Qutbi. Such a rival faction may well be led by Shaikh Muhammad al-Nuhayyan, the eldest of Fatima's sons and a dynamic personality who has carved out an important niche for himself in Abu Dhabi politics.[231] Moreover, in addition to their common bloodline, these younger sons are predominantly Western-university educated[232] and, as will be detailed in Chapter 4, given the recent emergence of more technocratic blocs in Emirati politics, the Bani Fatima bloc may be more favored by the UAE government than Shaikh Khalifa.[233] As such, Shaikh Zayed has been actively brokering a détente between the different al-Nuhayyan factions by distributing positions of power in the federal and Abu Dhabi administrations among his various sons, with the objective that all groups should recognize the succession.[234] Thus, on the one hand Shaikh Khalifa's position has been consolidated by a number of major appointments, including the chairmanships of Abu Dhabi's Executive Council, Abu Dhabi's Supreme Petroleum Council, and the Khalifa Committee, which as Abu Dhabi's highest financial body is responsible for the distribution of Abu Dhabi's funds. On the other hand, significant succession consolation prizes have included the appointment of Shaikh Sultan al-Nuhayyan as UAE deputy prime minister;[235] the 1993 appointment of Shaikh Muhammad al-Nuhayyan to the important position of army chief of staff;[236] the appointment of Muhammad's full brother, Shaikh Hazza al-Nuhayyan as head of national intelligence and security;[237] the creation of a new ministerial post in 2001, head of the presidential office, specifically for another of the Bani Fatima family, Shaikh Mansur al-Nuhayyan;[238] the promotion of the youngest of these brothers, Shaikh Abdullah al-Nuhayyan, to minister of information and culture;[239] and most recently the 2003 upgrading of Shaikh Hamdan al-Nuhayyan from his existing position as minister of state for foreign affairs to the new position of second deputy prime minister.[240] Finally, and perhaps most significant, the reported December 2003 creation of a deputy crown prince position for Shaikh Muhammad al-Nuhayyan[241] (believed to be the result of negotiations between prominent al-Nuhayyan and al-Maktum notables meeting in Geneva the previous year)[242] would seem to indicate Abu Dhabi's adoption of the same compromise succession arrangement undertaken by Dubai. In much the same way that the powerful Shaikh Muhammad al-Maktum has become the crown prince of his figurehead elder brother, it would seem likely that Shaikh Muhammad al-Nuhayyan will become the new crown prince of Abu Dhabi when Shaikh Khalifa succeeds Shaikh Zayed.[243]

Third, also related to power sharing and the distribution of consolation prizes, the increasing evidence of collective action both within and among the dynastic ruling families of the Gulf must be seen as another key stabilizing mechanism. Although it may be preferable for individuals to seek absolute rule, for the rest of the ruling family it is collectively preferable for them to prevent such an occurrence and instead to preserve the dominance of the family as a group. Conforming to a "prisoner's dilemma" model in which one's options have to be carefully considered alongside another's, collective action therefore promotes "groupthink" logic.[244] Thus the preservation of dynastic monarchy may rest on the crucial ability of the majority of family members to bandwagon against any breakaway factions, normally exiling the renegade princes or accommodating their supporters within the dynasty.[245] A key historical example of such collective action would of course be the replacement of Shaikh Shakhbut with his younger brother, Shaikh Zayed, as ruler of Abu Dhabi. By the mid-1960s several key members of the al-Nuhayyan family were concerned with their ruler's reluctance to delegate any of his administrative powers[246] or to channel any of the emirate's oil revenues into local development.[247] Consequently, in 1966 they approached the British and requested that Shakhbut be removed and that measures be taken to preserve law and order during the transition.[248] Thus, while it is popularly believed that the British ousted Shakhbut in favor of the more energetic and forward-thinking Zayed,[249] it was really more of an internal decision within the ruling family. By building upon his popular support as governor of Al-'Ayn and by offering his relatives positions of power in the new oil state, Zayed effectively became the leader of a bandwagon among the al-Nuhayyan dynasty, one that eventually grew to include every single member of the family except, unsurprisingly, Shakhbut's eldest son.[250] More recently, following the aforementioned 1987 coup attempt in Sharjah, a bandwagon soon emerged that included not only members of the Sharjah ruling family, but also members of the other Emirati ruling families. Indeed, although initially supported by Abu Dhabi,[251] Shaikh Abdul-Aziz and his supporters soon found themselves opposed not only by the many Sharjah notables still loyal to Shaikh Sultan, but also by the al-Maktum family of Dubai and even by the ruling families of other Gulf states.[252] Similarly, in summer 2003 the government of Abu Dhabi chose to send tanks to the smaller emirate of Ra's al-Khaimah in an effort to safeguard the octogenarian Qasimi ruler and his new crown prince following a controversial decision to remove power from the eldest son, Shaikh Khalid, who had effectively been regent for twenty years.[253] Accordingly, it would seem there is growing evidence that Emirati rulers can now be reinstated or considerably reinforced following collective action from other neighboring dynastic monarchies, which in turn suggests the emergence of a strong network of mutual support between these families.

## Conclusion

This chapter has provided an overview of how the UAE's polity and its traditional monarchies have managed to circumvent the shaikh's dilemma of assimilating new groups alongside old by carefully combining traditional sources of legitimacy with structural and material resources in an effort to create a stable and resilient "ruling bargain."[254] The polity has continued to draw upon personal legitimacy resources and, by fostering a patrimonial-clientalist system of privileges, loyalties, and vertical linkages, personal authority has remained a key component of the UAE's legitimacy formula even during an era of rapid population growth and urbanization. Moreover, by reviving and in some cases reinventing cultural, religious, and ideological resources, the polity has further augmented its position by unifying most segments of the population behind shared memories, common causes, and a greater sense of identity. Third, through astute constitutional engineering and the development of new bureaucracies and institutions it is also clear how the polity has managed to provide some degree of structural legitimacy while at the same time retaining its carefully managed patrimonial, or rather "neopatrimonial," network of relations.

At all levels, the region's substantial oil wealth has strengthened the UAE's legitimacy formula by providing enormous material resources and by facilitating the development of a distributive economy, which in turn has allowed for a powerful "rentier pact." Essentially, by providing the bulk of the population with a package of distributed wealth and a comprehensive welfare state, the rulers have been able to purchase political acquiescence and considerable popular support from both locals and expatriates. Moreover, this rentier pact has been particularly strong in the UAE given the relative weakness of the region's merchant elites at the beginning of the oil era. Unlike many of the other Gulf states, whose merchants were comparatively powerful when oil exports began, in the lower Gulf the merchants had suffered numerous setbacks and years of economic depression, thus making it easier for them to be absorbed into a new rentier coalition and less likely for them to press for political reform. Further relating to the UAE's material resources, there is little doubt that the region's favorable international relations with its powerful oil-purchasing and oil-investing allies have provided an important security umbrella. Indeed, without such protection and perceived support it would seem likely that the UAE and its monarchies would have eventually succumbed to the threat of more powerful expansionary states in an increasingly volatile region.

Finally, by evolving into large-scale dynasties complete with their own internal self-regulating mechanisms, the UAE's traditional monarchies have been able to warrant even better stability and far greater longevity. By carefully sharing positions of power in the new and more unitary rentier state, by safeguarding and guaranteeing the succession process, and by promoting greater collective action and bandwagoning against harmful factions, the ruling families have managed to avoid both internal divisiveness and damaging external influences. Essentially, the family itself has become an institution and has formed a layer of structural legitimacy in its own right. Indeed, as surrogate political parties, dynastic monarchies can be seen to have developed their own internal dynamic, a dynamic capable of making their members act positively for the group as a whole, and ultimately capable of reinforcing the existing neopatrimonial and materially based legitimacy formulae (see Figure 2.6).

**Figure 2.6 The Survival and Evolution of Traditional Polity**

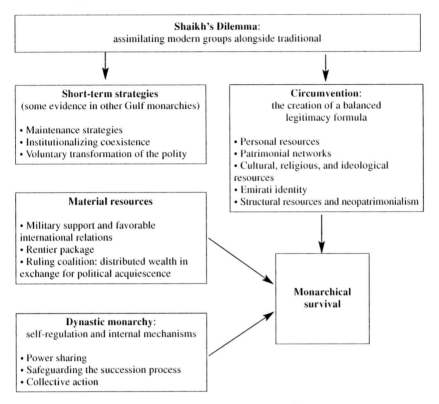

## Notes

1. UAE MINISTRY OF PLANNING (2001), p. 44. A GDP per capita of approximately $20,566 can be calculated using current prices from the listed figure of 75,477 dirhams.

2. The UAE's GDP per capita of $20,566 is higher than Italy's $19,962, and only just below the UK's $21,921. See UNITED NATIONS STATISTICS DIVISION (2002).

3. FREEDOM HOUSE (2001). Since 1972 Freedom House has published an annual assessment of states of freedom by assigning each country and territory the status of "free," "partly free," or "not free" by averaging their political rights and civil liberties ratings. The UAE was given a political rights score of 6 and a civil lib-

erties score of 5 (6,5). Those whose ratings average 1.0–2.5 are generally considered "free," 3.0–5.5 "partly free," and 5.5–7.0 "not free." Comparisons would include a score of (1,1) for the United States, (4,5) for Turkey, and (7,7) for Saudi Arabia.

4. LERNER (1958, 1964), p. 399.

5. See DEUTSCH (1961); and HUDSON (1977), pp. 11–12. Deutsch posits social mobilization as being an "interrelated set of growth processes including economic development, mass media exposure, interpersonal communications, urbanisation, and education."

6. HUNTINGTON (1968), p. 142.

7. Ibid., p. 140.

8. Ibid., p. 169.

9. Ibid., p. 191.

10. Ibid., pp. 179–191.

11. HALPERN (1963, 1965), p. 42. For a discussion of such preemptive action to reform from above, see NONNEMAN (2001), pp. 144–145.

12. HERB (1999), p. 23, a letter from T. C. Fowle, political resident in the Gulf, to Shaikh Sa'id al-Maktum, ruler of Dubai, 1 October 1938 (IOR:LP&S/12/3827).

13. Following merchant unrest and coaxed by the British, Shaikh 'Ahmad al-Sabah established a council in June 1938 comprising elected members. The Kuwaiti merchants had previously requested universal education, immigrant control, a government-sponsored hospital, and a demand that Kuwait work more closely with Iraq to improve cultural cooperation and trading links. See JOYCE (1998), pp. xiv–xv.

14. AL-ABED (2001).

15. HEARD-BEY (1982), pp. 356–357.

16. BBC MONITORING (2002).

17. See KAMRAVA (2002).

18. See "The Traditional Political Structure," p. 10 in this volume.

19. See "A Paralyzed Legislature?" p. 194 in this volume.

20. See U.S. LIBRARY OF CONGRESS (2001).

21. See U.S. CENTRAL INTELLIGENCE AGENCY (2001b).

22. See KAMRAVA (2002). As Kamrava describes, King Hassan and his son Muhammad VI, the patrons of such coexistence in Morocco, considered the role of democracy and the concept of political participation as "only letting political parties debate and fight over issues that in the grand scheme of things are politically marginal insofar as state-society relations are concerned" (p. 5).

23. HUNTINGTON (1968), p. 181.

24. HIRO (1987), pp. 31–36.

25. ISMAEL (1993), pp. 82–83.

26. Ibid., pp. 86–87.

27. Ibid., p. 185.

28. HUNTINGTON (1968), pp. 188–190.

29. See CORDESMAN (1997).

30. Personal interviews, Abu Dhabi, March 2001; Sharjah, December 2001 and March 2002.

31. See "Civil Society and Globalization, p. 266 in this volume.

32. See, for example, PRESS AFFAIRS DIRECTORATE OF SHARJAH EMIRI COURT, (1988), pp. 183–185, citing the level of financial co-option in Sharjah's civil society organizations.

33. See, for example, MADAD (2001).

34. U.S. DEPARTMENT OF STATE (2001), sec. 2(a).

35. KHALEEJ TIMES (2001), referring to an admission by the minister of

Islamic affairs that the ministry either provides written sermons or approves suggested topics by Islamic clergy in the UAE. Also, as will be discussed in the final chapter of this volume, over 99 percent of Sunni mosques are state-owned, with most of the Shi'a mosques receiving substantial government subsidies. See "The Co-option and Patronage of Civil Society," p. 269 in this volume.

36. See "The Federation of Emirates," p. 45 in this volume. Also see ANTHO-NY (2002), pp. 58–59.

37. ZABARAH (1982), pp. 43–44. Writing of the imam, Zabarah explains, "The traditionalist recognising that his powers are derived from his acceptance of traditional values, fights to preserve those values that are familiar to him, and those unfamiliar to him cannot be tolerated."

38. ZABARAH (1982), pp. 44–45.

39. HUDSON (1977), pp. 1–2, 7–11. In his "mosaic model" for conceptualizing change and legitimacy in traditional polities, Hudson emphasizes the persistence and resilience of selected primordial and parochial loyalties during rapid modernization, and even accepts that in some cases these traditional structures can be formalized and strengthened.

40. Like Hudson, David Easton reasoned that there were three main areas of resources available to traditional rulers: personal, ideological, and structural. See EASTON (1965), pp. 287–303; and HUDSON (1977), p. 18.

41. See "The Traditional Political Structure," p. 14 in this volume.

42. ENCYCLOPEDIA OF ISLAM (1960), p. 1114, for a definition of the bay'a principle.

43. As explained in Chapter 1, the Bedu's notion of citizenship underscored allegiance to a specific ruler rather than any sense of equality or territorial identity. See "The Traditional Political Structure," p. 14 in this volume. Also see NONNE-MAN (2001), p. 154.

44. HUDSON (1977), p. 84.

45. Personal interviews, Abu Dhabi, September 2002, with reference to Shaikh Zayed's ongoing popular support. For a discussion of the role of charisma in determining personal authority, see MOORE (1970), pp. 19–20.

46. Personal interviews, Abu Dhabi, September 2002, with reference to Shaikh Zayed's ongoing popular support. Also see KHOURY (1980).

47. AL-QASIMI (1999), p. 2. This is an extract from the speech made by the UAE's minister of economy and commerce to a conference convened by the Middle East Policy Council on 20 April 1999.

48. Personal interviews, Dubai, March 2001 and October 2002, with reference to the popular memory of Shaikh Rashid al-Maktum.

49. HUDSON (1977), p. 200. Hudson is quoting a "high-ranking subordinate" of Shaikh Rashid al-Maktum.

50. Personal interviews, Sharjah, December 2001; and Ra's al-Khaimah, December 2001. It is not uncommon to see impromptu convoys of 4x4s driving along the main streets of these cities waving flags and posters of their rulers.

51. See "Rentier Wealth and Favorable International Relations," p. 92 in this volume, with regard to the Iraqi monarchy's unpopular relations with Britain; and "Dynastic Monarchy and the Evolution of the Traditional Polity," p. 97 in this volume, with regard to the weaknesses associated with the Afghani and Libyan thrones.

52. See "The Traditional Political Structure," p. 14 in this volume.

53. For a similar discussion, see ABU BAKER (1995), pp. 122–123.

54. See, in this volume, "Dynastic Monarchy and the Evolution of the

Traditional Polity," p. 97, and "The Federal Decisionmaking Structure," p. 188.

55. ABDULLAH (1978), p. 138. Many of the young graduates were the returning sons of families who had exiled themselves to Doha during Shaikh Shakhbut's nonprogressive reign. See "Dynastic Monarchy and the Evolution of the Traditional Polity," p. 97 in this volume; and ABU BAKER (1995), p. 133.

56. ABDULLAH (1978), p. 140.

57. HUNTINGTON (1968), p. 186. See Huntington's argument with reference to Ethiopia.

58. ABU BAKER (1995), p. 258.

59. As a side note, the existence of this small local class has effectively displaced any conflicts between national classes and reproduced them between nationals and expatriates. See, for example, ABU BAKER (1995), p. 175.

60. Any visitor to the Gulf states is struck by the way traditional *dishdasha* and *abaya* are worn exclusively by the UAE nationals, almost as a uniform of privilege. See GAUSE (2000), p. 177; and CRYSTAL (1990, 1995), pp. 161–164.

61. For a similar discussion, see AL-RUMAITHI (1977), pp. 34–36.

62. HEARD-BEY (1999), p. 145.

63. It must be noted that a major social problem in the UAE stems from the freedom granted to Emirati men to marry women of any nationality or religion. Given that Emirati women are not yet granted the same freedom, there are a growing number of single Emirati women, as their men have taken wives from other Arab states, Africa, Asia, and even Russia.

64. A UAE government spokesman speaking in Abu Dhabi, March 2002, quoting Shaikh Zayed's speech regarding marriage funds in the UAE.

65. HEARD-BEY (1996), p. 397.

66. Ibid.

67. UAE MINISTRY OF INFORMATION AND CULTURE (1984, 1988).

68. FEDERATION OF UAE CHAMBERS OF COMMERCE AND INDUSTRY (1993), p. 34.

69. Personal interviews, Dubai, April 2001; and Al-'Ayn, April 2001. Also see "Diversification Through Agriculture," p. 128 in this volume.

70. MIDDLE EAST ECONOMIC DIGEST (1968), p. 558.

71. FENELON (1973), p. 106.

72. See OXFORD BUSINESS GROUP (2000), p. 70.

73. See WAM (2004).

74. See DAVIS (1991), p. 13.

75. FINDLOW (2000), p. 2.

76. See, in this volume, "Diversification Through Commerce and Tourism," p. 131, and "The Impact of Globalizing Forces on Contemporary Society and Culture," p. 262.

77. KHALAF (1999), pp. 85–106. Also see KHALAF (2000), pp. 243–261.

78. Personal interviews with Frauke Heard-Bey, Abu Dhabi, January 2004.

79. ABU 'ATHIRA (1987).

80. HUDSON (1977), p. 203.

81. Indeed, Islam can be interpreted to justify and legitimize absolute rule (a shepherd, *ra'iyy,* was to look after his flock, *ra'aiyya*). HUDSON (1977), p. 91.

82. See "The Co-option and Patronage of Civil Society," p. 269 in this volume.

83. See ABERCROMBIE, HILL, and TURNER (1994), p. 10: "Within the natural law tradition, the justice of social laws and institutions was thought to depend on their conformity to certain universal laws of nature. All human beings, by virtue of their membership in humanity and as part of this natural order, enjoyed certain natu-

ral rights, such as a right to freedom. Natural law theory concerned itself with the moral content of laws and developed the criterion that true laws could not be unjust laws."

84. See FIELD (1987), p. 18: "There has been an extraordinary and totally unnecessary increase in the number of mosques. Two years ago, James Bill, Professor of Government at the University of Texas, conducted his own survey and discovered that the number of mosques has tripled in the previous decade. Saudi Arabia had at least 20,000, one for every 100 adult male citizens."

85. I estimate that there is 1 mosque for every 150 male UAE nationals.

86. Close to the Abu Dhabi Officers Club one can see Shaikh Zayed Mosque, which as of early 2004 is nearing completion. It is believed that this will be the third largest mosque in the world (after Mecca and Casablanca).

87. SHARJAH LAW (2001).

88. Personal interviews, undisclosed locations, 2003. Inevitably these attempts were thwarted following strong complaints from Dubai.

89. The Saudi link would seem to have its roots in the 1989 Sharjah banking scandal, when the emirate's government defaulted on loans in excess of $500 million, bringing four commercial banks close to collapse. Saudi Arabia intervened with a rescue package. See "The UAE's Banking Sector and the Central Bank," p. 212 in this volume; and OXFORD BUSINESS GROUP (2000), pp. 71–72.

90. Personal interviews, Sharjah, March and April 2002.

91. See GAUSE (2000). Also see GAUSE (1994), pp. 31–39.

92. .See ABDULLA (1985), p. 285: "This was principally an Islamic organisation which pretended to be apolitical. Its major publications were religious in nature and only occasionally dealt with social issues. They did not represent any imminent danger to the political system though the association functions as an amorphous Islamic party."

93. The ECONOMIST (1981), p. 47.

94. Personal interviews, undisclosed locations, April 2002.

95. According to my personal research, al-Shehhi was a Ra's al-Khaimah citizen who then studied at the UAE University in Al-'Ayn. Following his graduation he received a generous overseas studies scholarship, which he used to travel to the United States. Personal interviews, undisclosed locations, 2003. Also, for a partially accurate report, see JOHNSTON (2001), p. 23: "How were the terrorists funded? There is no record of direct transactions of money from Bin Laden to any of the hijackers. However, American officials have traced 500,000 dollars used to pay for flight training, airplane tickets, car rentals and other logistics back to the United Arab Emirates. Atta received 100,000 dollars in his bank account from money-changers in Sharjah, one of the emirates. Marawan Al-Shehhi, believed to have piloted the second plane to the World Trade Centre, also received money through Sharjah. Jarrah is said to have met Iraqi intelligence officers in the UAE."

96. The arrest took place in October 2002, but details were withheld, including the arrest's location, which was reported to have been an "undisclosed Gulf state."

97. McGRORY (2002): "One of Al-Qaeda's most wanted terrorists has been arrested in the United Arab Emirates as he was about to launch a wave of bomb attacks on vital oil installations. Abdel Rahim Al-Nashri, a Saudi national, is seen as one of Al-Qaeda's top ten agents. He is said to be its head of operations in the Gulf. US authorities have been questioning him since his arrest in the Gulf at the end of October, though it is now suggested he was plotting suicide attacks including using oil tankers as weapons. A UAE official said yesterday that Al-Nashri was seized as 'he prepared to blow up economic installations inside the country.' The official said

'he planned operations aimed at the highest number of casualties among nationals and foreigners, but shifted to alternative plans when that failed.' He is alleged to have played a major role in the attack on the USS Cole in Yemen in October 2000 in which 17 US personnel died."

98. For a discussion of ideology and secular nationalism in conservative regimes, see APTER (1965), p. 266; and HUDSON (1977), pp. 21–22.

99. ABDULLAH (1978), p. 112.

100. AL-SAYEGH (1998), p. 98. Ironically these Arab merchants included members of the al-Futtaim and the al-Ghuhair families, who are now pressing for widespread reform and increased foreign investment. See ABU BAKER (1995), p. 139.

101. ABDULLAH (1978), p. 74.

102. See ABDULLA (1985), p. 96. Also see AL-NABEH (1984), pp. 121–123. Al-Nabeh contends that this group had close ties with the Dhufar Liberation Front in Oman.

103. ABDULLAH (1978), p. 144.

104. ANTHONY (2002), p. 25.

105. Ibid., pp. 83–84. Shaikh Saqr was exiled to Cairo at this time. See VAN DER MEULEN (1997), p. 209.

106. PECK (1986), p. 80.

107. ABDULLAH (1978), p. 144.

108. Also see ANDERSON (2000), p. 61. Anderson argues that nationalism can be limited due to the primacy of kinship and the nourishment and strengthening of existing kinship patterns and loyalties, as "this denies the notion of equality that under girds the nationalist conception of citizenship."

109. Examples of failing republican unions include the Wahda of Egypt and Syria (1958–1961); the Hashemite Arab Federal Union of Iraq and Jordan (1958); the Union of Arab States of Egypt and Yemen (1962); the Confederation of Arab Republics of Egypt, Libya, Syria, and the Sudan (1969–1972); and the Arab Maghreb Union of Algeria, Libya, Morocco, and Tunisia (1987). See ANTHONY (2002), pp. 18–19. Also see YAPP (1996), p. 43.

110. With reference to the Gulf monarchies, see HALLIDAY (2000), p. 290.

111. See WAM (2001b); WAM (2002); ECSSR (2002); HELLYER (2001), pp. 169–170 for a discussion on UAE aid for Iraq, pp. 172–173 on UAE aid for Palestine, and p. 177 on UAE aid for Kosovo; PECK (1986), p. 381; ABDULLAH (1978), p. 143; and HEARD-BEY (1982), p. 381 for a discussion of Abu Dhabi economic aid for developing Arab states.

112. ABDULLAH (1978), p. 112.

113. Recent examples include the 2002 rallies staged in Sharjah and Dubai, the latter of which was attended by Shaikh Muhammad al-Maktum, Dubai's crown prince.

114. OXFORD BUSINESS GROUP (2000), p. 23.

115. HALL (1987), regarding the boycott of Israel.

116. See "The Relationship Between Federal and Emirate-Level Structures," p. 199 in this volume.

117. HUDSON (1977), p. 4.

118. UAE government spokesman speaking in Abu Dhabi, March 2002, quoting part of Shaikh Zayed's 1966 accession speech.

119. See, for example, HUDSON (1977), p. 202.

120. FINDLOW (2000), pp. 16–17, 21–23.

121. Article 6 of the constitution states that one of the UAE's major purposes will be to "co-operate with its sister Arab states," that the UAE will become "part of the

great Arab Nation, to which it is bound by ties of religion, language and common destiny," and that Emirati citizens will be "one people, and one part of the great Arab Nation." See AL-MUSFIR (1985), pp. 108–109.

122. AL-MUSFIR (1985), p. 108. Also see FINDLOW (2000), pp. 21–23.

123. See PECK (1986), p. 381; ABDULLAH (1978), p. 143; and HEARD-BEY (1982), p. 381 for a discussion of Abu Dhabi economic aid.

124. FINDLOW (2000), pp. 29–30.

125. Interestingly, Findlow's responses from Al-'Ayn university students of Dubai and Ra's al-Khaimah origins were similarly emirate-specific (with only 15 percent claiming "UAE/Emirati" identity), again reflecting the relative economic power and proud histories of these emirates. See FINDLOW (2000), pp. 29–30. For a greater discussion of Dubai's commercial history, see "Substrategies: Abu Dhabi and Dubai—A Comparative Analysis," p. 154 in this volume; and for a discussion of Sharjah's perceived educational and cultural superiority, see "The Co-option and Patronage of Civil Society," p. 269 in this volume, with reference to educational, cultural, and environmental civil society organizations in the UAE.

126. For an explanation, see ABERCROMBIE, HILL, and TURNER (1994), p. 10: "Legal-rational authority is the characteristic form of authority in modern society. Within bureaucracy, a command is held to be legitimate and authoritative if it has been issued from the correct office, under the appropriate regulations and according to appropriate procedures. The authority of officials depends, not on tradition or charisma, but on a consensus as to the validity of rules of procedure which are perceived as rational, fair and impartial." Also see HUDSON (1977), p. 199.

127. A hakim being a regime with no constitution. See ABDULLA (1985), p. 139, with reference to Shaikh Rashid al-Maktum's hakim regime in Dubai prior to 1971.

128. HUDSON (1977), p. 199. Also see HUNTINGTON (1968), p. 12.

129. HALPERN (1963, 1965), p. 353.

130. Tilly argues that the origins of a strong state must lie in its fiscal ability and tax-gathering structures; for a good discussion of Tilly's views, see CRYSTAL (1990, 1995), p. 194. Similarly, Chaudhry argues that extractive structures are a crucial sign of state strength; see CHAUDHRY (1997).

131. See "The Federation of Emirates," p. 45 in this volume.

132. Personal interviews, Abu Dhabi, April 2001, December 2001, March 2002, and September 2002.

133. HUDSON (1977), p. 200.

134. A UAE government spokesman speaking in Abu Dhabi, March 2002, described there being "nine national government ministries, one state bank and one social security authority in the UAE, in addition to a plethora of emirate-specific government departments, e.g. Dubai's Department for Tourism and Commerce Marketing. Parallel to, and, on occasion, interlocking with, the federal institutions, each of the seven emirates also has its own local government. Although all have expanded significantly as a result of the country's growth over the last 27 years, these differ in size and complexity from emirate to emirate, depending on a variety of factors such as population, area, and degree of development" (personal interview with author).

135. See "Other Institutions, Parastatals, and Bureaucracies," p. 208 in this volume.

136. BUSINESS IN DUBAI (2001a), pp. 14–15, excerpt taken from a speech given in Switzerland in early 2001 by Shaikh Muhammad al-Maktum.

137. AL-QASIMI (1999), p. 2. This is an extract from the speech made by the UAE's minister of economy and commerce to a conference convened by the Middle East Policy Council on 20 April 1999.

138. See KAMRAVA (2000), p. 6, for a discussion of bureaucracies in developing states.

139. Ibid., pp. 4 5.

140. SALDAMANDO (2001b).

141. Personal interviews, Abu Dhabi, March 2001; Dubai, December 2001; and Sharjah, September 2001 and December 2001.

142. For further discussion of the UAE's constitution, see BATIKH (1997). Also see SHARAH (1995).

143. For a detailed analysis of government co-option and control over various civil society, religious, and press associations, see "The Co-option and Patronage of Civil Society," p. 269 in this volume.

144. HALPERN (1963, 1965), pp. 356–357.

145. BEBLAWI (1987), p. 51.

146. See "Greater Peripheralization and the Emergence of Rentier Structures," p. 34 in this volume.

147. GAUSE (1994), chap. 3, "Oil and Politics." Gause argues that the fourfold increase in oil prices between 1973 and 1974 made oil revenue the overwhelming controlling factor in the economies of the Gulf states. See Gause's tables 2a–2f for a statistical analysis of how oil came to dominate these economies.

148. Calculations based on a $29 barrel of oil. See STAUFFER (1987), pp. 29–30.

149. As Heard-Bey explains, Qatar is perhaps the best example of such rentier development, with Abu Dhabi closely following Qatar's development patterns due to its long history of Qatari immigration, and Dubai closely following due to its strong Qatari marriage links and shared currency up until 1971. Personal interviews with Heard-Bey, Abu Dhabi, January 2004. Also see ANTHONY (2002), p. 63; and CHATELUS (1987), pp. 121–123.

150. To give an idea of the relatively small numbers of workers involved in the UAE's oil industry, of the present-day work force of around 1,853,000 only 26,000, or 1.4 percent, are actively employed in the oil sector. Calculated from figures supplied by UAE MINISTRY OF PLANNING (2002c), p. 30.

151. CRYSTAL (1990, 1995), pp. 6–7. Moreover, as Crystal noted in her study of oil and politics, almost all other single-commodity-exporting states require at least some accommodation between the rulers and the economic elites who control the work force.

152. BEBLAWI (1987), p. 50.

153. See "The Traditional Political Structure," p. 14 in this volume.

154. BEBLAWI (1987), p. 52. For a more detailed explanation, see LUCIANI (1987), pp. 63–82.

155. PECK (1986), p. 93.

156. With regard to UAE nationals in Dubai, 10.4 percent of their per capita wealth is derived from government transfers. See DUBAI MUNICIPALITY (1999), p. 151.

157. BEBLAWI (1987), p. 50.

158. According to recent income surveys, only 0.4 percent of non-UAE national Arab income is derived from government transfers, with 0 percent of European and Asian income derived from such transfers. See DUBAI MUNICIPALITY (1999), p. 151.

159. It was estimated in 1997, for example, that the 300,000 Pakistani workers in the UAE (primarily in Abu Dhabi) were able to send home an average of $3,000 per year each, for a total remittance of about $1 billion. See VAN DER MEULEN (1997), pp. 71–72.

160. Personal interviews, Dubai, September 2002.

161. See "Greater Peripheralization and the Emergence of Rentier Structures," p. 34 in this volume.

162. CRYSTAL (1990, 1995), pp. 10–11, with reference to merchants in Kuwait and Qatar.

163. For a discussion of the massive extent of the oil resources of the UAE and the other GCC states, see AL-KAWARI and AL-SADUN (1996), p. 32.

164. For a discussion of this "fusion" that has evolved between the business classes and the political elites as a result of the pattern of capital accumulation, see AL-NAQIB (1991), pp. 204–207.

165. CRYSTAL (1990, 1995), p. 1.

166. Ibid., p. 196.

167. The UAE commands 9.8 percent of the world's proven crude oil reserves. In 1997 the UAE's petroleum exports amounted to nearly 800 million barrels, making it the world's sixth largest exporter. Iran's exports were around 944 million barrels and Russia's were around 910 million barrels. See U.S. ENERGY INFORMATION ADMINISTRATION (1997).

168. Qatar produces around 170 million barrels per year, making it only the world's eighteenth largest oil exporter, and Bahrain's oil industry has now all but closed down, with the emirate now ranked seventy-forth in global oil exports. See U.S. ENERGY INFORMATION ADMINISTRATION (1997).

169. With exports of over 400 million barrels per year, Kuwait is ranked just outside of the world's top ten oil exporters. See U.S. ENERGY INFORMATION ADMINISTRATION (1997).

170. See CRYSTAL (1990, 1995).

171. Personal interviews, Abu Dhabi, March 2001, with reference to the rentier compensation of former merchant elites.

172. See "Local Resistance and the Suppression of the Dubai Reform Movement," p. 37 in this volume.

173. See "The Relationship Between Federal and Emirate-Level Structures," p. 199 in this volume, with reference to the constitutional crisis.

174. Gause, Halliday, and Weitzman all contend that in addition to oil wealth and rentier networks, an explanation of the survival of these monarchies would be incomplete without also taking into account the external military and political support that many of these states have enjoyed. See GAUSE (2000); HALLIDAY (2000); and WEITZMAN (2000).

175. See "The Federation of Emirates," p. 45 in this volume.

176. See JOYCE (1998), pp. 93–114.

177. PECK (1986), p. 120.

178. Following the withdrawal of coalition troops from Kuwait and Iraq in early 1992, Iran calculated that the time was right to occupy all of Abu Musa. Furthermore, in 1999 Iran chose to build a town hall on the island and stepped up its military activities in the area. See OXFORD BUSINESS GROUP (2000), pp. 19, 26. From 2004 onward, there are even rumors that Iran plans to build a new state university on the island.

179. See "The Federation of Emirates," p. 45 in this volume.

180. Personal interviews with regard to Western military support, Abu Dhabi, April 2001 and April 2002 (at IDEX); and Dubai, December 2001 and September 2002.

181. The original managers of ADNOC were handpicked from Algeria and seconded to Abu Dhabi. See ABU BAKER (1995), p. 149.

182. This information is an updated combination of data gathered from ABDUL-LA (1985), pp. 107–114; AL-OTAIBI (1982), pp. 15–151; and OXFORD BUSINESS GROUP (2000), p. 48; in addition to personal interviews in Abu Dhabi in 2003.

183. See ABDULLA (1985), pp. 134–135; and AL-OTAIBI (1982), vol. 2, pp. 188–204.

184. See ABDULLA (1985), pp. 107–114; AL-OTAIBI (1982); and OXFORD BUSINESS GROUP (2000), p. 48. In addition, information was gathered from personal interviews with the author, Abu Dhabi, 2003.

185. For example, the longtime minister of petroleum and mineral resources, Manna Saʻid al-Otaibi, stated that during the period of colonial rule the agreements were drafted and prepared by the oil companies and that the rulers of the area were compelled to sign them under the pressure of British warships. See ABU BAKER (1995), pp. 147–148; and AL-OTAIBI (1977), pp. 39–40.

186. Personal interviews, Abu Dhabi, 2003.

187. ABDULLA (1985), p. 208.

188. Personal interviews with regard to Western military support, Abu Dhabi, April 2001 and April 2002 (at IDEX); and Dubai, December 2001 and September 2002.

189. See FOLEY (1998).

190. France's agreement followed Giat's $3 billion sale of nearly 400 "tropicalized" Leclerc main battle tanks to the UAE. See OXFORD BUSINESS GROUP (2000), pp. 58–59.

191. Personal interviews with regard to Western military support, Abu Dhabi, April 2001 and April 2002 (at IDEX); and Dubai, December 2001 and September 2002.

192. OXFORD BUSINESS GROUP (2000), pp. 57, 59. The Dubai Air Show is now the fourth largest in the world, after those in Farnborough, Paris, and Singapore.

193. Quoting Shaikh Muhammad al-Maktum, Dubai's crown prince and the UAE's minister of defense, speaking at the 2003 IDEX conference in Abu Dhabi. EMIRATES TELEVISION (2003).

194. WEITZMAN (2000), p. 41.

195. KEDOURIE (1984), p. 278.

196. See GAUSE (1992).

197. The 1991 Damascus Declaration effectively combined Gulf Arab financial resources with Egyptian and Syrian Arab manpower. See OXFORD BUSINESS GROUP (2000), p. 27.

198. Personal interviews with regard to Western military support, Abu Dhabi, April 2001 and April 2002 (at IDEX); and Dubai, December 2001 and September 2002.

199. For a further discussion of oil and favorable superpower relations, see AL-KHALEEJ ARAB STUDIES (1991), p. 3; and AL-HAMID (1997).

200. See KEEGAN (2002).

201. BUSINESS MONITOR INTERNATIONAL (2003b), p. 9. These groups were to boycott U.S. goods to show solidarity with the Palestinians and the innocent Iraqis.

202. Personal correspondence, Sharjah, March 2003 (with regard to the use of Dhafrah); personal interviews and my own eyewitness observations, Abu Dhabi, 2004 (with regard to billeting in the Abu Dhabi Hilton hotel).

203. Personal interviews, Dubai Chamber of Commerce and Industry, December

2001; and Abu Dhabi, April 2002. Both Dubai and Sharjah are now believed to have almost run out of oil.

204. CRYSTAL (1990, 1995), pp. 10–11.

205. Indeed, as Abu Baker has argued, distributive policies in the UAE have become as hard to reverse as universal suffrage in advanced capitalist countries. See ABU BAKER (1995), p. 174. For a similar discussion with reference to Kuwait, see KHALAF (1992), pp. 53–84.

206. CRYSTAL (1990, 1995), p. 2.

207. HERB (1999), p. 3. Herb claims in his comparative study of ruling families in the Middle East that the dominance of one large and cohesive family over the state is the key to survival, rather than oil wealth, education, military support, external political support, representative institutions, selective marriages, charismatic rulers, or any other factor.

208. See "The Traditional Political Structure," p. 14 in this volume.

209. HERB (1999), pp. 136–137. In 1948 the nephew of the ruler of Sharjah used his position as a wali to gain immense local popularity and power by supporting those who wanted a reduction in the pearling tax imposed by the ruler. By successfully defying the ruler he managed to build sufficient support to enable him to take over as ruler of nearby Ra's al-Khaimah.

210. ABU BAKER (1995), pp. 73–78.

211. Personal interviews, Al-'Ayn, February 2004. The most accurate al-Nuhayyan family tree is displayed in the National Museum in Al-'Ayn. Also see ANTHONY (2002), p. 106. Following the death of Zayed bin Khalifa in 1909, Khalifa declined to succeed and instead the second eldest son, Tahnun, assumed the mantle of leadership. Although Tahnun ruled with the bay'a of his family, his reign was troubled by ill health and he died of natural causes in 1912. This left the far less popular third son, Hamdan, in a vulnerable position, and in 1922 he was murdered by his two younger brothers, Sultan and Saqr. In due course Sultan became the new ruler, but in 1926 he was murdered by Saqr, and Sultan's sons (including Shakhbut and the contemporary Shaikh Zayed) were chased away. Crucially, however, this was the moment that the surviving Khalifa chose to reenter al-Nuhayyan politics. Disgusted by the behavior of his younger siblings, he sought to skip a generation by supporting the deceased Sultan's exiled sons. Therefore, uncle and nephews together conspired against Saqr and arranged for his assassination by a Baluchi slave eunuch (see VAN DER MEULEN [1997], p. 108), leaving the path clear for Shakhbut bin Sultan to succeed in 1928 (see ABU BAKER [1995], pp. 73–78). Thus, although Khalifa himself never became ruler of Abu Dhabi, his invaluable assistance to the Bani Sultan has never been forgotten, and even today his progeny continue to be recognized and rewarded for their loyalty.

212. VAN DER MEULEN (1997), pp. 124–125. Also see PETERSON (1988b), pp. 204–205.

213. PECK (1986), pp. 126–127. It is also important to appreciate an alternative argument that at this early stage not all of the shaikhs were interested in powerful positions. As Heard-Bey contends, many of Zayed's cousins preferred to continue hunting and spending their time as they wished, and as such may have been acting out of a sense of duty more than anything else by assuming these new posts. Personal interviews with Heard-Bey, Abu Dhabi, January 2004.

214. ANTHONY (1999). Also see VAN DER MEULEN (1997), p. 114. In particular, Shaikh Hamdan bin Mubarak al-Nuhayyan is the chairman of Gulf Air and the chairman of the Abu Dhabi civil aviation department.

215. HERB (1999), pp. 141–144. Shaikh Juma' was the younger brother of the

former ruler, Shaikh Sa'id; see VAN DER MEULEN (1997), pp. 184.

216. Personal interviews, Dubai, March 2001, with reference to the new job opportunities for prominent Al-Maktum members at the beginning of the oil era.

217. VAN DER MEULEN (1997), pp. 185–186, 189.

218. The current ruler being Shaikh Hamad bin Muhammad al-Sharqi, his brother being Shaikh Salih bin Muhammad al-Sharqi, and the deputy ruler being Shaikh Hamad bin Sayf al-Sharqi. See VAN DER MEULEN (1997), pp. 250–253.

219. In 1972 the aforementioned Shaikh Khalid al-Qasimi was assassinated in an attempted coup by the previously ousted Shaikh Saqr. This time Saqr was imprisoned by federal authorities. Also see PECK (1986), p. 128.

220. VAN DER MEULEN (1997), pp. 212–215; the first cousin in question being the relatively unambitious Shaikh 'Ahmad. With regard to appointing a crown prince it would seem that while Shaikh Sultan would favor his eldest son, Shaikh Muhammad, this is not a possibility given that his mother is from Dubai and that the powerful and dynamic Shaikh Faysal bin Khalid currently commands far greater respect from within the Sharjah community (and also, it would seem, from the al-Nuhayyan family given his previous high-profile appointments in the federal government).

221. BROWN (1998), p. 359.

222. HERB (1999), p. 184; see tab. 7.1, "Libya, the Gulf Monarchies, and Saudi Arabia Compared." Also see VAN DER MEULEN (1997), p. 60. Van Der Meulen argues that "from the standpoint of the rentier effect, Libya (with just over two million nationals) probably has more in common with the UAE and Kuwait than those two states have with their four GCC partners."

223. HERB (1999), p. 239.

224. Ibid., p. 9.

225. Ibid., p. 237.

226. Ibid., pp. 237–238.

227. Ibid., pp. 36–37.

228. ECONOMIST INTELLIGENCE UNIT (2000), p. 5.

229. It is also likely that the "passed over" Shaikh Hamdan may soon inherit Shaikh Maktum's prestigious position as federal prime minister, as the latter has expressed his disinterest in federal government affairs. See VAN DER MEULEN (1997), p. 187.

230. ECONOMIST INTELLIGENCE UNIT (2000), p. 7.

231. Ibid.

232. In particular, Shaikh Muhammad al-Nuhayyan, like Shaikh Muhammad al-Maktum, is Sandhurst educated. See ANTHONY (1999).

233. Personal interviews, Abu Dhabi, April 2001 and April 2002; and Al-Maktum Institute of Dundee, July 2002. Also see FOLEY (1998); and "Elite Interest Groups: Old Rentiers Versus New Rentiers," p. 225 in this volume.

234. ECONOMIST INTELLIGENCE UNIT (2000), p. 5.

235. See BUSINESS MONITOR INTERNATIONAL (1998); MIDDLE EAST RESEARCH INSTITUTE OF JAPAN (2002), statistics relating to UAE cabinet compositions; and POLSCI.COM (2001). In addition, information was gathered from personal interviews with the author, Abu Dhabi, September 2002.

236. ECONOMIST INTELLIGENCE UNIT (2000), p. 9.

237. See ANTHONY (1999).

238. BUSINESS MONITOR INTERNATIONAL (1998).

239. Shaikh Abdullah had previously been the ministry's undersecretary. See VAN DER MEULEN (1997), p. 123.

240. GULF NEWS (2003).

241. As reported by *Al-Jazeera*, 1 December 2003.

242. Personal interviews, Abu Dhabi, September–December 2003. Also, as reported by the Economist Intelligence Unit, it is believed that prominent UAE notables (from both Abu Dhabi and Dubai) were invited to Geneva in September 1999 to discuss Shaikh Khalifa's accession to the UAE presidency. See OXFORD BUSINESS GROUP (2000), p. 18.

243. For a detailed, if somewhat outdated discussion of possible succession scenarios in Abu Dhabi, see ANTHONY (1999). In particular Anthony implies that if such an arrangement were not to take place peacefully, then Shaikh Muhammad al-Nuhayyan, as army chief of staff, would "be able to bring to bear such formidable and potentially decisive assets as control of the armed forces, police, intelligence, and information" (p. 39).

244. See IRVING (1972). "Groupthink" is a concept that was identified by Janis Irving and refers to faulty decisionmaking in a group. Groups experiencing groupthink do not consider all alternatives and they desire unanimity at the expense of quality decisions.

245. HERB (1999), p. 47.

246. ABU BAKER (1995), p. 129.

247. It is believed that by 1966 Shakhbut had already lost the confidence of his family by being overly cautious in the use of oil revenue. Indeed, despite the pressing need for infrastructure, housing, schools, and general relief of poverty, Shakhbut had refused to spend more than a small fraction of oil revenue on these things, instead preferring to hoard against some undefined contingency. See OXFORD BUSINESS GROUP (2000), p. 130.

248. JOYCE (1999), p. 56.

249. For example, Majid Khadduri, writing in the early 1980s, pays particular attention to Zayed's 1966 visit to London as a guest of the Ottoman Bank. He claims that during Zayed's audience with the Windsors, the British explicitly hinted that a change in Abu Dhabi's leadership was required. See KHADDURI (1981), p. 309. With the benefit of hindsight and the knowledge of the Windsor's relatively apolitical role, it seems unlikely that this series of events was not preceded by at least some al-Nuhayyan input.

250. HERB (1999), p. 137. Shaikh Shakhbut's eldest son, Sa'id, eventually married into both the Bani Khalifa and the Bani Zayed branches of the al-Nuhayyan family. See VAN DER MEULEN (1997), p. 129.

251. See FEDERAL RESEARCH DIVISION (2003). It would appear that Abu Dhabi chose to withdraw its support and remain neutral in face of the growing bandwagon. However, it is interesting to note that Shaikh Abdul-Aziz now resides in al-Nuhayyan-built palaces in Al-'Ayn and Morroco, and that Shaikh Zayed appointed him to be one of his special envoys. See VAN DER MEULEN (1997), p. 211.

252. Personal interviews, Sharjah, April 2002 and September 2002, with reference to the 1987 coup and the support for Shaikh Sultan from both the Sharjah family and Dubai's al-Maktum family. Also see BROWN (1998), p. 359.

253. In June 2003 Shaikh Saqr al-Qasimi, ruler of Ra's al-Khaimah, chose to switch his crown prince appointment from Shaikh Khalid to the much younger Shaikh Saud. According to personal interviews, this decision may have been based on the ruler's desire to promote greater foreign investment in Ra's al-Khaimah (specifically allowing a new concrete production plant to be build), a policy for which the business-savvy Saud was seen as being better suited. Given that Khalid had been crown prince for nearly twenty years and had enjoyed a high profile in the

struggle with Iran for control over the disputed Tunbs islands, instability was feared and Abu Dhabi sent tanks to protect the palaces of the ruler and the new crown prince. In the event, based on my own eyewitness observations, the protests were entirely peaceful, with a number of Khalid's supporters declaring, "We will give our blood and souls for you, Khalid." Also see REUTERS (2003).

254. See KAMRAVA (2002).

# 3

# Socioeconomic Development and the Diversification Effort

A longside the consolidation of the polity and the preservation of politi-cal stability, which are themselves key prerequisites for successful modernization, the United Arab Emirates has undergone significant socioe-conomic development over the past thirty years as its "modernizing mon-archs" have sought to consolidate the material components of their ruling bargain while also attempting to adapt to their situation by carefully remov-ing and reducing some of the most patent weaknesses of their dependent economies. As such, viewed within the context of selective modernization shaped by inherited and persisting dependent circumstances, this chapter considers the UAE's major development plans and objectives and, crucial-ly, not only determines their level of achievement, but also highlights some of the key problems that have yet to be overcome and that continue to face the Emirati planners.

## Modifying Dependent Development

Orthodox neoclassical economic theory predicted the emergence of an interdependent world economy within which each national economy would seek to maximize its comparative advantage. In turn, it was suggested that this interdependence would eventually lead toward the long-term equaliza-tion of incomes,[1] and for some time many of the developing world's rulers accepted the inevitability of this argument. By the 1920s, however, the pre-vailing model had become one of "economic nationalism," as adverse eco-nomic conditions prompted many developing states to intervene and assist in building up and protecting their domestic industries.[2] While certain aspects of both these models did find some purchase among the planners and coordinators of the UAE's development strategies, these early econom-

119

ic development theories were nevertheless seen as insufficient in addressing the key concerns of the small and oil-rich Gulf state. Instead, the UAE's
continuing reliance on the export of a single primary product export, its
reliance on foreign technology, its international division of labor, and its
asymmetrical relationship with the oil-purchasing economies were seen as
being the most pressing issues.

Indeed, while the oil industry and its various requirements had certainly allowed the region to prosper and to escape from immediate poverty, it
was nonetheless feared that any long-term dependency would eventually
lead to serious structural problems and underdevelopment. Certainly, as
Samir Amin warned, even by the late 1970s there were already several very
marked features of economic disintegration beginning to appear in the
"dependent Arab oil economies" as a result of persisting peripheral relations with the core economies and unchecked dependent structures:

• The economic structure of most Arab countries had become more
externally orientated than that of any other group of countries in the developing world. Taken as a whole, the Arab world had become one of the most
fully integrated and potentially dependent regions in the contemporary
global economic system.
• Despite the availability of vast capital, industrialization remained
comparatively weak and desultory, trailing behind other developing regions
such as Latin America.
• Domination by the multinationals was leading to a corresponding
technological dependency. The Arab world imported virtually all its industrial means of production and depended more and more for its agricultural
development on multinational "agribusiness." As such, the economy of the
Arab world had become a disabled one, characterized by disjointed industrial development, growing consumerism and widening inequality in
income distribution, growing distortion of development orientation, and the
increasing waste of human and natural resources.
• Oil wealth, which rose astronomically after 1973, served only to
aggravate distorted development and to strengthen economic, military, and
cultural dependency on the West. Thus the illusion of wealth created by oil
was having the same effect on the Arab world as American gold had on
Spain in the seventeenth century: it was delaying the fundamental changes
that are necessary for any genuine renaissance.[3]

As such, in addition to straightforward growth and expansion, the
reversal, or rather the reduction, of dependency-related features soon
became a main feature of socioeconomic development planning in the
UAE. Certainly, if the UAE needed proof of the precariousness of its economy then the oil price fluctuations and slumps of the 1980s soon provided

clear indications as Saudi Arabia and other neighboring oil exporters were forced to contemplate austerity measures,[4] thereby highlighting the unpredictable nature of the international oil market and the dangers of relying on a narrow economic base and the demands of other economies. Moreover, it was recognized that many other external factors could also adversely affect the UAE's oil economy, including changing global energy consumption patterns resulting from stronger international antipollution legislation[5] and new oil-producing regions in Central Asia and Latin America coming on-stream.[6] Of course, further compounding this vulnerability was the continuing insistence of the core economies on purchasing only crude oil, thereby preventing any refinement or value addition to the commodity in the UAE. Indeed, as former Egyptian oil minister Hussain Abdullah recently explained to the Dubai Cultural and Scientific Association: "The real benefits of oil as a support for the industry were being gained by the West who refused our repeated attempts to sell them refined oil and insist on buying it from us as a crude product. We were not making enough profit from oil as far as selling it for a good price as well as refining it and manufacturing its products is concerned."[7] Internally, it was feared that any long-term dependency on oil rents and distributed wealth would lead to the emergence of a consumerist society as the population's purchasing power accelerated independently of their productive capacity. Ultimately this would lead to excessive imports and a serious trade imbalance, while of course also reducing employment incentives and creating a potentially parasitic national work force dependent on the labor of foreigners.

Initially, a partial solution to reducing the UAE's dependency on oil was seen to involve savings and investment. Undoubtedly, overseas assets have long been considered an important safety valve for the region's future, and such savings continue to play a key role in Abu Dhabi's financial planning. By investing billions of petrodollars abroad it was hoped that the UAE would be able to survive a postoil future and maintain its oil boom standard of living by relying on considerable interest payments. Certainly, the UAE's foreign investments have steadily increased over the years, with the central bank revealing in 1994 that almost 97 percent of its assets were placed overseas,[8] and with it being thought that the UAE's total investments abroad may now be close to the $400 billion mark.[9] However, no matter how substantial the interest payments, it was also accepted that such investments would never be able to provide long-term solutions for reducing the actual structures of dependency and the resulting domestic socioeconomic problems. Indeed, as early as the mid-1970s the UAE's planners had already begun to favor a more multidimensional approach based on economic diversification with the hope that the non-oil-based sectors and the necessary physical infrastructure could all be developed using the UAE's massive oil revenues. As such, the planners began to regard oil not merely as an expendable resource, but as a "gift from God" with which to develop a diverse, multiple-sector economy for future generations.[10]

Table 3.1 presents an official economic profile of the UAE and its constituent Dubai emirate. It is widely acknowledged, however, that govern-

**Table 3.1   Official Economic Profile of the UAE, 2001/2002**

|  | UAE Total | Dubai Only |
| --- | --- | --- |
| Population | 3,290,000 | 910,300 |
| GDP ($) | 67,662,000,000 | 17,512,000,000 |
| GDP per capita ($) | 20,566 | 19,244 |
| GDP by sector ($ millions/%) |  |  |
| Oil and gas | 18,978 | 1,492 |
|  | 28 | 9 |
| Agriculture and fisheries | 2,643 | 141 |
|  | 4 | 8 |
| Mining and quarrying | 190 | 20 |
|  | 3 | 0 |
| Manufacturing | 9,382 | 2,820 |
|  | 14 | 16 |
| Electricity and water | 1,332 | 294 |
|  | 2 | 2 |
| Construction | 4,754 | 1,422 |
|  | 7 | 8 |
| Trade | 6,223 | 2,866 |
|  | 10 | 16 |
| Hotels and restaurants | 1,476 | 782 |
|  | 2 | 4 |
| Transport, storage, and communications | 4,895 | 2,328 |
|  | 7 | 13 |
| Finance and insurance | 4,606 | 1,919 |
|  | 7 | 11 |
| Real estate | 5,358 | 1,714 |
|  | 8 | 10 |
| Government services | 7,494 | 1,618 |
|  | 11 | 9 |
| Other services | 1,575 | 598 |
|  | 2 | 3 |
| Less: imputed bank services | −1,244 | −496 |
|  | −2 | −3 |
| Nonoil foreign trade ($ millions/%) |  |  |
| Total | 30,428 |  |
|  | 100 |  |
| Imports | 22,667 |  |
|  | 74 |  |
| Exports | 1,610 |  |
|  | 5 |  |
| Re-exports | 6,151 |  |
|  | 20 |  |

*Source:* Dubai Department of Economic Development (2002), *Development Statistics, Goverment of Dubai,* pp. 15–21, using a fixed dollar exchange rate of 3.67.

ment-produced statistics in the Gulf states rarely provide an accurate or up-to-date picture, given the sensitivities associated with oil dependency and the successes or failures of development plans. Indeed, the UAE is very much subject to this rule, with many published reports failing to properly distinguish between the oil- and non-oil-related sectors of the economy. As such, the majority of figures provided throughout the body of this chapter have been compiled, wherever possible, from a number of cross-checked independent sources.

## Diversification Through Industrialization

Industrialization has historically been one of the most favored tools for the governments of developing states attempting to achieve economic growth and self-sufficiency. The UAE has been no exception, as in the 1970s the planners identified industrial expansion, specifically that of the non-oil-related manufacturing sector, as being the best hope for successful diversification.[11] In particular, as the 1979 Federal Industrial Law states, there were four main objectives associated with such development:

> 1. For the government to prepare a productive base capable of allowing manufacturing industries to thrive and thereby reduce the reliance on oil.
> 2. To give the manufacturing sector priority at all times with the aim of creating a sector capable of generating significant production linkages.
> 3. To encourage industrialisation as a way of providing foreign exchange.
> 4. To use the UAE's comparative advantage of low-cost energy to best effect by helping to make the UAE's industries regionally and internationally competitive.[12]

Moreover, with regard to the context of these aims, during this early period of Emirati development planning two different industrialization substrategies were prevalent elsewhere in the developing world: export-oriented industrialization (EOI) and import-substitution industrialization (ISI).

On the one hand, an EOI strategy based around large-scale industries was regarded as a means of quickly achieving industrialization and limited diversification. Although the plants would continue to rely on foreign technology, their growth would nevertheless serve to raise GDP, would provide a base for further domestic industrialization, and would make the best use of the UAE's comparatively low energy costs. It was reasoned that if the UAE could develop internationally competitive industries and thereby penetrate other regional markets, then the reliance on oil exports and the dependence on external economies could be reduced.[13] Indeed, as Mehran

Kamrava has shown, a number of developing states have embarked upon this strategy, some having met with considerable success in supplying other emerging markets with competitively priced and reliable goods.[14] On the other hand, while the alternative ISI approach was also to rely upon the importation of foreign technology, this was only to be a temporary stopgap measure until the UAE could substitute imported technology with its own domestic technology. Thus, foreign technology was to be used to build up a domestic industrial infrastructure that would eventually be able to use local technology to produce goods that would have otherwise been costly to import.[15] By the early 1970s there were already indications that both approaches were being employed in the UAE, with Kevin Fenelon having remarked on the clear-cut division between three different categories of manufacturing industries: the first being those of the EOI group, the second being the traditional manufacturing activities, and the third clearly being those of the ISI group:

> One [group] consists of large-scale, highly capitalised industries employ-
> ing the most modern technology, export-oriented and based on oil or natu-
> ral gas. The other group is composed of small, traditional and labour-
> intensive handicrafts working for a local market. In between there is a
> small though growing intermediate group, based like the first group on
> imported technology and machinery, but less highly capitalised and of
> more moderate size. For the most part, these industries serve local mar-
> kets and are engaged in servicing, repair, and maintenance, or manufac-
> ture such articles as soft drinks or cement blocks, which if imported
> would involve high transport costs in relation to their value.[16]

Furthermore, as Fatima al-Shamsi demonstrates in her study of industrialization in the Gulf, there are now clear signs that each of these strategies continued to be implemented in the UAE well into the 1980s and
1990s.[17] With reference to EOI in the UAE, a particularly strong example
would be the combination of natural gas, cheap energy, and large-scale
plants, especially in the resource-rich Abu Dhabi. Before the 1970s, the
UAE's considerable reserves of natural gas were underutilized, with the
only gas produced being a side product of oil drilling, over 90 percent of
which was simply flared off. However, one of the earliest EOI strategies
was to reverse this trend and to begin harnessing this potentially valuable
resource. Early success came with the establishment of three major gas
plants, one on Abu Dhabi's Das island, a second in Al-Ruways, and a third
in Dubai, each of which producing nearly 4 million metric tons per annum
by the mid-1970s.[18] Other key examples of early EOI plants include those
surrounding the Umm al-Nar refinery: deliberately built near downtown
Abu Dhabi (this was unnecessary, as the plants used corrosive material and
could have been built in a more remote area), it is believed that these plants

were also intended to be a visible symbol of industrialization, reminding the local population of their country's rapid development.[19] More recently, and as part of the UAE's continuing commitment to upstream gas developments, proposals for the Dolphin gas project were signed in the late 1990s, establishing Qatar as a major cosupplier and committing Abu Dhabi to the large-scale transportation and marketing of Qatari and Emirati natural gas to Dubai, Oman, and eventually Pakistan.[20] Alongside the main national gas companies of ADGAS and Atheer, other heavy export-oriented industries such as DUBAL (Dubai Aluminium) have also met with considerable success. Indeed, as the Economist Intelligence Unit estimated in 2000, aluminum exports have risen to account for nearly 60 percent of Dubai's nonoil exports, thereby placing DUBAL at the very heart of the emirate's industrial sector.[21] Crucially, in addition to aluminum, many other nonhydrocarbon-based heavy industries, including the UAE's various steel and plastics companies,[22] have also grown in number and in capacity over the years, and in several cases have become regionally and internationally competitive. Moreover, as Soheir el-Saba of the Dubai Chamber of Commerce and Industry explains, the future may be even more promising for EOI as the rising use of solar energy in Saudi Arabia and Kuwait extends to the UAE, thereby allowing for the development of new industries powered by a renewable energy source that, significantly for the diversification process, is entirely independent of the oil industry.[23]

Although, perhaps unsurprisingly, ISI-led growth has been less impressive given its concentration in smaller industries less able to benefit from the comparative advantages of the UAE's low-cost energy, there have nevertheless been appreciable results and important signs of technology substitution and diversification. Indeed, during the 1970s a number of uncomplicated small and medium-scale manufacturing firms were successfully established, each supplying a number of locally produced goods to the domestic market.[24] Most notable, construction goods such as piping and cement could be sold at competitive prices given the high cost of importing such bulky freight into the UAE.[25] The resulting reduction in such imports was reflected during this period, even during the massive construction boom, with the UAE's percentage of foreign trade to GDP gradually falling from 113 percent to 106 percent[26] and, in the case of Dubai, with the cost of imports being held in check at around 20 billion dirhams (at fixed prices) until the late 1980s.[27] Although the importation of such goods has risen in more recent years and continues to pose a serious structural problem for the Emirati economy, this does not necessarily indicate the failure of ISI. Indeed, there continues to be a significant rise in the number of new ISI projects, especially in the packaging and bottling industries, many of which initially licensed foreign technology but have now made successful substitutions.[28] As such, the perceived slowdown in ISI in the 1990s may have simply been due to the unsustainable growth of the early "easy stage": ISI was originally applied to relatively straightforward industries requiring only minor technology injections and minimal planning, but recent attempts to apply ISI to more technologically advanced industries may take more time and greater investment.

Overall, by applying a combination of these strategies, the UAE's nonoil manufacturing sector has grown steadily over the years from a practically negligible starting point in 1971, and now accounts for around 19 percent of the nonoil GDP, and more significantly for around 14 percent of the UAE's total GDP,[29] therefore indicating the increasingly important contribution of nonoil industries to the diversification effort. Moreover, although the sector's rate of growth may have slowed in recent years,[30] Al-Sharhan consultants do present a slightly more positive picture. Using data from the last few years and calculating projections for 2002 and 2003, they demonstrate that, by streamlining and improving efficiency, domestic industries are now rapidly increasing the value added to their manufactured goods. Indeed, arguing that the sector's growth in manufacturing value added is equally as important as the manufacturing sector's growth in contribution to the UAE's total GDP, they illustrate how, over the course of just five years, the sector's value added will more than double (see Figure 3.1).

With value added or "net output" being the difference between the total revenue of a firm and the cost of bought-in raw materials, services, and components, these figures would indicate that Emirati firms (in Dubai at

**Figure 3.1 Dubai's Manufacturing Sector:
Value Added to Domestic Manufactures, 2000 prices**

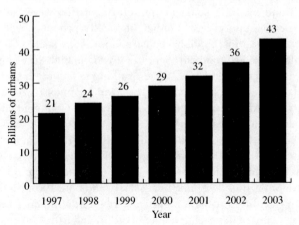

*Source:* Al-Sharhan International Consultancy (2001), "UAE Country Report 2001," Dubai, pp. 14–15.

*Note:* Figures for 2002 and 2003 are estimates.

least) are beginning to add more and more value to their bought-in materials and components by improving their processes of production.[31] If this trend is able to continue, the manufacturing sector's contribution to GDP will begin to grow more rapidly, thus renewing the sector's crucial diversification role.

### Fostering Technology Linkages with Foreign Firms

Further related to industrialization and diversification, the UAE's planners have attempted to generate meaningful technology linkages between infant Emirati firms and the many foreign firms that operate in the UAE. In particular, there has been a clear attempt to prevent the emergence of foreign enclaves and a "dual economy"—an asymmetrical economy in which little or no technology transfer takes place between foreign and local firms.[32] Certainly, by the late 1970s it was becoming increasingly clear that the oil sector, given its distinct role and its high degree of specialization, would never generate such linkages on its own, and that any "natural filter" of technology was unlikely to occur without more active government assistance.[33] As such, a number of high-tech foreign industries were targeted with schemes aiming to encourage, and in some cases enforce, the transfer of their technology and expertise to the UAE's diversifying domestic industries.

Indeed, by 1984 the UAE's Federation of Chambers of Commerce and Industry was already proposing that profitable foreign companies should be compelled to reinvest a significant portion of their revenue back into local enterprises. Furthermore, there were also calls for taxation and other restrictions to be imposed on these companies, as will be discussed in the following chapter. Although such measures were not implemented, their proposal nevertheless indicated the growing realization of the potential role that foreign companies could be made to play in the UAE's diversification process.[34] Although direct government intervention did not begin until the early 1990s, it nonetheless represented a very important step given that it took the form of a comprehensive arrangement requiring certain foreign firms, especially those having signed defense contracts with the UAE, to invest and assist in a number of commercial ventures with local partners. Administered by the newly formed "UAE Offsets Group" (chaired by the aforementioned Shaikh Muhammad al-Nuhayyan, Abu Dhabi's deputy crown prince), these domestic recipients of foreign technology transfers were seen to be offsetting the enclaves being created by the high-tech foreign arms manufacturers, many of which only required limited local manpower and most of which were thought unlikely to provide any genuine linkages with the domestic economy under normal circumstances. As such, the UAE's Offsets project can be seen as a clear attempt to take advantage of the world arms market and to promote vested interests in the UAE's stability and security,[35] while simultaneously escaping the "guns versus butter" quandary that has plagued many other developing economies.[36]

Specifically, the group's rules stipulate that such local "offsetting" ventures should yield accumulated profits of 60 percent of the arms procurement value over a period of seven years. In other words, by entering into profitable and sustainable joint ventures with members of the local private sector, the supplier would have to bring back to the UAE economy some sort of value addition worth 60 percent of the original contract. Furthermore, all projects have to be completed within seven years, and if the obligations are not met by the target dates, then the foreign company is penalized 8.5 percent of the unfulfilled portion of the obligation.[37] Although there have been some instances of offsets failure and ineffective technology linkages, most notably concerning Giat's missed targets,[38] there have nevertheless been a large number of highly successful collaborative operations, including:

- A language school with Boeing and McDonnell Douglas.
- A shipbuilding company with Newport News Shipping.
- An Abu Dhabi to Dubai seaplane shuttle service with Aerospatiale Matra.[39]
- An enzyme manufacturer in partnership with McDonnell Douglas.
- A healthcare center with Lockheed Martin.
- A solar energy panel manufacturer with GEC-Marconi.
- A fish-farming company with Dassault.
- Assistance with the aforementioned Dolphin gas project.[40]

Indeed, to date, the Offsets group has coordinated over thirty such projects, which, combined, are now valued at over $1 billion,[41] thus representing an important contribution to the UAE's productive base and, given their mandatory autonomy from the oil sector,[42] also representing an important contribution to the diversification of the UAE's manufacturing sector.

## Diversification Through Agriculture

Another major component of the UAE's diversification strategy has been the development of the agricultural sector. Although never likely to provide the same levels of growth and contributions to nonoil GDP as manufacturing and other sectors of the economy, the agricultural sector's improvement was nevertheless seen as necessary for reducing the UAE's dependency on imported foodstuffs and thereby achieving greater food security. In addition, the sector's development was also seen as a means of expanding the domestic market and complementing the growth of other local non-oil-related industries, especially the many dairy and poultry ISI industries, which rely heavily on agricultural products.[43] Third, the sustained growth of the agricultural sector, which employs a higher percentage of UAE nationals than any other sector (85 percent of all farm workers and 75 percent of all fishermen),[44] has assumed great socioeconomic significance in a country that has become increasingly overwhelmed by expatriate workers.[45]

In 1976 the directive documents of the UAE's Ministry of Planning emphasized the need to increase agriculture's contribution to the GDP, either by improving the productivity of the land itself (vertical expansion) or by increasing the total cultivatable area (horizontal expansion).[46] With regard to the former, there has been substantial government investment in the form of considerable subsidies, which have been used to slow the migration of farmers to the cities and to provide for superior equipment, irrigation, and water wells. Moreover, in practice, the subsidies have often extended far beyond these initial objectives and, as interviewees revealed, in the rural areas of Abu Dhabi and Dubai it is now possible for new farmers to walk into almost ready-made farms complete with housing, fencing, roads, and of course all the necessary farming equipment.[47] Also, there has been considerable investment in the development of new crop strains, with a number of agricultural trial stations now producing hardier crops better suited to the harsh desert conditions.[48] With regard to increasing the cultivatable area, the primary strategy has been to concentrate on afforestation. When asked by curious university students why the government was spending so much on planting trees in the desert, Shaikh Zayed famously claimed it was "so people could see what they looked like." The principal aim, however, has been to plant sufficient trees in order to reduce soil erosion and to help crops be better protected from the wind and sand. It has also been theorized that afforestation can stimulate increased rainfall, which would in turn lead to greater vegetation in previously desert regions.[49]

The first of these strategies, productivity gains, has led to a massive increase in agricultural output in recent years. Indeed, using Dubai as an example, vegetable production more than tripled from less than 2,000 metric tons in 1990 to over 6,000 metric tons in 1999.[50] Similarly successful has been the emirate's fruit production, which rose from just over 1,000 metric tons in 1990 to nearly 17,000 metric tons in 2000.[51] Most impressive, however, has been Dubai's dairy production, which rose from just 300 metric tons in 1981 to nearly 32,000 metric tons in 2000, representing a hundredfold increase in less than twenty years.[52] Equally promising, though undoubtedly far from cost-effective given the region's unforgiving climate, have been the results of the land cultivation strategy. Certainly, with figures made available by the Ministry of Agriculture, it can be demonstrated that there has been a substantial increase, 82 percent, of arable land since the mid-1980s (see Figure 3.2).

Further related to the growth of the agricultural sector has been the modest increase in Emirati fishing. Fishing has always been one of the region's main economic activities,[53] and although cautious of overfishing and unable to benefit from increasing land under cultivation, the industry has nevertheless benefited from productivity gains and government subsidies in recent years. Indeed, over the past decade the catches for Dubai and the other northern emirates have risen from 12,500 metric tons to 21,300 metric tons, thus representing a 70 percent increase in their annual fish production.[54]

Although the sector's growth is unlikely to lead to complete self-sufficiency given the many challenges of the desert and due to its reliance on subsidies from the allocative state,[55] these overall improvements have nevertheless considerably boosted the UAE's food security and, of course, have also directly and indirectly contributed to the diversification effort, especially by consolidating the UAE's many food-related ISI industries. Indeed, speaking at a recent Gulf food security conference, Sa'id al-Raqabani, the UAE's minister of agriculture and fisheries, underscored this considerable progress by claiming that the UAE had now managed to reach 83 percent sufficiency in vegetables, 80 percent in dairy products, 32 percent in eggs, 25 percent in meat, and 21 percent in poultry.[56] Furthermore, it is also worth noting that, with the exception of Saudi Arabia, the UAE

**Figure 3.2 Dubai Total Agricultural Area**

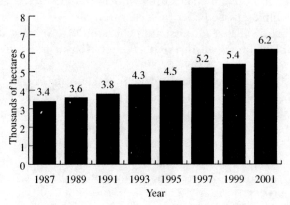

*Source:* UAE Ministry of Agriculture and Fisheries, "Dubai: Agricultural Holdings," in Dubai Department of Economic Development (2002), *Development Statistics,* Government of Dubai, p. 73.

now possesses a higher per capita agricultural product than any of the other states of the Gulf Cooperation Council (GCC) and, in addition to the impressive increases in production and arable land, the number of workers employed in the sector has more than tripled since the first development plans of the 1970s.[57]

## Diversification Through Commerce and Tourism

Alongside the industrialization of the domestic manufacturing sector and the development of the agricultural sector, in the mid-1970s the UAE's planners believed that the expansion of the commercial and tourist sectors would also play an important role in the growth of the UAE's diversified economy. Indeed, although on one level such activities may actually increase the UAE's dependence on external economies, the sectors were seen as a direct and effective means of building up non-oil-related activities that would not necessarily be reliant on foreign technology or foreign labor. Furthermore, as Ali Abdulsalam, a former director of the UAE Department of Planning explains, it was hoped that the development of these sectors would also contribute to the promotion of many of the region's traditional industries and various cultural and social activities, and more crucially would assist in developing the UAE's internal trading sector.[58]

By the early 1980s, with chambers of commerce in each emirate, an umbrella federation of chambers of commerce, and (in the case of Dubai) a World Trade Center, the UAE began to position and promote itself as a world-class commercial hub.[59] Moreover, in 1989 the government of Dubai underscored its commitment to the expansion of these sectors by establishing a Department of Tourism and Commerce Marketing, the first of its kind in the UAE. Essentially, the department sought to implement and support many of the original diversification plans within a more coordinated and effective framework through two objectives:

> 1. Contributing to economic diversification by promoting non-oil development; and creating new opportunities for the Dubai business community by attracting trade, investment and tourism.
> 2. Supervising tourist and archaeological sites, to lay down and implement plans and programmes that aim at encouraging tourism in the Emirate, to implement comprehensive media campaigns, to study projects related to tourism, to stage seminars and exhibitions inside and outside the Emirate, to regulate the services of tourist guides and others in the tourist sector, to license hotels and furnished apartments, to supervise restaurants, and to develop commercial relations between the Emirate and other countries.[60]

As these ambitious objectives indicate, the department was keen to transform the emirate of Dubai into the Gulf's leading trade zone and premier tourist destination. Some considerable successes have been achieved over a short period of time, and there is increasing evidence that similar strategies are beginning to be employed in the other emirates. Perhaps the greatest accomplishment so far has been the Dubai Shopping Festival (DSF), which was set up in 1996 with the aim of consolidating Dubai's status as an international shopping center, attracting much higher numbers of tourists, and boosting expenditure in all sectors and on all types of goods and services.[61] The DSF runs for approximately one month every year and claims to offer massive discounts in all participating stores and hotels.[62] Although, in practice, prices actually rise during the festival, the event's popularity and reputation nevertheless continue to increase.[63] More recently, the DSF's success has been complemented by the Dubai Summer Surprises festival, held during the out-of-season summer months, and the "Dubai, the city that cares" festival, held during the holy month of Ramadan.[64] Over the past few years, a number of other commercial events and festivals have also begun to be staged by the other emirates and their new tourism and commerce departments, most notably Sharjah's Ramadan festival and 'Ajman's Fantasia festival. In much the same way as the Dubai events, these have also appreciably boosted the local economies, with an increasing number of shoppers and tourists now being attracted to the smaller emirates.[65]

Regarding the actual growth of the UAE's commercial sector, perhaps the clearest indicator of expansion has been the sheer increase in the value and volume of international non-oil-related trade, especially in Dubai. Quite remarkably, the emirate's total nonoil foreign trade rose from a modest 8 billion dirhams in 1975 to nearly 112 billion dirhams in 2001 (measured at fixed 1995 prices), representing over 15 million metric tons of traded goods[66] (see Figure 3.3).

However, in addition to this fifteenfold rise in the total value of nonoil foreign trade and a 140 percent rise in the total volume of foreign trade since 1980,[67] the emirate's substantial increase in re-exporting activity over the past twenty-five years must also be taken into consideration. Certainly, given the UAE's historically high levels of imports, a problem that will be discussed later in this chapter,[68] the value and quantity of re-exports together with their relative contribution to total trade may provide an even more accurate indicator of the recent commercial expansion (see Figures 3.4 and 3.5).

Thus, with a massive increase in the value of re-exported goods between 1975 and 2001 (and with the volume of re-exported goods more than doubling between 1980 and 2001 from 0.9 million to 2.5 million metric tons)[69] and, as the above trend line indicates, with re-exports accounting for a much higher proportion of total trade, it is evident that the emirate is indeed generating considerable non-oil-related commercial activity.

**Figure 3.3 Value of Dubai's Nonoil Foreign Trade, 1995 prices**

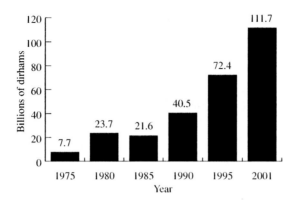

*Source:* Dubai Department of Ports and Customs, "Dubai: Non-Oil Foreign Trade—Total," in Dubai Department of Economic Development (2002), *Development Statistics,* Government of Dubai, p. 109.

**Figure 3.4 Value of Dubai's Re-exports, 1995 prices**

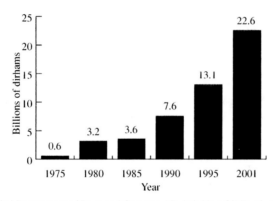

*Source:* Dubai Department of Ports and Customs, "Dubai: Non-Oil Foreign Trade—Total," in Dubai Department of Economic Development (2002), *Development Statistics,* Government of Dubai, p. 109.

Moreover, when compared to the value of foreign trade and re-exports for the other GCC states,[70] these figures clearly confirm Dubai's position as one of the main trading hubs of the Persian Gulf and the greater Middle East.

With reference to the actual growth of the UAE's tourist sector, the figures are similarly impressive, especially with the dramatic increase in the number of hotels, resorts, and other tourist-related establishments, and of course with the rising number of tourists and businesspeople now choos-

**Figure 3.5 Dubai's Re-exports:**
**Percentage of the Value of Total Trade, 1995 prices**

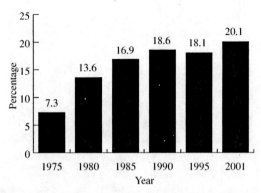

*Source:* Dubai Department of Ports and Customs, "Dubai: Non-Oil Foreign Trade—Total," in Dubai Department of Economic Development (2002), *Development Statistics,* Government of Dubai, p. 109.

ing to visit the UAE. Once again, Dubai has been at the forefront of such development, with its rapidly constructed tourist industry boasting nearly 300 hotels and now attracting nearly 3 millions visitors per annum,[71] compared with just 40 hotels and 0.4 million visitors in 1985[72] (see Figures 3.6 and 3.7).

Furthermore, given the major hotel developments that have taken place since 2000, including the Dubai Fairmont, the Dusit Dubai, and the Grand Hyatt, and given the only temporary decline in UAE tourism following the September 2001 terrorist attacks in the United States, these positive trends seem set to continue. It is also important to break down this sector and to show how the most rapid growth has occurred in the luxury tourist market, thus underscoring Dubai's objective of transforming itself into an important winter sun resort for affluent European holidaymakers, thereby boosting the emirate's supply of foreign exchange and further consolidating diversification.[73] Indeed, of the 265 hotels operating in 2000, 78 were either "deluxe" or "first-class" rated,[74] with many of the most prestigious Asian and international chains having chosen Dubai as the location for their flagship hotels.[75] Also, given that these deluxe hotels are far larger than most of the other hotels, they actually provide the bulk of tourist accommodation in the emirate. In fact, these 78 hotels account for nearly 20,000 of the total 31,000 hotel beds in Dubai and, more importantly, have enjoyed much higher occupancy rates than the other hotels, averaging nearly 70 percent, compared with less than 36 percent for some of the lower-class hotels.[76] These occupancy

**Figure 3.6 Number of Hotels in Dubai**

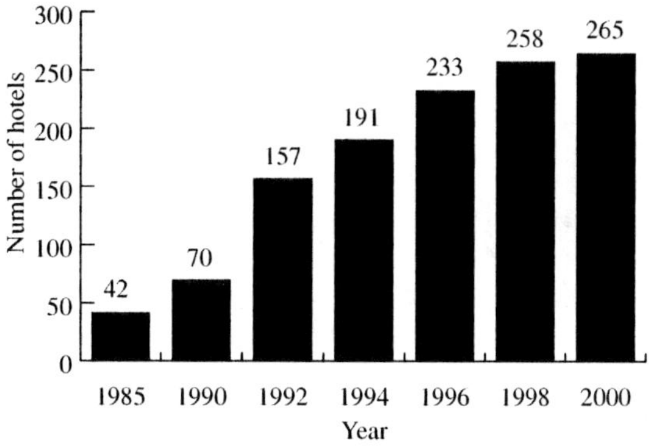

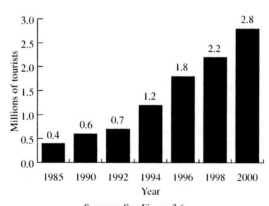

*Sources:* Dubai Department of Economic Development (2001), *Development Statistics,* Government of Dubai, pp. 167, 172; figures for 1985–1994 supplied by UAE Ministry of Planning; figures for 1995–1998 supplied by Dubai Department of Economic Development; and figures for 1999 onward supplied by Dubai Department of Tourism and Commerce Marketing.

**Figure 3.7 Number of Tourists in Dubai**

*Sources:* See Figure 3.6.

rates have therefore translated into a high and growing number of luxury tourists staying in Dubai: 1.8 of the 2.5 million visitors in 1999,[77] representing nearly 72 percent of the sector total and almost double the size of the emirate's resident population.

In much the same way as the commercial sector, the other emirates have also been able to follow Dubai's lead by developing their own international tourist industries. Indeed, Abu Dhabi now attracts around 18 percent of the UAE's tourists and hosts branches of most leading chains, including a Rotana, a Hilton, a Sheraton, and an Intercontinental. Furthermore, Abu Dhabi deserves a special mention for its upcoming Conference Palace Hotel, situated close to the Marina Mall breakwater. Due to open in 2005 in time for the annual GCC summit, the hotel is being constructed on an enormous scale, employing thousands of laborers and a team of hundreds of professionals. As one of the world's largest and most impressive buildings (combining a variety of Middle Eastern and Asian architectural styles), the final product will rival the aesthetics of the Taj Mahal and will easily eclipse Dubai's showpiece Burj al-Arab as the UAE's premier landmark. To a lesser extent, Sharjah also hosts many major international hotels, including a Rotana and a Holiday Inn, and quite remarkably manages to attract nearly 13 percent of the UAE's tourists,[78] despite the aforementioned decency laws and the emirate's ban on alcohol and sheesha smoking.[79] Furthermore, the UAE's many natural beauty spots in the mountains, its rock pools, and its relatively untouched Indian Ocean coastline are now also being developed, with the aim of providing additional destinations for those tourists hoping to travel a little farther afield. Examples of such projects include the recent recreation of a traditional village in the mountainous town of Hatta, the new Grand Hotel complex on the slopes of Jebel Hafit,[80] the launch of a luxury Le Méridien resort close to Dibba al-Fujairah,[81] the construction of new hotels on the coastal strip between Rol Dibba and Al-Faqit, and the construction of an aqua leisure park in the tiny emirate of Umm al-Qawain.[82] Significantly, where natural beauty does not exist, artificial beaches and breakwaters are also being created, and in the case of 'Ajman an entirely new corniche and seafront is currently being constructed with federal funds.[83]

Finally, in addition to their previously described role in the Emirati polity's legitimacy formula, the increasing number of cultural and sporting activities can also be seen as assisting and consolidating the growth of these important sectors. Certainly, the many museums, local art galleries, reconstructed forts, and "heritage villages" provide educational and charming distractions for the numerous tourists, most notably the pearling village, the Bedu village, and the Shaikh Sa'id art gallery, all of which line the creek side in Shindigha and provide Dubai's tourists with a pleasant open-air network of live entertainment, sights, and sounds. The emirate is also becoming a major tour stop-off point for many of the world's most popular acts, and in recent years has hosted the likes of Elton John, Bryan Adams, Enrique Iglesias, and Mariah Carey. Moreover, the growing number of sporting events, many of which have achieved world-circuit status, have undoubtedly boosted the UAE's commercial and tourist sectors by attracting wide audiences and greatly enhancing the UAE's international reputation. Key examples include the European golf tour's Dubai Desert Classic, the UAE's annual ATP and WTA tennis tournaments, Sharjah's international cricket tournaments, and most significantly the Dubai World Cup—the world's most lucrative horse race. In the near future these may be joined by the Dubai Grand Prix: a part-street, part-circuit race that will slot into the FIA's Formula One calendar either immediately before or after the existing Bahrain Grand Prix.

## The Physical Infrastructure for Diversification

Without a new infrastructure, the UAE's plans for industrialization and the development of the agricultural, commercial, and tourist sectors would have remained unattainable. While the UAE's evolving legal and financial infrastructures will be discussed in greater detail in the next chapter,[84] it is essential to underline here how the massive investments needed to create and maintain the physical infrastructure must be regarded as another key building block of the diversification strategy. Certainly, as Al-Sharhan consultants have described:

> [The UAE government] has continuously given high priority to the development of the country's infrastructure and has invested over 25% of its GDP annually in recent years to build the present modern system of seaports, roads and telecommunication services. This in turn has paid back handsomely enabling the once oil dependent state to now actively promote its non-oil sectors and draw in income from a myriad of sources thereby enabling the country to further reduce its dependence on oil reserves.[85]

Of course, it must be remembered that most of these impressive infrastructural improvements took place over just a few decades, with the Trucial states having previously been one of the most backward and undeveloped regions of the Middle East. Indeed, even as late as 1965, Fenelon observed on his visit that "there was not a single yard of surfaced public road in the whole of Abu Dhabi; the only bit of made road was a short stretch within the compound of the Political Agency between the Agent's house and his office. The airport runway was a strip of levelled sand, the office a tiny shed, and the customs and immigration offices a Land-Rover."[86] By the early 1970s, however, the situation had already begun to improve. Although Abu Dhabi and Dubai were still separated by over 100 miles of desert,[87] there were nevertheless many miles of brand new first-class roads, dual carriageways, and even a four-lane highway connecting Abu Dhabi and Al-'Ayn. As such, journeys between the outlying emirates, which had previously taken nearly a week, had been reduced to just two hours, and lorries were able to transport goods all over the region within a day. Moreover, in the space of just a few years, the airstrips were also changed beyond recognition as construction of new international airports capable of handling the largest aircraft began in Dubai and Abu Dhabi.[88] Ten years later, in the mid-1980s, the infrastructural developments were even more manifest, especially in the cities, with Malcolm Peck describing the enormous transformation he had observed in the centers of Abu Dhabi, Dubai, and Sharjah:

> The virtual absence of any physical structure more than ten years or fif-
> teen years old in Abu Dhabi reflects the extraordinary pace of change;
> only a few old buildings survive in Dubai and Sharjah. Glass, steel and
> concrete towers give the UAE's cities the appearance of transplanted
> Houstons rising above the flat sands of the Gulf. Almost overnight the
> greater part of the population has been displaced from traditional rural
> (and/or maritime) modes of existence to a setting of artificially sustained
> vegetation, broad boulevards, luxury hotels, and replicated Wimpys,
> Seven-Elevens, and Burger Kings, where only a scattering of barasti huts
> might have been found a generation ago.[89]

This fast-paced development was sustained throughout the 1990s and in many cases has continued unabated to the present day. Notable among the many achievements has been the completion of the Shaikh Zayed Highway, linking Abu Dhabi with Dubai: with twenty-four-hour lighting along its entire 210-kilometer stretch it is one of the longest roads in the Middle East.[90] Similarly impressive has been the continuing expansion of Dubai's international airport. Now hosting an award-winning passenger airline, the airport has grown under the auspices of Dnata[91] and the Dubai Cargo Village to become one of the world's major cargo-handling hubs, with over forty loading quays and with sufficient apron space to handle four jumbo jets simultaneously.[92] Moreover, with new terminals under construction and a modern underground rail network to link air passengers to the city center and the emirate's commercial and industrial districts, the airport looks set for further development in the near future.[93] With regard to seaports, there have also been considerable accomplishments in recent years, with the total tonnage handled by Port Rashid and Jebel Ali (the world's largest artificial harbor) having risen by over 75 percent in just five years, and with more than 100 shipping lines now calling at the UAE.[94] These important maritime infrastructural developments have consolidated and facilitated the growth of Dubai as a major trade transit hub, while also allowing the UAE to compete with other regional container ports in Aden and Salalah, both of which are situated much nearer to international lanes.[95]

With specific regard to the physical infrastructure required by the UAE's industrialization, there has been similarly rapid progress. Most notable have been the fully equipped export-processing zones (EPZs) that now exist in most of the emirates. In much the same way as the "ready-made" government farms in the rural areas, the aim of these EPZs has been to create an environment conducive to the development and rapid growth of manufacturing industries in the UAE. Lease office buildings (LOBs),[96] cheap energy, road links, and transport depots are all in place in an effort to provide new firms instantly with their entire required infrastructure. These zones have experienced massive growth over a relatively short period. Perhaps the best example of the EPZs has been the Jebel Ali Free Zone (JAFZ) southwest of Dubai. Although the original 1975 decision to create Jebel Ali envisaged the zone as being simply Dubai's second port,[97] in 1985 the Dubai Department of Industry began to operate the Jebel Ali Free Zone Authority with the objective of supplying all the necessary administration, engineering, and utility services required by its clients.[98] The zone expanded from a modest 298 companies in 1990 to over 2,000 by 2001, is now home to nearly 37,000 workers, and has attracted about $4 billion in investments.[99] For high-tech and media companies, other more specialist zones also now exist, including Dubai Internet City and Dubai Media City. Having opened in late 2000, their aims were to provide Internet and media-free zones with the entire necessary communications infrastructure in place for prospective computer-oriented firms.[100] A number of multinationals have been attracted by the high standards and impressive facilities, and the list of tenants now includes Microsoft, Compaq, IBM, and Hewlett-Packard.

## Social Growth

Also necessary for the successful diversification of the economy and of course an essential component of the described rentier package of distributed wealth and the political "ruling bargain," the UAE has made social growth another of its major priorities. In particular, education has been regarded as a key socioeconomic building block, one that will allow the country's youth to contribute in a better way to the national economy,[101] and one that will create a work force more capable of reducing the UAE's chronic dependency on expatriate labor than the present generation. Similarly, improved healthcare and a comprehensive welfare system have been seen as the necessary foundations for the creation of a healthy and happy society in which every individual can vigorously contribute to the UAE's future development.

Many of these aims were formally recognized in the early 1970s with the oil-financed actualization of social welfare and the provision of acquired rights being among the basic objectives of the UAE's first development plans: "These [social development objectives] were to be attained through a continuous improvement in the standard of living. . . . This was to be carried out on an equitable basis and in a manner which would emphasise and preserve the welfare benefits for the generations to come."[102] In the 1990s, after more than twenty years of sustained social development, the objectives remained much the same and, complemented by various other initiatives including the increased provision of facilities for women and expatriates,[103] continue to form part of an ongoing strategy to maintain and improve social growth for the UAE's expanding population. Indeed, in 1995 Sa'id Ghubash, the minister of economy and commerce, reaffirmed the government's commitment to these plans and reemphasized the importance of such development for the future of the UAE:

> The government of the UAE strongly believes in human development as a process of expanding and augmenting its people's choices. The most critical in the long list of these choices are to have a comfortable command of goods and services, to live a long and healthy life, to be educated, to feel safe and secure, and to have access to resources needed for an adequate standard of living. The choices people make are their own concern. However, the process of development must create a conducive environment that allows them to generate their full potentials.[104]

Given the relative simplicity of these goals and their clearly positive relationship with oil wealth and economic growth, most areas of social development enjoyed considerable success from a very early stage. Indeed, the provision and rapid implementation of educational and welfare services were already considered by the planners to have been "one of most remarkable achievements of the UAE during the period 1975 to 1980."[105] The continuing successes throughout the 1980s and 1990s were also regarded highly, and more recently, with a positive report in 2000 from the United Nations Development Programme (UNDP) on the UAE's first national human development statistics, the trend seems set to continue:

> The UAE has recently released its first national human development report. . . . It is the outcome of the nationally executed programme of "Sustainable Human Development Profile and Strategy for the UAE" begun in 1994. It shows how the UAE has risen from a global rank of 77 to 42 in just 8 years, and praises Shaykh Zayed's often cited vision that "true development is not measured by cement and steel buildings, but by developing the human being."[106]

Certainly, with specific regard to education, the number of primary and secondary schools, teachers, and students have multiplied, providing the UAE with one of the most developed systems in the Middle East, and one comparable to those of many Western states. Again, perhaps the most significant feature has been the speed of this progress, especially when one considers the region's rather modest background and its relatively recent urbanization. Among the most remarkable results have been the rise in the literacy rate of the UAE's youth, which is now estimated at 90 percent,[107] the gradual rise of primary and secondary school enrollment ratios, which now stand at 87 percent and 67 percent respectively,[108] and the doubling of Emirati secondary school graduates from 1991 to 2001 (see Figure 3.8).

In addition to this massive increase in the number of graduates, another important indication of improvement in the UAE's schooling system has been the steady decline in the student/teacher ratio. As the number of enrolled pupils has risen, the UAE has more than matched its population's needs, and the number of teachers has risen at an even higher rate, allowing the UAE's schools to provide an extremely conducive environment for both teaching and learning. Moreover, with ratios of around fifteen-to-one in primary schools, and just ten-to-one in secondary schools, the UAE's state sector ratios have been consistently lower than private sector ratios for much of the 1980s and 1990s.[109]

Similarly in the UAE's tertiary sector, there has been rapid expansion, with the number of universities and students increasing almost every year (with the enrollment ratio having risen from practically zero in 1971 to around 12 percent in 1999).[110] Sharjah provides a particularly strong example of recent development with its "University City," which now houses two large universities, a technical college, and various other training academies. Other, more recent examples include the expansion of the dual-campus Zayed University, the opening of the new Abu Dhabi University, and

**Figure 3.8 UAE Secondary School Graduates**

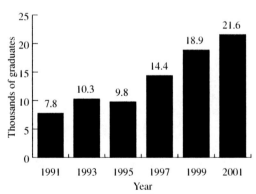

*Source:* UAE Ministry of Education and Youth, "UAE and Dubai: Secondary School Graduates," in Dubai Department of Economic Development (2002), *Development Statistics,* Government of Dubai, p. 209.

*Note:* Figures are for graduates of all types of secondary schools.

the forthcoming launch of the British University of Dubai. However, the success of the UAE's first university, situated in Al-'Ayn, probably provides the best measure of the UAE's tertiary education boom, given that it was established in 1978 and continues to enjoy consistently high growth (see Figure 3.9).

Evidently, the total number of students enrolled per annum has climbed from around 500 to over 16,000, representing a thirtyfold increase in just twenty-two years. Thus, as a result, the number of university graduates has now risen to nearly 3,000 per annum. Moreover, the UAE University in Al-'Ayn is an excellent example not only because of its considerable growth, but also because it provides a clear indication of the increasing importance attached to the educational development of UAE women (see Figure 3.10).

Clearly, female students have outnumbered males in every year group from 1983 onward, and now account for over three-quarters of all graduates and currently enrolled students. Given that the university specializes in the humanities and social sciences, these statistics would probably not be replicated in more technical and science-based colleges, which one may expect to be traditionally more male-dominated. Also, given that there has been a greater tendency for Emirati males to study abroad, these figures are perhaps unsurprising, but the increasing number of female students and graduates does point to an appreciable increase in female education at the highest levels and the continuing expansion of an important literary and skilled

**Figure 3.9 Students Enrolled and Graduates of UAE Univeristy in Al-'Ayn**

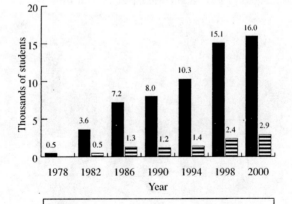

*Sources:* UAE University in Al-'Ayn, "UAE University Registered Students" and "UAE University Graduates," in Dubai Department of Economic Development (2001), *Development Statistics,* Government of Dubai, pp. 212–213.

**Figure 3.10 Graduates of UAE University in Al-'Ayn, by gender**

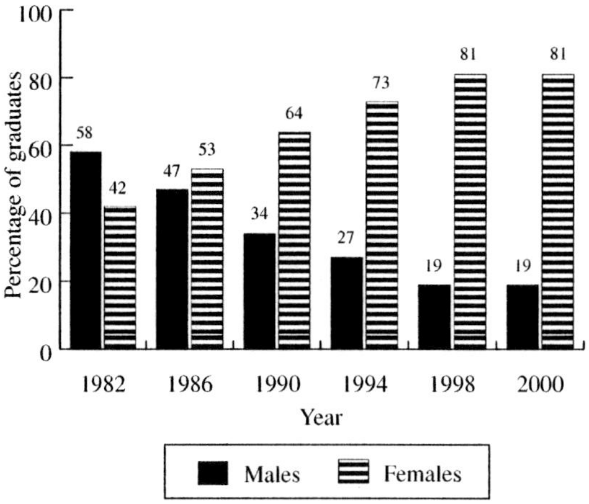

*Sources:* See Figure 3.9.
*Note:* Percentages calculated from listed totals by gender.

segment of the UAE's population.

With regard to healthcare, the UAE's attempts to create and maintain a welfare state have experienced similarly impressive results, especially given the region's rapidly increasing population.[111] Illustrating the scale of this challenge, in 1975 approximately 28,000 patients were admitted to health centers in the UAE, yet by 1995 this figure had reached nearly 100,000 per annum.[112] In most areas, this challenge has been met, and in many cases the level of care continues to improve. Almost all health-related problems can now be dealt with locally in first-rate hospitals, and the number of overseas consultations has fallen as the number of specialists resident in the UAE has risen. Indeed, focusing on Dubai, Figure 3.11 highlights some of the more tangible results in healthcare development.

Evidently, the provision of hospitals, health centers, and hospitals beds rose appreciably in just ten years, but even more impressive has been the considerable increase in healthcare professionals. Between 1990 and 2000, the number of medical doctors practicing in Dubai more than doubled, with the number of pharmacists, nurses, and other medical-related staff having risen by 66 percent.[113] As such, the population/doctor ratio continues to improve, having fallen from around 600-to-1 to just over 400-to-1,[114] thus placing the emirate close to the United States and ahead of the United Kingdom and many other European welfare states.[115] Furthermore, the number of hospital beds per thousand people has remained stable between two and three, despite the expanding population.[116] Finally, other important

**Figure 3.11 Healthcare Improvements in Dubai**

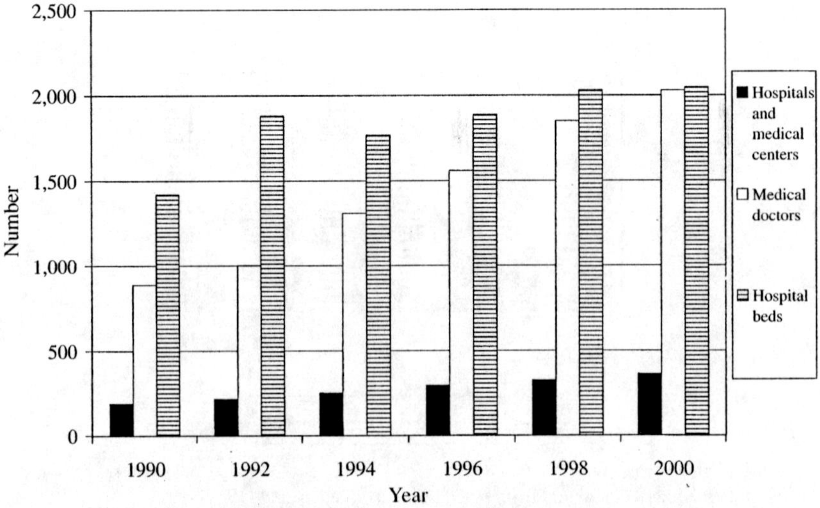

*Sources:* UAE Ministry of Health and Dubai Department of Medical Services, "Dubai: Health Centres," "Dubai: Hospitals," "Dubai: Hospital Beds," and "Dubai: Medical Doctors," in Dubai Department of Economic Development (2001), *Development Statistics,* Government of Dubai, pp. 181–182, 184.

*Note:* All figures include private healthcare.

indicators of these successful healthcare developments must include the UAE's average life expectancy at birth, which is now close to seventy-six years, and the falling infant mortality rate, which now stands at around 13 per 1,000, both placing the UAE comfortably within the world's top fifty healthcare systems.[117]

## Emiratization

As demonstrated in Chapter 1, expatriate labor has long been an important socioeconomic characteristic of the lower Gulf, with the pearling industry and its associated activities having always attracted large numbers of Indians, Iranians, and other nationalities to the main coastal towns.[118] However, by the early 1970s, the UAE's massive labor requirements for its oil-financed development projects soon led to far greater numbers of foreign workers, both skilled and unskilled, entering the work force and assuming semipermanent residence. Indeed, this influx continued more or less unabated until the 1990s, leaving the indigenous "locals" a minority in their own country and, as most would agree, rendering them totally reliant on the millions of foreigners who have built and continue to build the UAE. In much the same way as the need for diversification of the oil-dependent economy, the UAE's planners therefore recognized the need to reduce their population's persistent dependency on foreign labor and skills, not only to help achieve a more desirable level of labor self-sufficiency in both the private and public sectors, but also to control in a better way the many other socioeconomic problems that could result from the continuing presence of a large number of expatriate workers (both Arab and non-Arab). As such, not only has the need for greater "emiratization" of the work force been viewed within the context of labor nationalization, but it is also increasingly regarded as a necessary safeguard against the negative implications for the UAE's money supply growth resulting from salaries and other payments being transferred out of the country, as a check on the unhealthy gender imbalances arising from a predominantly male immigrant work force and as a curb on the perceived erosion of cultural and religious identities.

Illustrating the scale of this foreign presence, in 1968, three years before the creation of the UAE, a sizable but perhaps containable portion of the region's work force, 38 percent, was composed of expatriates.[119] By 2000, however, with a population of 3 to 4 million, recent surveys in the big cities have indicated that less than 17 percent of households comprise UAE nationals, and that over 70 percent of the municipal populations now comprise either Asian households or Asian labor collectives[120] (see Figure 3.12).

Indeed, it is now privately estimated that over 90 percent of workers may be expatriates, with the head of the Abu Dhabi planning department's statistics unit having recently admitted that UAE nationals now account for less than 7.5 percent of the private sector work force.[121] As Rawhi Abeidoh describes, this has of course been an enormous change over a relatively short period of time, a change that has led to increasing socioeconomic concerns for the UAE's future, even at the highest levels of Emirati politics:

> United Arab Emirates citizens are rapidly becoming a shrinking minority in their own country. UAE officials and businessmen say they are alarmed by what they see as a growing reliance on foreign workers who now form more than 90 per cent of the country's three million workforce. This is by far the highest percentage in the Gulf Arab states, their economies transformed by vast oil and gas riches. The UAE's rapid transformation from small tribal societies into a modern state with eight-lane highways and gleaming skyscrapers came at a heavy cost in a country where citizens have traditionally shied away from menial jobs. Foreigners now virtually dominate the private sector and form around 60 per cent of the public sector workforce, delegates said. According to the latest official census in 1997, the UAE population stood at 2.7 million, more than 75 per cent of it foreign. UAE officials privately say the figure was now around four million, 85 per cent of them for-

**Figure 3.12 Breakdown of Dubai Households, 1998**

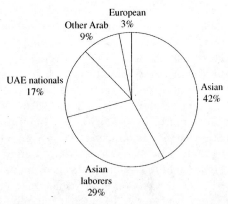

*Source:* Dubai Municipality (1999), "Results of Income and Expenditure Survey: Dubai City, 1997–1998," Administrative Affairs Department, Statistics Centre, p. 133.

eigners, mainly from India, Pakistan and other Asian countries. The expatriates-to-locals ratio is higher in the workforce as UAE immigration laws ban low-paid labourers from bringing in their families. In 1968, three years before the country's independence from Britain, UAE nationals represented 62 per cent of the workforce, said Matar Juma'a, head of the statistics unit at the Abu Dhabi government-planning department. "We are now less than 7.5 per cent," Juma'a added. The UAE does not issue a detailed breakdown of its population. "We are facing a grave issue that demands a swift solution. We are shackled and I want a solution now before I become a mere one per cent," said Muhammad Mazroui, secretary-general of the Federal National Council, the UAE's appointed parliament. Mazroui said a lack of laws setting limits on the country's need for foreign labour was also to blame for the situation. A study of the workforce in the private sector released last month found that construction and services employed the majority of the UAE's 1.4 million overseas workers, two-thirds of whom do not have a secondary education. Delegates said the flood of the foreign labour was wiping out the Arab character of the country where some areas now resemble parts of India or Pakistan.[122]

Until very recently, expatriates have dominated virtually all segments of the private sector and, as Abeidoh describes, even the public sector, 60 percent of which is now composed of foreigners. Perhaps most worrying of all, though, has been the increasing domination of expatriates in the middle and lower ranks of the government administration, areas one may have expected to remain the preserve of nationals, with official studies having estimated that more than four-fifths of Abu Dhabian and federal government employees may be foreigners, the majority of which may be non-Arab[123] (see Figure 3.13).

Thus, with non-Emirati Arabs accounting for 35 percent, and with a staggering 47 percent being non-Arab foreigners,[124] the size of the expatriate work force also has serious implications for the functioning of the government itself. Not only reliant on foreigners for the continuing success of its economy, the UAE has also become dependent on foreigners for the functioning of its bureaucracies and much of the day-to-day public administration of the country.[125] Indeed, as John Duke Anthony argues: "The expatriate community of advisors and technicians, though without citizenship status and theoretically in a category akin to other aliens in the area, exerts more real political influence than most local citizens and in many ways is considered crucial to the relatively smooth functioning of the political process."[126]

Even in the 1970s the government had recognized the potential problem of such "shackling,"[127] with the Abu Dhabi Department of Planning recommending in 1977 that state-sponsored encouragement was needed for far greater nationalization, or "emiratization," of the work force.[128] Essentially, in economic terms, it was felt that a continuing reliance on foreign labor would lead to persistently high development costs, and that the growing expatriate population would also adversely affect the UAE's money supply.[129] Indeed, even today a considerable portion of the money supply growth fails to find its way back into the UAE's banking system, and this is primarily due to the estimated $3.3 billion being repatriated overseas annually by foreign workers sending remittances back to their countries of origin.[130] Furthermore, by the mid-1980s there was also a growing consensus that without such an emiratization drive, the UAE's employment structure would become even more distorted, with fewer

**Figure 3.13 Breakdown of Abu Dhabi
Government Employees by Nationality, 1995**

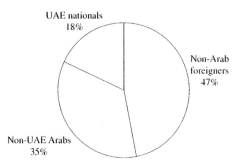

*Source:* Crown Prince Court, Department of Research and Studies (1996), "Development Indicators in the UAE: Achievements and Projections," Abu Dhabi, p. 95.

nationals capable or willing to undertake jobs normally associated with expatriate labor. Certainly, as Peck observed:

> As in the other wealthy oil states of the Arabian Peninsula, there is little evident connection in UAE society between wealth and work. As one analyst remarks, "the message is clear: without effort or self-denial one can simply accept a world made by others." As a result, there are incipient signs of the kind of social malaise already evident in Kuwait with its long history of very high per capita wealth and advanced welfarism. Some young men with large amounts of money and leisure at their disposal are tempted to spend them on such things as expensive cars and mistresses and to avoid meaningful employment.[131]

Greater emiratization has also been seen as an essential measure in lessening the growing gender imbalance in the UAE. Given that the vast majority of expatriate laborers are Pathan bachelors or married Keralite men unable to bring their spouses and families to the UAE (a minimum salary is required before a worker is eligible to invite family members to accompany him), this has inevitability led to a skewed demographic structure and a rather unpleasant atmosphere, with adult males vastly outnumbering adult females. Indeed, the results of the UAE's population censuses illustrate the scale of this imbalance over the years (see Figure 3.14).

As such, even though there were slight improvements in the 1990s, it is evident that of the 3 million or so registered in the census of 2000, more than two-thirds are male, thus making the UAE's population one of the most imbalanced in the world. Moreover, the proportion of males is probably even higher than this official figure given that many short-term contract workers are not included in census data. Also, given that the vast majority of the expatriates are based inside or close to the major cities, it is important to note that the gender imbalance will be much greater in these areas. Indeed, census statistics for the individual emirates show that the problem is most marked in the urban areas of Abu Dhabi, Sharjah, and especially Dubai, where the percentage of males has been consistently higher than the UAE average and now stands at around 71 percent.[132] Conversely, those emirates with less developed economies, smaller conurbations, and fewer labor-intensive activities, such as 'Ajman, Umm al-Qawain, and Ra's al-Khaimah, have much lower male-to-female ratios; but with males still accounting for around 59 percent of their populations,[133] gender imbalance is nevertheless still a nationwide problem. If more UAE nationals, both men and women, can be brought into the workplace and eventually be used to fill positions previously requiring expatriates, then it is hoped that this disparity and its negative social implications can be somewhat reduced.

With regard to the sociocultural impact of such a large population of foreign workers residing in the UAE, Sally Findlow, during her recent

**Figure 3.14 Breakdown of UAE Population, by gender**

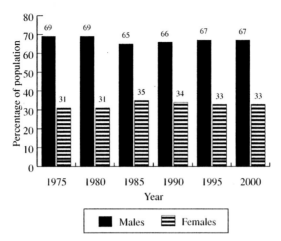

*Source:* UAE Ministry of Planning and Dubai Municipality, "UAE and Dubai: Population," in Dubai Department of Economic Development (2001), *Development Statistics,* Government of Dubai, p. 25.

investigation into emiratization, was informed that such factors were not important, and that the initiative was an entirely pragmatic policy designed to lessen the serious economic and demographic imbalances: "When pressed during my interviews, people either told me that culture was not an issue in this project, or they were non-committal. The impression was given that the action agenda is firmly a pragmatic one and that religious consider-ations and the nation's religious identity were not linked to this issue."[134] However, although not an official aim of the emiratization process, there is little doubt that it has also been seen as an increasingly necessary preventa-tive check on the perceived cultural and religious erosion resulting from the massive influx of expatriates. Indeed, while such erosion will be discussed in greater depth in Chapter 5,[135] it is important to emphasize here that many UAE nationals not only voice their misgivings over their minority status in the work force and their reliance on foreign labor, but also voice very deep concerns over their increasing cultural marginalization in a country domi-nated by non-Arabs and, in many areas, non-Muslims.[136] Moreover, given the crucial role of identity in the traditional polity, there is little doubt that emiratization is also considered a multidimensional strategy by the ruling elite, many of whom are keen to foster and preserve a distinct, loyal, and culturally rich Emirati Arab patrimonial class.

Finally, although of less direct interest to the UAE government and the planners, it is perhaps also worth considering that the emiratization strategy and indeed "Saudification" and the various other labor nationalization initiatives in the Gulf states are being increasingly viewed by both indigenous and Asian scholars as necessary measures for correcting what have developed into serious two-way population problems. It has been argued that massive labor migrations on the scale such as that between the Gulf and the subcontinent have caused marked gender imbalances and other socioeconomic problems for the supplier as well as the host countries. Indeed, as Peck noted in the mid-1980s, severe strains were already beginning to emerge in these South Asian supplier countries, with the cause often dubbed the "Dubai syndrome":

> Social strains are generated not only in the host societies by the presence of foreign workers, but in the latter's societies as well. Although many of the Asian labourers live in physically and psychologically difficult situations in the UAE and in its neighbour states, their wives left at home fall victim to frustration and attendant disorders dubbed "Dubai syndrome" (as coined by a Pakistani psychiatrist). The prolonged absences of heads of families cause a breakdown of social controls in some Asian settings, and the remittances that are sent back often create resentments and divisions in the workers' home communities.[137]

Moreover, twenty years later, these psychosocial problems are still very much in evidence, with recent Sharjah-based studies concluding that the majority of the millions of Asian expatriate workers not only suffer from some sort of psychological depression themselves, but also, due to their long periods of absence, are beginning to cause significant socioeconomic problems in their home countries.[138] Therefore, as part of a broader labor nationalization policy, if time limits or other restrictions can be placed on foreign workers, especially those unable to bring their families to the UAE, it is theorized that these pathologies can be somewhat reduced before conditions further deteriorate.

## Emiratization Strategies

With regard to the strategies themselves, the encouragement of nationals to participate in the work force actually has a long history in the region and, as such, the present-day emiratization initiative can be viewed as an extension of existing ideas and practices, albeit on a much more comprehensive scale. Indeed, with the beginning of *al-khawiya* (the oil exploration by foreign firms in the early 1930s) the rulers had already begun to insist that, as part of their concession agreements, the firms should be obliged to recruit and train some of the local population, rather than simply importing all of their labor.[139] Moreover, by the late 1930s, the ruler of Dubai had taken this agreement one stage further by insisting that Petroleum Development

Trucial Coast Ltd. (PDTC) employ only Dubai subjects.[140] Following the decline of the pearling industry, and faced with the prospect of unemployment, it was reasoned that Dubai locals needed far more stable jobs, and with the training provided by the foreign oil companies this early emiratization was seen as a suitable long-term solution.[141] Writing in the early 1970s, Fenelon remarked upon the apparent successes of these early initiatives, including those in Abu Dhabi, and described how the oil firms had been responsible for training a modest number of locals in skilled professions: "The contributions made by the oil companies in Abu Dhabi by providing training facilities for craftsmen and technicians have been of the greatest importance in producing a nucleus of skilled workers. A sizeable number of ex-trainees are now engaged in skilled jobs both inside and outside the oil industry."[142] Indeed, Abu Dhabi Marine Areas, one of the largest of the concession holders, had opened a number of such training centers with the twin aims of providing Abu Dhabi locals with greater responsibility within the organization and training them to such a level that they could eventually replace expatriate employees in technical and administrative departments. Similarly, the Abu Dhabi Petroleum Company (ADPC), the principal land-based concession holder, began to provide training facilities almost as soon as oil production began. Although many of the locals trained by ADPC subsequently left the company, they soon began to contribute toward other activities in the emirate, thereby continuing to fulfill the company's responsibility to the local population.[143]

By the late 1970s and 1980s the emiratization strategy became far more extensive, with the official economic and social development plans outlining a comprehensive program aiming to rehabilitate as many UAE nationals as possible by educating them, training them, and by giving them added incentives to participate and become an active part of the work force.[144] Indeed, the development of the UAE's education system was already a key priority, and with specific regard to emiratization a special emphasis was placed on courses and subjects relating to business practices and the professional skills demanded by other areas of the UAE's development. This commitment to investment in education was to be matched in the workplace by a number of government-sponsored schemes to encourage greater work experience and full-time employment. Prominent examples in recent years have included the Al-Futtaim Trading Group's summer courses offered to young UAE nationals, with the group claiming it intends to "pioneer the training of national personnel";[145] the work of the UAE Women's Federation, which aims to bring more young Emirati women into the workplace;[146] and the various Emirati-specific training programs offered by the major banks. Indeed, speaking about Mashriq Bank's role in the emiratization process, Abdul al-Ghurair, chief executive officer of Mashriq, explained why the bank was the first to launch such a program:

In our continuous quest for excellence, Mashriq Bank has never neglected to play the role of the responsible corporate, forever striving to create practical and innovative solutions in response to the direct needs of the UAE market. The contributions of Mashriq Bank in the process of emiratisation has been quite significant as we go ahead with our plans to increase the presence of UAE nationals in our bank.

Moreover, Mohammed al-Sayari, chairman of the bank's human resources department, explained how such a program would actually contribute to the emiratization process:

Our aim is to train 60 UAE nationals every year by running four courses throughout the year. The first 15 passed out in March and completed the programme successfully. Some are now working in Mashriq and some have started careers in other banks. The course concentrates on improving practical skills through on-the-job training rather than theory work. The course runs for five full working days to give the young nationals a feeling of the work place. They learn how to write a professional CV, how to behave in an interview and where to go if they have a problem. The training is definitely more practical than theoretical.[147]

In addition to these educational programs, there have also been more direct strategies, many of which have focused on the granting of specific privileges to UAE nationals with the aim of assisting their introduction into the workplace and reducing competition from expatriates. Certainly, as Abdullah Sultan Abdullah, the secretary-general of the Federation of the UAE Chambers of Commerce and Industry has explained, although the UAE's chambers do place great emphasis on training and qualifying nationals, this can only go so far, and in certain cases the government has had to intervene in order to provide additional incentives and encouragement.[148] Most recently this strategy has been reinforced by a new labor law aimed at regulating the employment of UAE nationals in the private sector. As part of the new law, UAE nationals will benefit from special pension funds and better guarantees of their rights as employees in the private sector.[149] Alongside these initiatives there have, of course, been more restrictive schemes, including the long-standing *kafil* sponsorship system, in which all non-Emirati entrepreneurs require a local partner, thereby ensuring that UAE nationals, even as parasites, have at least some involvement in the management and profits of the domestic economy. In addition, there have been specific emiratization quotas introduced, requiring certain companies to increase their percentage of Emirati employees over a set period. Once again, the banking sector provides a strong example, where up until the late 1990s locals accounted for just 12 percent of the work force. To redress this situation, the government chose to impose quotas, requiring all banks to increase their proportion of locals to 40 percent over the next ten years.[150]

As such, Mashriq Bank and many of the other banking houses have publicly stated their intention to have an "emiratization growth rate" of over 4 percent per year in an effort to meet these targets.[151] Moreover, it is worthwhile noting that in certain circumstances there have also been more extreme measures, including, for example, highly contentious directives such as the Ministry of Agriculture and Fisheries' decree that UAE nationals must captain all fishing boats. Explained by the minister as being a necessary step in order to "help check over-fishing and eliminate illegal practices resorted to by expatriate fishermen at sea"; in practice it is simply a part of the government's overall drive for emiratization in the agricultural sector.[152]

Third, and also deserving mention, are those emiratization strategies concerned not so much with the encouragement of UAE nationals, but rather the discouragement of expatriates or, more specifically, the discouragement of employers intent on hiring foreigners. Indeed, an important recent example would be a draft law released by the Ministry of Labor that will require companies to pay a fee for every foreigner they hire, thus making UAE nationals a more attractive alternative.[153] In addition, other more severe laws have aimed at stemming the flow of immigrant labor and actually reducing the size of the current expatriate population. Examples include the restrictions placed on new visas requested by unskilled workers from India and Pakistan,[154] and the introduction of lengthy immigration amnesties that have allowed all foreign workers without valid visas to leave the UAE with only minimal penalties. Indeed, it has been estimated that during the 1996 amnesty as many as 200,000 workers unexpectedly took advantage of the favorable terms and left before its deadline, thereby creating massive labor shortages.[155]

Given the enormity and complexity of the challenge, the results of these various emiratization strategies have been far less impressive than most would have expected (although it remains important to note that many serious observers had always remained skeptical).[156] The original objectives of the early 1980s, which proposed that national management and labor in all sectors would reach at least 25 percent of the UAE's total within five years,[157] have clearly not been met. Thus, unlike the comparatively straightforward diversification and welfare objectives, the nationalization of the UAE's work force has not been solved with financial packages and massive investment. Indeed, the experiences of the 1990s point to the opposite, given that the improved incentives, higher salaries, and pension schemes encouraged by the emiratization initiative may have actually priced UAE graduates out of the market. Certainly, many employers baulked at paying the $26,000 average salary for a local graduate in addition to the obligatory 12.5 percent pension contribution,[158] and much preferred to hire well-qualified and experienced South Asians at a fraction of the cost.[159] Nevertheless, although few of the official targets may have been reached, there has undoubtedly been a rise in the number of UAE nationals participating in very diverse areas of the work force, and with the rapidly increasing number of young Emiratis entering higher education, it is likely that emiratization, especially in managerial positions, will mushroom in the near future. Thus, although lacking the immediacy of the incentives, quotas, and sponsorship systems, the various emiratization education programs and the UAE's considerable investment in higher education may lead to important long-term results, especially in the nationalization of professional occupations, which is, after all, a far more realistic objective than nationalizing 25 percent of the total work force. Indeed, there are already important glimmers of hope, as the proportion of UAE nationals gaining such positions, in both the private and public sectors, has already appreciably increased. Again referring to the banking sector, the emiratization process has really taken hold since 2000, with UAE nationals now accounting for around 20 percent of the work force, thus representing a rise of nearly 8 percent over just a few years. Moreover, some banks have been particularly successful and, in the case of the Emirates Institute for Banking and Financial Studies (EIBFS), the general manager confidently expected their proportion of UAE nationals to rise to 23 percent by the end of 2004 as a direct result of fresh Emirati graduates.[160] Using a very different example, emiratization has also been extremely successful in the UAE's judiciary, a key area of the public sector. Although most judges are still foreign nationals, primarily from other Arab countries, the number of UAE nationals serving as public prosecutors and judges has nevertheless continued to grow,[161] and as the minister of justice, Muhammad al-Dhahiri, has claimed, nationals now account for 32 percent of the work force, a proportion likely to double within the next few years.[162]

## Substrategies: Abu Dhabi and Dubai— A Comparative Analysis

Given that Abu Dhabi and Dubai are by far the largest, wealthiest, and most populous members of the federation, there is little doubt that the developments that have taken place in these two principal emirates have most directly contributed to the UAE's overall diversification, social growth, and emiratization objectives. It is therefore essential to consider the important differences and substrategies that have emerged in these emirates. Although interemirate politics and the viability of the federation will be discussed in greater detail in the next chapter,[163] it is nevertheless crucial here to understand the relative flexibility of Emirati socioeconomic planning and to appreciate how, at least in some respects, this has led to mutually reinforcing and beneficial dual approaches.

Indeed, as the above analyses have shown, especially with regard to industrialization, commerce, and tourism, very often Abu Dhabi and Dubai have chosen to emphasize and pursue different elements of what remain very broad strategies. The immediate explanation for such divergent sub-strategies would of course be the relative differences in oil resources, with Abu Dhabi possessing some of the world's largest reserves, and with little secret being made of the more finite supplies in Dubai.[164] As the *Middle East Economic Digest* noted in the mid-1990s:

> The contrast between Abu Dhabi and Dubai, less than two hours apart by desert road, is striking. The capital city [Abu Dhabi] has risen as a glittering showcase for the modern Middle East, exuding an air of leisure and luxury. Dubai presents an altogether different aspect of the UAE with a sprawling townscape that hums to the rhythm of business. . . . Dubai has staked everything on trade, its traditional lifeblood. . . . Dubai's oil production is sustained by a huge re-injection programme and costly recovery techniques. Some analysts predict that Dubai may soon have to become a net oil and gas importer. Thus, for the long-term prospects, nothing less than massive development will do.[165]

Thus, as one might expect, Dubai has been pressed into more wholesale diversification, needing to promote the growth of ISI industries and rapidly expand its non-oil-related commercial and tourist sectors, while Abu Dhabi has instead been able to diversify at a slower pace and rely on its comparative advantage of cheap energy by concentrating on heavier oil-related and EOI industries. Furthermore, although unrelated to diversification, Abu Dhabi's massive oil wealth has also allowed the emirate to rely more heavily on oil-financed investments overseas. In many ways, the towering new headquarters of the Abu Dhabi Investments Authority (ADIA) along the city's showpiece Corniche Road can be seen as symbolizing the centrality of such a policy to the local administration.[166] Indeed, although the government of Dubai is reported to hold a fairly substantial $35 billion overseas, the undisclosed foreign assets held by ADIA (rumored to be in excess of $150 billion),[167] the Abu Dhabi ruling family (Shaikh Zayed's private office and his Panamanian conduit corporation are thought to have assets in the region of $50 billion),[168] and many private Abu Dhabi citizens (the 60,000 bona fide Abu Dhabian nationals hold over $160 billion among them)[169] are nevertheless believed to dwarf this figure.[170]

But a full explanation of how these different development paths have helped to shape the contemporary UAE cannot rest solely on the relative oil wealth and investment capabilities of the two emirates. Instead it must also be appreciated just how varied the pace of development had been for these two emirates during the first half of the twentieth century. It is often assumed that these emirates began the 1970s in much the same situation, as they had both been British-governed Trucial shaikhdoms and, as explained in Chapter 1, they possessed similar traditional social and political structures. However, while Abu Dhabi still remained something of a backwater even by the 1950s, Dubai had long since grown into the largest town of the lower Gulf. Indeed, when former British political agent Donald Hawley visited Abu Dhabi during this period, he felt obliged to remark on its comparative visible backwardness:

> The approach to the town, which is on an island, was appalling. High winds drove in the sea over miles of salt flats and only one narrow track, glistening with thick white cakes of salt, was passable. A square fort guarded a causeway (replaced only in 1968 with a bridge) and even the causeway was only built in the 1950s. Earlier, visitors had to drive through the shallows of the sea to reach Abu Dhabi. The town itself was a place of palm-frond houses, barastis, built on white sand among palm trees. A small market with tiny shops stood in higgledy-piggledy fashion between simple houses, and the streets were narrow and roofed with palm-fronds. Little was to be bought. The white palace of the ruler, turreted and crenellated like a Beau Geste fort, stood among the palms, dominating the place, with the red and white flag of Abu Dhabi fluttering over it.[171]

By the late 1950s, and in complete contrast to the "small dilapidated town" of Abu Dhabi,[172] Dubai was already beginning to display noticeable signs of prosperity and development. Certainly, as the early aerial photographs of the emirate illustrate, the town was already rapidly expanding, with an extensive commercial district in Deira and with many large merchant houses along the creek side.[173] Moreover, even following the oil boom and with Abu Dhabi developing into a modern city with much greenery, Dubai has always maintained a highly visible edge, and now of course boasts one of the most celebrated skylines in the Middle East.[174]

This manifestly differing pace of development can be best accounted for by the many underlying differences between the two emirates during the critical preoil period. Unlike Dubai, where prominent merchant families had been established for generations, Abu Dhabi's business community was really more of a post–oil boom phenomenon and, as Peck has noted, "therefore lacked the roots, scope and energy of its Dubai counterpart." Prominent Abu Dhabi families did of course succeed in launching themselves in business, but very often they lacked the necessary experience and had to rely on expatriate managers to carry out the daily affairs of their enterprises, whereas the stronger business traditions in Dubai allowed many leading families to assume a more hands-on role.[175] In most cases these early structural differences were the result of Dubai's long history of relative attractiveness over Abu Dhabi. Indeed, with regard to commerce and other coastal activities, Dubai had always possessed a geographical advantage over the other Trucial shaikhdoms, given its sheltered creek that extends much farther inland than any of the other inlets along the lower Gulf. Moreover, this considerable natural asset was further complemented by Dubai's relatively low tariff structure and the ruler's active encouragement of foreign trade (an encouragement that remains very much in evidence even today, with the entrepreneurial spirit of the ruling al-Maktum dynasty seen as being inextricably linked to the emirate's ongoing commercial success), especially compared to Abu Dhabi, where, as Miriam Joyce describes, the overly cautious rulers continued to restrict entry for foreign merchants and even merchants from the other Trucial states.[176]

Most significant, when the major ports on the Persian coast were forced to impose new customs regulations in the early 1900s, the towns of the Trucial coast suddenly became far more appealing prospects, and Dubai was best placed to accommodate the new influx of merchants.[177] Indeed, as D. K. Chaudhry, the general manager of the Persian Sharaf Shipping Agency, explains, much of the early success of the emirate's dhow trade and its commercial sectors can be attributed to the increasing tariffs in Iran[178] and the almost simultaneous abolition of the existing 5 percent customs duty in Dubai.[179] Certainly, the Shah's expanding control over southern parts of Iran had disrupted the relative freedom in the busy harbors of Lingah and Bushire, and consequently Iran's coastal business community began to shift its operations to Dubai.[180] As such, when German geographer Hermann Burchardt visited the area in 1904 he remarked that Dubai had been declared a "free port" and was therefore unsurprised to find an abundance of British and German merchandise in the port, and a large number of immigrants fresh from Lingah.[181] Thus, Dubai soon emerged as the main distribution center for imported goods along the coast from Qatar to Ra's al-Jibal (northeast of Ra's al-Khaimah), and even became the favored stopoff point for the British Indian Steam Navigation Company.[182]

Many states have been born from trading modes of production,[183] and as the century progressed and its commercial success continued to grow Dubai became one of these. By the 1920s it was becoming clear that the restrictions that had been strangling the economy of southern Iran were unlikely to lift. Thus, many of the Persian merchants who had taken up temporary residence in Dubai earlier in the century soon realized that they were unlikely to return to Lingah and decided to take up the ruler of Dubai's offer to settle permanently in the emirate.[184] These merchants had made great contributions toward Dubai's prosperity, and by deciding to remain they cemented Dubai's commercial preeminence. As such, business skills, entrepreneurship, and trading links with Asia and Africa were effectively transferred from Iran to Dubai. Indeed, these Persians even introduced the concept of wind towers to the region, and examples of this early form of air-conditioning can still be seen in the Bastakiyah quarter of Bur Dubai, where the ruler had originally donated land to the merchants. By the late 1940s the emirate received another boost following Shaikh Sa'id al-Maktum's fateful decision to accept Kuwaiti aid to dredge and improve Dubai's creek. Crucially, his neighbor, Shaikh Saqr al-Qasimi, had refused any such assistance at this time, thus allowing Sharjah's estuary to silt up in the 1950s, and with it his emirate's commercial potential.[185] In many ways this new comparative attractiveness of Dubai was formalized in the mid-1960s when the British decided that Dubai, rather than Sharjah (the residency's erstwhile base of operations), should host the headquarters of the Trucial States Council and the Trucial States Development Office. As explained in Chapter 1, these institutions administered considerable funds provided by the British Ministry of Overseas Development and brought a number of agricultural, medical, and technical experts to the emirate.[186] Thus, as Frauke Heard-Bey contends, their presence in Dubai gave the emirate a much more cosmopolitan air than the other shaikhdoms, and more importantly allowed Dubai's rulers to discuss projects informally with the foreign advisers and witness the office's achievements firsthand.[187] Finally, with regard to Dubai's continuing commercial advantages, in the 1970s the emirate was still benefiting from its free ports, especially following New Delhi's decision to impose duties on India's gold trade[188] and the Iranian government's renewed attempts to raise Lingah's tariff wall. Indeed, as a direct result of these new Iranian tariffs, often touching 40 percent, a fresh wave of Persian merchants began to transfer their businesses to Dubai. As before, these merchants recognized that it was far preferable to import goods through Dubai and then distribute them in the Arab world than it was to suffer the heavy infrastructural liabilities of trading through Iran. Furthermore, as Chaudhry also notes, by this stage the advanced development of Dubai's Port Rashid and its Port Jebel Ali megaproject had led many Iranian merchants to assume that Dubai would soon become the one convenient stopping point for long-distance shipping and therefore the most sensible location for any long-term commercial base in the Gulf.[189] Most recently, of course, external events in the early 1990s, this time on the Arabian coast of the Gulf, must have also provided Dubai with increased commercial opportunities vis-à-vis its entrepôt rivals. Indeed, although there is little concrete evidence to support such claims, it would seem likely that Dubai benefited enormously from the destruction of Kuwait in 1991 and from the Shi'a unrest in Bahrain three years later: in both cases it would appear that a significant number of businesses relocated to Dubai.[190]

Thus, in light of these different historical circumstances, it is apparent why Dubai's strong commercial traditions coupled with its comparatively modest oil wealth have facilitated and spurred a more rapid and wholesale diversification of the economy, especially in the non-oil-related trade sector. Conversely, Abu Dhabi's noncommercial foundations and its massive oil wealth have engendered a more oil-focused development strategy, using cheap energy to encourage the growth of heavy EOI industries and using oil revenues to finance large-scale overseas investments. Indeed, evidence of these differing diversification substrategies has become clearer as the UAE has matured, especially given the relatively small size of Abu Dhabi's nonoil sector and the increasingly large nonoil sector contributions being made to Dubai's economy (see Figure 3.15).

Thus, by the mid-1990s Dubai's nonoil economic sectors were already contributing 82 percent of the emirate's GDP. Perhaps most remarkable, over a period of just five years Dubai's nonoil economic sectors have continued to grow and now account for around 94 percent of the emirate's total GDP. Moreover, while Dubai's total GDP accounted for 24–25 percent of the UAE's total in 2000, its share of the UAE's nonoil GDP had risen to 34 percent by 2000,[191] demonstrating the emirate's far greater commitment to non-oil-related development than that of Abu Dhabi.

Second, with regard to attracting foreign direct investment, another key indicator of meaningful diversification and relative economic attractive-

**Figure 3.15 Comparison of Oil Sector and
Nonoil Sector Contributions to Dubai's GDP**

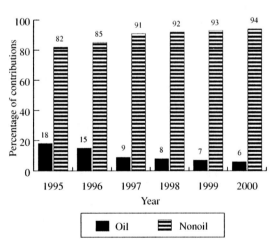

*Source:* UAE Ministry of Planning, "Dubai: GDP at Factor Cost," in Dubai Department of Economic Development (2001), *Development Statistics,* Government of Dubai, p. 42.
*Note:* Dubai's GDP at factor cost calculated on fixed 1995 prices.

ness, Dubai has been similarly successful and clearly ranks first among the emirates, attracting 54 percent of all non-oil-related foreign direct investment (FDI) in the UAE's manufacturing sector. This compares with Sharjah's share of 21 percent and 'Ajman's share of 10 percent. Accounting for just 9 percent, Abu Dhabi ranks only fourth,[192] indicating the emirate's different outlook on FDI and its preference for state-sponsored heavy industries[193] (see Figure 3.16).

Indeed, Abu Dhabi's commitment to heavy industries can be further confirmed by the fact that although the emirate hosts only 224 industrial establishments, a mere 10 percent of the total number of plants in the UAE, these plants account for more than half of the UAE's total manufacturing output. In comparison, Dubai has 817 plants, Sharjah 716, and 'Ajman 316. This clearly indicates the preference for lighter, smaller-scale ISI industries in Dubai and the northern emirates[194] (see Figure 3.17).

Third, and also with regard to the comparative success of Dubai's nonoil development, it is important to note the appreciable improvements in the emirate's labor productivity scores, especially in its diversifying sectors. Using data from 2000, Figure 3.18 compares labor productivity scores for the various economic sectors in Dubai with the UAE averages. Thus, if compared to the labor productivity statistics for the entire UAE, it is evident that in the three main nonoil sectors Dubai has enjoyed significantly higher productivity than the other emirates, particularly in the commercial sector, where the emirate has now achieved internationally competitive labor productivity rates (indicated by a score substantially higher than 1.0). Only in the agricultural sector does Dubai fall short of the UAE average, indicating the emirate's historical preference for coastal and trading activities, and Abu Dhabi's greater development of its hinterland.

**Figure 3.16 Distribution of Nonoil-Related**
**Foreign Direct Investment in the UAE**

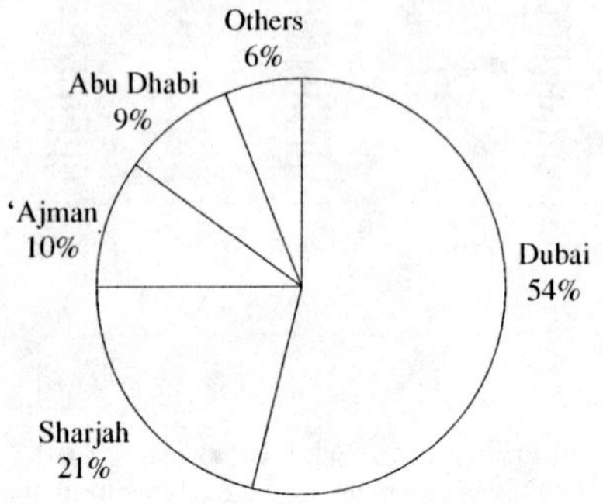

Source: UAE Ministry of Finance and Industry (2001), Abu Dhabi.

**Figure 3.17 Total Manufacturing Plants in the UAE, all sizes**

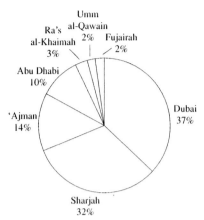

*Source:* Al-Sharhan International Consultancy (2001), "UAE Country Report 2001," Dubai, pp. 14–15.

**Figure 3.18 Labor Productivity Scores:
Dubai Compared with the UAE Average**

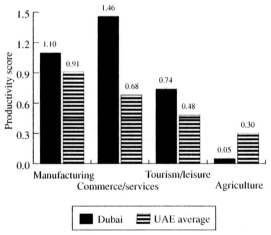

*Sources:* UAE Ministry of Planning, "UAE and Dubai: Employment by Economic Sectors" and "UAE and Dubai: GDP at Factor Cost and per Capita, 2000," in Dubai Department of Economic Development (2001), *Development Statistics,* Government of Dubai, pp. 30, 44.

*Note:* Calculated from Dubai's total GDP of 54.741 billion dirhams in 2000 using sector shares of total employment and total GDP.

Despite these marked differences between Abu Dhabi and Dubai, there is a growing consensus that such diversity will bring added strength to the federation and will eventually provide the UAE with the best of both worlds. Indeed, as *Business Monitor International* has claimed, the differing macroeconomic strategies of Abu Dhabi and Dubai can be regarded as complementary rather than divisive and are likely to ensure that the UAE's overall economy remains resilient and prosperous even in times of low oil prices.[195] Abu Dhabi can draw upon massive financial reserves if the oil industry falters, whereas Dubai can provide greater diversification and more diverse employment opportunities for the emiratization process. Moreover, Jamal al-Suwaidi of the Emirates Centre for Strategic Studies and Research (ECSSR) has also emphasized these positive aspects of the relationship, explaining how Abu Dhabi needs to support Dubai's rapid development, as "keeping Dubai strong is important for the federation and important for the future of the federation." Thus, even though Dubai's contribution to the federal budget is low,[196] he recognizes that Dubai's expanding nonoil sectors are more likely to solve the employment/emiratization problem than Abu Dhabi.[197] Similarly, as Muhammad al-Fahim has acknowledged, it is increasingly believed that Abu Dhabi will be unable to achieve many of the UAE's long-term goals on its own, as "its economy is built on selling oil to build infrastructure whereas Dubai's more diversified and imaginative development projects offer a means whereby job creation can be encouraged."[198]

As a result, there has been growing evidence of greater financial and physical links between the two emirates. One such link may be the widely rumored decision by Abu Dhabi to donate 100,000 barrels of oil a day to support Dubai's development projects. At current prices, this "gift" represents more than $650 million a year.[199] Physical links have included the recent opening of the Maqta-Jebel Ali natural gas pipeline, which by 2005 will feed 700 cubic feet per day from Abu Dhabi into Dubai's industrial zones as part of the aforementioned Dolphin gas project.[200] Indeed, as the Economist Intelligence Unit reports, this UAE-Qatar landmark gas deal provides the clearest indicator to date of closer economic ties between Abu Dhabi and Dubai.[201] As such, much of the UAE's recent economic development can be seen to have taken place within a context of increasing coexistence between two different but mutually supportive economies. As Chapter 1 emphasized, the UAE survived the initial dangers of the early years due to its ability to balance and include the different demands and concerns of the individual emirates. Similarly, the federation's socioeconomic development planning has not led to uniformity and adherence to one rigid strategy, but has instead embraced a number of substrategies that, at least in this case, have complemented and reinforced the UAE's overall development. Moreover, there is every indication that this coexistence and flexibility will continue for the foreseeable future: Abu Dhabi will continue to pursue its long-term strategies of "economic nationalism"[202] by developing government-sponsored heavy industries and downstream operations such as oil refinery, gas-processing, and polyethylene plants, while in contrast it is predicted that Dubai's macroeconomic strategy will remain more neoliberal and oriented toward private sector activity, with the government providing the infrastructure and focusing on the international promotion of the emirate[203] (see Figure 3.19).

## Readily Identifiable Development Problems

Despite the visible success of most areas of diversification, infrastructure building, and social development, and despite the existence of mutually beneficial dual development strategies in the two principal emirates, the UAE has nevertheless been faced with certain other development problems, many of which have remained unresolved. The most notable persisting concerns have included chronic overconsumption and a continual trade imbalance despite the modest expansion of the UAE's productive sectors (thus realizing the described fears of the early development planners),[204] the expensive and wasteful duplication of investments, and the substantial disequilibrium between the constituent emirates.

First, with regard to excessive consumption, there has long been a concern that oil wealth and strong purchasing powers will lead to distressingly high levels of consumer imports, which will in turn present serious long-term problems for the growth of domestic manufacturing, and of course for the UAE's balance of payments.[205] In short, it was feared that the UAE's parochial function was being limited not only to that of an oil producer but also to that of a completely open-ended market for consumer and luxury goods manufactured in the core capitalist countries.[206] Indeed, many of these pessimistic predictions were soon justified as the UAE's balance of payments surplus began to fall from highs of nearly 39 billion dirhams in 1980 to less than 2 billion dirhams in the mid-1990s.[207] Similarly, the UAE's trade balance fell from over 50 billion dirhams to less than 15 billion dirhams over the same period, leaving the UAE with the lowest trade balance of all GCC states by some considerable margin.[208] Moreover, in the specific case of Dubai, the most commercially developed of the emirates, imports rose from around 7 billion dirhams in 1975 to a staggering 83 billion dirhams in 2001, and although as shown there has been an appreciable increase in re-exporting activity, these imports still represent around 74 percent of total nonoil trade (and with approximately half of these being accounted for by straightforward consumer durables)[209] (see Figures 3.20 and 3.21).

Thus, despite a number of plans to set both governmental and private

**Figure 3.19 Abu Dhabi and Dubai: A Comparative Analysis**

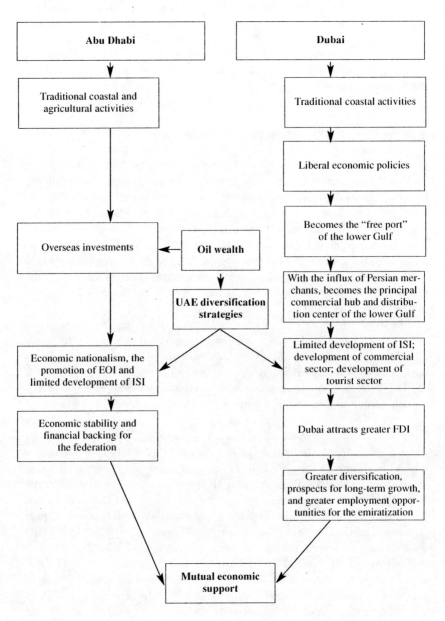

consumption limits,[210] over the past twenty-five years relatively little has been achieved. Certainly, with accelerating imports and an increasingly dominant consumption structure, the issue would seem to retain much of its original urgency, especially as the UAE's explicated attempts to reduce reliance on oil by boosting the nonproductive commercial sector can be seen as having actually compounded the problem—the much-vaunted low tariff rates (especially in Dubai), the government's defraying of the infra-structural costs for transportation and importation, and extremely high

**Figure 3.20 Dubai Nonoil Foreign Trade, 1975**

Re-exports 7%    Exports 1%

Imports 92%

*Source:* Based on data from Dubai Department of Ports and Customs, "Dubai: Non-Oil Foreign Trade—Total," in Dubai Department of Economic Development (2002), *Development Statistics,* Government of Dubai, pp. 109, 114.

*Note:* Calculated from values for nonoil foreign trade given at fixed 1995 prices.

**Figure 3.21 Dubai Nonoil Foreign Trade, 2001**

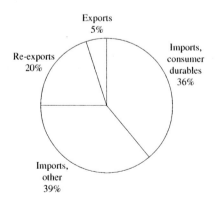

Exports 5%

Re-exports 20%

Imports, consumer durables 36%

Imports, other 39%

*Source:* See Figure 3.20.

*Note:* Calculated from values for nonoil foreign trade given at fixed 1995 prices.

credit facilities for the encouragement of local entrepreneurship all being very clear examples,[211] in addition of course to the lack of any form of income tax and all of the other patrimonial and rentier-related subsidies described in the previous chapter.[212] Indeed, as al-Shamsi notes of this conundrum: "Great emphasis has been put into encouraging the non-oil sector, and that share of the GDP has increased. However, such development has its shortcomings . . . a prevalence of high income and consumption sustained without recourse to local production and the existence of high levels of conspicuous investment."[213]

Similarly, despite the potential effectiveness of Abu Dhabi and Dubai's duai development paths, the UAE's spectacularly costly duplication of investments and a lack of regionwide cooperation, especially between the larger and smaller emirates, have also persisted and continue to undermine the overall diversification strategy.[214] Particularly strong and much discussed examples would include the UAE's disorganized development of its airports and factories, and the apparent absence of any meaningful coordination between these projects.[215] Indeed, even in the mid-1970s Sa'id 'Ahmad Ghubash, the UAE's minister of planning, was already complaining of this problem:

> Economic necessity will require the eventual cessation of the costly duplications of projects that have occurred throughout the UAE since it was established. UAE officials recognised that this duplication of projects only wastes time and money that could be used more effectively elsewhere. The intense rivalry between the various emirates and the important status issue dictated that if one emirate acquired an airport or factory then a similar one had to be built in the other emirates.[216]

Writing in the mid-1980s, Peck also emphasized this lack of coordination and the resulting unnecessary duplications:

> Abu Dhabi, Dubai, Sharjah and Ra's al-Khaimah all have airports that service both international and domestic flights. This overbuilding, prompted by inter-emirate rivalry, has left the latter two facilities underutilised. Abu Dhabi, on the one hand, recently opened a new, large civilian airport to handle its traffic. Dubai, with the busiest airport in the Gulf, is upgrading its facilities.[217]

Clearly, this underutilization of major airports was a direct result of so many facilities having been built in a relatively small country. Of course, the problem is still very much in evidence today, with new international airports in Al-'Ayn and Fujairah and with foreign airlines now cutting back their flights to the Sharjah airport as a result of the continuing expansion of Dubai International only a few miles away.[218] In fact, Dubai airport is closer and now far more accessible to most parts of Sharjah than is the Sharjah airport.[219] Similarly, with regard to the UAE's airlines, there has been much the same problem. Although jointly owned between Abu Dhabi, Bahrain, Qatar, and Oman, Gulf Air was originally intended to be the UAE's principal carrier, but has experienced difficulties in recent years and has always faced stiff competition from its award-winning Dubai-based rival, Emirates Airways. Furthermore, in late 2003 such duplication became even more marked with the launch of a third "national carrier," the Abu Dhabi–based Etihad Airways. Designated by an Abu Dhabian Emiri decree as being the "national airline of the United Arab Emirates" and now chaired by Shaikh 'Ahmad al-Nuhayyan,[220] one cannot help but feel this is a direct response to Shaikh 'Ahmad al-Maktum's highly successful Dubai operation.[221] Certainly, the joke is now wearing thin as few other countries of a similar population and geographic size as the UAE have successfully supported two major airlines, let alone three.[222]

The problem would therefore appear to remain the lack of any high-level organization of development projects between the emirates. Thus, although interemirate political relations will be considered more closely in the next chapter, it is important to note that persisting rivalries, overlapping local government departments, and the continuing lack of certain federal ministries (most significantly the absence of a UAE Ministry of Tourism), have clearly clouded any overall vision and in many cases have led to underused facilities, aborted projects, and gigantic resource waste. Indeed, it later emerged that one of the causal factors behind the 1987 coup attempt in Sharjah was Shaikh Abdul-Aziz al-Qasimi's opposition to the ruler's sanctioning of expensive and unnecessary "prestige projects," including the airport, an unfinished television station, and several empty museums.[223] As such, the initial lack of coordination and necessary period of transition predicted by the planners of the early 1970s still remains a significant issue.[224] In many ways it has become even more of a concern than before given that the shock-absorbing effects of oil wealth may have allowed the UAE to survive the duplication and disorganized spontaneity of the 1980s and 1990s,[225] but in a future of potentially greater scarcity, and in a future requiring greater diversification, such haphazardness may prevent more long-term sustainable growth.

Closely associated with duplication, another considerable problem has been the lack of equilibrium between the various emirates. Indeed, the need for a reduction in regional disparity (in much the same way as the reduction in the UAE's reliance on oil, foreign technology, and foreign labor) has long been a key concern of the development planners, many of whom believed that if the different emirates could better pool and balance their resources then socioeconomic growth would be more achievable for the entire country.[226] Moreover, and clearly addressing another major feature of dependency theory, it was understood that greater equilibrium would also serve to prevent any "superexploitation" of the UAE's less well-developed areas by either indigenous or foreign forces.[227] As such, in 1975 the development planners clearly stated their objective of "finding the optimum allocation of projects according to the relative importance of each emirate."[228] Specifically, the strategy was to ensure that the smaller non-oil-producing emirates were to be targeted for appropriate federally funded developments based on their individual characteristics, while all major development projects were to be better supervized to ensure more balanced investments and the best possible utility for the country.

A major and immediate obstacle to this strategy was Article 23 of the UAE's provisional constitution, which stated that the "natural wealth and resources of each emirate should remain the public property of that individual emirate." Although such articles allowed for greater flexibility and guarded against political fragmentation,[229] they also effectively set apart the rich from the poor, thus hindering full economic integration at an early stage.[230] To a limited extent some of the UAE's regional imbalances were improved during the 1970s, as the federal government, at that stage funded almost entirely by Abu Dhabi, began to intervene and assist outlying regions that would have otherwise remained underdeveloped and would have fallen into further decline. Indeed, as a by-product of the UAE's expanding physical infrastructure, many previously remote regions became better connected and more assimilated with the national economy than ever before. In particular, certain coastal and desert regions that had recently been linked by new roads and telecommunications, but that remained reliant on traditional economic activities such as fishing and date farming, were targeted to receive additional development grants in an effort to prevent worsening disparity. A strong example of this regeneration program would be the island of Dalma, which as described in Chapter 1 had long been one of the lower Gulf's most prosperous pearling centers.[231] Unlike the nearby island of Das, which had been transformed into an offshore oil terminal for ADMA in the early 1970s (complete with company accommodation, restaurants, cinemas, and bowling alleys),[232] Dalma possessed no oil, and following the collapse of the pearling industry it became entirely reliant on fishing. Consequently, the population of the once bustling island fell to less than a hundred by the late 1970s,[233] and seemed set to fall even further as the result of increasing migration to the cities. Yet as a present-day Dalma resident explains, the community's decline was successfully held in check at this time, as the island (after becoming a major construction site for a royal palace complex and various other developments), along with the remote interior towns surrounding the Liwa oases, began to receive substantial government aid.[234] Indeed, as Heard-Bey explains:

> The increase in oil company activities eventually diverted most of the manpower away from the pearling industry, which was already at a low

ebb in the 1950s. With this the importance of Dalma also declined. In the later 1970s the small community of tribal fishermen was given new incentives to stay there by the establishment of government-financed houses, schools, new mosques, a market complex, and a small hospital; free transport to and from the island by helicopter was organised by the army; several construction projects are proposed for the island. Thus, Dalma, like the Liwa and Bida Zayed and the Al-'Ayn area, entered the era of departmentalised administration, co-ordinated by government institutions in Abu Dhabi town.[235]

However, despite these hinterland aid packages, the sustained growth of Sharjah's manufacturing sector throughout the 1980s, and the expansion of Fujairah's Indian Ocean ports in the early 1990s, most of these regional developments have remained dwarfed by the progress of the two principal emirates. In fact, the growth of Fujairah's ports peaked in 1996 and actually began to decline following an aggressive advertising campaign by the Dubai Ports Authority, which claimed that Dubai remained the ultimate destination for the majority of incoming cargo and therefore that it still made sense for shipping companies to use Port Rashid and Jebel Ali.[236] Certainly, as the Economist Intelligence Unit has noted, the vast bulk of the UAE's development projects continue to be undertaken in Abu Dhabi and Dubai, while the smaller emirates continue to have very few commercially viable ventures apart from some small-scale tourism[237] (and, as the Oxford Business Group reports, even these infant tourist industries are now being compromised as most tour operators working out of Dubai are reluctant to recommend anything more than short stays in the Indian Ocean coastline hotels when pricing an overall "Dubai package").[238]

Indeed, as the UAE's indicators for the period 1975–1995 illustrate, its regional disparities, at least in terms of economic development, have persisted, and the goal of greater equilibrium would seem as elusive as before. Although Abu Dhabi's share of the UAE's GDP fell from nearly 71 percent to 61 percent, this still represented by far the greatest contribution. Moreover, with Dubai's share of GDP rising from 20.5 percent to 24 percent, the two major emirates still accounted for over 85 percent of the UAE's GDP in 1995, despite Dubai's declining oil revenues. In contrast, the combined share of the four smaller emirates accounted for just 7 percent of GDP in 1995, and although this is nearly double the 1975 share of 4 percent, it nevertheless represents a very small increase in total contributions over a considerable twenty-year period.[239] Furthermore, it can be argued that the vast bulk of this share is actually made up of remittances from nationals who commute to work in other parts of the UAE. Many Sharjah nationals of course work in Dubai, but more illustrative of this phenomenon are the large groups of young male nationals from Ra's al-Khaimah and Fujairah who share apartments in either Dubai or Abu Dhabi during the working week and return to their faraway home emirate only at the weekends.[240] These GDP breakdown figures therefore indicate not only that few major wealth-generating developments exist in the outlying regions, but also that the northern emirates are in danger of becoming satellites dependent on "foreign aid" from their more affluent neighbors[241] (see Figures 3.22 and 3.23).

Finally, although the problem is unlikely to be resolved in the near future, and although regional disequilibrium will remain a feature of the UAE's lopsided development for some time, a number of revival projects and developments are in the pipeline or on the horizon, and at the very least these underscore the planners' continuing commitment to reducing regional disparity. Such examples include the Offsets Group's proposed ventures in the northern emirates and in Al-'Ayn,[242] and the generous sponsorship of coastal restoration projects and festivals in 'Ajman by the National Bank of Dubai and the UAE's telecom company, Etisalat.[243] The western desert region of Abu Dhabi has also been earmarked for future development with a multimillion-dirham project already under way in an effort to transform what is probably the UAE's least developed area into a network of rural tourist attractions. Among others, these will include settlements close to Liwa and in Ghayathi, near the Saudi border.[244] Moreover, there have been comprehensive plans drawn up by some of the smaller emirates in cooperation with the federal government and the UNDP, and given time these may also lead to greater regional development. In particular, Ra's al-Khaimah recently launched its "UNDP-RAK Vision," a plan aiming to achieve sustainable growth in the non-oil-producing emirate by promoting Ra's al-Khaimah-specific policies for the expansion and diversification of its econ-

**Figure 3.22 Contributions to UAE GDP, 1975**

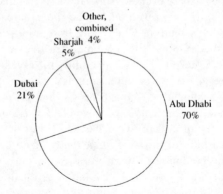

*Source:* Crown Prince Court, Department of Research and Studies (1996), "Development Indicators in the UAE: Achievements and Projections," Abu Dhabi, p. 54.

**Figure 3.23 Contributions to UAE GDP, 1995**

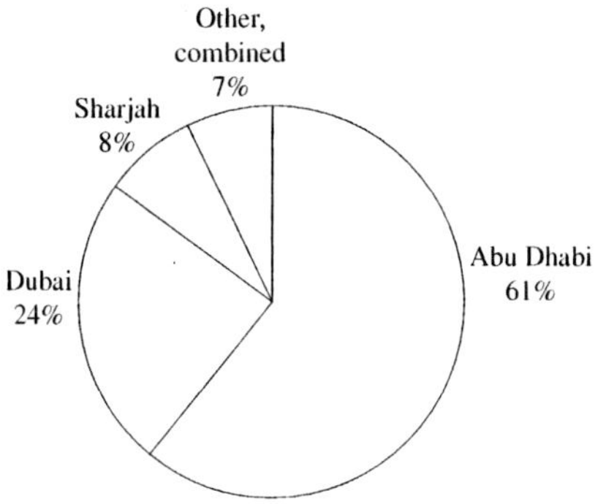

*Source:* See Figure 3.22.

omy. Indeed, as part of his official announcement, the ruler, Shaikh Saqr, stated his clear intentions to boost the emirate's relatively small contribution to the UAE's economy and to reduce the gap between Ra's al-Khaimah and the three larger emirates.[245]


## Conclusion

By the mid-1970s the UAE's economy was already heavily reliant on overseas demand for its oil exports, on foreign technology for the functioning of its industries, and on foreign labor for supplying both its skilled and unskilled work forces. Thus, in an effort to promote greater self-sufficiency and more sustained autonomous growth, and of course to ensure the longevity of the crucial material components of their ruling bargain, the "modernizing monarchs" and their development planners initiated a number of strategies that aimed to reduce some of the most damaging features of their dependent development. In particular there were calls for the greater diversification of the economy, specifically the promotion of the UAE's non-oil-related sectors and the encouragement of technology linkages and transfers between foreign and domestic enterprises; the creation of a first-class educational and welfare state to provide for a trained and healthy work force; and the "emiratization" of labor, to encourage UAE nationals to assume positions previously requiring expatriates (see Figure 3.24).

With regard to diversification, over the past thirty years the UAE has experienced the modest growth of its non-oil-related industries and in some cases, particularly in the ISI manufacturing sector, has managed to encour-

**Figure 3.24 Socioeconomic Development Strategies in the UAE**

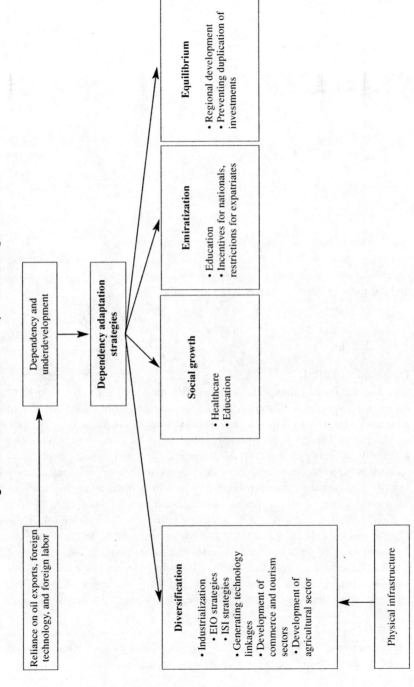

age the transmission and domestic substitution of foreign technologies. Perhaps more significant, the UAE's commercial and tourist sectors have expanded considerably over this period. While not reducing dependency on foreign economies as such, these sectors have nevertheless greatly reduced the reliance on oil. Furthermore, although with understandably less impressive results, the agricultural sector has also grown, providing an additional non-oil-related contribution to the UAE's GDP, while of course providing greater food security. Finally, underpinning these developments has been the creation of a brand new physical infrastructure of roads, ports, industrial parks, and communications. Financed by the UAE's remaining oil wealth, this infrastructure continues to expand, facilitating fresh diversification opportunities and better ensuring a stable and prosperous postoil future. Thus, although the oil sector remains the greatest contributor to the UAE's GDP, accounting for somewhere between a quarter and a half of all exports,[246] and although the various diversifying sectors have periodically suffered bouts of sluggish growth,[247] the nonoil sector has nevertheless become extremely significant, especially given the small timescale and the region's comparative backwardness as late as the 1960s.

Social growth has been equally forthcoming, again of course aided by the UAE's massive oil-financed investments. A large number of schools and universities staffed by qualified and experienced teachers and lecturers have provided the UAE's youth with the highest standards of education, with small class sizes, and with excellent facilities. Similarly, the quantity of hospitals and medical centers has mushroomed over this short period, with the ever-increasing number of medical professionals ensuring low doctor-to-patient ratios and providing effective care for almost all conditions within the UAE. These accomplishments have therefore not only symbolized and consolidated the welfare state component of the rentier coalition, but also demonstrated the planners' clear commitment to human development in the UAE and the conception of an educated and strong Emirati population.

Although by comparison the emiratization of the labor force has met with only limited success, and the UAE remains as reliant as ever on foreign labor, there have been a number of promising signs, especially in recent years, that point to the much greater emiratization of managerial, professional, and high-level public sector positions in the very near future. Moreover, given that this has been an area of strategy that has not directly benefited from oil wealth, and indeed may have been hampered by financial incentives that have priced UAE nationals out of the market, these results have been far more difficult to achieve. Indeed, it would appear that the planners have been forced to adopt a multidimensional approach, relying not only on wealth inducements for locals and restrictive practices such as quotas and visa limitations for expatriates, but also on greater educational and motivational opportunities for the increasing numbers of UAE graduates. Certainly, by providing and sponsoring vocational courses, internships, and other professional training programs, the government has successfully begun to place far higher numbers of young UAE nationals than ever before into both public and private sector jobs, many of which previously required the expertise of expatriate workers.

In addition to these broad strategies, the relative flexibility of the UAE's federal system has allowed for the pursuit of differing substrategies, especially in the two largest and wealthiest emirates, Abu Dhabi and Dubai. Quite simply, Abu Dhabi's substantial oil wealth has engendered a more cautious diversification strategy based around heavy EOI industries that aim to maximize the emirate's comparative advantages of cheap energy and abundant natural resources. On the other hand, Dubai's rich history of commercial development and the entrepreneurial spirit of the ruling al-Maktum dynasty, coupled with more modest and depleting oil reserves, has instead promoted far more rapid and far truer diversification. Indeed, with an emphasis on smaller ISI industries largely unrelated to the oil sector and with the massive expansion of its commercial and tourist sectors, Dubai's nonoil sector has long since accounted for the vast bulk of the emirate's GDP. Crucially, these differing strategies are now regarded as complementary and mutually reinforcing, as Abu Dhabi's considerable wealth and heavy industries can continue to provide the UAE's financial backbone and support the other emirates, while Dubai's more diversified economy and strong commercial links can better promote the UAE internationally and can better contribute to the emiratization strategy by providing more varied and appropriate employment opportunities for UAE nationals. Thus, far from conflicting, the UAE's substrategies may become a vital factor in ensuring successful future socioeconomic development.

Finally, however, a number of critical development problems have periodically surfaced and in some cases have remained unresolved. Indeed, despite the planners' best efforts, the UAE has remained heavily oriented toward consumption rather than production, with a resulting trade imbalance and a declining balance of payments. Furthermore, despite the evidence of increasing cooperation between Abu Dhabi and Dubai, there has also been the highly visible duplication of projects in the different emirates, with expensive and unnecessary developments often taking place in adjacent territories, many of which have remained underutilized and empty. Third, there has been the continuing concern of regional disequilibrium, with the wealth and development gap between the oil-producing emirates and the other emirates remaining almost as great as it was thirty years ago. In much the same way as the plans for emiratization, these have not been problems that can easily be addressed by greater investment and oil-financed development projects. Instead, given their nature, it would appear that a number of internal pathologies must be responsible, perhaps stemming from the primarily allocative nature of the state, the persistent consumerist mentality of the rentier population, the lack of interemirate coordination, the absence of effective interdepartmental cooperation, and presumably, on occasion, the mismanagement of resources and a lack of transparency. Thus the next chapter will focus on these more deeply entrenched disadvantages of what would appear to be the UAE's inherited and reinforced dependent circumstances. Indeed, both present and future attempts to modify features of the socioeconomic development path will continue to be undermined by the hidden costs of the UAE's ruling bargain, its political instability, and the persistence of traditional forces.

## Notes

1. For a discussion of orthodox economic development theories, see ARNDT (1987).

2. For a discussion of economic nationalism, see HARRIS (1987).

3. AMIN (1982), pp. 56–78, summarized in SHARABI (1988), pp. 133–135.

4. Regarding the collapse in oil prices in the mid-1980s, see PRADO (1996). Also, for a discussion of the continuing trend toward austerity measures in Saudi Arabia, see U.S. EMBASSY TO SAUDI ARABIA (1999).

5. For a more recent example, see KHALEEJ TIMES (2001) for a report on Hussain Abdullah (the former undersecretary for Arab and international Affairs at the Ministry of Petroleum in Egypt) speaking in May 2001 to the Dubai Cultural and Scientific Association: "Another major threat is the Kyoto Protocol which aims to decrease the intensity of carbon dioxide in the air because 50 years down the road it might lead to an unbearable increase in the earth's temperature and might cause disasters. If the industrialised countries signed this protocol, they might be forced to rationalise the consumption of power and look for alternatives, because oil production increases the quantity of $CO_2$ in the air."

6. For a more recent example, see LOCKWOOD (1996) for a discussion of the emerging oil-producing Central Asian states.

7. KHALEEJ TIMES (2001).

8. UAE CENTRAL BANK (1994).

9. Combined Abu Dhabi and Dubai foreign assets would appear to total around $395 billion. See "Substrategies: Abu Dhabi and Dubai—A Comparative Analysis," p. 154 in this volume, for a more detailed breakdown.

10. Personal interview with a representative of the research studies department in the Dubai Chamber of Commerce and Industry, December 2001.

11. It must also be remembered, however, that at this time "industrialization" was very much a buzz-word in Arab states, and with many of the UAE's development plans being drawn up by Egyptian expatriates it is important not to overemphasize the significance of these early industrial laws. Personal interviews with Frauke Heard-Bey, Abu Dhabi, January 2004.

12. AL-SHAMSI (1999), pp. 83–84.

13. Personal interview with a representative of the research studies department in the Dubai Chamber of Commerce and Industry, December 2001.

14. KAMRAVA (2000), pp. 42–43.

15. Personal interview with a representative of the research studies department in the Dubai Chamber of Commerce and Industry, December 2001.

16. FENELON (1973), p. 70.

17. AL-SHAMSI (1999), pp. 86–89.

18. GCC DEVELOPMENT PLANS: UNITED ARAB EMIRATES (1982), p. 50.

19. Personal interviews with Frauke Heard-Bey, Abu Dhabi, January 2004.

20. ECONOMIST INTELLIGENCE UNIT (2000), p. 30. See also OXFORD BUSINESS GROUP (2000), pp. 54–55. The second phase of the project will involve an underwater pipeline from Oman to Pakistan.

21. ECONOMIST INTELLIGENCE UNIT (2000), p. 33.

22. These include the Abu Dhabi Polymers Company (Borouge) and ADNOC's partner chemicals firm Borealis. See OXFORD BUSINESS GROUP (2000), pp. 90–91.

23. See EL-SABA (2002).

24. AL-SHAMSI (1999), p. 88.

25. A prime example being Portland Cement (with nine factories across the UAE and a tenth under construction in Ra's al-Khaimah). See OXFORD BUSINESS GROUP (2000), pp. 90–91.

26. GCC DEVELOPMENT PLANS: UNITED ARAB EMIRATES (1982), p. 17.

27. DUBAI DEPARTMENT OF ECONOMIC DEVELOPMENT (2001), p. 110. Imports valued at fixed 1995 prices.

28. A good example is the Sharjah-based London Dairy. As an ice cream manufacturer and packager, the firm originally licensed British technology, but in recent years has substituted domestic technology.

29. UAE MINISTRY OF PLANNING (2001), p. 44. All calculations based on figures for 2001 and at current prices.

30. U.S. CENTRAL INTELLIGENCE AGENCY (2001c). For 1997 estimates on industrial growth; some recent estimates put the industrial production growth rate in the local nonoil manufacturing sector at close to zero.

31. See BANNOCK, BAXTER, and DAVIS (1992), p. 438, for a definition of *value added*.

32. KAMRAVA (2000), p. 43.

33. AL-SHAMSI (1999), pp. 83–87.

34. PECK (1986), p. 111; and MIDDLE EAST ECONOMIC DIGEST, (1984), p. 73.

35. EL-DIN (1997), pp. 120–123. As el-Din argues, another aspect of these local joint ventures has been to encourage strategic alliances with multinationals, and given that these projects and their financial gains are output based, this has led to such companies developing a vested interest in the future security and stability of the UAE.

36. Ibid.

37. Ibid.

38. FOLEY (1998). Also see KEMP (1997); JANE'S DEFENCE WEEKLY (1997); and BLANCHE (1997).

39. OXFORD BUSINESS GROUP (2000), p. 60.

40. AL-SHARHAN INTERNATIONAL CONSULTANCY (2000), pp. 29–30.

41. ECONOMIST INTELLIGENCE UNIT (2000), p. 35.

42. OXFORD BUSINESS GROUP (2000), pp. 60–61.

43. ABU DHABI PLANNING DEPARTMENT, ECONOMIC DIVISION (1976), pp. 21–22.

44. GCC DEVELOPMENT PLANS: UNITED ARAB EMIRATES (1982), p. 46.

45. ECONOMIST INTELLIGENCE UNIT (2000), p. 28.

46. ABU DHABI PLANNING DEPARTMENT, ECONOMIC DIVISION (1976), pp. 21–22.

47. Interview with Sulayman Khalaf, Dubai, April 2001; and personal interviews, Al-'Ayn, April 2001.

48. FENELON (1973), pp. 46–50.

49. PECK (1986), p. 107.

50. UAE MINISTRY OF AGRICULTURE AND FISHERIES (2001e), p. 75.

51. UAE MINISTRY OF AGRICULTURE AND FISHERIES (2001d), p. 78.

52. UAE MINISTRY OF AGRICULTURE AND FISHERIES (2001b), p. 80.

53. See "The Traditional Economic Structure," p. 5 in this volume.

54. UAE MINISTRY OF AGRICULTURE AND FISHERIES (2001c), p. 83.

55. See "Domestic Pathologies," p. 185 in this volume.

56. RAO (2002), quoting Sa'id al-Raqabani, minister of agriculture and fisheries, speaking at the second GCC Food Security Conference in early 2002.

57. CROWN PRINCE COURT, DEPARTMENT OF RESEARCH AND STUDIES (1996), pp. 31, 76. The number of agricultural workers in the UAE rose from 23,156 in 1975 to 67,500 in 1995.

58. GCC DEVELOPMENT PLANS: UNITED ARAB EMIRATES (1982), p. 56. Ali Abdulsalam recognized that unless such development took place, then the UAE's small geographic and demographic size would restrict the potential market capacity and restrain the growth of any domestic industries, thereby short-circuiting the UAE's overall diversification strategy. Also see GCC DEVELOPMENT PLANS: UNITED ARAB EMIRATES (1982), pp. 18–19; and CROWN PRINCE COURT, DEPARTMENT OF RESEARCH AND STUDIES (1996), p. 26; data provided by UAE Central Bank Economic Bulletins for 1979, 1982, 1987, and 1992; by the UAE Ministry of Planning Statistical Abstracts 1975–1995; and by the UAE Ministry of Finance and Industry.

59. DUBAI DEPARTMENT OF ECONOMIC DEVELOPMENT (1999), p. 257.

60. Ibid., p. 247.

61. Ibid., p. 221.

62. See http://www.mydsf.com for the official Dubai Shopping Festival (and Dubai Summer Surprises) website.

63. Personal interviews, Dubai, March 2001 and March 2002.

64. See http://www.mydsf.com.

65. Personal interviews, Sharjah, December 2001.

66. DUBAI DEPARTMENT OF PORTS AND CUSTOMS (2002), p. 109. Values for nonoil foreign trade given at fixed 1995 prices.

67. The 169 percent increase in volume is calculated from 1980 to 2001, as 1975 remains unavailable. DUBAI DEPARTMENT OF PORTS AND CUSTOMS (2002), p. 109.

68. Ibid. Imports currently account for around 75 percent of the total value of nonoil trade.

69. Ibid.

70. Personal interview with a representative of the research studies department in the Dubai Chamber of Commerce and Industry, December 2001.

71. DUBAI DEPARTMENT OF ECONOMIC DEVELOPMENT (2001), pp. 167, 172. Figures for 1985–1994 supplied by the UAE Ministry of Planning; figures for 1995–1998 supplied by the Dubai Department of Economic Development; and figures for 1999 onward supplied by the Dubai Department of Tourism and

Commerce Marketing.
    72. Ibid.
    73. Personal interviews with representatives of the Radisson, Metropolitan, and Le Méridien hotel chains, Dubai, December 2001 and October 2002.
    74. DUBAI DEPARTMENT OF ECONOMIC DEVELOPMENT (2001), p. 167. Figures supplied by the Dubai Department of Tourism and Commerce Marketing.
    75. Personal interview, Dubai Hilton Creek, December 2001, following the hotel's opening.
    76. DUBAI DEPARTMENT OF ECONOMIC DEVELOPMENT (2001), p. 171. Figures supplied by the Dubai Department of Tourism and Commerce Marketing.
    77. Ibid., p. 172.
    78. See UAE MINISTRY OF PLANNING (1995).
    79. See "Cultural and Religious Resources," p. 77 in this volume. Unlike Dubai and Abu Dhabi, which attract Western luxury tourists, Sharjah predominately attracts Russian and eastern European tourists. Indeed, during the 1980s many tourists from the Soviet Union would travel to Sharjah to purchase luxury goods in the Al-Wahda street district.
    80. Jebel Hafit is a natural beauty spot in the mountains close to Al-'Ayn.
    81. Le Méridien Aqabar Beach stands close to Dibba. Its restaurants and bars benefit enormously from alcohol prohibition in the nearby Sharjah-administered town of Khor Fakkan.
    82. See TRIDENT GUIDE (1996).
    83. Between 2001 and 2003, 'Ajman's seafront was extensively redeveloped with a long corniche and an extended beach.
    84. See, in this volume, "The Judiciary and Related Institutions," p. 211, and "The UAE's Banking Sector and the Central Bank," p. 212.
    85. AL-SHARHAN INTERNATIONAL CONSULTANCY (2000), p. 61.
    86. FENELON (1973), p. 18.
    87. PECK (1986), p. 51.
    88. FENELON (1973), p. 18.
    89. PECK (1986), p. 66.
    90. Personal interviews, Dubai, March 2001.
    91. Dnata is the cargo-handling branch of Emirates Airways.
    92. DUBAI DEPARTMENT OF ECONOMIC DEVELOPMENT (2001), p. 257. Since the early 1990s, the village's total cargo-handling tonnage has risen almost fourfold.
    93. AL-JANDALY (2003). Dubai's rapid rail transit system will be completed by 2010 and will ease the strain on Dubai's roads by providing fast links to the city center, to the border with Sharjah, and to Jebel Ali.
    94. DUBAI DEPARTMENT OF ECONOMIC DEVELOPMENT (2001), p. 243.
    95. ECONOMIST INTELLIGENCE UNIT (2000), p. 18.
    96. Large lease office buildings can be seen close to the entrances of the Jebel Ali Free Zone southwest of Dubai. They provide ready-made office space for new firms at an affordable rent.
    97. Personal interviews with Frauke Heard-Bey, Abu Dhabi, January 2004.
    98. DUBAI DEPARTMENT OF ECONOMIC DEVELOPMENT (1999), p. 241.
    99. DUBAI DEPARTMENT OF ECONOMIC DEVELOPMENT (2002), p. 255.
    100. ECONOMIST INTELLIGENCE UNIT (2000), p. 5.
    101. Indeed, as Enver Khoury explains, "The UAE does not consider education as a mere public service to be provided to citizens but as a productive investment that yields a return in the future." See KHOURY (1980), p. 75.

102. GCC DEVELOPMENT PLANS: UNITED ARAB EMIRATES (1982), p. 10.

103. See, for example, WAM (2001a).

104. UAE MINISTRY OF INFORMATION AND CULTURE (1995), p. 97, taken from a speech by Sa'id 'Ahmad Ghubash, minister of economy and commerce.

105. GCC DEVELOPMENT PLANS: UNITED ARAB EMIRATES (1982), pp. 18–19.

106. UNDP-UAE (2000c).

107. UNESCO (2001). Literacy rates rose from 81.8 percent in 1987 to 91.1 percent in 2001 for fifteen- to twenty-four-year-olds.

108. UNESCO (2000, 2001), regarding the net enrollment ratios (the percentage of children of the relevant age attending school).

109. UAE MINISTRY OF EDUCATION AND YOUTH (2001a, 2001b, 2001c); figures for government sector schools taken from ratios published on p. 199, ratios for private sector schools calculated from teacher and student totals listed on pp. 208–209.

110. UNESCO (1998, 1999), regarding the net enrollment ratio (based on a five-year age group following the secondary school–leaving age).

111. GCC DEVELOPMENT PLANS: UNITED ARAB EMIRATES (1982), pp. 62–63. The planners foresaw this challenge in the early 1970s: "The health care system would primarily face difficulties in setting up the best programmes to suit the changing conditions of society which will result from the large increase in the volume and type of expatriate population."

112. CROWN PRINCE COURT, DEPARTMENT OF RESEARCH AND STUDIES (1996), p. 95. Figures are for Abu Dhabi emirate.

113. UAE MINISTRY OF HEALTH and DUBAI DEPARTMENT OF MEDICAL SERVICES (2001f, 2001g), pp. 185–186. Figures include pharmacists.

114. UAE MINISTRY OF HEALTH and DUBAI DEPARTMENT OF MEDICAL SERVICES (2001b), p. 188.

115. WORLD HEALTH ORGANIZATION (2002).

116. UAE MINISTRY OF HEALTH and DUBAI DEPARTMENT OF MEDICAL SERVICES (2001b), p. 188.

117. U.S. CENSUS BUREAU (2002).

118. See "The Traditional Social Structure," p. 10 in this volume.

119. ABEIDOH (2000). Calculations based on quoted figures.

120. DUBAI MUNICIPALITY (1999), p. 133. With regard to Dubai the survey indicated that 17 percent of households were local, 8.9 percent were nonlocal Arab, 3.2 percent were European, 41.9 percent were Asian, with the remaining 29 percent of the population composed of collective laborers (based in labor camps).

121. ABEIDOH (2000).

122. Ibid.

123. CROWN PRINCE COURT, DEPARTMENT OF RESEARCH AND STUDIES (1996), p. 95.

124. Ibid.

125. See ABDULLA (1985), p. 213; and ANTHONY (1975), p. 115.

126. ANTHONY (1975), p. 114.

127. For a further discussion of the demographic problem, see BILAL (1990).

128. ABU DHABI PLANNING DEPARTMENT, ECONOMIC DIVISION (1976), pp. 14–16.

129. GCC DEVELOPMENT PLANS: UNITED ARAB EMIRATES (1982), p. 17.

130. AL-SHARHAN INTERNATIONAL CONSULTANCY (2000), p. 54.

131. PECK (1986), p. 68.

132. UAE MINISTRY OF PLANNING (2002e), p. 25.

133. Calculated from official figures reported in GULF NEWS (2002).

134. FINDLOW (2000), p. 34.

135. See "The Impact of Globalizing Forces on Contemporary Society and Culture," p. 262 in this volume.

136. Personal interviews, Dubai, 2001–2002; Abu Dhabi, 2001; and Sharjah, 2001–2002.

137. PECK (1986), p. 72.

138. 'AHMAD (2003), reporting the findings of Ali Harjan, a leading Sharjah-based psychologist.

139. HEARD-BEY (1982), p. 252.

140. See HAWLEY (1970), p. 212, for details on Article 14 of the 1937 agreement with PDTC.

141. HAWLEY (1970), p. 212.

142. FENELON (1973), p. 98.

143. Ibid., pp. 98, 100–101.

144. ABU DHABI PLANNING DEPARTMENT, ECONOMIC DIVISION (1976), p. 14.

145. AL-MUSHARRAKH (2000), quoting Jassim al-Banay, Al-Futtaim's "emiratization manager."

146. WAM (2001a).

147. LANGLEY (2000).

148. BUSINESS IN DUBAI (2001c), p. 26.

149. BIBBO (2002), as explained by Khazraji, undersecretary of the Ministry of Labor and Social Affairs.

150. AL-SHARHAN INTERNATIONAL CONSULTANCY (2000), pp. 12–13.

151. LANGLEY (2000).

152. See, for example, RIZVI (2000), quoting A. Abdulrazzaq, the director of fisheries in the Ministry of Agriculture and Fisheries and head of the Fishing Regulations Committee, speaking to the *Khaleej Times* about the ministry's plans.

153. AL-SHARHAN INTERNATIONAL CONSULTANCY (2000), pp. 12–13.

154. Ibid.

155. ECONOMIST INTELLIGENCE UNIT (2000), p. 5. Also, with regard to the 2002 amnesty, see BUSINESS MONITOR INTERNATIONAL (2003b), p. 8.

156. Personal correspondence, June 2003.

157. AL-SHAMSI (1999), pp. 83–84.

158. ECONOMIST INTELLIGENCE UNIT (2000), p. 14.

159. Personal interviews, Dubai, April 2002.

160. BUSINESS IN DUBAI (2002a), p. 2, quoting from Humaid al-Qutami, general manager of EIBFS.

161. U.S. DEPARTMENT OF STATE (2001), sec. 1(e).

162. KHALEEJ TIMES (2001), from a lecture at the Zayed Centre for Coordination and Follow-Up by Muhammad bin Nakhera al-Dhahiri, the minister of justice, Islamic affairs, and the Awqaf (an institution to collect donated wealth and supplement Islamic expenditure).

163. See "The Relationship Between Federal and Emirate-Level Structures," p. 199 in this volume.

164. Personal interview with a representative of the research studies department in the Dubai Chamber of Commerce and Industry, December 2001. The UAE holds around 9.3 percent of the world's proven oil reserves, and of this Abu Dhabi

accounts for 90 percent, Dubai for around 5 percent, and the other emirates for much smaller shares. The Oxford Business Group reported in 2000 that Dubai's reserves would last for another ten to fourteen years at current rates of production. See OXFORD BUSINESS GROUP (2000), p. 47.

165. MIDDLE EAST ECONOMIC DIGEST (1994), p. 14.

166. The Samsung-ADIA complex close to the British embassy will be completed in 2005, easily eclipsing the Hilton's Burj Baynunah to become Abu Dhabi's tallest building.

167. In 2000 the Oxford Business Group estimated ADIA's investments to be in the region of $150 billion. See OXFORD BUSINESS GROUP (2000), p. 47. Also see p. 43, where it is estimated that 60 percent of this $150 billion is believed to be invested in equity markets in the developed world, with the remainder invested in the emerging markets of Southeast Asia.

168. OXFORD BUSINESS GROUP (2000), p. 43. The information regarding the Panamanian "Financiera Avenida" was gathered from personal interviews, undisclosed locations, 2003.

169. OXFORD BUSINESS GROUP (2000), p. 31.

170. ECONOMIST INTELLIGENCE UNIT (2000), p. 47.

171. HAWLEY (1970), pp. 241–242.

172. THESIGER (1991), p. 262. Thesiger is describing his reaction upon arriving in Abu Dhabi from Sulaiyil in 1950.

173. Aerial photographs of the preoil era are held in Shaikh Sa'id al-Maktum House in Shindagha, Dubai.

174. MANNAN (2001): "The impressiveness of Dubai's skyline has been generating encomiums from near and far in recent times, especially after the opening of the Burj al-Arab and Emirates Towers."

175. PECK (1986), p. 109.

176. JOYCE (1999), pp. 48–49, with particular reference to Shaikh Shakhbut al-Nuhayyan.

177. HEARD-BEY (1982), pp. 189–191.

178. AL-JUM'A SUPPLEMENT (1981), p. 11, quoting D. K. Chaudhry, the general manager of the Sharaf Shipping Agency.

179. ABDULLAH (1978), p. 104. Also see HEARD-BEY (1982), p. 243, where the considerable tax exemptions in Dubai are described, with 200 boats and 4,000 men being exempt from customs duties.

180. AL-JUM'A SUPPLEMENT (1981), quoting D. K. Chaudhry, the general manager of the Sharaf Shipping Agency.

181. ABDULLAH (1978), p. 104. Abdullah mistakenly refers to this traveler as Burckhart, a Swissman. It was in fact Burchardt, a German, who was most notable for his writings on Yemen, where he was in fact ambushed and killed shortly before World War I. Personal interviews with Frauke Heard-Bey, January 2004.

182. HEARD-BEY (1982), pp. 189–191.

183. AMIN (1978), pp. 84–85.

184. HEARD-BEY (1982), p. 245.

185. ANTHONY (2002), p. 82.

186. See "Britain and the Path to Federation," p. 41 in this volume.

187. HEARD-BEY (1982), p. 265.

188. See "The Traditional Economic Structure," p. 5 in this volume; GREEN (1968), p. 171; HAWLEY (1970), p. 205; and OXFORD BUSINESS GROUP (2000), p. 45. Following India's independence, the New Delhi government chose to levy duties on gold, thereby boosting Dubai's attractiveness as a gold market and establish-

ing the emirate as a base for informal gold trading with the subcontinent.

189. AL-JUM'A SUPPLEMENT (1981), quoting D. K. Chaudhry, the general manager of the Sharaf Shipping Agency.

190. For a limited discussion of this subject, see OXFORD BUSINESS GROUP (2000), p. 21.

191. UAE MINISTRY OF PLANNING (2001), p. 44. GDP for 2000 calculated at 1995 prices.

192. UAE MINISTRY OF FINANCE AND INDUSTRY (2001).

193. This poor performance has also been blamed on the absence of an official stock market and the lack of official trading. See ABU DHABI ECONOMY (1999), pp. 17–18.

194. AL-SHARHAN INTERNATIONAL CONSULTANCY (2001), pp. 14–15.

195. BUSINESS MONITOR INTERNATIONAL (1997), pp. 5–6.

196. See "The Relationship Between Federal and Emirate-Level Structures," p. 199 in this volume, for an account of Dubai's troubled federal budget contributions.

197. EVERETT-HEATH and DUTTA (2002), pp. 27–30, quoting Jamal Sanad al-Suwaidi of the Emirates Centre for Strategic Studies and Research.

198. Ibid.

199. Ibid. Corroborated with personal interviews, Dubai Chamber of Commerce and Industry, December 2001; and Al-Maktum Institute of Dundee, July 2002.

200. EVERETT-HEATH and DUTTA (2002), pp. 27–30.

201. ECONOMIST INTELLIGENCE UNIT (2000), pp. 4–5.

202. See HARRIS (1987) for a discussion of "economic nationalism" and economic development theories.

203. BUSINESS MONITOR INTERNATIONAL (1997), pp. 5–6.

204. See "Modifying Dependent Development," p. 119 in this volume.

205. GCC DEVELOPMENT PLANS: UNITED ARAB EMIRATES (1982), p. 15.

206. ABDULLA (1985), p. 192.

207. CROWN PRINCE COURT, DEPARTMENT OF RESEARCH AND STUDIES (1996), p. 32.

208. Ibid., pp. 32, 76.

209. DUBAI DEPARTMENT OF ECONOMIC DEVELOPMENT (2002), p. 114; imports valued at fixed 1995 prices. Also see GCC DEVELOPMENT PLANS: UNITED ARAB EMIRATES (1982), p. 15.

210. GCC DEVELOPMENT PLANS: UNITED ARAB EMIRATES (1982), pp. 15, 46. A number of restrictions on spending were proposed but none were implemented.

211. For such a discussion, see ABU BAKER (1995), pp. 176–177. In particular, Abu Baker describes how the Abu Dhabi Chamber of Commerce and Industry persuaded the UAE Central Bank to lower the payments required for letters of credit: although reluctant, the central bank caved in to the pressure.

212. See, in this volume, "Patrimonial Networks," p. 73, and "Rentierism," p. 87.

213. AL-SHAMSI (1999a), p. 4.

214. AL-SHAMSI (1999), pp. 83–84. Also see ABDULLA (1985), p. 240.

215. BROWN (1998), p. 360.

216. OVERTON (1983), p. 184, taken from Overton's interview with Sa'id 'Ahmad Ghubash in Abu Dhabi in 1976.

217. PECK (1986), p. 100.

218. In 2002 the German carrier Lufthansa reduced its flights to Sharjah. Moreover, Lufthansa is now the only Western airline still serving the airport. Dubai's third terminal will open sometime in 2005.

219. It would appear from recent airport throughput statistics that Sharjah has become primarily an air freight hub. See OXFORD BUSINESS GROUP (2000), p. 111.

220. For details of the 5 November 2003 Emiri decree, see http://www.etihadairways.com.

221. Shaikh 'Ahmad bin Sa'id al-Maktum is the uncle of the present ruler, not to be confused with the fourth of Shaikh Rashid's sons, Shaikh 'Ahmad bin Rashid al-Maktum.

222. Personal interviews, Dubai, November 2003.

223. BROWN (1998), p. 359. Also see FEDERAL RESEARCH DIVISION (2003). It was believed that by 1987 Shaikh Sultan had amassed debts of nearly $920 million following several ambitious construction projects. On assuming power, Shaikh Abdul-Aziz made a news broadcast claiming that his brother had voluntarily stepped down due to economic mismanagement.

224. ABU DHABI PLANNING DEPARTMENT, ECONOMIC DIVISION (1976), p. 19.

225. RIZVI (1993), p. 666.

226. See AL-MUSFIR (1985), p. 136.

227. Personal interviews, Dubai Chamber of Commerce and Industry, December 2001. Also see AMIN (1982), p. 41, for a discussion of superexploitation.

228. GCC DEVELOPMENT PLANS: UNITED ARAB EMIRATES (1982), p. 17.

229. See "The Federation of Emirates," p. 45 in this volume.

230. RIZVI (1993), p. 665.

231. See "The Traditional Political Structure," p. 14 in this volume. With further reference to the comparative prosperity of the island during the pearling era, Dalma's three old mosques (most notably Meirikhi Mosque) in many ways symbolize the wealth that the community once enjoyed. Personal interviews with Peter Hellyer, Abu Dhabi, April 2004.

232. Personal interviews with an ADMA pilot, Abu Dhabi, August 2003.

233. FENELON (1973), p. 3.

234. Personal interviews with a resident of Dalma island, Abu Dhabi, January 2004.

235. HEARD-BEY (1982), p. 112.

236. OXFORD BUSINESS GROUP (2000), p. 113. Fujairah and Khor Fakkan's combined share of the UAE's port traffic fell from around 33 percent in 1996 to around 28 percent in 1998, while Dubai's rose from 59 percent to nearly 63 percent over the same period.

237. ECONOMIST INTELLIGENCE UNIT (2000), p. 28.

238. OXFORD BUSINESS GROUP (2000), p. 105.

239. CROWN PRINCE COURT, DEPARTMENT OF RESEARCH AND STUDIES (1996), p. 54, a comparison between 1975 and 1995.

240. Personal interviews, Abu Dhabi, March 2004.

241. VAN DER MEULEN (1997), pp. 69, 83.

242. See BUSINESS MONITOR INTERNATIONAL (2001).

243. KHALEEJ TIMES (2002a).

244. IBRAHIM (2002).

245. UNDP-UAE (2000a).

246. AL-SHARHAN INTERNATIONAL CONSULTANCY (2000), pp. 23–25. Al-Sharhan claims that 22 percent of GDP is accounted for by the oil sector. See U.S. CENTRAL INTELLIGENCE AGENCY (2001c), which claims 45 percent of

total exports are oil-related. See OXFORD BUSINESS GROUP (2000), p. 47, which claims that 30 percent of GDP is oil-related.

247. See ABU DHABI PLANNING DEPARTMENT, ECONOMIC DIVISION (1976), pp. 9, 18, for agricultural sector growth. See U.S. CENTRAL INTELLI-GENCE AGENCY (2001c) for 1997 estimates on industrial growth.

# 4

# Domestic Pathologies
# and the Political Process

While the United Arab Emirates has enjoyed moderately successful socioeconomic development since the 1970s, and while the planners have managed to reduce some of the most manifest weaknesses resulting from the UAE's dependency on oil, foreign technology, and foreign labor, there have however been a number of significant under-the-surface pathologies that have continued to undermine the development path. Certainly, as the previous chapter indicated, a number of readily identifiable development concerns would appear to have their roots in deeper and far more complex internal problems, perhaps connected to the allocative nature of the rentier state, the domestic political process, the lack of interemirate coordination, the lack of interdepartmental cooperation, the need for greater transparency, and the interaction of conflicting interest groups. Crucially, without contradicting the growing economic neoliberal emphasis on internal factors shaping development,[1] I seek in this chapter to demonstrate that such pathologies are in many ways by-products of the same reinvigorated traditional structures that allowed for the consolidation of the polity and the reinforcement of the dependent client elite in the first place. Indeed, I will show how many of these persisting complications can be seen as the hidden cost of the UAE's political stability and therefore the long-term price that must be paid in order to circumvent the shaikh's dilemma and escape the inevitability of the early modernization theories.

## Domestic Pathologies

A number of theoretical models have been devised in an effort to explain the relative impact of domestic pathologies in developing states, and elements of these can be readily applied to the UAE. First, in light of the various development problems discussed in the previous chapter, it is necessary to consider the inherent weaknesses of a political economy that is still by and large dominated and financed by oil—an allocative, subsidy-based, rentier state that is still able to rely primarily on hydrocarbon resources, and that therefore by definition lacks the impetus to build up the kind of productive sector so desperately needed by the development planners and the diversification strategists. Indeed, although there have been concerted attempts to create a multisector economy in the UAE, Giacomo Luciani, Ali Khalifa al-Kuwari, and other scholars have argued convincingly that such efforts will ultimately always be limited, as developing a domestic nonoil economic base in many ways still represents something of a bonus rather than a necessity for such states:

> Growth in the domestic economy is one of the various luxuries that the state can buy with its oil income in one case, it is an essential precondition for its existence and survival in others. . . . [T]he strengthening of the domestic economic base may be included, but not necessarily so. Even if this happens to be one of the goals of the state. . . . [T]he strengthening of the domestic economy is not reflected in the income of the state, and is therefore not a precondition for the existence and expansion of the state.[2]

As demonstrated, despite improvements in import-substitution industrialization, hydrocarbon resources are still behind many of the UAE's manufacturing activities, especially in Abu Dhabi, as many plants remain geared toward heavy export-oriented plants reliant on cheap energy.[3] Similarly, the agricultural sector continues to rely heavily on government subsidies (providing ready-made farms, equipment, irrigation, etc.),[4] which are of course a luxury that can only be afforded by an oil-rich allocative state. Moreover, as also explained in the previous chapter, allocated wealth has indirectly hindered the emiratization drive, as UAE nationals have been priced out of the market and in many cases have been stripped of incentives to enter the work force.[5]

Related to this employment issue, given that the vast bulk of the privileges and rewards described in the analysis of the UAE's legitimacy formula are directly reliant on rentier subsidies, the problem can in fact be reduced all the way down to the level of individual UAE nationals. With free housing and healthcare, nationals are provided with a constant safety net; with generous marriage funds, nationals are no longer required to resource huge dowry payments of their own; with entirely free higher education, nationals are not required to perform any kind of cost benefit analysis with regard to their future careers; with extremely favorable loans and business sponsorship systems, nationals can emerge unscathed from private sector misadventures;[6] and of course with purchasing power being artificially high given the lack of any major financial demands such as income tax or accommodation costs, the UAE's most popular leisure activity, shopping, has led to a heavily dominant consumption culture. Thus, while rentierism has provided great wealth, has allowed for social growth, and would seem to have engendered much needed stability, in many other instances the phenomenon has either created or done little to curb long-term development problems. In effect, citizenship in the UAE has become a financial asset, thus removing any need for meaningful and productive service. Given the enormous human impact of rentierism, this particular pathology must therefore be seen as all-encompassing: a malaise that both directly and indirectly effects almost all aspects of development in the UAE, and that must be kept in mind, at least in the background, when considering the country's various other shortcomings.

Building upon these implications, and of course again related to the earlier discussion of the survival of traditional monarchy and the polity's increased reliance on patrimonial networks alongside seemingly modern institutional structures, another important starting point would be the neopatrimonial model of pathologies. There is little doubt that the ruling families continue to dominate the UAE's political system, continue to control the highest offices of state, and, significantly, administer the bulk of the state's allocated wealth. It would seem reasonable, therefore, to hypothesize that patrimonial elites direct policy formulation while the more modern bureaucracies simply act as augmentations of the patrimonial network and as tools for policy implementation. In this scenario

> the bureaucracy is turned into an extension of a self-serving patrimonial elite which provides no coherent or dynamic administrative leadership. Particularistic distrust prevents the delegation of authority, stifles initiative, and frustrates teamwork and the co-ordination of functions. The chain of command is unreliable: legal prerogatives of office may give little real authority where power derives from personal connections and loyalties or legal commands are short-circuited by "personal fiefdoms."[7]

Indeed, Raymond Hinnebusch summarizes how such a neopatrimonial political process and the resulting pathologies can greatly affect development policy:

> Development policy is subverted by a patrimonial strategy of control in which economic rationality is subordinated to the creation of clienteles, co-optation, and payoffs of potential opposition. In such an uninstitutionalised regime, instability and fragmentation paralyse or induce swings in policy, rendering it incoherent, and effective instruments of policy implementation are wholly lacking. In short, state policy, put in the service of narrow group interests, is "irrational" from the point of view of the larger society.[8]

Thus, given this hybrid of traditional groups and new institutions, one would expect to find considerable competition between the various patrimonial elites and their clients over policymaking and the management of the state's resources.[9] Moreover, one would expect to uncover a system far removed from the Weberian ideals of legal-rational priorities, issues, and procedures, and therefore a political process likely to significantly impede and slow socioeconomic development.

Furthermore, the neopatrimonial expansion of the UAE's bureaucracies may also lead to the emergence of self-interested bureaucratic interest groups whose members may seek to secure themselves and their careers as well as consolidating the future of their particular institution within the hybrid political network. Certainly, as Fred Riggs has argued, such a behavioral pattern may lead to additional pathologies as bureaucracies and their staffs pursue irrational motives in an effort to further their own interests rather than those of greater society or indeed even the patrimonial elites.[10]

Finally, while such models may be able to highlight the particularistic struggles that can take place within neopatrimonial structures, they do not take into account the actual nature and complexity of the elite's orientation at the apex of this system.[11] Indeed, as Immanuel Wallerstein noted in the 1970s, such elites cannot always be viewed as homogeneous entities pursuing the narrow interests of patrimonial politics, as they will very often have conflicting economic interests, with some favoring an "open" economy while others favor some form of protection.[12] Certainly, with new generations of Western-educated and professional technocrats, many of whom control big businesses and are now beginning to gain positions of high office, the UAE's patrimonial elite and, in Hisham Sharabi's more Marxist terminology, its "dominant rentier class,"[13] is becoming distinctly heterogeneous, with a clear divide emerging between those conservatives seeking to perpetuate oil-derived rentier wealth and those "new rentier" reformers attempting to liberalize the economy in order to exploit fresh sources of economic rent. Thus, recognition of these domestic elite interest groups and their differing development priorities and preferences must form another crucial layer of understanding.

## The Federal Decisionmaking Structure

At the federal level, the UAE's decisionmaking structure comprises a split executive, with a "president for life" chairing a supreme council of the various hereditary rulers, and a prime minister presiding over an appointed council of government ministers. Underneath this executive operates a unicameral (and supposedly legislative) council comprising selected representatives from the seven emirates. As one might expect, given the described neopatrimonial model, the powerful executive is almost entirely dominated by members of the ruling families and representatives of other notable Emirati families; and, most important, it is largely unrestrained by the weak and ineffective legislature, which has primarily served as an optional consultative body allowing for the limited co-optation of other privileged families.

At the apex of this decisionmaking structure is the institution of the presidency, with the president acting as the head of state, representing the UAE in foreign relations, performing both procedural and ceremonial functions, and serving as an important bridge between the two executive bodies:

> [He] convenes meetings of the Supreme Council of Rulers. He also represents the UAE in foreign relations, supervises the implementation of federal laws and decrees. He appoints the Prime Minister with the approval of the Supreme Council of Rulers, and then selects the Council of Ministers with the approval of the Prime Minister. Perhaps most importantly, given his sole responsibility for calling joint meetings between the Supreme Council of Rulers and the Council of Ministers he plays a crucial role in linking the UAE's two highest political bodies.[14]

As Enver Khoury described in his study of the UAE's political system, this linking role has often allowed the president to balance and regulate conflicts within the political system, thus satisfying his monarchical need to reinforce personal legitimacy and his position at the center of patrimonial power.[15] Indeed, the presidency of the UAE is entirely synonymous with the traditional rulership of Abu Dhabi, the largest and wealthiest of the constituent emirates, with Shaikh Zayed al-Nuhayyan having been reelected to the position every five years by the six other rulers.[16] Moreover, with Abu Dhabi being by far the largest contributor to both the federal budget and the UAE's GDP,[17] this historical association of the presidency with the ruler of Abu Dhabi has now been informally accepted by the other emirates.[18] Thus, barring any major interemirate challenge or, as discussed in Chapter 2 regarding dynastic monarchies, any internal power struggle among the al-Nuhayyan family, it would seem likely that Shaikh Zayed's eldest son and crown prince, Shaikh Khalifa, will succeed as both ruler of Abu Dhabi and as president of the UAE. Accordingly, in much the same way that many of the republican Middle Eastern states have been described as "presidential monarchies," the UAE can be seen as having evolved into a "monarchical presidency," with a continuously reelected royal president.

Comprising the seven hereditary rulers, the Supreme Council of Rulers (SCR) is the UAE's highest federal authority, with the power to initiate policy, to review and reject laws passed by the ministerial government, to declare a state of "defensive war" or martial law, to admit new members to the federation, and to appoint or dismiss any civil servant including the judges of the federal supreme court, the prime minister, and even the president. Officially, the SCR's annual sessions last for eight months of the year, during which time four formal meetings are supposed to take place,[19] but, given that no constitutional provision exists for enforcing such regular meetings, these have often been infrequent. Indeed, over the years the rulers have generally preferred the ease of informal gatherings, and this essentially traditional process has often left major controversial issues in abeyance, sometimes even to the detriment of the national interest.[20] Moreover, while the SCR's procedural issues are in theory decided by a simple majority, with each of the seven members having a single vote, in the case of more substantive matters both the rulers of Abu Dhabi and Dubai in addition to at least three of the five other emirates must approve all decisions and ratifications. Thus, at this highest level, the UAE's formal political process serves to underscore the supremacy of Abu Dhabi and Dubai.[21] Finally, with regard to social formation, the SCR naturally remains the most exclusive of the UAE's political institutions, with its members having always been the seven respective emirs, all of whom are descendants of the "paramount shaikhs," or *tamima,* of the long-established tribal dynasties originally supported and favored under the British Trucial system. Indeed, Abu Dhabi is represented by Shaikh Zayed, the head of the al-Nuhayyan family, with Dubai represented by Shaikh Maktum al-Maktum, Sharjah and Ra's al-Khaimah represented by Shaikh Sultan and Shaikh Saqr (their respective Qawasim rulers), 'Ajman represented by Shaikh Humayd of the al-Na'im family, Umm al-Qawain represented by Shaikh Rashid of the al-'Ali family (the Mu'alla clan), and Fujairah represented by Shaikh Hamad of the Sharqiyin family.[22]

The Council of Ministers (COM) is effectively the UAE's formal cabinet, with its members responsible for most of the day-to-day running of the federation. Although clearly subordinate to the SCR, the COM is nevertheless responsible for formulating the bulk of the UAE's policies, and can initiate its own legislation after receiving ratification from the SCR. In addition, the COM approves the federal budget, oversees all public expenditure, and supervises all decrees, regulations, supreme court decisions, and international treaties.[23] Currently, there are nearly thirty members of this executive, including seventeen government ministers and five ministers of state, along with the president, the vice president, the prime minister (currently also the vice president), two deputy prime ministers, the governor of the central bank, and (on occasion), the UAE's permanent representative to the United Nations and the UAE's ambassador to the United States.[24]

Although each of the seven emirates is represented by at least one minister, the COM, in a fashion similar to that of the SCR, is also clearly structured in favor of Abu Dhabi and Dubai, with these considerably more affluent emirates controlling the most significant portfolios. Originally, six of the ministries were allotted to Abu Dhabi (including foreign affairs, interior, and information), while the premiership in addition to three other important ministries were given to Dubai (including defense and finance); three were given to Sharjah; two each were given to Ra's al-Khaimah and Fujairah; and one each was given to the smallest emirates, 'Ajman and Umm al-Qawain.[25] This composition of the cabinet was first negotiated in 1971 and was eventually formalized in 1996 when the constitution was finally made permanent. Thus, over the years the allotments have remained relatively unchanged, with the main additions having instead come from newly created cabinet posts for Shaikh Zayed's younger sons, including the previously discussed minister of state for the presidential office[26] and more recently with the appointment of a second deputy prime minister[27] (see Figure 4.1).

Conforming to the neopatrimonial model, the COM's social formation is perhaps best viewed as an extension of monarchical authority, with many of the ministerial posts being occupied by either key members of the various ruling families (around 40 percent of posts)[28] or by representatives of other long-established and powerful tribal families. Most obvious, in much the same way that the president's role is an overlapping one, the UAE's prime minister, Shaikh Maktum al-Maktum (as the ruler of Dubai and also the vice president), serves on both the COM and the SCR. Shaikh Muhammad al-Maktum, Dubai's crown prince, is also represented in the cabinet, serving as the minister of defense, as is his older brother, Shaikh Hamdan al-Maktum, who serves as the minister of finance and industry. In addition to Shaikh Zayed, Abu Dhabi's ruling family is well represented by

**Figure 4.1 Distribution of Ministerial Portfolios in the UAE**

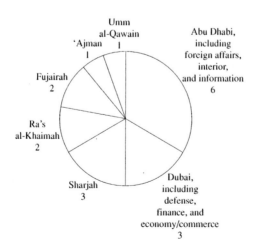

*Source:* Economist Intelligence Unit (2000), "United Arab Emirates," London, p. 7.

Shaikh Sultan al-Nuhayyan, the deputy prime minister; by Shaikh Hamdan al-Nuhayyan, the second deputy prime minister and the UAE's minister of state for foreign affairs (and the de facto foreign minister since the actual ministry is headed by a token 'Ajmani);[29] by Shaikh Nuhayyan al-Nuhayyan, the minister of higher education and scientific research; and by Shaikh Abdullah al-Nuhayyan, the minister of information and culture. Other royals currently include Sharjah's Shaikh Fahim al-Qasimi, who heads the Ministry of Economy and Commerce, and Umm al-Qawain's Shaikh Humayd al-Mu'alla, who serves as the UAE's minister of planning.[30] Examples of prominent nonroyal families serving in the COM have included Abu Dhabi's al-Dhaheri (the Dhawahir), the al-Suwaidi (the Sudan),[31] and the al-Otaibi.[32] Indeed, Muhammad al-Dhahiri currently heads the Ministry of Justice and Islamic Affairs while Muhammad al-Badi al-Dhahiri is the minister of interior. Sultan al-Suwaidi serves as the governor of the central bank,[33] and in the past 'Ahmad Khalifa al-Suwaidi was the UAE's first ever minister of foreign affairs,[34] with Manna Sa'id al-Otaibi having presided over the UAE's Ministry of Petroleum and Mineral Resources for many years,[35] and Otaibi bin Abdullah al-Otaibi having served as the minister of state for cabinet affairs until the mid-1970s.[36] Finally, however, as revealed in the earlier discussion of broader patrimonial networks and their contribution to the ruling bargain,[37] in recent years a number of ministerial posts have also been granted to members of other Emirati families, often those possessing both professional experience and overseas postgraduate education. Certainly, the number of these "technocrats" in the UAE's cabinet is steadily increasing and their expanding role in federal politics will be detailed later in this chapter.

The UAE's legislature, or more accurately its consultative chamber, consists of the unicameral forty-member Al-Majlis al-Watani lil-Ittihad, or Federal National Council (FNC). In 1971 it was quite naturally assumed that the relatively small local populations of the constituent emirates could be sufficiently represented by a few people chosen from among the leading merchant families and those tribal elders who had traditionally held the confidence of their people.[38] Thus, by consolidating the principle of *shura* (consultation), it was intended that the FNC would function as a contemporary federal majlis, offering the people direct democracy via respected intermediaries. Indeed, as Kevin Fenelon remarked soon after its creation, the FNC was certainly structured in such a way that it could raise local issues and debate all matters of public interest before the responsible ministers. Furthermore, in theory the FNC was to be informed of all government decisions, was to be able to ratify all international treaties signed by the UAE, and (to ensure the independence of its views) its members were to be excluded from all other public posts and ministerial portfolios.[39]

However, unlike the parliamentary legislatures normally associated with democracies, the FNC, in much the same way as the COM, has remained entirely appointive, with the seven rulers (and in the near future perhaps also their wives)[40] being required to select rather than elect the FNC representatives for their emirates.[41] Moreover, again resembling the COM, this selection procedure is further controlled so as to favor the two wealthiest emirates. Thus, while eight members each are chosen from Abu Dhabi and Dubai, only six members each are chosen from Sharjah and Ra's al-Khaimah (despite having larger populations of UAE nationals),[42] and just four each are chosen from the smaller emirates of Fujairah, 'Ajman, and Umm al-Qawain[43] (see Figure 4.2).

Regarding the social formation of the FNC, the institution's membership can again be interpreted as an attempt to incorporate representatives of prominent nonruling families into the neopatrimonial political process, even if they are granted little real authority. Certainly, as Fatma al-Sayegh has shown in her study of merchants in the UAE, these FNC members, especially those from Dubai, often represent the new generations of the merchant elite families who previously dominated the Trucial states.[44] Furthermore, in a fashion similar to that of the COM, there has also been an appreciable increase in the number of distinguished professionals (often from less well established families) serving as FNC members, and these technocrats are now even represented by the FNC's speaker, Muhammad al-Habtur.[45] Other recent examples would include Juma' Belhoul, Hussein al-Mutawa, and Tariq al-Tayir,[46] along with a number of other well-known businessmen, respected doctors, and experienced lawyers. Indeed, Dubai-based lawyer Muhammad al-Roken provides a typical example of the latter. Educated in the United Kingdom and having taught at the University of the

**Figure 4.2 Distribution of FNC Members**

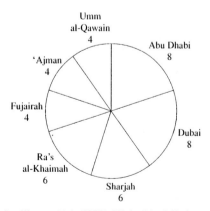

*Source:* Economist Intelligence Unit (2000), "United Arab Emirates," London, p. 7.

UAE in Al-'Ayn, al-Roken is a published researcher and academic in addition to practicing general commercial law in both local and federal courts.[47] Indubitably, such well established legal experts are seen as best placed for representing the individual emirates in a federal council that advises on pending draft legislation (see Figure 4.3).

It is also important to highlight the many weaknesses that are now increasingly associated with the FNC and the UAE's legislature. Quite apart from its nonelected membership and its inappropriateness for the UAE's ever expanding population, the original powers described by Fenelon have rarely been put into practice, often rendering the FNC a purely advisory body and more of a civilized "talking shop" than anything else, with its members limited to discussing and reviewing only the legislation referred to it by the COM.[48] Moreover, for the most part the FNC is seldom able to submit any of its reports directly to the president or the SCR; instead all queries and findings have to be referred to the relevant minister, thus locking it into a subordinate role underneath the COM.[49] Indeed, writing in the mid-1980s, Malcolm Peck had already noted how

> its real power is virtually nil because it does not initiate legislation but only offers recommendations on draft laws issued by the Council of Ministers, which is not, in turn, obliged to accept any of the FNC's proposals. Although the FNC may prove to be a useful exercise in developing political expertise and leadership and might someday provide the basis for a real legislature, it is now only a consultative institution and debating forum, entirely dominated by the Council of Ministers.[50]

There are, of course, occasions when the system has worked, and the FNC, often supported by special committees,[51] has managed to have its suggestions incorporated into government policy, but as the following recent case studies will suggest, the FNC's powers have continued to remain limited, with the council often unable to extract information on more substantive matters from the COM. Furthermore, when information is gathered and recommendations are made, often following serious delays, there appears to be little evidence of FNC proposals actually being implemented unless they reinforce existing government policy. Certainly at present there appears to be no official requirement or even precedent for the COM or the individual minister in question to address the FNC's concerns within a specific time frame, or indeed for them to reply at all.

## A Paralyzed Legislature?

First, the FNC's standard procedure normally follows a pattern whereby a member or a group of members will submit a query or request to the rest of the council. This will normally be concerned with a pressing matter that these

**Figure 4.3 The Decisionmaking Structure**

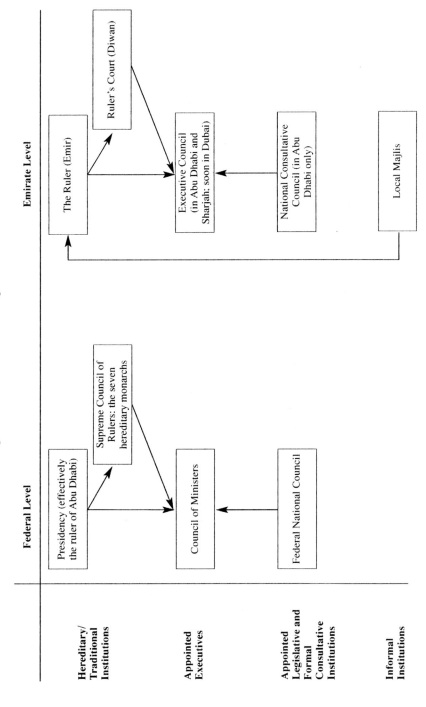

members wish to debate. Following approval from a majority of other FNC members, the matter can then be referred to the COM, usually in the form of a recommendation to the relevant federal minister. In theory, the minister should then promptly discuss the matter with the FNC or an appointed special committee of FNC members; if deemed necessary, the minister should then seek to initiate policy with the approval of his colleagues in the COM.

An example of this process is the July 1990 meetings of the FNC concerning the question of foreign real estate ownership in the UAE. A request was submitted to discuss government policy on this issue, culminating in an FNC recommendation to "prevent foreigners from owning real estate without fixed restrictions in an effort to preserve the UAE's resources in the interest of future generations." Unsurprisingly, given that the content of this recommendation was already a long-standing feature of government policy, the proposal was forwarded directly to the SCR.[52] Similarly, the FNC's March 1994 recommendation to uphold the UAE business statutes that require foreign ownership of businesses to be limited to 49 percent was entirely compatible with the aforementioned kafil sponsorship system,[53] another well established policy. Predictably, the recommendation was met with a swift and detailed response, with the relevant minister attending the FNC's discussion, demonstrating exactly how the ministry was tackling the problem, and agreeing to refer the FNC's concerns to the COM.[54] Also successful was the FNC's May 1993 proposal for greater investment in youth antidrug awareness. Closely related to the government's ongoing development of the Supreme Council for Youth and Sports, the proposal was forwarded to the SCR and the necessary policies were soon drawn up.[55]

However, with regard to more complicated matters requiring either the modification of existing legislation or the initiation of new policy, the FNC's recommendations and criticisms have not been so well received. A strong example would be the long-running FNC debate over the alarming size of the expatriate work force and the need for drastic new emiratization measures. Indeed, in 1990 a request was submitted to discuss the measures being taken by the Ministry of Labor and Social Affairs to address what was then believed to be a work force with a national composition of just 15 percent. This eventually took the form of a recommendation stating that the FNC's members accepted the continuing need for expatriate manpower, but that they were nevertheless alarmed by what appeared to be an "uncontrolled random increase." As such the COM needed to issue legislation forcing both public and private sector establishments to employ a portion of trained nationals as part of their work force.[56] Delayed by the Kuwaiti crisis, the debate was resumed in May 1991 with the FNC deciding to send several members to brief the prime minister on their renewed demands.[57] Given the previously discussed emiratization strategies, such strong demands were not completely in step with the government's more cautious approach to solving this sensitive problem,[58] resulting in the matter being temporarily shelved and little further interaction taking place between the FNC and the COM on the subject. Indeed, it was not until May 1994 that the minister of labor and social affairs finally attended an FNC discussion on the nationalization of labor, and it was not until January 1996, nearly six years after the original recommendation, that the FNC at last began to receive relevant draft legislation from the COM.[59] Another similar example of slow and ineffectual procedure would be the FNC's June 1993 request to discuss the performance of the Ministry of Information and Culture in improving the cultural content of mass media in the UAE. Although the minister attended the initial meeting and agreed to refer the matter to the COM, when in March 1994 the FNC remained dissatisfied with the ministry's progress, especially with regard to the lack of television programs relating to Emirati culture, the minister failed to attend the FNC's scheduled debate. Moreover, when the minister finally did attend in April 1994, he promised to provide the FNC with a detailed letter outlining all of the ministry's forthcoming television and radio projects, but it was not until April 1996, two years later, that the FNC actually received such a letter.[60]

The worst instances of FNC paralysis, however, have been those occasions when formal recommendations and requests have failed to elicit any response from the minister in question. As one might expect, this has often occurred regarding issues connected with substantive and highly sensitive matters such as national security, political reform, and oil policy.[61] While the FNC's abortive attempts to press for limited political reform will be considered in greater depth below, the recent oil-related requests provide another very clear insight into the FNC's subordinate relationship with the COM. In January 1994 a query was submitted by FNC members with regard to the distressing escalation of petrol prices in the UAE. In the normal manner, a request for information was presented to the minister of petroleum and mineral resources emphasizing the FNC's concern that petrol prices were much higher in the UAE than in any of the other GCC states. Moreover, the FNC requested that the ministry fully explain its plans for reducing the prices and eliminating the hardships faced by local businesses reliant on petrol products. Unable to bring the minister to question and unable to extract any information from the COM, despite following the established procedure, the FNC was forced to postpone its petrol-related questions indefinitely.[62]

## The Emirate-Level Decisionmaking Structure

At the emirate level, the rulers' courts, or diwan, preside over local governments, most of which possess their own civil services, economic affairs departments, public works departments, finance departments, and in some cases even their own oil departments, civil aviation authorities, and internal security organizations. Moreover, Abu Dhabi operates its own executive council, a sixteen-member organization chaired by the crown prince and made up of heads of Abu Dhabi local government departments, in addition to a national consultative council, which acts as a scaled down emirate-level version of the FNC.[63] Similarly, Sharjah also has an executive council comprising twenty-six nominated members of the ruling family and the local elite, which, as explained earlier, was formed in 1987 by the reinstated ruler following the coup leader's promise for greater political participation in the emirate.[64] Likewise, following the February 2003 announcements, Dubai will establish an executive council to supervise its large number of local government institutions.[65] Indeed, reflecting the emirate's greater diversification and the development of its nonoil sectors, there are unsurprisingly a number of additional government departments and authorities at the local level in Dubai. Among others, these include the aforementioned Department of Tourism and Commerce Marketing,[66] the Department of Ports and Customs, the Dubai Ports Authority, the Jebel Ali Free Zone Authority, the World Trade Center Association, and a Department for Economic Development.[67]

In addition to these formal emirate-level structures, the region's majalis, although originally an integral part of the traditional tribal hukumah and now perhaps less able to cope with the demands of large urban populations, nevertheless continue to provide an important informal consultative channel between the citizen and the ruler.[68] In fact, as the UAE's minister of information and culture explains, these majalis have, like the more modern institutions, tried to adapt to the country's needs and in some cases still serve as useful forums for raising topics of debate more directly affecting the individual and their specific emirate:

> Just as the modern institutions have developed in response to public need and demand, however, so the traditional forms of tribal administration have adapted. With many relatively routine matters now being dealt with by the modern institutions, so the traditional ones, like the majalis, have been able to focus on more complex issues rather than on the routine matters with which they were once heavily involved. . . . On matters more directly affecting the individual, such as the topic of unemployment among young UAE graduates, debates often tend to begin in the majalis, where discussion can be fast and furious, before a consensus approach is evolved that is subsequently reflected in changes in government policy.[69]

Indeed, even the United Nations Development Programme in the UAE has reported on the continuing relevance of informal majalis in emirate-level politics. In particular, the frequent discussions over issues such as the role of women, the management of the expatriate population, and youth employment prospects have led the majalis to be recognized by the UNDP as providing an important forum for local social and political development.[70] Certainly, the rulers and their courts are aware of this function, with Abu Dhabi having deliberately augmented its majalis to include not only established tribes but also the many urban families and other groups who had previously lacked such local participation.[71] Similarly in Dubai there are currently plans to allow for elected regional majalis in various parts of the emirate by early 2005.[72] Finally, it is also notable how a number of local businesses have sought to embrace such forums, with many now promoting open majalis between managers and employees in an effort to raise issues of concern and improve the workplace environment[73] (see Figure 4.3).

## The Relationship Between Federal and Emirate-Level Structures

Under the terms of the UAE's constitution the federal government is responsible for a wide range of matters, including defense, foreign policy, immigration, nationality, communications, health, justice, and education.[74] As such, while local branches, offices, and institutions exist throughout the emirates, the majority are in theory subordinate to the COM's ministries, based in the federal capital of Abu Dhabi. Furthermore, although the constitution does enable local-level powers to provide public services, to maintain law and order, to uphold standards, and to enforce local ordinances,[75] at present the individual emirates are all obliged to contribute half of their revenue to the federation. Indeed, as Shaikh Abdullah al-Nuhayyan describes:

> All the emirates contribute to the federal budget and the federal budget funds projects in all of the emirates, including the three emirates that have no oil and gas production. Thus, while Fujairah, for example, has no oil revenues, the federal government funds projects in Fujairah, that are, in turn, funded by the contributions to the federal budget made by oil producers like Abu Dhabi and Dubai. The oil revenues of the emirates that do have oil are used through the medium of the federal budget to fund development in the emirates which do not have oil.[76]

Under this redistributive system, Abu Dhabi and Dubai, the two major oil-producing emirates, have therefore been required to make larger contributions, and, as Shaikh Abdullah contends, federal spending is shared proportionately by the seven members depending on their domestic populations and their specific needs. Thus it would appear that some aspects of the federal-emirate relationship, especially with regard to financial contributions, are now becoming formalized or at least better accepted by the constituent emirates. However, this was not always the case, with the past thirty years providing a rich history of federal-emirate struggles, and even now (as

Shaikh Abdullah admits) with the individual governments of the seven emirates still retaining certain autonomous powers and often maintaining duplicate and parallel local government departments, many of which overlap existing federal institutions.[77]

Thus, critical to a fuller understanding of the UAE's decisionmaking structure is the relationship between its federal, centralized political institutions and the local, emirate-level structures. Significantly, in many respects the term "federation" is something of a misnomer. Although the UAE is widely acknowledged to be one of the most successful examples of Arab unity and federation, it is really more of a confederation. True federations, such as the United States and Australia, normally represent groups of regions or states that maintain their own local governments and laws, but are also united with a central government that is responsible for defense, foreign policy, and other matters of national interest.[78] But there has so far been little real unity under the UAE's surface, with many crucial policy areas having often remained outside of federal control. Indeed, although the federation is undoubtedly evolving, the UAE at present remains more of a loose confederation, with its constituent emirates more closely resembling the Swiss cantons than the federated U.S. states or the six Australian regions.[79]

The first signs of potential disunity were acts of violence, when after just one year of federation a number of interemirate territorial disputes escalated into bloody tribal skirmishes. Most of these confrontations were the result of border disagreements within the complex patchwork of villages and settlements in the hinterland of the northern emirates—a particularly violent example being the 1972 dispute between tribesmen of Sharjah and Fujairah, which left twenty dead and many more wounded.[80] As described in Chapter 1, many of the tribes and villagers claimed allegiance to specific rulers, sometimes even to those in different and faraway shaikhdoms, and were therefore reluctant to recognize any newer, more central forms of authority.[81] A combination of Union Defence Force (UDF) coercion and negotiations were eventually able to settle most of these issues and reduce the frequency of the outbursts. However, until the housing boom of the late 1970s and the increasing urbanization of the Bedu during the 1980s, the prospect of tribal insurgence remained a serious threat to political stability and domestic security, especially in the rural areas. Indeed, speaking in 1977 Shaikh Zayed specifically referred to this ongoing problem, emphasizing the need for greater cooperation and a stronger union: "Unification steps must be continued and deepened and legislation supporting the federation must be a prime importance and above boundary disputes and individual disputes."[82]

By the mid-1970s significant divisions over the direction of federal policymaking and, moreover, serious doubts over the future of the federation itself began to emerge. While many of those high up in the political system believed that the federation was little more than a transitional stage preceding the establishment of a more coherent state. There were many others, however, especially in Dubai, who continued to believe that the relative autonomy of each separate emirate was the federation's greatest strength, as it better preserved the region's tribal democratic systems and all of the other emirate-specific characteristics that would be lost under a more centralized state.[83] As such, these conflicting views led to political struggles over delicate matters such as oil and immigration. As these were policy areas that required the individual emirates to relinquish control over what were seen as their private resources and their means of livelihood, immediate consensus was understandably unforthcoming, with the local rulers and their governments reluctant to concede existing powers. Indeed, this was especially the case with regard to oil, as Dubai and Sharjah, the second and third wealthiest oil-producing emirates, preferred to retain full autonomy over their oil policies and were disinclined to contribute a large share of their oil revenue to the federal budget and the Abu Dhabi–based federal ministries.[84] This problem stemmed primarily from Article 23 of the provisional constitution, a clause that allowed the individual emirates to manage independently their own hydrocarbon industries.[85] Such emirate-specific articles may have provided much needed accommodation during the early federal negotiations,[86] but in this case, with no formal provisions for future regulations to ensure proportional contributions to the federal budget, the clause effectively inhibited any greater financial centralization. Similarly, when the federal government called for a more uniform immigration policy to enforce passports, residence visas, and work permits, some of the local governments were hesitant to cooperate, preferring to retain control over the rate of immigration in their own particular emirate rather than hand over power to a distant ministry in Abu Dhabi.[87]

Eventually, this increasing lack of cooperation and unwillingness to integrate and contribute led to the first major crisis in UAE politics. When in 1976 the time came to draw up a new and more permanent constitution,[88] a committee of twenty-eight prominent citizens and legal experts was formed to consider the matter. Essentially this committee was divided between those who continued to regard themselves as representatives of their native emirate and who sought to promote the preferences of their particular Emir, and those "independents" who saw the creation of a new constitution as an ideal opportunity for updating many aspects of Emirati political life. Indeed, as Zaki Nusseibeh, Shaikh Zayed's former press secretary, explains, these independents, many of whom can be considered among the first generation of Emirati technocrats given their educational and professional backgrounds, sought greater centralization at the expense of individual interemirate politics and intended to remove Article 23 in order to encourage more efficient wealth distribution.[89] As a reflection of these differing views, the committee's draft of the new constitution was something of a compromise: Article 23 would be abolished, but each emirate would still be able to retain 25 percent of its hydrocarbon income.[90] However, when the draft was forwarded to the SCR later that year, the rulers of Dubai and some of the other emirates chose to reject the signing of such a constitution and insisted on retaining the original provisional constitution. This direct challenge to the federal vision prompted Shaikh Zayed to threaten his resignation from the presidency. Given his level of personal commitment to the federation, and given Abu Dhabi's single-handed financing of the federation during its early years,[91] Zayed argued that the other emirates should have been more appreciative and more enthusiastic in accepting moves toward a more permanent and centralized government.[92] Furthermore, as Adnan Pachachi, Zayed's former personal political adviser (and now chairperson of the post-Ba'thist Iraqi Governing Council),[93] explained, this threat of resignation was coupled with an offer to move the capital from Abu Dhabi if it would bring about a more viable federation, such was Zayed's dedication to the UAE's future stability.[94] Regardless of the motives, the bluff could not be called, as the other rulers recognized the important mediating role of their illustrious and statesman-like president, and of course his control over the largest and most powerful of the emirates. Thus Abu Dhabi managed to remain the center of the federation, but only after a costly four month crisis just five years after the creation of the UAE.[95]

Nevertheless, less than two years later the tensions again resurfaced, this time over the issue of the UAE's armed forces. In 1978 Shaikh Zayed decided to appoint his second eldest son, Shaikh Sultan al-Nuhayyan, as commander in chief of the UDF, despite his being only twenty-three years old.[96] Given that Shaikh Muhammad al-Maktum, the third eldest son of Dubai's ruler, was the UAE's defense minister, many in Dubai and the northern emirates interpreted this move as a clear attempt by Abu Dhabi to assume even greater control over the federation and what remained of their non-UDF incorporated local armies (most notably the Dubai Defence Force, the Sharjah National Guard, and Ra's al-Khaimah's Badr Brigade).[97] Indeed, Shaikh Rashid al-Maktum reportedly threatened to pull Dubai out of the UAE along with Ra's al-Khaimah and Umm al-Qawain unless the decision were reversed.[98] Thus, although the situation was eventually defused following a clearer definition of the two posts,[99] the dispute nevertheless highlighted the continuing reluctance of the smaller emirates to fully integrate with Abu Dhabi.[100] Indeed, in a similar fashion to the proposed centralization of oil and immigration policies, the amalgamation of the various emirate-level armed forces became an increasingly unlikely prospect. In fact, in the late 1970s Shaikh Rashid actually tripled expenditure on the Dubai Defence Force while making no effort to coordinate with the UDF.[101] Certainly, as Frauke Heard-Bey explains, the individual rulers continued to derive much power and prestige from their respective militaries, and many were unwilling to hand over such control to a more centralized command:

> Before the 1970s the various armed forces had always been the traditional manifestation of a ruler's standing. Therefore, the political price to be paid for trying to enforce amalgamation and thereby alienating some rulers would have been disproportionate to the fighting strength which these forces would have added to the capability of the newly formed federal forces.[102]

But the most serious disagreement did not occur until the following year, when a widely supported multipart memorandum for reform was submitted to the SCR. In 1979 the Islamic revolution in nearby Iran and the ensuing threat of Shi'a insurgency in Sunni Muslim states led to the fear of a "fifth column" of Islamic revolutionaries in the Gulf. Second, the Soviet invasion of Afghanistan and the anticipated U.S. reaction left many expecting a superpower conflict close to the Gulf. Third, at this same time Sadat, the Egyptian president, attended the Camp David meetings and set in motion the Egyptian-Israeli peace process, a controversial diplomatic move that divided the Arab world and clearly placed the conservative Islamic rulers of the Gulf states in an awkward position.[103] Given this increasingly uncertain regional political climate, many groups in the UAE called for a strengthened federation, a more unified leadership, and an end to the interemirate squabbles of the 1970s. Essentially, therefore, the "independents" were reacting to regional instability by renewing their backing for Shaikh Zayed's drive for greater centralization. Crucially, the resulting memorandum was drawn up by members of both the COM and the FNC, and was also believed to represent the views and concerns being expressed in more informal assemblies such as the majalis. In particular, the memorandum called for an end to the autonomy of the individual emirates, stating that they should unify in the national interest. Quite significantly, it also called for the SCR, which had been meeting less and less frequently, to meet monthly to decide policy, and for it to devolve far more of its policy-making powers to the COM. Although evidently not the memorandum's main emphasis, it was also requested that the FNC be given full legislative powers (thereby elevating the council from its limited consultative capacity)[104] and an "expanded base of membership," perhaps paving the way for public elections.[105]

The result was a protracted five-month-long "constitutional crisis." Demonstrations were held across the UAE and Shaikh Zayed enjoyed much popular support from a number of diverse groups ranging from students to local businessmen, all of whom were calling for greater unification.[106]

Predictably, the opposition came from the rulers of Dubai and Ra's al-Khaimah, the emirates that had earlier opposed the permanent constitution and blocked any proposed military amalgamation. The claim was that such a move toward a more centralized state as demanded by the memorandum was clearly unconstitutional given the loose nature of the federation outlined by the original statute. Furthermore, Dubai argued that any unification of services was only justified if better results could be promised than the existing emirate-level services. As a relatively prosperous oil-producing emirate with an independent revenue, it was clear that Dubai was still unwilling to contribute any great quantity of its wealth to the development of the smaller emirates via the medium of a federal budget.[107] Indeed, as Valerie Yorke explained of Shaikh Rashid, Dubai's ruler and the main challenger to Zayed's leadership, "It was said that Shaykh Zayed was in the union for what he could put into it; Shaykh Rashid for what he could get out of it."[108] However, this issue of revenue contribution perhaps clouds the fundamental political differences between the emirates at this time. In many ways, what Dubai really preferred was not an end to unity, but simply that the UAE remained a much looser federation or, as described earlier, more of a confederation—a collection of states in which the central authority never exceeded the total of all the individual authorities. Undoubtedly Shaikh Zayed and the 1979 proposals were seen as exceeding this total.

The crisis was only resolved with the help of outside mediation from experienced Kuwaiti negotiators, and the compromise solution has remained in place ever since, albeit now with a new generation of rulers. A new cabinet was formed and Shaikh Rashid was appointed prime minister. Thus, in addition to serving as the federation's vice president, the ruler of Dubai was to take on the extra function of presiding over the COM. Shaikh Zayed and his supporters hoped that this greater and more direct involvement from Dubai in federal matters would encourage Dubai to remain a part of the UAE and to take a more active interest in improving the services provided by the federal ministries. The agreement worked and Dubai soon began to contribute 50 percent of its oil revenue to the federal budget,[109] with the two smaller oil-producing emirates of Sharjah and Ra's al-Khaimah also beginning to contribute by the mid-1980s.[110] Thus, although the other aspects of the memorandum regarding the increased powers of the COM and the expansion of the FNC were not implemented, the crisis can nevertheless be viewed as something of a watershed in federal politics, as its resolution not only averted the secession of Dubai and the eventual breakup of the UAE, but also demonstrated that, if necessary, political opposition to the hereditary SCR could be mobilized.

Alongside this centralization debate, another important aspect of federal politics (and again a source of confusion and tension) has been the persistence of relatively autonomous foreign relations maintained by the various emirates. Although in theory the constituent emirates were to be represented by the federal foreign affairs ministry and the president, a number of disputes during the 1970s and 1980s served to undermine the UAE's international standing, with different emirates pursuing different objectives based on their individual interests. Perhaps the most damaging of these early disagreements were those concerning OPEC, as the UAE's provisional constitution permitted each emirate to either take up or abstain from OPEC membership.[111] While Abu Dhabi had decided to follow Saudi Arabia's lead and had joined the international oil cartel in 1966,[112] Dubai had instead opted to remain an independent producer. Thus, when the time came to create a federal oil ministry in the early 1970s, it soon became apparent that such an institution would have little control over oil and oil-related foreign policies outside of Abu Dhabi. This lack of control became particularly problematic for Abu Dhabi from 1974 onward when OPEC began to treat the UAE as a single entity rather than recognizing Abu Dhabi's individual membership. Consequently, when OPEC production quotas were first introduced in the early 1980s, Abu Dhabi was obliged to take the sole responsibility for ensuring that the UAE's overall oil production met these requirements. With Dubai regularly refusing to accept any pro rata share of the necessary cutbacks, Abu Dhabi was often forced to underproduce in order to stay within the quota.[113] Moreover, by the mid-1980s Dubai's unrestrained production was not only leading to tense relations between Abu Dhabi and OPEC, but also attracting the unwanted attention of Iraq. Embroiled in a costly and lengthy conflict with Iran, Iraq was threatening to punish all fellow OPEC members that persistently violated the designated quotas; this list of offenders included not only Iraq's future victim, Kuwait, but also the UAE.[114] Indeed, although when OPEC's Roberto Subroto visited the capital in 1987, Shaikh Zayed assured him that the UAE was "at the forefront of preserving the unity and cohesion of OPEC"; at the same time, however, the UAE was strongly suspected by OPEC of actually being the worst offender by producing an estimated 20 percent above its assigned quota.[115] In 1988 the supervision of Abu Dhabi's embattled oil industry was finally reorganized under the Supreme Petroleum Council. This effectively sidelined the powerless federal ministry, assumed sole responsibility for ADNOC (the main Abu Dhabi oil company),[116] and unilaterally declared a higher oil output for Abu Dhabi, regardless of Dubai.[117] In many ways, this new emirate-specific oil council can be seen as symbolizing Abu Dhabi's grudging acceptance of the limitations of federal control over not only oil policy, but also the other emirates' interactions with neighboring states and foreign organizations. Today, despite its checkered history, Abu Dhabi does manage to adhere to OPEC's quota for the UAE,[118] but this task is perhaps only easier because of the declining oil reserves in Dubai and Sharjah.

Moreover, the 1970s and 1980s also saw divided opinion over superpower relations. The majority of the emirates were naturally inclined to the Western powers given the region's long association with Britain and their continuing reliance on Western advisers and skills for their respective development programs. Remarkably, however, Ra's al-Khaimah, still the most reluctant member of the federation, attempted to seek support from the Soviet Union in the late 1970s (having come full circle from its afore-mentioned U.S. overtures in 1971)[119] in an effort to create a new breakaway state that would have included Sharjah, and that would have involved seizing a part of Oman.[120] Furthermore, in the 1980s during the height of the Iran-Iraq War, Ra's al-Khaimah again sought to further its own interests by offering Iraq the opportunity to establish airbases in its territory in exchange for greater independent recognition in the Arab community[121] (and presumably the opportunity to liberate its two Iranian-occupied islands).[122] Significantly, the war also resulted in a split between the six other emirates, with Abu Dhabi, 'Ajman, and Fujairah also supporting Iraq, Dubai, Sharjah, and Umm al-Qawain chose to support Iran, their primary trading partner and the home of many of their merchant expatriates.[123] Thus, as Peck noted at the time: "Dubai and Sharjah's pro-Iranian stance subjected the UAE's federal government, which has the sole responsibility for conducting foreign political and diplomatic relations, to embarrassment and pressure from Saudi Arabia and other Gulf neighbours."[124] Although the UAE has presented a more unified front in recent years, divisions over foreign policy have persisted, with some of the emirates reluctant to support the Desert Storm coalition in 1991,[125] and only mixed support for the U.S.-led invasion of Afghanistan in 2001. (Until September 11, 2001, many of the strongly anti-Iranian emirates had favored a "Sunni axis" comprising the UAE, Saudi Arabia, Pakistan, and the Afghani Taliban, in an effort to curb potential Shi'a expansion.)[126]

In summary, it is perhaps useful first to consider Fatma al-Sayegh's view that federal-emirate relations have evolved over three distinct phases: the early years, 1971–1979, can be seen as having been the "creation of the federation," during which federal institutions were being built and teething troubles were being resolved; 1980–1986 can be seen as the period of "accepting the federation," during which the seven emirates conceded some of their former powers in the national interest; and the period from 1987 to the present can be viewed as the "maturity of the federation," during which many of the former difficulties have been overcome and those that have remained unresolved have been effectively contained.[127] Indeed, in recent years the federation has certainly strengthened as the threat of internal rivalry has subsided and as the federal institutions have become better established. Furthermore, the resolution of the majority of outstanding boundary disputes, the establishment of a central bank, and the increasing contributions to the federal budget from the other emirates have all combined to create a more cohesive federation.[128] Perhaps the most important development, however, has been the greater integration of Dubai. Agreeing to accept a permanent constitution and, also in 1996, finally agreeing to integrate its tiny but highly symbolic local army into the federal command were clear signs that Dubai had chosen to concentrate on its ambitious economic development program while accepting Abu Dhabi's leading role as the financial backbone and protector of the federation. Indeed, in 1997 Dubai officials were even quoted as saying: "There is no obvious need to maintain an independent force in Dubai because the UAE armed forces GHQ provides a fully fledged and cost-effective defence capability."[129] Thus, with declining oil revenues and with the need to pursue greater diversification, it would appear that Dubai has relinquished its claims to regional leadership and now prefers to assign otherwise costly services to federal control.

It is also clear that any "maturity of federation" view remains decidedly and overly optimistic. In many areas it is evident that the strained and loosely defined relationship between federal and emirate-level powers has led to significant divisions that, on occasion, have led to policy disputes over key issues such as immigration, military integration, and budget contributions. While some of these differences have certainly abated over the years, there are nevertheless certain gray areas that have persisted, and over time these may resurface and again play a determining role in the federation's future. Indeed, in addition to the obvious differences over critical matters such as oil policy and foreign relations, there are a number of other very recent internal inconsistencies that continue to undermine the federal framework. Each emirate, for example, maintains its own independent police force. While all emirate-level internal security organs are theoretically branches of one federal organization, in practice they operate with considerable independence.[130] Second, the UAE's shari'a courts, which are administered by each emirate and which are supposed to answer to the federal supreme court, still do not always do so. In 1994 the president decreed that the shari'a courts would have the authority to try almost all types of criminal cases, but this decree has not yet affected the emirates of Dubai and Ra's al-Khaimah, which have lower courts independent of the federal system and special Shi'a councils to act on matters pertaining to Shi'a law.[131] Third, although a federal law was discussed in the mid-1990s with regard to establishing a federal stock exchange (strangely, despite having the second largest market by capitalization in the GCC, the UAE had no formal bourse at this time), a draft did not emerge until 1999, and even then this was largely redundant, as Abu Dhabi and Dubai were refusing to agree on a common location, instead preferring to go their own separate paths.[132] Indeed, as discussion of the UAE's banking sector later in this chapter will reveal, such an exchange has recently begun operating in Dubai, with seemingly no linkage to Abu Dhabi.[133] Fourth, although of seemingly less importance, the lack of an integrated national public transport system continues to symbolize a lack of cohesion in many people's eyes. The UAE must be one of the few countries in the world where buses will go from one city to another city just a few hours away, but will make the return journey completely empty (leaving passengers to take taxis) because the necessary paperwork is not yet in place between the different emirate-level transport companies.[134]

Finally, with more specific regard to development pathologies, it is also clear how the numerous interemirate disputes and other internal problems that have arisen as a result of opposition to federal policies may in many cases have directly affected the UAE's socioeconomic planning. The divisions in wealth distribution and the initial reluctance to commit to the federal budget certainly contributed to the uneven development and regional disequilibrium described in the previous chapter, and can therefore be seen as a causal factor behind many of the problems being addressed by the development planners today. Second, the lack of coordination and the distrust of federal control must also have exacerbated the described duplication of investments, with interemirate rivalry leading to inappropriate and often wasteful developments that may have been avoided under a more comprehensive federal development plan.[135] Third, as the majority of indigenous scholars will readily concur, the significant overlap between federal and emirate-level powers and the constant need for informal consultation between the various bodies must be seen as having slowed the overall formulation and implementation of development policies,[136] especially given that federal laws often require further enabling legislation in the individual emirates.[137] Indeed, as Heard-Bey explains:

> This can be a cause for the tardiness of some legislation . . . and this opportunity for emirate level input does not necessarily improve the draft or make the law more universally enforceable. . . . [L]ocal legislation, which is passed by the individual emirates in most instances still retains the hallmarks of their rulers, who are used to acting directly and even autocratically, when they perceive the need for their regulatory intervention.[138]

## Other Institutions, Parastatals, and Bureaucracies

### Chambers of Commerce and Industry

Established in 1976, the Federation of UAE Chambers of Commerce and Industry serves as both an umbrella organization and as a general forum for members of all the emirate-level chambers of commerce.[139] Broadly speaking, the organization's objectives have been to enhance cooperation between the commercial sector and the government, to promote better coordination between traders and manufacturers in different economic sectors, and to provide reconciliation and arbitration in instances of commercial and industrial dispute.[140] To this end, the chamber collects and processes data, commercial statistics, and other pertinent information from its members before finally submitting its suggestions to a federal board of directors. Consisting of the directors of each of the seven individual chambers in addition to a second delegate from each emirate, this board annually elects a chairman on a rotation system to ensure greater regional representation and to improve the unity of the federal chamber.[141] If the board deems the chamber's recommendations appropriate, these are then forwarded to the relevant minister or government department, and on occasion may also be raised in specialist commercial and industrial committees hosted by the FNC.[142] Indeed, recent examples of such involvement include the chamber and the legislature's joint reviews of draft ordinances on commercial transactions, trade licenses, and the protection of Emirati industries.[143]

More significant than this umbrella organization, however, are the constituent local chambers, as these deal with most of the UAE's day-to-day commercial and industrial administration, and are of course responsible for appointing the directors and associates who then serve on the federal board. Unsurprisingly, given the described pace of commercial development in the emirate, the Dubai chamber was the first such institution, established by Emiri decrees in 1965 and 1975 to be an "autonomous and non-profit-making institution" responsible for regulating economic life in Dubai.[144] Essentially the chamber is responsible for reviewing all legislation and orders relating to commercial and industrial activities such as trademark laws and the various free zone laws required by the new export-processing zones. To fulfill this task, the chamber hosts a research and studies department employing economic analysts and industrial experts to advise its director,[145] and more recently has begun to host a number of business oriented conferences and symposia for the benefit of its members and other interested parties. These have been held on a wide variety of subjects, including business contracting, human resources, arbitration of disputes, management of technology, and the implications of the UAE's World Trade Organization (WTO) membership.[146] A good early example would be the 1988 conference on the subject of the usefulness of free zones for promoting investment in Dubai. Attended by representatives of the Ministry of Finance and Industry, the Islamic Development Bank, and the Islamic Bank of Dubai, it was hoped that a forum could be created for informed members to voice their opinions and concerns on what was to become a controversial and far-reaching development for Dubai. Indeed, much discussion was generated with several papers delivered on the subject of the Jebel Ali Free Zone, with reports made on the success of similar EPZs in other GCC states, and with an informative report from the United Nations Industrial Development Organization (UNIDO) being presented on the international experience of free zones.[147]

Similarly, the Abu Dhabi Chamber of Commerce and Industry (ADCCI) has also played a key role in local development and commercial affairs. In much the same way as the Dubai chamber, the ADCCI has hosted a number of seminars and conferences for the benefit of its members and, in addition, has hosted numerous exhibitions and has invited numerous trade missions to the emirate in an effort to increase foreign investment and to boost the diversification of the local economy.[148] A strong example of the former would be the chamber's 1993 symposium on industrial investment opportunities in Abu Dhabi.[149] Attended by the ADCCI's members in addition to a number of prominent UAE and Gulf-based institutions, including the Gulf Investment Organization, Emirates Industrial Bank, and Gulf Industrial Consultations, the event reportedly led to an "enriched dialogue" between the chamber and the government that eventually led to the drafting of policy recommendations based on the findings and agreements of the conference guests and representatives.[150]

Despite these instances of successful and meaningful interaction, the UAE's chambers have been routinely criticized for their inflexible hierarchical structure and their otherwise limited participatory opportunities. Indeed, the Dubai chamber not only excludes a number of categories of small businesses from membership,[151] but also still lacks a formal assembly for Dubai businessmen, industrialists, and other members to meet and discuss their concerns with each other. Moreover, the chamber has also been slated for having no real procedure for normal members to contact the board of directors, the latter of which has remained dominated by members of key families, many of whom (such as the al-Tayir and the al-Mulla families) also hold important ministerial portfolios, FNC positions, and other overlapping responsibilities.[152] The Abu Dhabi chamber provides another interesting example given that its organizational structure has changed considerably over the years. As former member Salam al-Saman describes, the board of directors was originally made up of elected members of Abu Dhabi's business community. As the chamber grew in size and numbers, however, the board expanded to over twenty positions, all of which came to be filled by appointment, including members of influential Abu Dhabian families such as the aforementioned Dhawahir.[153] Crucially, the chairmanship of the Abu Dhabi chamber also became a permanent, nonelected position, and is now held by Shaikh Sultan bin Khalifa al-Nuhayyan, the crown prince's eldest son and the chairman of the crown prince's court.[154] Thus, many observers have contended that with this apparent reinvigoration of patrimonial client networks, the Abu Dhabi chamber's organization is no longer appropriate for a modern institution claiming to represent the emirate's business community.[155] Certainly, in addition to shouldering more responsibilities, providing greater chamber-sponsored advice for investors, introducing more comprehensive services aimed at meeting the needs of Abu Dhabi businessmen, and addressing many of the usual business community concerns, it has also been argued that, like Dubai, the emirate's chamber needs to provide more direct channels of communication between the nonelected board and its members.[156]

## The Judiciary and Related Institutions

The judicial branch of the federal government is represented by a federal supreme court and a number of courts of first instance. This federal supreme court is made up of a president and five judges, all of whom are appointed by the UAE's president and the COM.[157] At the formal request of the individual emirates these judges can act as adjudicators between the different emirates or between an emirate and the federal government. Moreover, like the FNC, the supreme court also has a consultative role, deciding on the constitutionality and viability of the federal laws drafted by the COM (although, as explained, in practice the status of these laws often depend on further enabling legislation in the individual emirates).[158] The courts of first instance adjudicate administrative, commercial, and civil disputes between the federal government and individuals, leaving local matters to the emirate-level judicial bodies.[159] In theory, these emirate-level shari'a courts, which deal primarily with criminal cases, are also answerable to the federal supreme court, but as demonstrated these often maintain independence from the federal system, especially in Dubai.[160] Supporting these institutions at all levels, the UAE's judicial staff has mushroomed to satisfy the needs of the rapidly expanding population. As the minister of justice, Muhammad al-Dhahiri, claims, the population now comprises a greater number of carefully monitored and well qualified professionals capable of ensuring independence and promoting greater transparency from within the system. Indeed, speaking recently at the Zayed Centre for Coordination and Follow-Up, al-Dhahiri chose to reemphasize his ministry's continuing commitment to these key objectives:

> We have an independent judicial system that does not accept interference in its work from whatever quarters. The judiciary is closely watched by the supreme authority in the country, the Supreme Council of Rulers, to ensure that justice is administered efficiently and with fairness, and also to ensure that nobody other than the Supreme Court of Appeal should interfere in court cases.[161]

However, as the U.S. Bureau of Democracy, Human Rights, and Labor indicated in its comprehensive 2001 report, while the UAE's judicial institutions are now generally independent, there is still considerable room for improvement and further development.[162] The federal government remains opposed to any form of external monitoring of the UAE's judicial system and its prisons, many of which are reported to be overcrowded and lacking in basic amenities such as air-conditioning. Some of the prisons are believed to have "secret wings" where large numbers of South Asian inmates are housed indefinitely in appalling conditions.[163] Furthermore, an archaic "blood money" compensation system continues to be applied across the UAE, especially in the event of motoring accidents, which can lead to financial interventions and long-term incarceration for those unable to pay. Moreover, many of the courts (except those in Dubai) still impose harsh corporal punishments on both Muslim and non-Muslim offenders, with sentences of 40 to 200 lashes not uncommon for "moral'" crimes such as adultery and prostitution[164] (although mutilations have now been phased out, with such sentences recently overturned by the supreme appeals court).[165] Perhaps the most severe weakness, however, is found in the long bureaucratic delays that have often left prisoners languishing behind bars for several months beyond their court-mandated release dates.[166] For the most part, these delays have been blamed on the restricted access to legal counsel. The accused is usually only permitted to seek counsel after the police have finished their investigation, thereby allowing the police to question suspects for long periods before they can be released.[167] Even more serious, and implying an underlying lack of genuine autonomy, these delays have also been blamed on the frequent involvement of the aforementioned rulers' courts, or diwan, which still reserve the right to review sentences and to return cases to the courts. Occasionally, in cases of personal interest, there have also been alleged instances where rulers of other emirates have attempted to intervene in local cases.[168]

## The UAE's Banking Sector and the Central Bank

As late as 1960 there were still only two banking houses represented in the Trucial states, and both of these were foreign: Eastern Bank and the British Bank of the Middle East (BBME).[169] However, when Shaikh Rashid al-Maktum chartered the National Bank of Dubai in 1963,[170] other locally chartered banks soon followed suit and by the time of federation fifteen other foreign banks from Britain, Pakistan, Iran, and Jordan had joined these. Understandably, the main weaknesses during this early period were the lack of basic controls and accountability. Indeed, as Fenelon noted in the early 1970s, apart from seeking permission to operate (which was granted by the ruler), the UAE's banks had to follow very few other guidelines. Certainly, the currency boards, which had been established earlier by the British, were concerned primarily with the issue and redemption of coins and notes, and occasionally with the provision of a few statistics, rather than with providing a regulatory framework for the UAE's financial institutions.[171] As such, by the mid-1970s the need for far greater control over the banking sector had become a major priority, especially given the UAE's increasing need to provide a sound financial base in support of its industrial and commercial development.[172]

While some controls to prevent the overextension of credit and the excessive expansion of foreign banks were implemented during the late 1970s,[173] the establishment of the UAE Central Bank in 1980 was the first major step forward. Replacing the currency boards, the bank was set up to control credit policy while fostering more balanced economic growth and to advise the government on all monetary and financial matters.[174] Indeed, along similar lines to other state banks such as the Bank of England, the UAE Central Bank is regularly represented at the meetings held by the Ministry of Finance and Industry and the Ministry of Planning, and on occasion is required to submit reports to the International Monetary Fund (IMF) and other international agencies.[175] In much the same way as the chambers of commerce, the bank is organized around an appointed board of directors,[176] many of whom hold multiple high-level positions in the UAE's business community, and are sometimes even prospective ministers.[177] Along with a treasury department and a department of current accounts, the board is advised by a banking supervision department, a research and statistics department, and an internal audit department, all of which can make recommendations for future resolutions.[178] Essentially, the supervision department ensures the financial soundness of all UAE-based financial institutions and, crucially, their compliance with the provisions of federal law and monetary policy. Recent departmental recommendations have included the need for important measures such as the requirement for certified stockbrokers,[179] the upward revision of the cash reserve requirement (CRR) for commercial banks in an effort to improve the sector's stability,[180] and the curbing of any bank's excessive concentration of credit to a single borrower.[181] The research and statistics department provides the board with annual and quarterly reports advising on the success or failure of current policies such as the UAE's pegging of the dirham to the dollar, the viability of offshore banking projects in the UAE, and the possibility of liquidating the bank's certificates of deposit.[182] Similarly, in addition to checking the bank's various transactions, the internal audit department is also given the task of supplying monthly reports to the board. Significantly, these reports not only concentrate on the external auditor's findings and provide the bank's management with suitable responses to the auditor's questions, but also contain recommendations for improved performance and better internal organization. In recent years such recommendations have included the setting up of a department to advise on the automation of banking services, the need for a system to compensate those with damaged banknotes, and a scheme to reward employees who obtain higher academic qualifications.[183]

Another important financial institution, especially given the UAE's plans for greater industrialization, has been the Emirates Industrial Bank (EIB). Created in 1982 under the 51 percent ownership of the Abu Dhabi government (with 49 percent held by a consortium of local banks),[184] its express aims were to promote economic growth and to assist in reducing the dependency on oil by encouraging the development of the industrial sector. Essentially, the EIB has acted as a federal vehicle or "parastatal": providing aid to the establishment of new, non-oil-based private industries, while consolidating the UAE's existing industries.[185] Among others these new ventures have included ice cream factories, shoemakers, and paint manufacturers.[186] Indeed, since its inception it is estimated that the bank has "soft loaned" in excess of $330 million to various would-be local entrepreneurs.[187] Moreover, given that the bank supposedly seeks to promote long-term diversification, it is noteworthy that these loans are carefully monitored to ensure that the most suitable industrial projects are given the necessary assistance. As such, its activities have often taken the form of comprehensive feasibility studies, financial and engineering analyses, marketing and legal consultations, and supplying UAE firms with essential industrial information.[188]

Also worthy of mention have been the more recent attempts, especially the aforementioned unilateral efforts in Dubai, to expand the UAE's financial markets further by establishing more tightly regulated stock exchanges (as it was believed that many players who preferred the ease of the original over-the-counter trading system were indulging in widespread insider-trading abuses).[189] The first example of such a bourse came in early 2000 when the Dubai Financial Market opened for business. Although it suffered from a slow start, it nevertheless showed much promise. Certainly, as the Economist Intelligence Unit noted, "trading volumes were low in the first few months, but moves to allow foreign investors to buy shares and the imminent opening of a sister bourse in Abu Dhabi should boost liquidity."[190] In early 2002 it was announced that this financial market would be supplemented by the opening of the Dubai International Financial Centre (DIFC), which, as the crown prince claimed, would allow Dubai and the UAE to join the international financial markets of London, New York, and Tokyo. Indeed, as the chairman of the center's board elaborated: "We want to be able to satisfy the regional needs of business and investors by building a hub in Dubai. We want to create a place for regional blue chips to find financial solutions and a place for international banks to seek regional investment opportunities."[191] Similar (though completely separate) projects are under way in Abu Dhabi, with the Emirates Global Capital Corporation having been launched with the express purpose of implementing Abu Dhabi's ambitious $3.3 billion Sadiyat project. This was to be an island free zone bridging the time zones between Asia and Europe by housing an international stock exchange, a futures exchange, a commodities exchange, and an offshore banking center.[192] Although this particular project has since changed direction and, as will be described later in this chapter, is now destined to become a real estate development,[193] there is nevertheless every indication that such an Abu Dhabi–based bourse will soon be established.[194]

In summary, the UAE's banks and financial institutions have undergone significant development since the mid-1970s, a trend that is set to continue for the foreseeable future, thereby further strengthening and complementing the overall diversification effort. Impressively, by 2001 there were already well over 430 banks in the UAE, with no fewer than 324 of these being locally chartered, and with over 100 of these being based in Dubai alone.[195] Indeed, when gauging the size and development of the banking and financial system relative to the domestic economy, the UAE fares particularly well, especially given its ratio of money to the GDP. Certainly, as Alan Richards explains: "[The ratio of money to GDP] stands at about 54% in the UAE. That's comparable to 59% in the USA and 51% in Ireland. So we are dealing, at this very simple macro indicator level, with a developed financial system."[196] Furthermore, it had also been claimed that the UAE has enjoyed relatively good macroeconomic policy consistency due to its central bank, and, although the government does not formally guarantee deposits, the UAE is also believed to enjoy relatively low moral hazards given the government's relative wealth and implicit guarantees.[197] In addition, the UAE has been seen as providing increasingly respectable regulatory oversight by requiring all commercial banks to adopt new administrative structures more representative of their shareholders,[198] and by promoting simultaneous deregulation and reregulation it is also hoped that the banking sector's accountability and disclosure will be further enhanced. Indeed, as Richards explains:

> One can only hope that in the next thirty years the UAE will continue to modernise its banking system by simultaneously deregulating (privatising certain key banks), and also re-regulating (making them conform to international standards of information disclosure). If they do this, I suspect that in 2030 the UAE banking system will be a fully developed component of the global financial system.[199]

However, despite the many improvements, the UAE's banking sector still exhibits a number of serious problems and for many of these it continues to draw both domestic and international criticism.[200] Most obvious, the sector strictly conforms to an "oligopoly with a competitive fringe model" dominated by a few large banking houses preventing free competition, and, more significant, there is also still believed to be very poor transparency of information:

> In general it is believed that the UAE's banking system suffers from a relatively low level of disclosure. Quoting a recent assertion made by Standard & Poors, "the disclosure falls short of international best practice and even compares unfavourably with some regional peers like Saudi Arabia." Any analysis of the UAE's banking system must thus take into account a rather high information risk.[201]

Moreover, in much the same way as the UAE's other political institutions and bureaucracies, and most crucially for the sector's regulatory future, the central bank's real powers and autonomy have remained rather questionable, especially given the appointed board's clear incorporation into the neopatrimonial network, and the organization's historical inability to assert control over emirate-level authorities. Indeed, the central bank has only had as much or as little power as the individual emirates and their ruling families have been prepared to give it. It has tried with only limited success to control unmonitored loans to directors and to demand disclosures of balance sheets in certain emirates. Furthermore, its powers of persuasion and assistance with regard to mergers and disasters among the UAE's numerous commercial banks have also been dwarfed by those of the emirate-level governments and other interested parties.[202] Certainly, the mergers that took place in the mid-1980s in Abu Dhabi and Dubai were entirely the work of the two local governments, since it was they rather than the central bank that put up the necessary funds. In 1985, when the Ra's al-Khaimah government failed to provide the necessary funds to rescue the Ra's al-Khaimah National Bank, the UAE Central Bank was also powerless in intervening.[203] Similarly in 1989, when Sharjah's four commercial banks came close to collapsing (after the Sharjah government defaulted on loans in excess of $500 million), it was a Saudi rescue package rather than the central bank that saved the day.[204] By far the most notable example of such failure, however, was the scandal involving the Bank of Credit Commerce International (BCCI) in Abu Dhabi in the early 1990s. Although a new UAE Central Bank board of directors was appointed to try to assert more control and restore confidence in the UAE's banking sector,[205] the central bank was nevertheless relegated to a secondary bystander role as the local Abu Dhabi government and ruling family assumed complete responsibility for the restructuring and subsequent closure of the branches. Indeed, as the following case study will demonstrate, quite remarkably the UAE Central Bank was to play only a minimal part in what was destined to be the region's most serious and damaging financial catastrophe.

## The BCCI Scandal

Collapsing in 1990–1991 against a backdrop of scandal and corruption, the demise of the Bank of Credit Commerce International was a major source of discomfort for the UAE, the home of many of the bank's largest and most influential backers. The ensuing international investigation lifted the lid on a world of patrimonial politics, unethical dealings, and criminal practices, thereby exposing the weaknesses of the UAE's banking sector, the lack of judicial independence, the high levels of bureaucratic self-interest, and the overall opaqueness of the state's political process. This was especially true for Abu Dhabi given the bank's close links to the emirate's local government and its seemingly undefined relationship with representatives of members of the al-Nuhayyan ruling family, some of whose personal fortunes had played a key role in the bank's history since its establishment in 1972.

Originally, Abu Dhabi's planners and advisers may have seen the bank as a means of building up a strong financial base capable of supporting the nonpetroleum sector, thereby complementing the emirate's early diversification efforts. Certainly, as the *Washington Post* reported, Abu Dhabi's attempts to buy up the BCCI could in some ways be seen as the realization of the emirate's long-term ambition to transform itself into an offshore banking center using the BCCI as a "flagship bank."[206] Ultimately, however, the crisis that unfolded in the early 1990s had severe consequences for the UAE's international credibility, seriously delaying any such transformation. Indeed, as U.S. senators Hank Brown and John Kerry reported in their 1992 investigation, the BCCI was found to have hosted an almost criminal structure centered around an "elaborate corporate spider-web . . . which was both an essential component of its spectacular growth, and a guarantee of its eventual collapse."[207] Furthermore, their explanation of the bank's ability to evade regulation seems to have placed particular emphasis on the weaknesses arising from its multilayered, top-down, and non-legal-rational structure, not dissimilar to the pathologies normally associated with neopatrimonialism:

> Unlike any ordinary bank, BCCI was from its earliest days made up of multiplying layers of entities, related to one another through an impenetrable series of holding companies, affiliates, subsidiaries, banks-within-banks, insider dealings and nominee relationships. By fracturing corporate structure, record keeping, regulatory review, and audits, the complex BCCI family of entities created by Abedi [Agha Abedi being the founder of the BCCI] was able to evade ordinary legal restrictions on the movement of capital and goods as a matter of daily practice and routine. In cre-

ating the BCCI as a vehicle fundamentally free of government control, Abedi developed in the BCCI an ideal mechanism for facilitating illicit activity by others, including such activity by officials of many of the governments whose laws BCCI was breaking.[208]

Specifically, this impenetrable layering of the BCCI's corporate structure was believed to have facilitated the operation of a number of illegal mechanisms ranging from shell corporations, secrecy havens, kickbacks for front men, and the use of falsified documentation. Moreover, as a result of its closed patrimonial structure, the bank was able to maintain a high level of opaqueness, easily avoiding existing controls in the UAE and, as the investigation claims, allowing its administrators and their associates to engage in a wide range of international criminal activities including money laundering, gun running, the management of prostitution, the facilitation of income tax evasion, and perhaps most significantly the financing of terrorist organizations.[209]

Given that Abu Dhabi represented the BCCI's largest depositors, borrowers, and shareholders (the Abu Dhabi share was estimated at 77 percent),[210] it is of little surprise that many of the bank's structural failings were seen as being inextricably linked to its long association with the emirate's local government, especially as Abedi had long been granted the powers of attorney to act in the name of Shaikh Zayed.[211] Indeed, as UK-based auditor Price Waterhouse informed the Bank of England, the relationship between the two entities was not only "very close," but also "far beyond the ordinary relationship of a bank to either its shareholders or depositors."[212] Moreover, while Abu Dhabi persistently presented itself as a victim and claimed only a passive role in the affair, its lack of cooperation in providing key documents and witnesses left the international community less convinced and even more determined to unravel the layers of deceit.[213] While many questions have been left unanswered, the investigators nevertheless exposed several of the less desirable features of the UAE's political structures in the course of their study. Of these, perhaps the most pertinent to this discussion were the findings regarding the lack of any clear division between the polity and the judiciary, the continuing ability of BCCI-connected individuals to arbitrarily manipulate the UAE's judicial system, and of course the lack of disclosure surrounding the extent of involvement of representatives of members of the ruling family and other notables in the BCCI's affairs.

Although members of the al-Nuhayyan family held more than $750 million worth of the BCCI's shares by the time of its collapse, their total contribution to the bank's capitalization quite remarkably appears to have been only $500,000: the initial start-up contribution paid to the bank by Shaikh Zayed in the early 1970s. Indeed, as the investigation claims, the

majority of these supposed shares were acquired as a result of fake "investments" whereby the shaikhs' representatives (possibly without the knowledge of their employers) would make payments on a risk-free, guaranteed-
return basis, thereby allowing the bank to project an illusion of substantial
royal backing:[214] "Price Waterhouse specifically found that representatives
of the ruling family of Abu Dhabi acquired shares on the basis of guaranteed rates of return and buy-back arrangements, with the result that they
were not at risk for their ostensible 'shareholdings' of the BCCI."[215]
Determining the level of actual participation from these "front men" proved
less straightforward due to a lack of information and numerous logistical
obstacles. Nevertheless, as the investigation did uncover, there had
undoubtedly been a long and familiar association between the BCCI and
the ruling family for many years, with the bank and its advisers having
"handled almost every financial matter of consequence for the Shaykh and
his family, as well planning, managing, and carrying out trips abroad, and a
wide range of services limited only by the desires of the Al-Nuhayyan family itself."[216]

Central to this close relationship was the founder of the BCCI, Agha
Abedi, who for over twenty years created and managed a network of foundations, corporations, and investment vehicles for Abu Dhabi's ruling family, of a complexity similar to the network he had created at the BCCI itself.
Consequently the BCCI handled the financial arrangements for many of
these entities, managed a variety of Abu Dhabi's portfolio accounts in dollars, and "provided members of the ruling family with personal services
ranging from Shaykh Zayed's own modest needs to the more elaborate
requirements of his sons and members of his retinue."[217] Certainly, given
the previously described rise of the unitary state and the expansion and
demands of the evolving dynastic monarchy, it is quite conceivable that the
BCCI's finances quickly became so intermingled with the finances of Abu
Dhabi that it became difficult even for BCCI insiders to determine where
one left off and the other began.[218]

Even more conclusive than the long-standing association with Abedi
was the Abu Dhabi government's strong links with two other prominent
BCCI bankers: al-Mazrui and Iqbal. For more than fifteen years, Ghanim
al-Mazrui served Shaikh Zayed as a financial adviser and manager, and as
such he was a central figure in the al-Nuhayyan financial network.
Furthermore, from 1981, al-Mazrui also served on the board of directors
of BCCI itself, in his capacity as secretary-general of the Abu Dhabi
Investments Authority, an organization that at that time held around 10
percent of the BCCI's shares, and that continues to handle the principal
government investments of Abu Dhabi.[219] As such, al-Mazrui represented
a clear three-way connection between the employees of the ruling family,
the BCCI, and an important local government institution, a link that effec-

tively blurred the financial autonomy of one entity from another. However, although the auditors and investigators discovered that al-Mazrui had received substantial personal financial benefits from the BCCI, had made bogus loans to members of the ruling family, and had lied about his earlier misdemeanors, when he finally confessed to Abu Dhabi authorities in 1990 he was not held in custody and was even permitted to remain in place as the head of Abu Dhabi's working group to deal with the BCCI. Given that he was neither fired nor forced to resign from positions of trust he had clearly violated, his existence brought into question the accountability of the emirate's regulatory and judicial processes, and again indicated the significant role that may have been played by higher-ups:

> Al-Mazrui's continued role in handling Abu Dhabi's response to the collapse of BCCI raises additional questions. One possible explanation is that Shaykh Zayed and the ruling family are remarkably tolerant of incompetence, deception, fraud, and the personal enrichment of top advisors. Alternative explanations are that Al-Mazrui's improprieties had previously been sanctioned by higher-ups, or were consistent with ordinary practices in the Emirate.[220]

Similarly, when the time came to appoint a new team to manage the Abu Dhabi–based rebuilding of the BCCI, Zafar Iqbal, the former head of the Bank of Credit Commerce Emirates (BCCE, a BCCI-affiliated UAE-based bank) was selected. This was also seen as being highly controversial given Iqbal's previously close ties with employees of the ruling family and his perceived lack of banking expertise. As the investigation claimed, based on reports by junior BCCI staff: "[Iqbal] had long had a close personal relationship with important employees of the ruling family of Abu Dhabi. . . . Within the bank [the BCCE], Iqbal was not considered to be an expert on much besides pleasing Abu Dhabi."[221]

With specific reference to the independence of the emirate's judiciary during the affair, al-Sayegh, Abu Dhabi's chief witness and a BCCI employee, argued that one of the main difficulties in making available key documents to foreign investigators was that Abu Dhabi's legal system forbade such interference, as it was based on a separation of powers to ensure that the executive branch could never exercise any influence over the judicial process. As such, he contended that there were no shortcuts that could be undertaken in order to supply more quickly the much needed documents and witnesses. However, as the BCCI investigators uncovered, this claim was highly inaccurate, as the judicial system at this time was found to be far from autonomous, with many examples of external influence and manipulation, thus reinforcing the belief that important witnesses and information were being deliberately withheld.[222] Indeed, one particularly weak area was believed to be the UAE's detainment law, which appeared to have been left completely open to outside interference:

> Following his arrest, an accused may not be detained for more than forty-eight hours [unless there is an order by the prosecutor] to detain him provisionally pending interrogation for a period of seven days subject to renewal for further periods not exceeding fourteen days. . . . [A judge may] extend the detention for a period not to exceed thirty days, subject to renewal.[223]

This law, especially regarding the possibility of "renewal," was believed to be serving as a primary mechanism for keeping accused BCCI officials and other staff with connections to representatives of the ruling family away from international investigators:

> These final provisions were the basis for the ordering of the summary arrest of the BCCI officials suspected of being involved in the irregularities and fraudulent activities, and their detention since, as under the interpretation given the law, the phrase "subject to renewal" allows the judge to continue to hold the accused from month to month so long as the prosecution wishes, without any limit whatsoever, for years, decades, or life, if matters remain under investigation. Indeed, Subcommittee staff have interviewed one knowledgeable Pakistani insider about BCCI and Abu Dhabi who spent years in prison in Abu Dhabi without trial, after being involved in a dispute with a representative of the ruling family.[224]

Moreover, the separation of powers was also called into question with regard to the federal civil court's "protective custody" of many of the BCCI's records. In al-Sayegh's prepared testimony it was stated that the court restricted access to these records to the majority shareholders and that the UAE prosecutor, appointed by Shaikh Zayed, "ordered that the documents . . . remain confidential for reasons not explained."[225] Thus, given that the majority shareholders were members of the Abu Dhabi ruling family and their guardians, and given the apparent closeness of the judiciary to the ruling family, the senators' rather damning report concluded:

> Given the fact that Shaykh Zayed, according to his own attorneys in submissions with the Federal Reserve, owns most of Abu Dhabi's resources and land, and that the laws themselves are styled as decrees by Shaykh Zayed, in consultation with other bodies and officials who are appointed by Shaykh Zayed, not by popular vote at elections, the notion that the United Arab Emirates' justice system is somehow completely independent from the interests of the ruling family of Abu Dhabi stretches credulity.[226]

Although clearly oversimplistic and expressing little appreciation of the intricacies of the complex Emirati political process, such a statement nevertheless indicates the extent of damage that can still be caused by such neopatrimonial pathologies not only to domestic development, but of course also to the UAE's high standing in the international community.

### The Drive for Greater Transparency

While the alleviation of the UAE's more serious bureaucratic pathologies, especially those deriving from the persistence of informal neopatrimonial networks and the lack of institutional independence, may be extremely difficult to overcome, attacking opaqueness and improving accountability have become increasingly regarded as more realistic and immediate objectives. Indeed, the drive for greater transparency has attracted much support in recent years from a wide number of sources, including, most notably, the Dubai government and ruling family, whose very future rests on the creation of a successful diversified economy and the establishment of a sound international reputation in order to compensate for the emirate's declining oil revenues.[227] Broadly speaking, this drive has thus far consisted of three identifiable sets of initiatives: the rulers' and ministers' frequent personal attempts to expose opaque bureaucracies, the attempts to mobilize the UAE's press as a greater organ of accountability, and most significantly the creation of new formal organizations and legislation capable of institutionalizing and enforcing better answerability.

The crown prince of Dubai, in much the same way as the old Venetian Doges, has personally spearheaded his emirate's drive to reduce corruption and incompetence. Indeed, Shaikh Muhammad al-Maktum has attempted to shake up Dubai's civil service, sometimes even resorting to early morning raids on government offices and firing any officials not present at their desks.[228] Furthermore, he has also publicly called upon the editors of all local newspapers to act as "watchdogs to ensure that governments and their bureaucracies correct their mistakes and take the right decisions in the interests of the people." Along similar lines, the UAE's minister of information, Shaikh Abdullah al-Nuhayyan, has openly encouraged all federal institutions and bureaucracies to become more sophisticated in their approach to press and public criticism and "not to regard it as disloyal, or even traitorous." Moreover, Shaikh Abdullah has also called for information services such as the Internet to be embraced by both the press and public, and to be used as tools to encourage greater bureaucratic accountability.[229] Although highly visible, these individual efforts and royal interventions are by themselves unlikely to lead to any wholesale improvement. Certainly, while there have been cases where the press has criticized alleged inefficiencies in the provision of government services and in the judicial system,[230] these are still extremely rare and the strengthening of the UAE's press should be viewed as more of a long-term objective. Indeed, as the next chapter will explain, the UAE's media remains in a considerably weakened state, caught between existing government controls and the continuing self-censorship exercised by the many cautious expatriate journalists.[231]

Instead, it would seem that significant improvements in transparency, at least in terms of public relations, are far more likely to result from the work of strong organizations granted the powers they need to enforce better accountability in the UAE's bureaucracies. A good example would be the work of a recently created "anticorruption unit" in Dubai, another of Shaikh Muhammad's initiatives. In February 2001 the unit first came into effect and soon began investigating and arresting a large number of officials in the Dubai customs, ports, and immigration services on charges of corruption. Six suspects were detained, including the director-general of Dubai's customs authorities, and these were soon joined by a further fourteen, including the head of the immigration section of Dubai International Airport. All were accused of taking part in the embezzlement of millions of dollars, thus leading to the first public acknowledgment of corruption by the Dubai authorities. Initially, the accusations and findings considerably shook the political and business environment in the city, but many have contended that by exposing the great extent of corruption in Dubai, the long-term benefits have been considerable. Indeed, with signs that the emirate is now beginning to "get its house in order," it is believed that more foreign investors will be inclined to consider the UAE as a viable option.[232]

Similarly, new anti-money-laundering organizations and legislation have been seen to encourage greater formal accountability in the UAE's financial sector. Certainly, under the 1987 federal law concerning the promulgation of the penal code, the UAE was one of the first countries to adopt specific anti-money-laundering articles. In 1993 these articles were reinforced by the central bank's requirement for comprehensive customer identification for the opening of all accounts, including those purportedly for charitable institutions. In 1999 an "anti-money-laundering and suspicious cases unit" was established and given access to all relevant authorities, and in 2000 this was followed by the formation of a national anti-money-laundering committee responsible for all such policy in the UAE. In late 2001 an anti-money-laundering law was passed by the COM and duly approved by the FNC, in an almost immediate response to the widespread accusations of Al-Qaida funding following the September 2001 terrorist attacks.[233] Early the following year this was strengthened by a further law (Federal Law no. 4 of 2002) allowing the UAE's financial authorities to seize dubious funds while investigations take place, and resolving many earlier legal contradictions regarding the confidentially of bank accounts.[234] As such, by February 2002 at a meeting of the Financial Action Task Force (FATF) held in Hong Kong, the UAE was declared to have finally established a comprehensive anti-money-laundering system, comprising all the necessary laws, regulations, and procedures, and was said now to be "in a very good position to co-operate in the internationally declared fight against money laundering." Moreover, the team also affirmed that any deficiencies in the UAE's previous anti-money-laundering systems had now been eliminated.[235]

In the near future, these anticorruption and anti-money-laundering organizations and legislation will be augmented by other transparency initiatives. One important example will be the UAE Central Bank's forthcoming establishment of a customer credit worthiness database. This database will oversee all transactions and will aim to reduce the number of fraud-related incidents that have historically plagued the UAE's financial sector (most infamously the Madhav Patel scandal of 1999, which severely crippled a number of local banks and amounted to over $400 million of unrecoverable funds).[236] For the first time, a database will gather financial information on selective clients along with details of their operations, the magnitude of their business, and the nature of their transactions.[237] At a more grassroots level will be the Dubai government's forthcoming "Excellence Program," which will play host to a number of projects including a "mystery shopper" operation designed to call anonymously on government departments and directors and rate their performance. Indeed, as the program's sponsor explains: "Some people think that closed doors can hide . . . the fact that this applies to some directors . . . who did not come up with a single idea or project during the whole year. What are they waiting for, while their colleagues have succeeded in transforming their departments into active cells."[238]

Similarly, it is also hoped that the Dubai International Finance Centre can play a key role in promoting the UAE's drive for transparency.[239] Indeed, as emphasized by its chairman, Anis al-Jallaf, there will be a brand new regulatory and executive system set up in the DIFC with strong regulatory codes and rules based on respected international standards. Moreover, it is intended that the DIFC's regulatory agency will be divided into a council and a commission to ensure the separation of oversight and execution. As such, al-Jallaf argues that the DIFC will be "even more tightly regulated than the developed markets. We have to be more careful because of the scrutiny we will come under from the USA and the dangers of money laundering."[240] Thus, given that the DIFC's main priority will be to reach a high level of internationally recognized transparency, al-Jallaf expects that the institution will soon gain recommendation from the Organization for Economic Cooperation and Development (OECD), and that all operations based in the DIFC will be accredited entities, with their headquarters in either a member country of the FATF or a country committed to the Wolfsberg principles and guidelines relating to money laundering.[241]

## Elite Interest Groups:
## Old Rentiers Versus New Rentiers

Far from homogeneous, the UAE's powerful client elite can increasingly be divided into two main socioeconomic interest groups: the conservatives and the reformers. Although both are clearly components of a dominant class seeking to perpetuate rentier wealth and rent-channeling structures, there are important differences between those "old rentiers" remaining reliant on oil-derived economic rent and aiming to maintain the status quo, and those "new rentiers" seeking fresh and less finite sources of economic rent from non-oil-related activities such as the leasing of real estate and the ownership of business parks. To facilitate the development of these more diversified sources of rentier wealth, the new rentiers have been pressed to seek a number of liberalizing reforms in an effort to remove existing restrictive practices, to attract greater foreign investment, and to boost the UAE's international credibility. Crucially, on occasion, these proposed reforms have led to significant conflicts, sometimes at the highest levels, with the more conservative elements of the Emirati elite keen to block any potentially destabilizing initiatives or amendments to existing legislation. Moreover, although the differing substrategies of cautious oil-related development in Abu Dhabi and more vigorous diversification in oil-scarce Dubai are increasingly seen as mutually beneficial, the UAE's interelite conflict can in some ways still be interpreted as a struggle between the two principle emirates.[242]

For the most part, the UAE's prominent conservatives, many of whom are believed to be supported by Shaikh Zayed and his crown prince, Shaikh Khalifa,[243] are either closely related to the ruling families or associated with the UAE's oil industry. Many have been understandably reluctant to permit sweeping changes lest their oil-related sources of revenue be jeopardized or their high-level positions be lost. Certainly, examples of such conservatives would include many of the members of the previously discussed Dhaheri family. Originally from Buraimi and now one of the most influential Abu Dhabian families (for primarily historical reasons),[244] the Dhawahir presently hold more than twenty-five senior positions in the UAE's hierarchy, including executive posts in the Abu Dhabi National Oil Company, the federal judiciary, the Abu Dhabi financial department, and the UAE University in Al-'Ayn.[245] Similarly, the Bin Yousefs, another prominent Abu Dhabian family, have for some time also been closely linked with the emirate's oil industry. Although, as Business Monitor International reported, Yousef bin Omair Yousef resigned as minister of petroleum and resources in the early 1990s,[246] this was only because of the federal ministry's impotence and his subsequent lack of control over oil-related policies. Significantly, he was soon appointed general manager of

ADNOC and later became the secretary-general of the Supreme Petroleum Council, which, as described in Chapter 4,[247] now formulates the bulk of Abu Dhabi's oil policies and has therefore become one of the most powerful bodies in the UAE.[248] Other such examples would include members of the al-Masud, the al-Mazari', the al-Fahim, the Hawamil, the bin Aweidah, and the aforementioned al-Suwaidi and al-Otaibi: seven large families who between them have a controlling interest in many of Abu Dhabi's leading hydrocarbon-related industries and organizations.[249]

In contrast, the UAE's most prominent reformers have tended to be those businessmen and families with closer links to the non-oil-related sectors, and therefore those with a greater personal interest in successful diversification. Moreover, many of these are believed to have a more technocratic background, with the majority having studied abroad, holding academic qualifications, and in some cases also having had professional and entrepreneurial experience. Prime examples of such technocrats would include the influential and well-renowned businessmen Muhammad al-Abbar, Majd al-Futtaim, Juma' al-Majid Abdullah, Abdul-Rahman Bukhatir, and various members of the Behruzian family. As director-general of Dubai's economic development department, the North American–educated al-Abbar has been instrumental in formulating and implementing many of the emirate's recent economic reform programs and, as the Economist Intelligence Unit claims, deserves much of the credit for their apparent success. Indeed, he is believed to have championed a number of liberal economic strategies in an effort to boost local businesses, including his own highly successful Emaar Properties, which has now achieved considerable international status. Similarly, al-Futtaim, another household name in Dubai, has been a major driving force behind a number of thriving property developments and business ventures. Moreover, in much the same way as al-Abbar, he has been seen to have embraced free market economics, and is now thought to wield an enormous liberalizing influence in Dubai's rapidly developing financial sector.[250] Al-Majid Abdullah, again from Dubai, can be regarded as another key member of this new technocratic elite. His business and educational interests are much in evidence in the emirate, with many successful local enterprises to his name, with his vice chairmanship of both Emirates Bank International and the UAE Central Bank, and with his establishment of a cultural foundation dedicated to local scholarship.[251] On a slightly smaller scale, Bukhatir represents the leading business family in Sharjah: not only is he the chairman of the National Bank of Sharjah, but he is also the owner of Duhatir Investment Limited, a co-owner of Gulf Consolidated Services and Industries Company, and a shareholder in the Sharjah Economic Development Company.[252] In Fujairah, the Behruzian family are similarly influential, with many owning a number of commercial and financial holdings in the emirate, and with some having established local manufacturing firms.[253] Other notable examples would include members of the Galadiri, the al-Ghurair, the al-Gurg, the Nabudah, the bin Lutah, and the Shirawi: these Dubai merchant families (many being of Iranian origin)[254] all have enormous holding companies in addition to having representatives on most of the city's prominent boards of directors (including the Chamber of Commerce and Industry, the Arab Heavy Industries Company, the Dubai Insurance Company, the Dubai Islamic Bank, the Bank of Oman, and the Emirates National Bank).[255]

Crucially, as a greater proportion of the UAE's youth begin to experience higher education and professional environments, and as the need for diversification and reform becomes even more pressing, it is believed that the size and relative political weight of this more technocratic group will continue to grow. Although the traditional rulers have always carefully sought to accommodate and incorporate such "modern groups" into their polities,[256] in more recent years there have been very visible signs that the technocrats are finally beginning to assume many more positions, sometimes even those previously occupied by powerful conservative families. Indeed, there has been much evidence that the technocrats may now even be gaining a foothold in the COM, which is the most influential nonhereditary political institution in the UAE and is responsible for the bulk of day-to-day policy formulation.[257] Either as a result of growing pressure or out of a genuine desire to achieve broader representation, in 1997 Shaikh Zayed admitted to the COM a group of Western-educated professionals with considerable experience in commerce, banking, and other non-oil-related activities. Furthermore, despite their youthfulness, these new appointees were not restricted to minor cabinet portfolios, with Muhammad Kharbash even being appointed as head of the Ministry of Finance and Industry,[258] one of the UAE's key development-related ministries.

In 1998 the influence of the technocrats was further enhanced after another Western-educated graduate, Muhammad al-Habtur, won an election to become speaker of the FNC. Although the FNC only commands limited legislative powers, the position of speaker is nevertheless of great significance, not least because it is one of the few genuinely elected positions in the UAE's political system. Indeed, whereas all previous speaker elections had been uncontested formalities, the 1998 election was fiercely fought. Democracy was in action given that both the proreform al-Habtur and his more conservative opponent canvassed for support from individual FNC members.[259] Most important, al-Habtur's victory was far from unanimous, with *Al-Wasat* newspaper reporting the result as being twenty-four to fifteen, with only one abstention.[260] Furthermore, given that voting patterns did not necessarily reflect regional or family origin,[261] the split would seem to confirm that politically opposed blocs and differing elite orientations do exist underneath the surface of UAE politics, and that, as in most other states, the political elite is far from being a single unit.

Thus, given this increasing strength of technocratic reformers alongside the continuing presence of powerful conservatives, it is of little surprise that a number of major "new rentier" versus "old rentier" development-related policy struggles have surfaced in recent years, which on occasion have led to counterpolicies and attempts to slow and block controversial reforms. Certainly, some of the more notable examples to promote liberalizing reforms would include the following:

• The liberalization of property rights. Traditionally only UAE nationals have been allowed to own property, but these rules are now being relaxed and changed by those seeking to open up the UAE economy and attract greater foreign direct investment. In 1999, al-Abbar's Emaar Properties allowed GCC citizens and even wealthy non-GCC citizens to purchase ninety-nine-year leases at its exclusive Emirates Hills development. Similarly, in 2000, Union Properties, a subsidiary of the al-Majid Abdullah–linked Emirates Bank International, announced it would offer thirty-year leases to foreigners on selected developments. In much the same way, in the commercial sector, Dubai Internet City has allowed investors to purchase fifty-year renewable leases from the year 2000 onward. Thus, as the case studies below will reveal, although these developments have remained within the letter of the law, it is quite clear that, by offering such long-term leases, the reformers clearly have attempted to bypass the existing restrictive legislation.

• The liberalization of business ownership laws. In 1997 the governor of the UAE Central Bank recommended to the COM that some of these restrictions be relaxed and that non-nationals should be allowed to invest in the public offerings of a future stock exchange with the intention of pushing the UAE's capital market toward maturity and further expansion. Following approval, al-Abbar's Emaar Properties once again led the way by being the first listed Emirati company to allow foreigners to buy shares: up to 20 percent of its equity at first, then eventually rising to 49 percent.[262]

• The provision of investment work-arounds for non-UAE nationals. By providing nonvoting investment opportunities for foreigners, some of the UAE's banks have attempted to create an investment alternative for those restricted by the current regulations. The first of such schemes, the Emirates Equity Fund, was sponsored by Emirates Bank International and offered more than 30 million dirhams worth of open-ended units. As BSP Management Consultants claims, other banks are soon expected to follow suit.[263]

Those examples to block liberalizing reforms and augment existing restrictions would include the following:

• The introduction of "exclusive agency" agreements in which certain UAE-based companies have been given the sole distribution rights for imported goods. These were intended to eliminate the threat of competition in certain areas, thereby safeguarding the interests of established UAE enterprises.[264]

• The introduction of a 4 percent customs duty, imposed by the federal government on most goods since 1994.[265] Although a relatively low figure, Dubai's merchants have relied upon a tax-free trading environment for much of the twentieth century.[266] Indeed, as the *Middle East Economic Digest* notes, many of the UAE bankers have vigorously opposed this policy, cautioning that the duty may impede Dubai's further growth as a trading center if companies find more attractive alternatives such as Hong Kong or Singapore.[267]

• The constant efforts to maintain the ban on foreign ownership of real estate in the UAE, as demonstrated in earlier discussion of the FNC's July 1990 recommendations.[268]

• The efforts to reinforce the kafil sponsorship system and the minimum 51 percent ownership share by nationals in all UAE businesses, as noted in the earlier discussion of the FNC's March 1994 recommendations.[269]

• Calls from some members of the FNC for the government to impose a 5 percent corporation tax on non-UAE companies, thereby weakening the competition.[270] While many domestic companies would surely thrive under free market conditions, it was feared that a number of companies, especially the many infant light manufacturing industries, would suffer without some form of protection.[271]

• The opposition to Dubai Media City and the proposed plans to allow greater freedom for Dubai-based media companies. Indeed, as was reported in 2001, a number of FNC members recoiled at the prospect of potentially uncontrollable and culturally eroding media outlets: "The FNC members generally expressed deep reservations about what kinds of content the media companies setting up in the trade free zones like the Media City would be producing. Some said that the content might erode the national culture and morals. Such nervousness is understandable, as the individual Emirates establish the free zones, and the federal government has no authority or control over their activities."[272]

### Foreign Property Ownership

This first of three case studies highlighting these "new rentier" reforms and their greater impact on socioeconomic development considers in detail the controversial issue of foreign property ownership, or rather foreign long-term leasing and the struggle to overcome the existing federal property

laws. Attempting to establish new sources of economic rent, improve foreign investment, and of course boost the diversification of the economy,
many have sought to challenge or circumvent the ban on non-national property ownership by either bending regulations or working around restrictions. Perhaps the first example of such an endeavor was the result of a
strategic alliance formed between Dubai's crown prince, Shaikh
Muhammad al-Maktum, and al-Abbar's Emaar Properties. Significantly,
for much of the early and mid-1990s, Emaar Properties had confined its
activities to the construction and letting of condominiums on the shaikh's
donated land, and both parties had been content to restrict the sale of completed apartments to UAE nationals, thereby upholding the foreign ownership ban. However, by 1997 an important change had taken place. Emaar
announced the launch of Emirates Hills, a 700 million dirham golfing-cum-
residential project that would overlook the Emirates Golf Club, close to
Dubai's busiest commercial center. Given the scale of the project, Shaikh
Muhammad began to take a more active role by personally supervising its
progress.[273] Thus, with a powerful supporter and benefactor, al-Abbar
finally began to contradict publicly the existing laws by underscoring his
commitment to foreign ownership: "We have had strong response [for
Emirates Hills] from citizens of Abu Dhabi, Dubai, Saudi Arabia, and
Kuwait, and even from expatriates. We will also allow locally incorporated
companies to purchase the villas."[274] Thus, for the first time in the UAE's
history, residential plots were being marketed not only to Emirati and GCC
citizens, but also to "those 'others' that can either buy fully built-up villas
or plots."[275]

Moreover, Emaar's much publicized follow-up project, the Westside
Marina, further consolidated the reformist al-Abbar/Shaikh Muhammad
position. Indeed, in much the same way as Emirates Hills, the project's stated objective was not so much to meet the needs of the local population, but
rather to increase the attractiveness of Dubai to foreign investors.
Specifically, it was to comprise:

> A marina complex with mixed usage low, medium and high-rise buildings
> along with comprehensive infrastructure features, complete with shopping
> centres, swimming pools and golf courses . . . which would accommodate
> the expected growth of Dubai for tourists, international expatriates, and
> UAE and GCC citizens. Properties within the community complex would
> also be available for UAE, GCC and other companies, he added.[276]

Thus, by condoning the long-term leasing of property to all interested parties, regardless of nationality, the marketing aims of these two projects have
strictly speaking been outside of UAE law. However, given that both
Emirates Hills and the Westside Marina have been resounding successes for
Dubai's real estate sector, Emaar appears to have set a precedent, with

many other developers having followed their lead.

By far the most ambitious and noteworthy of these new property developments have been the creation of two vast Palm Island complexes built on artificial atolls off the coasts of Jebel Ali and Dubai's Jumeirah Beach. With their 120 kilometers of artificial sandy beaches, a monorail linking their palms' various fronds, high-rise hotels, and 3,000 luxury villas, the Palm Islands will join the Great Wall of China as being among the few artificial structures visible from space. The project has reportedly cost over 15 billion dirhams and has been funded primarily by the government of Dubai along with a number of local and international banks. Crucially, although not under the auspices of Emaar Properties, this project is personally supervised by Shaikh Muhammad. Furthermore, in much the same manner as the groundbreaking al-Abbar developments, the properties on the Palm Islands are being made available to overseas buyers on hundred-year leases.[277] Accordingly, while this does not actually constitute foreign ownership, the semipermanency of the proposed leases and the overall objectives of the project are best viewed as careful work-arounds of the law.

Significantly, it would appear that even the UAE's federal ministries are now beginning to recognize the importance of these successful developments in Dubai, and as a recent communiqué from the Abu Dhabi–based Ministry of Information and Culture indicates, it would seem that the reformers' strategies are gradually being accepted, even if not yet officially approved: "In general, expatriates are not allowed to buy properties in the UAE, however it is now possible to do so in some emirates, for example, Dubai. The ambitious Palm Island Project—the world's largest man-made island shaped like palm trees, being developed by the Dubai Government, offers villas to be sold on a free-hold basis."[278] In addition, the pioneering role of Dubai-based companies such as Emaar Properties, and their use of long-term leases as legal loopholes, are now also being acknowledged by the ministry:

> Last year Dubai Lands and Properties Department has announced that expatriates, including non-resident foreigners, can now buy property in Dubai in the form of 99-year leases with properties managed by Emar Properties. Earlier, only GCC citizens were entitled to this privilege, now foreigners are entitled to the same rights as UAE citizens and Gulf nationals as far as buying, selling and renting lands and property in Dubai is concerned.[279]

Finally, in the past few years there have been indications that such developments are also beginning to take shape in other emirates, even in Abu Dhabi, where previously all land was owned by the ruler.[280] A good example is the Sadiyat Island project. As described earlier in this chapter, the development was originally intended to house an offshore financial market in Abu Dhabi.[281] However, as the Economist Intelligence Unit reports, it now appears that the project has become a real estate development, offering ninety-nine-year leases and free zone status to prospective foreign companies and investors.[282] Thus, in Abu Dhabi it would seem that there are also efforts being made to bypass the existing property restrictions by exploiting ambiguities such as long-term leases and offshore status. Sadiyat Island and a number of similar projects under way in the smaller emirates may therefore indicate that Dubai's example and the strength of the reformers are having a liberalizing influence across the UAE's previously restricted real estate sector.

### Commercial Ventures and Free Zones

Another important source of new rentier wealth has been the economic rent accruing from the leasing of free zone plots and industrial parks to productive tenants. Thus, in much the same way as the efforts to reform and circumvent real estate laws, there have also been clear attempts to relax and avoid the existing foreign business restrictions. Indeed, without such liberalization it is undoubtedly feared that potential foreign investors will be put off by the 49 percent cap on foreign business ownership and the much maligned *kafil* sponsorship system requiring all foreign businesses to take on an Emirati partner. Once again, Dubai's technocrats have been at the forefront of this mission, with the creation of the massive Jebel Ali Free Zone in the mid-1980s having already clearly confirmed their intentions. As demonstrated in Chapter 3, the JAFZ was to serve as a major non-oil-related industrial export-processing zone for both domestic and foreign firms, and as such there was a pressing need to remove all unpopular commercial restrictions.[283] Thus, in 1985, a local Dubai law was passed with the express aim of providing the JAFZ Authority with greater freedom and exemptions from existing UAE business regulations. Specifically, the law empowered JAFZ companies to be released from all export fees and turnover taxes, and most crucially allowed all of the zone's foreign companies to be exempt from local partner conditions and to claim full repatriation of the invested capital.[284]

In recent years a number of innovative development projects have attempted to follow this pattern, with many of the new free zones and parks also claiming to permit 100 percent foreign ownership. Indeed, if the Dubai-based Emaar Properties can be viewed as the pioneer of residential real estate development in the UAE, then Dubai Investments Park Development Company (DIPD) can be regarded as its commercial equivalent. In 1998 the firm was seeking approval to allow foreigners to hold a majority stake in ventures in its business park situated close to the JAFZ.

Certainly, although general manager Khalid Kalban accepted that the park was likely to remain distinct from Jebel Ali and its free zone status, he nevertheless stated his "hope for 100% foreign ownership in the business park."[285] Since then, the DIPD intensified its marketing campaign to attract foreign investors and businesses by offering them first-rate infrastructure with complete freedom from any restrictions.[286] Backed by a new Dubai decree in 2000 to promote such freedom in commercial developments, these promises were soon realized. Although the "Dubai Technology, Electronic Commerce, and Media Free Zone Law no. 1" was not a federal law, it was nonetheless the first of its kind in the UAE, again underscoring the emirate's strong commitment to liberalization of the UAE's economy. Indeed, by expanding upon the earlier JAFZ enabling legislation, this new local ordinance responded to the needs of the business community by allowing for a number of significant amendments and relaxations of the existing restrictions:

- *Article 9:* "Entry into leases of plots and buildings may extend to periods of up to 50 years, with any establishment in the free zone, to enable it to carry on its activity according to terms and conditions agreed upon."
- *Article 15:* "Free zone establishments shall be exempt from all taxes, including income tax, with regard to their operations in the free zone. They shall also be excluded from any restrictions on repatriation and transfer of capital, profits and wages in any currency to any place outside the free zone for a period of 50 years."
- *Article 16:* "Assets or activities of the free zone establishments shall not be subject to nationalisation or any measures restricting private ownership throughout the period of their activities in the free zone."
- *Article 17:* "Free zone establishments may employ or hire whomsoever they choose in their operations in the free zone, provided that such employees are not subject to any countries politically or economically boycotted by the UAE."
- *Article 18:* "The operations of free zone establishments or employees, within the free zone, shall not be subject to the laws and regulations of Dubai Municipality, the Department of Economic Development of the Government of Dubai, or the powers and authority falling within their jurisdiction."[287]

Essentially, therefore, these articles formalized the practice of granting long-term leases to foreign firms while guaranteeing them exemption from any possible nationalization of industry and from any future implementation of taxation, such as the proposed 5 percent corporation tax.[288] Furthermore, they also granted all free zone companies exemption from municipal laws, thereby effectively placing them outside of federal law.

Benefiting from this custom-made legislation, a flurry of new ventures have sought to maximize these new advantages. One such example would be the Dubai Airport Free Zone, which became operational in late 2000. Close to the city center, the zone began to offer prospective high-tech companies a number of incentives, many of which relied heavily upon the recent relaxations. Indeed, in much the same way as the JAFZ, but without needing a specific Emiri decree, the zone was able to promise tax exemptions, 100 percent foreign ownership, and 100 percent repatriation of capital and profits.[289] An even stronger example of such a development has of course been Dubai Internet City, another of Shaikh Muhammad's personally supervised projects. Certainly, the city seems intent to capitalize on all of the benefits granted by the new law, as its marketing brochure reads:

> 100% foreign ownership, 0% problems! To attract IT and internet-focused companies, Dubai Internet City will offer an extremely attractive set of benefits. In addition to 100% foreign ownership, companies will also get land on renewable leases of up to 50 years. They can move into ready-to-operate-from offices or build their own offices. The aim is to facilitate immediate commencement of business operations. Towards this end there will be a "single-window" for all government clearances, including those pertaining to trade licences and work permits.[290]

Thus, given the many similarities between these objectives and the described articles, developments such as Dubai Internet City can be regarded as direct products of this new legislation. Moreover, as these new free zones grow in size and number, they may catalyze further amendments to existing UAE regulations. Indeed, it is believed that Dubai Internet City's requirements for more comprehensive Internet access may soon even lead to a relaxation in the UAE's telecommunications restrictions. For a long time the topic of Internet access has been a delicate issue in the UAE, with freedom of use currently being sacrificed for state control. However, with a clear reference to Dubai Internet City, a spokesman for the federal government recently raised this very issue of censorship by stating that

> the current regulations enforced in the UAE may need to be examined and even dropped altogether as a concession to the fact that electronic information knows no borders and it is virtually impossible to stop its flow in and out of the UAE. . . . [B]usinesses located in the Dubai Internet City would soon be able to by-pass the Etisalat proxy server [the imposed intermediate server and information filter] for the purposes of sending and receiving electronic information.[291]

Lately there have also been indications of similar efforts to reform and liberalize the UAE's financial zones. Indeed, it has been reported that the aforementioned Dubai International Finance Centre will attempt to defy current UAE laws in much the same way as the commercial and industrial parks. Moreover, this challenge will be especially significant for the reformers given that the DIFC, lacking any official free zone status, will not be able to rely upon the Dubai 2000 legislation and, as is widely believed, has not yet received support from the UAE Central Bank. Certainly, as Sultan al-Suwaidi, the governor of the central bank, has stated, the DIFC remains "entirely a Dubai initiative, with no connection to either the Central Bank or any other UAE institution."[292] However, despite its ambiguous status, the chairman of the DIFC, al-Jallaf, has confidently stated that the center's offices and banks "will not be operating under the laws and regulations of the UAE," and that "100% foreign ownership will definitely be permitted."[293] Unsurprisingly, al-Jallaf's bold statement soon received support from Shaikh Muhammad, who reiterated that the DIFC would parallel international laws and conventions similar to those in the United States and the United Kingdom, rather than local UAE laws.[294] It would therefore seem likely that the DIFC, in a similar fashion to Emaar Properties and the DIPD, will at first be operating outside of UAE law, perhaps until fresh legislation is introduced in order to disable the existing restrictions.

Last, in the same way as the other emirates have slowly begun to follow Dubai's lead in liberalizing property markets, there are now also signs of greater commercial freedom emerging in other parts of the UAE. Indeed, in what has been described as an unprecedented move, the Sharjah economic department has drawn up a framework that will allow 100 percent foreign ownership in certain Sharjah businesses. Moreover, although this Sharjah Service Agent Law is still in the draft stages and has yet to be approved, it is thought unlikely that any opposition will be able to block such development, especially given the spate of legislation and exemptions in neighboring Dubai. Similarly in Fujairah, it has been reported that the emirate's local government has drawn up plans to boost its local industries by allowing for 100 percent foreign ownership. With the only major port on the UAE's Indian Ocean coastline, the emirate intends to become the region's main distribution point for the Indian and East African markets, and by sharing the same views as Dubai's reformers there has been an increasing realization that such objectives can only be met if existing federal regulations are removed.[295]

## The Foreign Investment Debate

As both of these case studies have demonstrated, many of the reformers' attempts to amend and circumvent existing restrictions have been directly related to the issue of foreign direct investment, whether regarding foreign ownership of residential real estate, foreign ownership of commercial and industrial plots, or even foreign ownership of financial centers. The reformers clearly hope that by liberalizing the UAE's laws, a more competitive commercial environment will develop and greater foreign investment can be attracted to the region, thereby bringing new technologies to the country and reducing the UAE's reliance on oil, while also providing a fresh source of rent. Indeed, as A. W. Galadiri, a prominent member of the aforementioned merchant elite family, famously stated in the early 1980s: "I am against any laws that come in the path of free enterprise. As our only investment is capital, we should not put obstacles in the path of its growth."[296] Conversely, more conservative groups have always contended that such developments and attempts to relax regulations may have dangerous consequences for the future of the UAE's economic structures. Indeed, as explained in the previous chapter, it is thought that the transfer of technology and skills between foreign and domestic enterprises may prove unattainable unless unaccompanied by emiratization, joint ventures, or other government-sponsored initiatives.[297] Moreover, it is undoubtedly feared that any greater liberalization may further encourage technology enclaves and dual economies, especially if the free zones remain distinct from the domestic productive base. Finally, the conservatives have also argued that creating the free zones is shortsighted, given that such zones are essentially onshore tax havens, and that their autonomous existence may make it difficult for the UAE to implement corporation tax or any other form of control in future years.[298]

In a recent study on this debate by the Dubai Chamber of Commerce and Industry, results indicated that there are indeed such identifiable groups for and against greater FDI in the UAE, in addition to a sizable third group stressing the need for a more moderate path. First, with regard to the conservatives, it was noted that there are a considerable number of officials and observers in the UAE who continue to stress the need to proceed with caution when "opening the door to FDI." These conservatives have pointed out a number of the negative implications of an overly liberal approach to investment in the UAE, and have voiced their intention to oppose such policies as and when they are brought to discussion. Muhammad al-Khuri, the president of the International Central Circle Group, emphasizes not only the tax-related drawbacks associated with unrestrained FDI, but also its worsening effects on the UAE's already imbalanced population structure and the considerable risks posed to local UAE markets if a high value of FDI were to be suddenly withdrawn. As such, al-Khuri argues: "What is important is not to go for more foreign investments, but to lay down the basis and controls that govern existing investments and find out the best methods of benefiting from them and avoiding negative effects which may arise as a result of their expansion."[299]

In contrast, the study also highlighted the opinions of certain proreform officials who contend that FDI plays a crucial role in all developed countries and that, with a veiled reference to the oil-dependent Abu Dhabian economy, a financial surplus in the hands of citizens cannot be considered a valid reason for conservatism and the restriction of FDI. Moreover, this group also argues that the risks of greater FDI far outweigh by its important benefits, the most important of which are seen to be technology linkages, the provision of jobs and training for nationals, and the diversification of the productive base. These officials also claim that low FDI and economic isolation will ultimately lead to higher costs and reduced competitiveness, reminding their opposition that other developing states such as Singapore, Malaysia, and Korea have all succeeded in embracing FDI while seeming to overcome the associated problems and dangers. Advocates of greater FDI have included FNC member Musallam bin Hum, who maintains that if such investments do not duplicate local projects then they are wholly advantageous to the UAE, and that 100 percent foreign ownership in the free zones is entirely acceptable.[300] Similarly, Muhammad Yasin, the director general of Emirates Commercial Centre, has joined these supporters of greater FDI by claiming that "more FDI would support the local economy and lead to equilibrium in the trade balance, diverting the UAE from being an importer of products and exporter of investments to a recipient of investments."[301] Moreover, Jasim al-Shamsi, the director of the budget department of the Ministry of Finance and Industry, shares this structural view, arguing that greater FDI in the manufacturing sector will eventually improve the UAE's integration with international production systems, and that instead of fearing the creation of foreign enclaves, local UAE companies should instead embrace FDI, as foreign investors are likely to allow them to improve penetration of export markets by providing them with important contacts and information such as the location of the best distribution outlets.[302] Also, in much the same way, Muhammad Shihab, an economics expert in the federal planning department, believes that greater FDI is entirely beneficial to the UAE and that the fears of multinational dominance and loss of national identity have been greatly exaggerated. Indeed, in an interview with the chamber he stated:

> The UAE, being a mono-resource economy country, where oil dominates the local resources, should strive to develop its local investments and attract FDI to lessen dependence on the oil revenue in its development process. The importance of FDI in the UAE is not restricted to being a means of economic development, but should be considered as a factor which helps in increasing the country's economic integration in the international economic system as well.[303]

The third group identified by the chamber's study were those moderates who stress the need for a balance between reforms and conservatism. Essentially, the moderates maintain that by introducing appropriate laws and regulations, the benefits of FDI can be maximized while at the same time preserving national heritage and avoiding the dangers of unbridled foreign investment. Such foreign investment laws would prevent economic dumping and other harmful consequences of FDI, while also directing FDI into the most beneficial sectors.[304] To this end, these moderates have called for an institution capable of both promotion and restraint, citing the successful examples of moderate strategies in Taiwan and Japan, where FDI has been both encouraged and limited, and where foreign companies have transferred much of their technology within a comprehensive package of industrial policies.[305] Indeed, Muhammad al-Assouri, the director of research in Emirates Industrial Bank, sums up this group's preference for such a dual strategy: "We [the UAE] should act as an open market allowing free and fair competition, but at the same time, we should prepare our public and private institutions and companies for the inevitable forthcoming competition. This way the UAE will have an effective role in the new global economic relations."[306]

## Conclusion

In addition to the negative and all-pervading effects of rentierism on the national population and the kind of subsidy-based nonproductive culture it has promoted across the state, the development efforts of the UAE's modernizing monarchies and their polities have suffered from a number of other significant internal pathologies. In particular, reinvigorated neopatrimonial networks, bureaucratic self-interests, and differing client elite orientations have frequently subverted rational policymaking and the policy implementation process, thereby undermining the planners' attempts to modify the UAE's circumstances and alleviate some of its more pressing problems.

The UAE's decisionmaking structure at the federal level is still dominated by hereditary rulers and their appointees in what would appear a hybrid neopatrimonial government of seemingly modern institutions grafted onto powerful traditional authorities. Moreover, although a legislature does exist, the unicameral nonelected chamber of appointed representatives has remained in a paralyzed state, often unable to exercise its constitutional rights and frequently incapable of questioning or restraining the executive. Furthermore, at the emirate level, local governments and departments continue to exist, some of which are subordinate but many of which run parallel to and overlap their federal counterparts. Certainly, there have been numerous occasions when the fabric of the union has been stretched to breaking point, often over vital issues of national interest such as oil policy, foreign affairs, and defense. Thus, while the federation has certainly strengthened in recent years with the greater incorporation of Dubai, it is nevertheless still more accurate to consider the UAE as something of a loose confederation, with its relatively autonomous and at times uncoordinated emirate-level powers continuing to shape the state's development.

Also capable of influencing Emirati development have been the various other institutions, parastatals, and bureaucracies tasked with policy implementation and advisory roles. The various chambers of commerce, judicial institutions, and financial institutions are also very much part of a rigid neopatrimonial network of nonelected appointments and close ties to the traditional polity. Furthermore, in certain circumstances these institutions have suffered from a number of other pathologies, including bureaucratic self-interest, opaqueness, and a lack of genuine independence. Indeed, the BCCI scandal of the early 1990s can be seen as a prime example of the devastating effect of such a combination of pathologies, with the management and fortunes of one of the UAE's most prominent development-related institutions having been inextricably linked to the traditional polity, the offending bureaucracies having prevented disclosure in the interests of self-preservation, the major regulatory bodies being powerless to intervene, and the host emirate's local government and legal system left vulnerable to external interference and corruption.

Finally, the increasing struggle over the future of Emirati development between the reformers and conservatives highlights the nonhomogeneous nature of the UAE's client elite. Although both orientations are of course components of the same dominant rentier class deriving income from economic rent, the reformers can be seen as "new rentiers" while the conservatives can be seen as "old rentiers." Essentially, the new rentiers have sought fresh sources of economic rent from non-oil-related activities such as the letting of real estate and commercial free zones, while the old rentiers have sought to perpetuate the steady flow of oil revenues. A number of controversial issues, such as foreign property ownership, foreign business ownership, and foreign direct investment, have led to protracted disputes between those attempting to liberalize the economy and foster the growth of these non-oil-related activities, and those attempting to preserve the status quo and safeguard what they believe to be the UAE's national interests. Thus, with conflicting legislation, work-arounds, pioneering projects, and attempts to circumvent existing regulations, the interactions of these opposing elite interest groups must be regarded as another major domestic influence on the UAE's socioeconomic development.

## Notes

1. See, for example, TODARO (1994), p. 85; and WORLD BANK (1985), p. 1, cited in TOYE (1987), p. 35. Todaro explains: "Contrary to the claims of the dependence theorists, the neoclassical counterrevolutionaries argue that the Third World

(many don't even accept this terminology) is underdeveloped not because of the predatory activities of the First World and the international agencies that it controls but rather because of the heavy hand of the state and the corruption, inefficiency and lack of economic incentives that permeate the economies of developing nations."

2. LUCIANI (1987), pp. 69–70. Writing specifically on the Gulf states, Ali Khalifa al-Kuwari offers a similar view; see AL-KUWARI (1978).

3. See "Diversification Through Industrialization," p. 123 in this volume.

4. See "Diversification Through Agriculture," p. 128 in this volume.

5. See "Emiratization Strategies," p. 150 in this volume.

6. Indeed, as Van Der Meulen argues, these business subsidies and advantages give the illusion of private sector growth, but such growth should be more accurately seen as a "rentier multiplier effect." VAN DER MEULEN (1997), p. 280.

7. HINNEBUSCH (1989), p. 7.

8. Ibid., p. 3.

9. Ibid.

10. See RIGGS (1991), pp. 485–504, cited in JREISAT (1992), p. 11.

11. HINNEBUSCH (1989), p. 3.

12. See WALLERSTEIN (1979), cited in RANDALL and THEOBALD (1998), p. 145.

13. See SHARABI (1988) for a discussion of a neopatrimonial dominant class.

14. PECK (1986), p. 122.

15. KHOURY (1980), p. 87.

16. Technically, the Supreme Council of Rulers is supposed to elect by secret ballot both the president and the vice president every five years, with five of the seven members needing to agree. See AL-NABEH (1984), p. 49. However, such a ballot has never been needed; personal interviews, Abu Dhabi, March 2004.

17. Abu Dhabi contributes around 70 percent to the federal budget, with Dubai contributing around 15 percent, and the remainder being provided by federally-owned enterprises such as Etisalat. See OXFORD BUSINESS GROUP (2000), p. 45.

18. ECONOMIST INTELLIGENCE UNIT (2000), p. 6. In 1996 the provisional constitution was formalized, with Abu Dhabi chosen as the capital and the seat of the presidency.

19. See Article 46 of the federal constitution. Also see PECK (1986), p. 122; and AL-NABEH (1984), pp. 48–49.

20. HEARD-BEY (1999), p. 136.

21. ECONOMIST INTELLIGENCE UNIT (2000), p. 6.

22. POLSCI.COM (2001); and personal interviews, Abu Dhabi, September 2002.

23. PECK (1986), p. 122.

24. Information gathered from BUSINESS MONITOR INTERNATIONAL (1998); MIDDLE EAST RESEARCH INSTITUTE OF JAPAN (2002); POLSCI.COM (2001); and personal interviews, Abu Dhabi, September 2002.

25. ECONOMIST INTELLIGENCE UNIT (2000), p. 7.

26. See BUSINESS MONITOR INTERNATIONAL (1998).

27. GULF NEWS (2003).

28. Calculated from COM members lists supplied by BUSINESS MONITOR INTERNATIONAL (1998); MIDDLE EAST RESEARCH INSTITUTE OF JAPAN (2002); POLSCI.COM (2001); personal interviews, Abu Dhabi, September 2002; and ANTHONY (1999).

29. VAN DER MEULEN (1997), p. 259. The minister of foreign affairs, Rashid

al-Na'imi, is from 'Ajman and shares the same clan name as the ruler, but he is of the greater tribe and not a member of the emirate's ruling family.

30. POLSCI.COM (2001); GULF NEWS (2003); and personal interviews, Abu Dhabi, September 2002.

31. See ANTHONY (1999).

32. PECK (1986), p. 126. For other examples, see AL-RUMAITHI (1977), p. 35.

33. POLSCI.COM (2001); and personal interviews, Abu Dhabi, September 2002.

34. 'Ahmad Khalifa al-Suwaidi currently heads the Arab Cultural Foundation. See ANTHONY (1999).

35. PECK (1986), p. 126; and U.S. CENTRAL INTELLIGENCE AGENCY (2001a).

36. See ABU BAKER (1995), p. 212.

37. See "Patrimonial Networks," p. 73 in this volume.

38. HEARD-BEY (1999), p. 135.

39. FENELON (1973), p. 24.

40. It would seem likely that if there are to be female FNC members in the near future, Shaikha Fatima will be responsible for drawing up a list of suitable candidates. See BUSINESS MONITOR INTERNATIONAL (2003a).

41. See RIZVI (1993), p. 665, for a discussion of Article 69 of the UAE's provisional constitution.

42. Ra's al-Khaimah has around 88,000 UAE nationals, Sharjah has around 67,000, while Abu Dhabi has around 60,000, and Dubai has only 41,000. See VAN DER MEULEN (1997), p. 202.

43. ECONOMIST INTELLIGENCE UNIT (2000), p. 7.

44. AL-SAYEGH (1998).

45. See "Elite Interest Groups: Old Rentiers Versus New Rentiers," p. 225 in this volume. It must be noted, however, that although the al-Habtur are not one of the top ten nonruling Dubai families, they nevertheless control around twenty local businesses and at one point held the chairmanship of the Commercial Bank of Dubai. See ABDULLA (1985), p. 151.

46. These were members during the FNC's twelfth term (2000–2002). See http://www.almajlis.gov.ae.

47. Information provided by Busit, Al-Roken, and Associates law firm, Dubai.

48. ECONOMIST INTELLIGENCE UNIT (2000), p. 7. Also see AL-AKIM (1989), pp. 23–24.

49. FENELON (1973), p. 24.

50. PECK (1986), p. 123.

51. In April 1996, for example, the FNC formed a combined committee to follow up the execution of the presidential directions aimed at providing greater employment opportunities for national graduates. A recommendation was drawn up for presentation to the COM stressing the passive consequences ensuing from large numbers of unemployed nationals. In June 1996 the document was reviewed by the COM and many of its suggestions were incorporated into the government's plan. See AL-NUHAYYAN (2000b), pp. 147–148.

52. AL-NUHAYYAN (2000b), p. 184.

53. See "Emiratization Strategies," p. 150 in this volume.

54. AL-NUHAYYAN (2000b), pp. 122–123.

55. Ibid., pp. 143–144.

56. Ibid., p. 185.

57. Ibid., p. 186.

58. See "Emiratization Strategies," p. 150 in this volume.

59. AL-NUHAYYAN (2000b), p. 188.

60. Ibid., pp. 178–179.

61. Indeed, the Council of Ministers can prohibit the FNC from discussing any matters relating to national security. See AL-NABEH (1984), pp. 53–54.

62. AL-NUHAYYAN (2000b), p. 121.

63. ECONOMIST INTELLIGENCE UNIT (2000), p. 8.

64. PETERSON (1988a), p. 101; and HEARD-BEY (1996), pp. 411–412. Also see "Dynastic Monarchy and the Evolution of the Traditional Polity," p. 97 in this volume.

65. Personal correspondence, Dubai, February 2003.

66. See "Diversification Through Commerce and Tourism," p. 131 in this volume.

67. For more information, see DUBAI DEPARTMENT OF ECONOMIC DEVELOPMENT (2002), pp. 222–271.

68. RIZVI (1993), p. 666.

69. UAE MINISTRY OF INFORMATION AND CULTURE (1995), p. 28.

70. UNDP-UAE (2000c).

71. PETERSON (1988a). Also see AL-WASAT (1994).

72. WAM (2003).

73. HEARD-BEY (1999), p. 145.

74. Articles 120 and 121 of the constitution stipulate eighteen different areas that should be federally controlled. See AL-MUSFIR (1985), pp. 113–114.

75. Article149 of the constitution permits the individual emirates to promulgate legislation not specified in Articles 120 and 121. See AL-MUSFIR (1985), p. 115; and UNPAN (2002).

76. KAWACH (2002b), quoting Shaikh Abdullah al-Nuhayyan, the UAE's minister of information and culture, responding to allegations of financial disunity within the federation.

77. Ibid.

78. Taken from the CAMBRIDGE INTERNATIONAL DICTIONARY OF ENGLISH (2002): "Federation—a group of regions or states united with a central government which has control over some things such as defence, but with each region having its own local government and laws, or the act of forming such a group" (p. 84).

79. Analyst and historian John Duke Anthony would appear to concur with this view: "The UAE, to date, is everything in the way of a loose confederation of states that the American republic's founding fathers—and the secessionist south's leaders half a century later—sought to achieve, but found impractical and ineffective. Here, as nowhere else in the Middle East, or for that matter anywhere else in the developing world, is a confederation that works." See ANTHONY (1999).

80. ANTHONY (1981), p. 27.

81. See "The Traditional Political Structure," p. 14 in this volume.

82. WAM (1977).

83. HEARD-BEY (1982), pp. 387–393.

84. Personal interviews, Abu Dhabi, September 2002, with regard to oil revenue contributions to the federal budget.

85. HEARD-BEY (1999), p. 135.

86. See "The Federation of Emirates," p. 45 in this volume. In fairness to Dubai, John Duke Anthony claims that one of the emirate's secret unwritten conditions on joining an Abu Dhabi–dominated federation was that it would never have to con-

tribute anything toward the federal budget other than for federal services specifically extended to Dubai. See ANTHONY (2002), p. 115.

87. HEARD-BEY (1982), pp. 387–393.

88. The original provisional constitution, signed in 1971, was intended to be
replaced by a more permanent constitution after five years.

89. OVERTON (1983), p. 186, citing an interview in 1976 with Zaki Nusseibeh,
press secretary to Shaikh Zayed. In the mid-1970s, Nusseibeh predicted that these
"independents" would become "a new generation of educated citizenry that identifies with the federal system, leading the forces of localism to appreciably diminish.
Also, these younger people of the Emirates who are becoming part of the federal
bureaucracy will be the ones holding the union together."

90. HEARD-BEY (1999), pp. 137–138.

91. It is believed that Abu Dhabi was the sole financier of the federal government until 1974. See AL-MUSFIR (1985), p. 137.

92. HEARD-BEY (1982), pp. 387–393.

93. Personal interviews with Frauke Heard-Bey, Abu Dhabi, January 2004.
Standing alongside General Bremner of the United States, Pachachi delivered the
Arabic press release to the international media following the capture of Saddam
Hussein in late 2003.

94. OVERTON (1983), taken from Overton's interview with Adnan Pachachi,
Zayed's personal political advisor, in Abu Dhabi on 25 May 1976.

95. HEARD-BEY (1982), pp. 387–393.

96. MIDDLE EAST ECONOMIC DIGEST (1978), p. 48. Since 1993 Shaikh
Muhammad al-Nuhayyan has been the army chief of staff; see "Dynastic Monarchy
and the Evolution of the Traditional Polity," p. 97 in this volume. With regard to
Shaikh Sultan's age, see VAN DER MEULEN (1997), p. 121.

97. AL-NABEH (1984), p. 62. The Dubai Defence Force had approximately
1,000 men at this time, with the Sharjah and Ra's al-Khaimah forces having about
250 men each. Also see VAN DER MEULEN (1997), p. 242.

98. MIDDLE EAST ECONOMIC DIGEST (1977), p. 3.

99. It would appear that the duties associated with the two posts were more
clearly defined, thereby reducing the likelihood of overlapping responsibilities.

100. AL-NABEH (1984), p. 62.

101. AL-MUSFIR (1985), p. 161.

102. HEARD-BEY (1996), p. 390.

103. As described, a key component of the rulers' legitimacy formula was strict
adherence to Islamic values and the support of the Palestinian cause. With Egypt,
one of the leading Arab states at that time, being drawn into closer relations with
Israel, the UAE and the other Gulf states were placed in an awkward situation, not
least due to their ongoing boycott of Israeli goods and personnel.

104. PECK (1986), p. 131; and HEARD-BEY (1982), pp. 397–401.

105. HEARD-BEY (1982), pp. 397–401.

106. Personal interviews, Abu Dhabi, October 2002, with regard to the 1979 constitutional crisis.

107. HEARD-BEY (1982), pp. 397–401.

108. YORKE (1980), p. 42.

109. HEARD-BEY (1982), pp. 397–401.

110. AL-SAYEGH (1999), pp. 15–16.

111. See UNDP-POGAR (2002).

112. Saudi Arabia, Iran, Iraq, Kuwait, and Venezuela founded OPEC in 1960. In
December 1966 Abu Dhabi joined. See OXFORD BUSINESS GROUP (2000), p.

49; and PLATTS GLOBAL ENERGY (2002).

113. BROWN (1998), p. 361.

114. Ibid.

115. Ibid., p. 724.

116. Ibid., p. 361. Also see ECONOMIST INTELLIGENCE UNIT (2000), p. 8. Indeed, as the Economist Intelligence Unit notes, the Supreme Petroleum Council is now effectively a federal institution given that the federal oil ministry was downgraded in the 1990s with much of its formal power being transferred. As one would expect given the UAE's continuing reliance on oil exports, the Supreme Petroleum Council plays a major role in the policymaking process, as it approves all oil-related policies and development projects for the companies falling under the umbrella of the state-owned Abu Dhabi National Oil Company.

117. BROWN (1998), p. 366.

118. GULF NEWS (2002).

119. See "The Federation of Emirates," p. 45 in this volume.

120. Information gathered from personal interviews in Ra's al-Khaimah, September 2002. For an independent confirmation, also see UNDP-POGAR (2002).

121. Ibid. This rather maverick orientation is perhaps best explained by the emirate's proud history and, as described in Chapter 1, its constant need for greater recognition and some kind of parity with the wealthier oil-producing emirates.

122. See "The Federation of Emirates," p. 45 in this volume.

123. Also, given that many of these Iranian merchants represented a significant Shi'a minority and the aforementioned potential "fifth column," it seems plausible that Dubai, Sharjah, and Umm al-Qawain preferred to have Iran on their side, rather than plotting against them.

124. PECK (1986), p. 133.

125. Personal interviews, Abu Dhabi, September 2002, with regard to UAE foreign policy.

126. Personal interviews, undisclosed locations, 2003.

127. AL-SAYEGH (1999), pp. 15–16.

128. Dubai now contributes around 15 percent of the federal budget. See OXFORD BUSINESS GROUP (2000), p. 45.

129. MIDDLE EAST ECONOMIC DIGEST (1997). Also see FOLEY (1998).

130. U.S. DEPARTMENT OF STATE (2001), sec. 1.

131. Ibid., sec. 1(e). Also see OXFORD BUSINESS GROUP (2000), p. 115.

132. OXFORD BUSINESS GROUP (2000), p. 79.

133. See "The UAE's Banking Sector and the Central Bank," p. 212 in this volume.

134. For example, one can readily take a Dubai transport bus to Al-'Ayn, but because Al-'Ayn is part of Abu Dhabi, there is no return service. Similarly confusing is the journey between Abu Dhabi and Dubai, which one can travel using Al Ghazal transport for 20 dirhams in one direction, but where one must pay 33 dirhams for a Dubai transport service on the way back.

135. OVERTON (1983), p. 184, based on a 1976 interview with Sa'id 'Ahmad Ghubash, the UAE minister of planning. Also see "Readily Identifiable Development Problems," p. 163 in this volume, for a description of duplicated investments.

136. ECONOMIST INTELLIGENCE UNIT (2000), p. 7. Also see ABDULLA (1985), p. 212; and KHALIFA (1979), p. 60.

137. See, for example, "Commercial Ventures and Free Zones," p. 232 in this volume, with regard to the "Dubai Technology, Electronic Commerce, and Media Free Zone Law" of 2000.

138. HEARD-BEY (1996), pp. 415–416.

139. This forum is referred to as the "Federation of UAE Chambers of Commerce and Industry General Assembly."

140. FEDERATION OF UAE CHAMBERS OF COMMERCE AND INDUSTRY (1994b), pp. 11–12.

141. Ibid., p. 5.

142. Ibid., pp. 11–12.

143. Ibid., p. 21.

144. DUBAI CHAMBER OF COMMERCE AND INDUSTRY (2001), pp. 1–8.

145. Ibid.

146. FEDERATION OF UAE CHAMBERS OF COMMERCE AND INDUSTRY (1994a), pp. 14–15.

147. Ibid., pp. 45–46.

148. Ibid., pp. 14–15.

149. Ibid., p. 47.

150. Ibid., pp. 45–46.

151. DUBAI CHAMBER OF COMMERCE AND INDUSTRY (2001), pp. 1–8. According to Article 6 of the Emiri decree establishing the chamber, membership was to include all "except small businesses or those whose profession depend on personal efforts rather than financial resources."

152. Personal interviews, Dubai, March 2002. With regard to the al-Tayir family, 'Ahmad al-Tayir is currently the minister of communications and Matar al-Tayir is currently the minister of labor and social affairs; also, as mentioned, Tariq al-Tayir is one of Dubai's Federal National Council representatives. See "The Federal Decisionmaking Structure," p. 188 in this volume. Muhammad al-Mulla was the former minister of transportation in addition to being a longtime member of the Dubai chamber's board of directors; see ABU BAKER (1995), p. 222.

153. ABU DHABI ECONOMY (1999), p. 4. Also see "The Federal Decisionmaking Structure," p. 188 in this volume.

154. ABU DHABI ECONOMY (1999), p. 4.

155. Personal interviews, Abu Dhabi, April 2001.

156. ABU DHABI ECONOMY (1999), p. 4.

157. PECK (1986), p. 123.

158. ECONOMIST INTELLIGENCE UNIT (2000), p. 7.

159. PECK (1986), p. 123.

160. U.S. DEPARTMENT OF STATE (2001), sec. 1(e).

161. KHALEEJ TIMES (2001), from a lecture at the Zayed Centre for Coordination and Follow-Up by Muhammad bin Kakhira al-Dhahiri, the minister of justice, Islamic affairs, and the Awqaf.

162. U.S. DEPARTMENT OF STATE (2001), sec. 1.

163. Personal interviews, undisclosed locations, September 2003. For independent eyewitness accounts, see http://www.uaeprison.com.

164. U.S. DEPARTMENT OF STATE (2001), sec. 1.

165. Personal interviews, Fujairah, September 2002. It was revealed that in 1998 an expatriate Arab judge imposed mutilation sentences on two offenders in Fujairah; this sentence was soon overturned by the supreme appeals court.

166. U.S. DEPARTMENT OF STATE (2001), sec. 1(d).

167. Ibid., sec. 1(e).

168. Ibid.

169. FENELON (1973), pp. 80–83.

170. OXFORD BUSINESS GROUP (2000), p. 86.

171. FENELON (1973), pp. 80–83.

172. ABU DHABI PLANNING DEPARTMENT, ECONOMIC DIVISION (1976), p. 14.

173. A limit of eight branches was placed on each foreign banking house, thus allowing local banks such as the National Banks of Abu Dhabi and Dubai to dominate. See PECK (1986), pp. 111–112.

174. ECONOMIST INTELLIGENCE UNIT (2000), pp. 38–39.

175. UAE CENTRAL BANK (1991), p. 43.

176. UAE CENTRAL BANK (1996).

177. In recent years these directors have included the bank's deputy chairman, Juma' al-Majid Abdullah, who also serves as vice president of Emirates Bank International, and Muhammad Kharbash, who now serves on the Council of Ministers as minister of state for finance and industry. See APS REVIEW (1998).

178. UAE CENTRAL BANK (1991), pp. 39–47.

179. Ibid., pp. 39–41. This recommendation was made in 1991.

180. AL-SHARHAN INTERNATIONAL CONSULTANCY (2000), p. 43. This recommendation was made in 2000.

181. See UAE CENTRAL BANK (1994).

182. AL-SHARHAN INTERNATIONAL CONSULTANCY (2000), pp. 41–42.

183. Ibid., pp. 43–45.

184. OXFORD BUSINESS GROUP (2000), p. 88. The EIB was created following Federal Law no. 1 of 1982. See ABDULLA (1985), p. 250.

185. DUBAI DEPARTMENT OF ECONOMIC DEVELOPMENT (1999), p. 267.

186. See EMIRATES INDUSTRIAL BANK (1983); these examples being Galadiri Ice Cream, Gulf Shoes, and Arabcoat.

187. The majority of these soft loans have provided UAE nationals with capital for new industrial ventures. See OXFORD BUSINESS GROUP (2000), p. 88.

188. ABU DHABI PLANNING DEPARTMENT, ECONOMIC DIVISION (1976), p. 14; and personal interviews, Dubai, March 2002.

189. Personal interviews, undisclosed location, 2003. For an independent confirmation, see OXFORD BUSINESS GROUP (2000), p. 79.

190. ECONOMIST INTELLIGENCE UNIT (2000), p. 6.

191. EVERETT-HEATH (2002), p. 4, quoting Anis al-Jallaf, chairman of the DIFC's board of directors.

192. ECONOMIST INTELLIGENCE UNIT (2000), p. 6. Also see OXFORD BUSINESS GROUP (2000), p. 83.

193. ECONOMIST INTELLIGENCE UNIT (2000), p. 41. Also see "Foreign Property Ownership," p. 229 in this volume.

194. Personal interviews, Abu Dhabi, March 2002.

195. UAE CENTRAL BANK (2002), p. 155.

196. RICHARDS (2001), pp. 7–11, quoting Alan Richards speaking at the 20 April 1999 conference convened by the Middle East Policy Council.

197. Ibid.

198. ECONOMIST INTELLIGENCE UNIT (2000), pp. 38–39.

199. RICHARDS (2001), pp. 7–11.

200. The Hong Kong and Shanghai Banking Corporation (HSBC) and other organizations including Business Monitor International recently stated that the prevailing regulatory and commercial environment in the UAE would have to improve rapidly in order for high levels of investment to be maintained. Indeed, in the second quarter of 2001 Business Monitor International quite explicitly called for greater transparency concerning the UAE's economic data, and tighter federal legis-

lation to counteract persistent fraud. See BUSINESS MONITOR INTERNATION-
AL (2001), p. 15; and HSBC MIDDLE EAST (2001).

201. RICHARDS (2001), pp. 7–11.

202. RIZVI (1993), p. 669.

203. Ibid.

204. OXFORD BUSINESS GROUP (2000), pp. 71–72.

205. HEARD-BEY (1996), p. 400.

206. See MUGSON (1991a, 1991b); HOAGLAND (1991); and TRUED and
GURWIN (1992).

207. KERRY and BROWN (1992), pp. 102–140; in particular, see "Executive
Summary: BCCI Constituted International Financial Crime on a Massive and
Global Scale."

208. Ibid.

209. Ibid.

210. OXFORD BUSINESS GROUP (2000), p. 71.

211. KERRY and BROWN (1992); in particular, "Abu Dhabi: BCCI's Founding
and Majority Shareholders."

212. Price Waterhouse Report sec. 41 to the Bank of England, June 1991, sec.
1.33, cited in KERRY and BROWN (1992), "Abu Dhabi: BCCI's Founding and
Majority Shareholders."

213. Referring to the statements made by al-Sayegh, Abu Dhabi's witness in the
BCCI investigation, cited in KERRY and BROWN (1992), "Abu Dhabi: BCCI's
Founding and Majority Shareholders."

214. Ibid. Regarding Shaikh Zayed's initial share, also see MIDDLE EAST ECO-
NOMIC DIGEST (1982), p. 31.

215. Price Waterhouse Report sec. 41 to the Bank of England, June 1991, cited in
KERRY and BROWN (1992), "Abu Dhabi: BCCI's Founding and Majority
Shareholders—Abu Dhabi's Ownership Interest in BCCI."

216. KERRY and BROWN (1992), "Abu Dhabi: BCCI's Founding and Majority
Shareholders—Findings."

217. Ibid.

218. See "Dynastic Monarchy and the Evolution of the Traditional Polity," p. 97
in this volume, for a discussion of the unitary state.

219. Referring to the statements made by al-Sayegh, Abu Dhabi's witness in the
BCCI investigation, cited in KERRY and BROWN (1992), "Abu Dhabi: BCCI's
Founding and Majority Shareholders—Ghanim al-Mazrui."

220. Price Waterhouse Report sec. 41 to the Bank of England, June 1991, cited in
KERRY and BROWN (1992), "Abu Dhabi: BCCI's Founding and Majority
Shareholders—Ghanim al-Mazrui."

221. Based on staff interviews in the BCCI and BCCE, cited in KERRY and
BROWN (1992), "Abu Dhabi: BCCI's Founding and Majority Shareholders—Abu
Dhabi's Commitments in April–May, 1990."

222. KERRY and BROWN (1992), "Abu Dhabi: BCCI's Founding and Majority
Shareholders—Al-Sayegh's Testimony and Answers to Questions."

223. Extracts, Federal Law no. 6 of 1973, Federal Law no. 10 of 1973, Federal
Law no. 3 of 1983, cited in KERRY and BROWN (1992), "Abu Dhabi: BCCI's
Founding and Majority Shareholders."

224. KERRY and BROWN (1992), "Abu Dhabi: BCCI's Founding and Majority
Shareholders—Al-Sayegh's Testimony and Answers to Questions."

225. Ibid.

226. Ibid.

227. See "Substrategies: Abu Dhabi and Dubai—A Comparative Analysis," p. 154 in this volume, with regard to Dubai's diversification strategy.

228. Personal interviews, Dubai, December 2001.

229. BUSINESS MONITOR INTERNATIONAL (2000), pp. 9–10.

230. U.S. DEPARTMENT OF STATE (2001), sec. 2(a). Newspapers began publishing articles critical of alleged inefficiencies in the delivery of services by the Ministries of Health, Education, and Electricity and Water. In August the English-language daily newspaper *Gulf News* featured a two-part exposé on life in the Dubai women's central prison. A rare look into a women's correctional facility, the series included interviews with both UAE national and foreign prisoners, describing in depth a typical day in the prison.

231. See "The Co-option and Patronage of Civil Society," p. 269 in this volume.

232. BUSINESS MONITOR INTERNATIONAL (2001), pp. 4–5.

233. KHALEEJ TIMES (2002d). Also see "Cultural and Religious Resources," p. 77 in this volume.

234. ZA'ZA (2004).

235. KHALEEJ TIMES (2002d).

236. AL-SHARHAN INTERNATIONAL CONSULTANCY (2000), p. 41; and OXFORD BUSINESS GROUP (2000), p. 75. Patel absconded in May 1999 owing nearly $400 million to local and international banks. Fifteen banks suffered, and some nearly collapsed.

237. AL-SHARHAN INTERNATIONAL CONSULTANCY (2000), p. 41.

238. BUSINESS IN DUBAI (2001b), p. 6, the program's sponsor being Shaikh Muhammad al-Maktum.

239. See "The UAE's Banking Sector and the Central Bank," p. 212 in this volume.

240. EVERETT-HEATH (2002), p. 4.

241. BUSINESS IN DUBAI (2002a), pp. 8–9.

242. ECONOMIST INTELLIGENCE UNIT (2000), p. 22. Also see "Substrategies: Abu Dhabi and Dubai—A Comparative Analysis," p. 154 in this volume.

243. ECONOMIST INTELLIGENCE UNIT (2000), p. 23.

244. Between 1926 and 1928 the Dhawahir assisted the exiled sons of deceased Shaikh Sultan al-Nuhayyan by offering them refuge until they were able to dispose of the murderous Shaikh Saqr al-Nuhayyan.

245. Hadaf al-Dhahiri is the vice president of the UAE University in Al-'Ayn. See ANTHONY (1999).

246. BUSINESS MONITOR INTERNATIONAL (1997), p. 17.

247. See "The Relationship Between Federal and Emirate-Level Structures," p. 199 in this volume.

248. ECONOMIST INTELLIGENCE UNIT (2000), p. 9; and BUSINESS MONITOR INTERNATIONAL (1997), p. 17.

249. See ABDULLA (1985), p. 153; ABU BAKER (1995), pp. 155, 240; and VAN DER MEULEN (1997), pp. 139–145.

250. ECONOMIST INTELLIGENCE UNIT (2000), p. 9.

251. One such example being the Juma' al-Majid Cultural Foundation east of Deira, where a number of Arabic-language books and journals are made available to the public.

252. ABDULLA (1985), p. 156.

253. Ibid., p. 157.

254. The Galadiri and the al-Gurg (*gurg* translates as "wolf" from Farsi) are Shi'a

families descended from the merchants who transferred their business interests from Iran to Dubai earlier in the twentieth century. See "Substrategies: Abu Dhabi and Dubai—A Comparative Analysis," p. 154 in this volume; and VAN DER MEULEN (1997), pp. 195–199.

255. ABDULLA (1985), pp. 148–153. Also see ABU BAKER (1995), pp. 243–246.

256. See earlier discussion of Shaikh Zayed's policy in the late 1960s to accommodate certain graduates into his administration, and Shaikh Khalid al-Qasimi's attempts to give young graduates a role in the Sharjah government. See ABDUL-LAH (1978), pp. 138, 140; and "Patrimonial Networks," p. 73 in this volume.

257. See "The Federal Decisionmaking Structure," p. 188 in this volume.

258. See APS REVIEW (1998).

259. Personal interviews, Abu Dhabi, March 2001.

260. AL-WASAT (1997).

261. Personal interviews, Abu Dhabi, March 2001.

262. JOHNSON (1997). Michael Johnson is an associate of BSP Management Consultants, Abu Dhabi.

263. Ibid.

264. MIDDLE EAST ECONOMIC DIGEST (1994), pp. 14–16.

265. Ibid.

266. See "Substrategies: Abu Dhabi and Dubai—A Comparative Analysis," p. 154 in this volume.

267. MIDDLE EAST ECONOMIC DIGEST (1994), pp. 14–16.

268. AL-NUHAYYAN (2000b), p. 184.

269. Ibid., pp. 122–123.

270. ECONOMIST INTELLIGENCE UNIT (2000), p. 23.

271. Personal interviews, Abu Dhabi, March 2002: "There are many efficient and dynamic organisations that would be more than capable of successfully competing in a liberalised economy without any of these restrictive rules and regulations. Indeed there are numerous Dubai- and Abu Dhabi–based family companies ranging from Arabian sword vendors and tailors to cake shops and luxury soap manufacturers which not only offer value for money and efficient service, but have also embraced the opportunities of e-commerce and Internet marketing. Equally, however, there are also many other groups that realise their businesses would be inefficient and uncompetitive in such an environment. Obvious examples would include those family businesses reliant on outdated technology and of course the many infant light manufacturing industries striving to make economies of scale."

272. SALDAMANDO (2001a), pp. 59–60.

273. GULF NEWS (1997).

274. GULF NEWS (1998b).

275. GULF NEWS (1997).

276. GULF NEWS (1998a).

277. THEODOULOU (2002).

278. UAE MINISTRY OF INFORMATION AND CULTURE (2002); see http://www.uaeinteract.com, the ministry's official website.

279. Ibid.

280. As described in Chapter 2, the Khalifa Committee allocates land to UAE nationals and can administer the property for them. Through this mechanism the ruler retains the actual title to the land. See OXFORD BUSINESS GROUP (2000), p. 65.

281. See "The UAE's Banking Sector and the Central Bank," p. 212 in this volume.

282. ECONOMIST INTELLIGENCE UNIT (2000), p. 41.

283. See "The Physical Infrastructure for Diversification," p. 137 in this volume.

284. FEDERATION OF UAE CHAMBERS OF COMMERCE AND INDUSTRY (1994a), pp. 36–37.

285. KHALEEJ TIMES (1998b).

286. KHALEEJ TIMES (1998a).

287. DUBAI GOVERNMENT (2000), issued by Shaikh Maktum al-Maktum in 2000.

288. ECONOMIST INTELLIGENCE UNIT (2000), p. 23.

289. AL-SHARHAN INTERNATIONAL CONSULTANCY (2000), pp. 25–30.

290. Taken from Dubai Internet City's 2001 official brochure.

291. HOBBY (2001). Gerard Hobby is an associate of Al-Tamimi Consultants.

292. EVERETT-HEATH (2002), p. 4, quoting Jamal Sanad al-Suwaidi of the Emirates Centre for Strategic Studies and Research.

293. Ibid., p. 5.

294. BUSINESS IN DUBAI (2002a), pp. 8–9.

295. AL-SHARHAN INTERNATIONAL CONSULTANCY (2000), pp. 25–30.

296. Quoted in ABDULLA (1985), p. 177.

297. See, in this volume, "Fostering Technology Linkages with Foreign Firms," p. 127, and "Emiratization," p. 144.

298. Personal interviews, Abu Dhabi, March 2002 and January 2004.

299. BUSINESS IN DUBAI (2001c), pp. 19–21.

300. Ibid., pp. 20–22.

301. Ibid.

302. Ibid.

303. Ibid.

304. Ibid., pp. 18–19.

305. Ibid., pp. 16–18.

306. Ibid., pp. 18–19.

# 5

## Globalization and the
## Prospects for Civil Society

W ith the described reforms of the UAE's "new rentiers" clearly
encouraging the much touted forces of globalization and the new
economy, this chapter assesses the seemingly ambiguous impact of such
increasing external influences on the UAE's dependent development and
the future of its domestic structures. On the one hand, globalizing forces, as
extensions of the same international forces that created the dependent structures in the first place, may continue to reinforce the UAE's dependency-
related domestic pathologies; on the other hand, something of a second
wave of globalization may be capable of surmounting such obstacles and
engendering genuinely liberalizing reforms.

### The Globalization Dilemma

Internationalized economies with widespread interstate activities have
existed for centuries, but in most cases individual national economies
remained distinct and predominant. In more recent years, however, there
has been a growing trend toward a more globalized economy in which
such individual economies have been "subsumed and re-articulated into
a system by international processes and transactions."[1] Globalization can
therefore be viewed as both an evolution and a qualitative shift from
internationalization as it supplies functional integration to the previously
dispersed economic activities of separate national economies.[2]
Furthermore, although globalization has been regarded by political scientists as being primarily a characteristic of economic activity, it is also
a multidimensional force with the power not only to subsume national
economies but also to reshape national identities. Indeed, as many planners in the developing world have realized, while globalization may on

251

the one hand offer an escape route avoiding future economic marginal-ization, at the same time it may also have serious implications for their indigenous political systems, societies, and cultures.

If the slogan of the annual Dubai Shopping Festival, *"One World, One Family, One Festival,"* is to be taken literally,[3] it would seem that the UAE, or at least Dubai, is prepared to embrace wholeheartedly the forces of globalization. It would appear that the government of Dubai and its business community are both welcoming and actively encourag-ing foreign investment, international communications, and many of the other developments commonly associated with globalization. Indeed, in citing a recent speech by Dubai's energetic and reforming crown prince, David Hirst illustrates this point well:

> Early last year His Highness General Shaykh Muhammad bin Maktum [*sic*] announced at a press conference that the Internet revolution and the "new global economy" were coming to Dubai. It was an incongru-ous spectacle: so traditional a figure, in distinctive black dishdasha, delivering a pep talk like some wired and with-it corporate executive. As "synergy," "internet-enabled solutions," "cycle-time reduction" and suchlike flashed across a screen behind him, he swore he would have his globalised "government@Dubai" fully in place within 18 months or else.[4]

Moreover, in the near future globalization in Dubai is predicted to reach even higher levels following the much publicized "Dubai 2003," a mas-sive event that hosted members of the World Bank, the IMF, and other international organizations. This gathering was seen as confirming Dubai's position at the crossroads of the new global economy, and as the event's coordinator, Ibrahim Belselah, has described, "it offered the opportunity for Dubai to reach out to global investors and decision-makers while affirming the emirate's credibility and stability."[5] But has this same proglobalization attitude been shared by the other emirates and interest groups? As the earlier case studies regarding foreign property ownership and foreign business ownership have indicated, there has clearly been little consensus, with many of the more conservative "old rentiers" remaining firmly opposed to such reforms and wary of the per-ceived dangers of greater global integration. Certainly, by building upon the previous chapter's discussion of the role of foreign direct investment,[6] it would appear that there is now also something of a national debate between those seeking to maximize the benefits of "benign globalization," and in contrast those wishing to maintain and augment the existing restrictions and regulations in an effort to preserve not only the UAE's national economy but also its distinct national socie-ty and culture.

To complicate the matter further, it would seem that neither camp has been able to present a definitive argument in their favor, given the paucity of real-world examples from other developing states experiencing similar conditions. Furthermore, on a more conceptual level, the abundance of both convincing pro- and antiglobalization literature has only served to fuel the debate, especially as both schools of thought would appear to be directly applicable to the UAE's development. Predictably, the antiglobalization writings of Samir Amin[7] and others reinforce dependency theory by tying globalizing forces to the capitalist interests of the core economies and the notion of unequal "underdevelopment." As such, globalization is seen as a collection of predatory socioeconomic forces that will eventually incorporate and undermine peripheral nation-states in order to allow for the greater expansion of capitalist markets. Therefore, within such a framework, globalization is seen as leading to the loss of control over domestic economies and resources, generating disequilibrium and fragmentation within developing states,[8] and of course also threatening national identity and eroding social cohesion. Thus, mindful of these dangers, the solutions suggested by the antiglobalization theorists and many of the UAE's conservatives have centered around a more activist nation-state capable of regulating potentially harmful forces and offering greater protection. In contrast, much of the recent proglobalization literature has provided support and solutions for those reformers seeking to liberalize the UAE's economy and welcome the forces of globalization.[9] Indeed, arguing that greater global integration, labor migration, improved communications, and other manifestations of "convergence" will not only bring economic improvements but also provide long-term social and political benefits,[10] the proglobalization theorists suggest that developing states should not resist such changes, but should instead remove all obstacles in order to facilitate this inevitable transformation.

## The Historical Antecedents of Globalization

As Frauke Heard-Bey notes in her study of the Trucial coast, for a long period the shared waters of the Gulf region served not only as conduits between the various shaikhdoms, but also as an economic lifeline to the rest of the world.[11] Indeed, this lifeline became especially evident at the turn of the twentieth century, when a common regional interest in the profitable pearling industry began to encourage far greater contact and cooperation between the various towns and ports. Although certainly stunted by the described British exclusivity agreements and the region's subsequent incorporation into the British-Indian economic network, international trade, overseas markets, and labor migration nevertheless all became key features of the lower Gulf's economic life during this early period.

More recently, following the creation of the federation in the early 1970s, there began a fresh wave of greater regional and international economic integration. At this time the UAE's planners were concentrating heavily on a broad strategy of diversification, requiring the UAE's non-oil-related sectors to expand in an effort to reduce the economy's reliance on its single primary product export. Such a strategy, especially with regard to the UAE's domestic export-based industries and commercial activities, therefore called for a far superior framework of cooperation not only between the UAE and the other Gulf States, but also between the UAE and potential international markets.[12] Thus, from the 1970s onward, the attempts to establish greater trade links led to a plethora of mutually beneficial industrial, commercial, and tourist agreements linking the UAE with many other states, predominantly those in South Asia and Africa, but also with some as far afield as Singapore and Brunei.[13] Indeed, thirty years later many of these bilateral agreements are still in place, and can therefore be regarded as important antecedents of the region's more recent global economic integration.

Similarly, with regard to the sociocultural globalization of the region, by the late nineteenth century the lower Gulf was already beginning to experience greater cultural influences from other parts of the Middle East and North Africa. Certainly, as Muhammad Abdullah explains, this was especially evident following the opening of the Suez Canal in 1869:

> Steam navigation routes reconnected the lower Gulf with Egypt after a rupture of about three hundred years. These new lines of communication also brought to the Gulf, as well as international mail, Cairo daily newspapers and literary magazines, thus helping to foster more of a political awareness within the educated groups. This was especially significant given the fact that before the First World War the Gulf did not even possess an Arabic printing press.[14]

Moreover, during this period the region's previously narrow economic links with the Indian subcontinent also began to expand to include much greater cultural stimulation. Indeed, as the pearling industry reached its zenith, the international trading hub of Bombay had already grown rapidly in size and diversity, with the city widely regarded as a cosmopolitan cultural center and as a symbol of "British-western civilisation."[15] Given Bombay's close links with the Trucial coast, particularly with Dubai, there is little doubt that much of this foreign influence also began to filter through to the lower Gulf. Bombay, like Cairo, possessed many printing presses, and a mixture of Indian- and Egyptian-published volumes duly found their way into private libraries along the Trucial coast.[16] Furthermore, as Fatma al-Sayegh describes, the increasingly frequent contact with Indian and other Arab merchants in Bombay was already leading to a much greater awareness of world developments and stimulated much greater political thinking among those in the lower Gulf.[17]

Of course by the time of the oil booms, the massive influx of foreign workers together with the vast consumption of imported goods, improved communications, and the Emiratis' newfound ability to travel overseas, all considerably accelerated the region's sociocultural global integration. Indeed, even in 1973, just two years after the creation of the federation, Kevin Fenelon remarked how "the presence of a large number of expatriates, drawn from many nations, cannot but have a great influence in breaking down conservatism, old habits, and prejudices against other ways of life, such as might have been felt in more isolated communities."[18] Moreover, Fenelon also foresaw the influence of mass media and foreign travel on Emirati society and culture:

> Television and radio have done much to widen horizons, as these media penetrate into the home and thus reach all members of the family, including the women's quarters. The almost universal possession of transistor radios has brought the happenings of the outside world into relatively remote regions. In the towns, modern cinemas that show films in Arabic, English and Indian languages are very popular, again providing links with the outside world. Merchants are well travelled, and it is not unusual for them to travel abroad several times a year. Many now are bringing their families on visits to Beirut, Cairo and Europe. In Oxford Street, London, ladies from the Gulf can be seen not infrequently in the summer doing their shopping, masked and veiled as they would be at home—a striking combination of the ultra-traditional with the most modern.[19]

Writing ten years later, Malcolm Peck made similar observations, especially with regard to the increasing number of foreigners in the UAE's schools and universities. Certainly, by focusing on the example of UAE University in Al-'Ayn, he demonstrated how in the late 1970s and early 1980s local UAE students were beginning to come into much greater contact than ever before with foreign students and staff. In particular, he highlighted the Palestinian contingent of students, which at that time composed the largest nonlocal student body in the UAE. The assumption was that increasing interaction with such groups would soon widen the sociocultural horizons of Emirati students, and at the very least make them more receptive toward ideas such as Arab nationalism than previous generations.[20] Although Arab nationalism has never really taken a firm hold in the UAE,[21] there is nevertheless little doubt that Peck's broader sociocultural predictions are being realized as expanding expatriate contingents continue to exchange ideas and experiences with the local youth.

## The Impact of Globalizing Forces
## on the Contemporary Economy

In more recent years, one of the most debated features of increasing economic integration and globalization has been the seemingly inevitable
increase in international competition, and of course the extent to which this
will affect the UAE's domestic businesses. Unsurprisingly, in much the
same way as the foreign investment question, the UAE's reformers and
conservatives have remained at odds over the way in which the government
and local Emirati enterprises should best adapt to these changes. On the one
hand, many local Dubai businessmen appear positive and seem ready to
accept a more liberal and global trading environment. Certainly, as 'Ahmad
al-Shaikh argues, Dubai family-based businesses will always have a place,
and, although they may have suffered initially due to international competition, they are nevertheless going to be well suited to change as their small
size will allow for more streamlined decisionmaking and less bureaucracy:
"As such, their growth should be fast, and as long as laws are introduced to
improve the transparency of family businesses, they can hope to reap the
benefits of international markets, e-commerce, and improved global communications."[22] On the other hand, however, Muhammad al-Meshrikh, a
member of the Sharjah Chamber of Commerce and Industry, offers a more
cautious perspective. Claiming that family-owned businesses cannot possibly hope to compete "in an open market with multinationals that own
expert houses and huge capitals," he contends that globalizing forces will
soon require the UAE's family firms to either merge or to go public simply
in order to survive.[23] Although, as of yet, there are perhaps too few examples to accurately assess the impact of these forces on domestic businesses,
it would seem that the proglobalization thinkers can nevertheless draw
much comfort from the many small family enterprises, especially those in
Dubai and Abu Dhabi, which have clearly seized the opportunities of globalization and which have definitely begun to prosper in a greater international market. Among others, these have ranged from Arabian sword vendors and tailors to cake shops and luxury soap manufacturers, all of which
not only offer value for money and efficient service, but also have adopted
the concepts of e-commerce and Internet marketing in order to expand their
customer bases.[24]

An equally complex issue has been the debate over globalization versus regionalization, with many UAE nationals arguing that another major
economic impact of greater globalization has been the stagnation and
sidelining of the UAE's regional economic integration with the other Gulf
states and the rest of the Arab world. Indeed, claiming that the UAE is now
pursuing globalization without first promoting regionalization, many have
asserted that individual national economies also need to be part of a strong

regional economy, which can be used as a safety net in times of crisis and instability as, in the event of an economic downswing, it is thought likely that the multinationals and other foreign companies will be the first to withdraw their investments from the UAE. Thus it is argued that greater regionalization should be seen as a necessary first step in order to consolidate the national economy and to provide a more effective launch pad from which to enter the global economy.[25] Although it is perhaps again too early to judge the long-term effects of globalization over regionalization, as with the implications for domestic business, there are nevertheless already clear indications of such unbalanced economic integration. Certainly, as the statistics in Figure 5.1 highlight, there is now little doubt that the UAE's key trading partners have become almost exclusively nonregional, non-Arab economies. Clearly, in the case of Dubai, the central hub of the UAE's trading activities, almost all of the emirate's imports currently originate from Western or Asian trading partners (see Figure 5.2), with Iran, traditionally the UAE's highest-placed regional partner, now ranking just twentieth. Similarly, if Dubai's re-exporting activity is excluded,[26] it would appear from the available figures that, in addition to the aforementioned consumption/import bias and the resulting trade imbalance,[27] almost all of the major trading partners for the UAE's exports are either Western or Far Eastern, with formerly significant regional partners such as Bahrain, Kuwait, and Yemen now placed well outside of the top ten.

Moreover, with regard to investments, there is also believed to have been a discernible shift away from regional investment toward more global

**Figure 5.1 Total Value of Dubai Imports from
Major Nonoil Trading Partners**

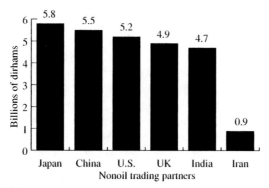

*Source:* Dubai Department of Ports and Customs, "Dubai: Major (Non-Oil) Trade Partners—Imports," in Dubai Department of Economic Development (2001), *Development Statistics,* Government of Dubai, p. 129.

**Figure 5.2 Total Value of Dubai Exports from
Major Nonoil Trading Partners**

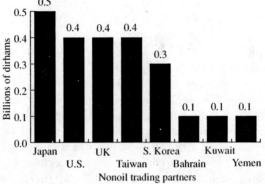

*Source:* Dubai Department of Ports and Customs, "Dubai: Major (Non-Oil) Trade Partners—Exports," in Dubai Department of Economic Development (2001), *Development Statistics,* Government of Dubai, p. 130.

investment. Indeed, writing in the early 1990s, J. E. Jreisat had already high-lighted the fact that although total Arab foreign investment was around $65 billion (almost all of which was held by the governments, banks, and ruling families of the Gulf), only 5 percent of all surplus funds accumulated by these oil rich states was actually invested back into the region.[28] Similarly, with regard to foreign direct investment, it has been shown by Sari Hanafi in his recent study of the "paradoxical effects of the UAE's political economy" how the UAE has become increasingly reliant on FDI from multinationals, with relatively little input from the Arab region. Specifically, the Jebel Ali Free Zone and the UAE's other export processing zones are seen as being particularly strong examples of this trend, and have been accused of being geared entirely toward globalization while doing little to support and pro-mote regional integration. Indeed, by 2000 the Jebel Ali Free Zone com-prised over 1,000 registered companies, of which about 32 percent were Asian, 30 percent were European, 14 percent were North American, and less than a quarter were Arab or Middle Eastern[29] (see Figure 5.3).

Thus, Hanafi convincingly argues that Arab investors have shied away from investing in such zones, claiming they feel less integrated with the structures than their European and North American counterparts. It is also widely believed that many Arab investors are now reluctant to invest in the UAE and the other Gulf states given the long history of restrictive business practices and ownership regulations, such as the aforementioned kafil spon-sorship system. Indeed, citing the experiences of many Palestinian busi-nessmen and investors in the UAE, Hanafi claims that even though some of

**Figure 5.3 Regional Distribution of Jebel Ali
Free Zone Companies, 2000**

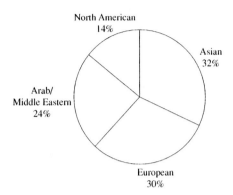

*Sources:* Sari Hanafi (2001), "Globalisation Without Regionalisation: The Paradoxical Effects of the Political Economy of the United Arab Emirates," excerpt and statistics from a presentation given at the "Globalisation and the Gulf" conference at the University of Exeter, July 200,1; and for investment statistics, Jebel Ali Free Zone Authority (2000), Jebel Ali, Dubai.

these restrictions are now being relaxed the old memories are taking time to fade, and that many prefer to invest elsewhere, believing that the UAE is specifically targeting Western investors and multinationals.[30]

Another significant effect of globalizing forces on the UAE's national economy has been the increasing presence and involvement of supranational economic organizations, most notably the World Trade Organization, the International Monetary Fund, and the United Nations Development Programme. Although again it is perhaps rather premature to ascertain the relative positive or negative impact of such globalizing influences on the UAE, it is nonetheless important to note that in some cases the ink has already dried on agreements signed between these organizations and the UAE, and in the very near future a number of these will come into effect, thereby permanently altering domestic economic structures. Moreover, as with all other globalization-related issues in the UAE, it is also important to recognize the deep divide that has emerged between the supporters and opponents of such involvement. While the most controversial of these future changes are likely to result from the region's increasing cooperation with the IMF, which is already believed to be urging the GCC states, including the UAE, to strengthen their extraction capabilities and maybe even to levy some form of income tax,[31] the UAE's contentious membership of the WTO remains the most visible example at present.

Regarded as institutionalizing the national economy's integration into the global economic system, many local observers contend that WTO membership can only have long-term benefits for the economies of the Gulf states.[32] Most notable, it is believed that the technical and organizational assistance now being provided to the Arab Monetary Fund by the WTO will soon enhance multilateral trading in the Arab region, thereby dispelling any of the above mentioned concerns over globalization without regionalization.[33] Furthermore, many UAE businessmen and industrialists argue that WTO membership will soon lead to very tangible benefits resulting from the improved copyright controls and international patent law outlined by the WTO's Trade-Related Aspects of International Property Rights (TRIPS) agreement. Certainly, it would seem that the UAE's infant industries require much greater protection from copying and infringement by third parties, which remains a very real problem given the slew of copyright-breaking products that flow into the region from South Asia and the Far East. Indeed, as Muhammad al-Jabil, a prominent Dubai banker, has explained, in recent years many of the UAE's new computer programming and media companies have faced a serious threat from computer pirates operating throughout the country. Following the TRIPS agreement, however, al-Jabil claims that pirated software has already begun to disappear from the UAE's computer stores, allowing copyrighted products to claim a greater market share.[34] Other clear examples of beneficial patent control include the rapid growth of the UAE's indigenous pharmaceutical industry. For some time, the UAE's pharmaceutical companies (most notably Julphar,[35] Globalpharma, and Gulf Inject[36]) have struggled to establish their products alongside the plethora of low-cost, nonpatented imports that have filled the shelves of most pharmacies, but following TRIPS their position appears to have been greatly strengthened.[37]

In addition, other perceived advantages of WTO membership have included the proposed loosening of existing monopolies in the Gulf. Although such openings have not yet taken place, the UAE's WTO monopoly exemptions expired in 2003 and the government may soon be required to promote full competition in previously monopolized sectors. A prime example will be the telecommunications sector, where Etisalat's monopoly position[38] will be reduced by 2005 as a direct result of the UAE's WTO agreements. Many nationals and resident workers argue that this will lead to lower prices and improved Internet products, especially as new independent service providers will be able to offer competitive alternatives.[39] Indeed, even the highly influential director-general of the Dubai Chamber of Commerce and Industry, Abdul Rahman al-Mutawi, would appear to concur, arguing that "Etisalat's monopoly position cannot stay that long . . . it has to find a less costly way of providing service to customers."[40] Also, excepting these potentially harmful monopolies, given that membership in the WTO still allows for a wide array of special customs and trade practices specific to particular members, many contend that the UAE and the other

Gulf states need not fear any real loss of control over their national economies. Indeed, as the UAE's minister of economy and commerce, Shaikh Fahim al-Qasimi, has explained, although the UAE committed itself to the General Agreement on Tariffs and Trade when it joined the WTO in 1996, the country nevertheless still maintains the right to impose special duties on imports in order to protect indigenous infant industries from harmful competition, and to prevent other undesirable aspects of greater openness such as economic dumping.[41] Furthermore, as Al-Tamimi Consultants note, many of the existing restrictions on foreign firms based in the UAE will be unaffected by WTO membership. For example, the aforementioned 49 percent cap on foreign capital participation will remain unchanged, at least by the WTO, given that this specific Emirati business requirement applies equally to all WTO members operating inside the UAE, and therefore does not violate the organization's principles of fair trade.[42] Similarly, the UAE's continuing requirement that all registered commercial agents be 100 percent nationals of their respective country does not violate the General Agreement on Trade in Services. Thus, although fellow WTO member Bahrain has already voluntarily removed such a requirement, and the United States has lobbied heavily for such change elsewhere in the Gulf, the UAE remains well within its rights to retain these restrictions until it feels more comfortable to incorporate them into its own WTO "Schedule of Commitments."[43]

In contrast, the opponents of WTO membership and the UAE's agreements with other international organizations have argued that such affiliations and commitments will soon lead to costly changes to the economic structures of the Gulf states.[44] Indeed, presenting the flip side to the question of monopolies and the example of Etisalat (which has, after all, been credited with allowing the UAE to achieve the highest teledensity of any Arab state),[45] these opponents contend that it may be unwise to open up certain key components of the UAE's technological infrastructure to foreign and non-state-controlled competition during what remains a relatively early stage of the UAE's development. Moreover, it is also feared that despite the current WTO-permitted UAE-specific restrictions, other future WTO agreements may still seek to remove the necessary layers of protection currently enjoyed by many of the UAE's infant industries. Without these layers, it is argued that some of the more recently established industries, including the UAE's booming textile and ready-made clothes firms, are likely to falter as they will face stiff competition from Asian and African imports.[46]

Furthermore, it has also been argued that at present there are insufficient long-term economic incentives to balance the losses likely to result from such a removal of protection. Indeed, as Ali Merza of the UNDP has demonstrated, membership in the WTO does not even provide any real assistance in the restructuring of economic systems for developing states. Also, as the UAE and the other Gulf states already have clear development strategies in place, they are believed to be capable of implementing their own changes when deemed necessary.[47] In addition, the UAE and its oil-producing neighbors are seen to be especially disadvantaged by such membership given that they continue to rely on oil and gas products that, as of yet, remain outside of the WTO's list of reciprocal concessions. Thus, until hydrocarbons are explicitly included by the WTO, the Gulf states have few major financial incentives to join. Moreover, although the opponents accept that membership of the WTO does not interfere with a country's right to employ its own citizens first, it is nevertheless feared that such WTO affiliation may still affect the UAE's future labor national-ization strategies, with "emiratization" legislation becoming harder to adopt as the UAE becomes increasingly expected to conform to interna-tional norms and reduce "restrictive practises."[48] Finally, it has also been noted that WTO membership may lead to certain unwanted political com-plications for the UAE and other Arab states. Indeed, as 'Ahmad Jiyad explains, although the UAE currently only grants most-favored-nation sta-tus to other GCC states,[49] and still tends to rely on its long-established bilateral "double taxation" treaties with other friendly countries,[50] the terms of WTO agreements may eventually require the UAE to grant the same favorable trade conditions to all other WTO member states, includ-ing boycotted states such as Israel.[51]

## The Impact of Globalizing Forces on Contemporary Society and Culture

Alongside economic considerations, the impact of globalization on a devel-oping state's society and culture has also been recognized as a key motor of change,[52] and the UAE has been no exception, with accelerating and often highly intrusive sociocultural globalizing forces having caused local divi-sions between those fearing and those ready to embrace such changes. First, with regard to the opponents, perhaps the greatest concern has been over the perceived "cultural contamination" of the UAE. Indeed, although the UAE's Arab League for Educational, Scientific, and Cultural Organization (ALESCO) representatives now no longer publicly speak of a cultural invasion, and have instead begun to express their desire to promote "fairness among other equally worthy cultures,"[53] there is little doubt that a significant number of UAE nationals continue to blame globalizing forces for the near-destruction of their country's heritage (turath).[54] Certainly, as Sulayman Khalaf explains in his case study of Emirati culture, much of the lower Gulf's heritage was lost over the past thirty years,[55] especially during

the oil booms of the 1970s and 1980s, when many of the region's traditional buildings were rapidly replaced with tenements and skyscrapers and
when many began to exchange their traditional ways of life for seemingly
more Western and urban lifestyles.

As such, many in the UAE and the other GCC states have reacted to
the eroding effects of globalization by initiating something of a modern-
day cultural revival. Indeed, as Khalaf notes: "Cultural revival is growing
so fast as to reach levels of national industry in the Arabian Gulf societies
[with] heritage revival appearing at this time juncture as an expanding
national cultural industry."[56] Indeed, museums were simply not necessary
in the region in earlier times as traditional activities remained a part of
everyday life, but as Khalaf argues, there is now seen to be an increasing
need for "living museums" and "imagined communities" such as the
Dubai Heritage Village, the Pearling Village, and the recently constructed
Hatta Heritage Village, all of which have been created and promoted by
the emirate-level tourism departments. Of course, this speedy reaction to
potentially damaging globalizing forces is of particular significance, especially given the government's in-built need to preserve and create "living
memories" to remind the population of their culture and heritage.[57]
Certainly, as this book has demonstrated, not only are these museums and
heritage centers seen to be performing an increasingly necessary role in
the UAE's economic diversification through tourism strategy, but they
have also served to reinforce an integral component of the traditional polity's legitimacy formula.

Related to this cultural erosion, the impact of globalizing forces on the
UAE's national language, Arabic, has also roused considerable opposition
and has prompted strong reactions, often from the highest levels. Indeed,
long considered a symbol of advanced civilization and a source of great
pride in the Arab world, the Arabic language is now becoming increasingly
marginalized in the UAE. With massive and diverse non-Arab expatriate
populations from the subcontinent and East Asia, in addition to significant
British and European minorities, English has quickly become the lingua
franca for almost all private sector gatherings ranging from board meetings
to secretarial functions. Indeed, English is now the primary language in
some of the major semigovernmental organizations, such as Dubai's
Emirates Airways. Similarly, Hindi is universally understood and frequently used by the less educated sections of the population engaged in retailing,
transport, construction, and other blue-collar activities. In fact, even many
of the young UAE nationals are now well acquainted with Hindi, having
been brought by up Asian caregivers. Moreover, while other globalizing
forces such as English-language television (including Arab-run English television stations),[58] films, DVDs, radio stations, and pop music are of
course also contributing to this marginalization of the Arabic language, per-

haps the most important factor, at least for the UAE's youth, will be the increasing use of English in their secondary and tertiary education. Certainly, for those schooled in the private sector, English will have been their primary medium of instruction from an early age.[59] Correspondingly, at the university level there are a growing number of UAE national students who prefer to continue their education at the new English-language institutions such as Zayed University, the American University of Sharjah, and the American University of Dubai, rather than Arabic-only institutions such as the University of Sharjah and the UAE University in Al-'Ayn. Indeed, in her recent study of the UAE's national identity, Sally Findlow supports this pro-English view by demonstrating the changing attitudes of Emirati students toward the use and necessity of Arabic. In a 1999 survey, she investigated student preferences for English and Arabic in UAE colleges, finding that nearly half of respondents were in favor of solely English instruction, 30 percent wanted to have mixed English and Arabic instruction, and only 23 percent preferred to be taught in Arabic, simply claiming that it was "their language" (see Figure 5.4).

Understandably, groups such as the Arabic Language Protection Association have attempted to limit this erosion of the national language by unwanted globalizing forces. As Abdullah al-Madfa, the association's chairman, explains, the main aim has been to

> preserve the Arabic language from an awkward mix of foreign vocabularies and dialects, and to limit the negative influences of the multicultural environment on the UAE's official language. A quick observation of the language used at present indicates a looming catastrophe. The new generations are becoming more and more distant from their native tongue, favouring other languages such as English. This has given rise to a new

**Figure 5.4 Language Preferences of UAE Students, 1999**

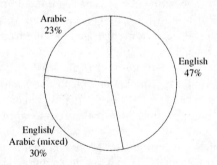

*Source:* Sally Findlow (2000), "The UAE: Nationalism and Arab-Islamic Identity," Abu Dhabi, Emirates Centre for Strategic Studies and Research (ECSSR), ECSSR Occasional Paper no. 39, p. 33.

form of broken Arabic that combines various accents emerging on the surface.[60]

Among its activities have been plans to correct misspelled Arabic shop signs and street names, plans to introduce new and more interesting Arabic-language lessons in schools, and plans to increase the number of Arabic-language tutors for expatriate workers. Significantly, these initiatives have found much support from government organizations, especially in Sharjah, where in an effort to check the spread of English and broken Arabic, the ruler decreed in late 2002 that all public departments shall in future use only Arabic in their correspondence and meetings.[61] Interestingly, at Zayed University in Abu Dhabi and Dubai, although English clearly still remains the key focus, there has also been evidence of such an initiative in recent years, with a new "Arabic across the curriculum program" having been designed to ensure that all students continue to practice from at least some Arabic-language material in the course of their studies.[62] Indeed, one of the most frequent complaints made by the university's Department of Arabic and Islamic Studies is that while many of their students are practically fluent in English, they continue to make very basic grammatical errors in their Arabic assignments.

Although by no means universally supported, perhaps the most popular feature of greater sociocultural globalization in the UAE has been the improvement in global communications, especially given its perceived positive effects on improving government accountability and transparency. Indeed, as Mai Yamani notes with reference to the Gulf states, transnational media including satellite television stations and Internet sites have considerably loosened the state's grip over information and therefore reduced the relevance of state-controlled media. In particular, Yamani highlights the Kuwaiti crisis as being a major turning point for public perception, arguing that the credibility of state television in the Gulf was irreversibly damaged as a result of its delayed and sanitized broadcasts regarding the Iraqi invasion and the cross-border forays into Saudi territory.[63] Gulf citizens could simply no longer rely on their own television stations for reliable information and instead switched their loyalties to global satellite channels such as CNN and the BBC. Moreover, although more closely related to regionalization, these global-scale events were also seen as improving Arab media, by leading to greater demands for more probing and comprehensive Gulf news services capable of providing accurate information and reducing government opaqueness. Perhaps the strongest example of such development has been the creation of the Qatari-based Al-Jazeera satellite station, which, as Gerd Nonneman explains, "has broken through these traditions [of submissiveness, narrowness, and dogmatism], and as a consequence has become one of the favourite sources of information in the Arab World (even if avoiding criticism of Qatar's own ruler), however much regional regimes at times fulminate against it."[64] Indeed, in 1994 the BBC World Service assisted in training Al-Jazeera's Arab production crew, and as part of their training the staff were encouraged to be more critical and questioning of government officials, a trend that appears to have been followed by most of the other Gulf satellite television stations in recent years. Certainly, as Yamani asserts, Al-Jazeera and these other stations have led to something of a cultural competition between Gulf television stations as each attempts to produce the most sensationalist programming.[65] Thus, although the UAE's television stations have remained more cautious than their Qatari and Bahraini counterparts, it nevertheless remains possible that the snowball effect taking place elsewhere in the Gulf may eventually lead to changes in the UAE's media, thereby complementing the existing transparency initiatives.

## Civil Society and Globalization

In his revealing study of neopatriarchal society and political change, Hisham Sharabi contends that many of the existing power structures in the Arab world cannot be overcome simply by revolution, modernization, or development. Instead, it is argued that the state-society relationship needs to fundamentally change from one of authoritarianism to one capable of humanizing social relations and liberating political life.[66] Thus, for long-term political development and a shift in the existing order, Sharabi and many others believe that there first needs to be greater and more genuine civil society in the Arab world. Indeed, with regard to the UAE, this would seem a particularly sound hypothesis given the confirmed stability of its political structures and the resistance of its neopatrimonial networks to rapid socioeconomic development and the forces of modernization.

### Preconditions for the Emergence of Civil Society

What exactly is meant by "civil society," and how should the term be best applied to the UAE? In her survey of civil society in southern Arabia, Sheila Carapico explored the strength of associational life and the proliferation of voluntary associations.[67] Working within a similar framework to de Toqueville's earlier study of civil society,[68] she demonstrated that in Yemen there existed a network of institutions and associations that "operated in a pluralistic, continuously contested public space or public civic realm, a zone between the state and private sectors." Moreover, she contended that the existence of such a zone in the emerging Arab states could serve as a "layer or buffer between government and households . . . representing a third, non-governmental, non-profit making, voluntary sector of modern society."[69] Crucially, it was also suggested that such a layer might include many seemingly traditional and tribal groups: a key factor with regard to the study of Emirati associational life given the previously described tribal nature of society in the lower Gulf.[70] Writing with a more general reference to the developing world, Mehran Kamrava has largely concurred with Carapico's view, while also highlighting the potential political power of civil society and, on a more individual level, also emphasizing the existence of the many important social actors that often constitute civil society:

> Civil society gives rise to a very specific type of organisation, one that is social in its genesis and composition but can be political in its agendas and initiatives. It is an organisation that is formed out of the independent, autonomous initiatives of politically concerned individuals. These social actors are united by a common concern, often rallying around a specific issue (e.g., greater political space, less literary censorship, etc.). But irrespective of their specifics, if their demands on the state were met, they would either directly or indirectly result in a greater opening up of the political process.[71]

Thus, in light of these definitions, examples of such civil society organizations could be seen to include a wide variety of voluntary and socially oriented associations ranging from women's organizations, charities, and expatriate community centers, to those with potentially greater political motivations such as human rights organizations, religious groups, media societies, and workers' associations. Second, as Carapico asserts, any evidence of independent intellectual production, including newsletters, poetry readings, and literary journals, must also be considered, as these all form part of what Europeanists would define as being the "civic realm." Third, any voluntarily organized, nongovernmental, and noncommercial events such as academic seminars, conventions, demonstrations, and celebrations can also be considered a part of civil society, not least because they also provide an important outlet for the dissemination of ideas and the creation of public opinion.[72] Finally, complementing these organizations, certain social actors can be identified in most emerging civil societies, and as Kamrava has shown these can include a wide range of motivated persons, such as politicians, intellectuals, and journalists.[73]

Despite visibly possessing many examples of these associations and actors, civil society in the UAE has remained weak, at least on one level, due to the absence of certain key prerequisites. First, there is clearly a severe lack of "civic space." Indeed, in their highly relevant study of resurgent associational life in Eastern Europe following the demise of the

USSR, M. A. Weigle and Jim Butterfield emphasized the necessity of autonomous civic space above all else. In particular, it was argued that, without an institutional base capable of defining such space, a country's associations and actors would be rendered incapable of participation and voluntary organization.[74] As Carapico notes, in most states this civic space can usually be determined by an interrelated set of four factors:

1. The level of suppression or liberalization as determined by the regime.
2. The existence of a legal framework and constitutional framework that either excludes, tolerates, or fosters civil society organizations.
3. The level of public infrastructure necessary for the growth of civil society organizations (e.g., communications, buildings, etc.).
4. The availability of economic resources for public, private, and voluntary-sector investment.

Together these factors effectively set the parameters within which associations and actors can press for greater tolerance, expanded services, and clearer separation of private from public wealth.[75] Thus, on first inspection the UAE would appear to meet many of these preconditions, as both the regime and constitutional framework seem relatively tolerant of associational life, and the level of public infrastructure and the availability of economic resources are undoubtedly far higher than in most other developing states. However, as will be revealed, the UAE's civic space has actually remained extremely limited, with a number of under-the-surface circumstances combining to prevent and discourage the emergence of genuinely independent associations. Certainly, as Carapico described of nearby Yemen, "civil society is rarely a binomial event, either there or not, but instead a variable that assumes different forms under different circumstances."[76]

Moreover, alongside these four factors regarding civic space, another important precondition for the emergence of civil society must also be considered, especially given the UAE's demonstrated reliance on large numbers of resident expatriates.[77] Specifically, it has been argued that for successful growth there must exist a homogeneous national culture, rather than smaller cultural subgroups that are likely to retain their own specific norms, rituals, and status. A vibrant civil society may therefore require a nationally uniform cultural milieu where there is seen to be a "standardisation of idiom" and where people are bound "not by segmentary, exclusivist institutions that differentiate, but rather by associations that are unsanctified, instrumental, revocable and yet effective."[78] The many disparate groups of expatriates working and living in the UAE, many with little common middle ground, can therefore be seen as blocking this necessary precondition. Indeed, as former U.S. ambassador to the UAE William Rugh claims:

The UAE is not a "melting pot." Many separate and distinct social and ethnic groups reside in the UAE side by side, each maintaining its own cultural identity and tolerating the other in a "live and let live" environment. The largest groups—Indians, Pakistanis, Bangladeshis, and Filipinos as well as the smaller ones such as the British, all have their own schools, their own clubs, and their own places of worship, and they tend to spend their leisure time with their own people. The foreigners learn just enough Arabic to get by. Many spend a minimal amount of their earnings, sending most of the money home to relatives.[79]

Although there are of course countries such as India where large subgroups do exist and civil society does thrive, the subgroups in the UAE are often temporary workers unwilling to involve themselves in what is perceived to be an alien society. As Rugh noted, this has led to an overall lack of engagement and a general sense of apathy in most of the expatriate groups. Moreover, by citing a rare example of street protests by Pathans in the UAE, he showed how the wealth and employment security offered by the rentier state was easily sufficient to quell any sustained civil society activism by expatriates:

In December 1992 when a mob of Hindus in the Indian city of Ayodhya destroyed the Bahri Masjid Mosque, and Muslims protested in many places, Muslims in the UAE (mainly Pakistani) also took to the streets. . . . These demonstrations lasted only about two days, however, as the government promptly rounded up several hundred suspects and deported them. The protests suddenly stopped. Jobs were more important.[80]

Indeed, given their cautious acceptance of their employers' sponsorship and their strictly temporary view of life in the Gulf, which is often regarded as a steppingstone to other countries and as a quick means of making money,[81] the majority of the UAE's resident expatriates are extremely weak civil society actors lacking any strong cultural and institutional ties with the constituencies they serve or claim to represent.[82]

### The Co-option and Patronage of Civil Society

An investigation of the underlying problems that appear to be restricting Emirati civic space, alongside the fragmented cultural milieu and the wealth-driven objectives of most of the population, reveals some of the main weaknesses of contemporary civil society in the UAE. In particular, very few civil society associations are able to gain any genuine autonomy, with almost all being organizationally and financially tied to government ministries and ruling families, and with many of the more independent expatriate societies now facing increasing restrictions and regulations. Thus, as demonstrated in Chapter 2, even though there has of yet been little pressure for the polity to pursue a repressive maintenance strategy,[83] there are nevertheless subtle indications of greater control being exercised over the UAE's many civil society organizations.

Certainly, in her study of the history of Emirati civil society, Fatma al-Sayegh has emphasized this trend, arguing (albeit indirectly) that although there exists a long tradition of civil society in the region, in recent years almost all organizations have suffered from increasing government co-option:

> Civil society started before independence; in 1967 the first female society was established in Ra's al-Khaimah. Arab communities also were established before independence, and in 1978 there were 17 of them. During the 1980s many other civil society organisations appeared, all of which were dependent on government support. . . . [T]heir development has been dependent largely on the development of the legal and executive bodies of the society itself.[84]

Indeed, while the Federal Social Welfare Societies Law of 1974 did allow for the establishment of community societies, it is important to note that most public assemblies and associations in the UAE now require government approval, and all private associations must now be licensed by local authorities. This follows an amendment in 1981 that effectively suspended the issuing of licenses to such associations, reasoning that their existence posed a "significant threat to internal security."[85] Moreover, even though by the end of 1999 there were still estimated to be more than 100 associations operating without such licenses, a forthcoming amendment will ensure that all of these "illegal" associations are soon brought under the government umbrella. In fact, this amendment will require all societies to legalize their status within six months of the new law, otherwise they will be automatically dissolved. Furthermore, as a senior official from the Ministry of Labor and Social Affairs explained in late 2001, the law will give the ministries full "legal authority to oversee their activities" by allowing for the supervision of all their programs, projects, and financial performances.[86]

By measuring, or at least indicating, the extent of this co-option and dependence on government support, the following case studies will demonstrate some of the problems faced by the wide variety of UAE-based organizations.

*Cultural/educational/environmental groups.* As one of the longest-running cultural organizations in the UAE, the Emirates Association for the Revival of Folk Arts provides a good example of the increasing co-option of civil society. Formed in the 1980s as a voluntary organization aiming to revive traditional folk arts and protect Arab traditions from the influence of modern

trends, the association issued 20,000 shares to its members and those interested in its activities in order to raise funds. However, before long the association was granted "federal status," and although its activities remained
seemingly autonomous, its budget began to be administered and allocated
by the Ministry of Finance and Industry.[87] In much the same way, the
UAE's environmentalist groups also provide very clear examples of financial support from federal ministries. Normally associated with political
activism in campaigning for animal rights and antipollution measures in
most countries, the UAE's groups, such as the Environment Friends
Society and the Emirates Environmental Group, have remained more
restrained, concentrating on more limited goals regarding the UAE's nature
reserves. These more sanitized objectives are undoubtedly due to the high
level of co-option by the state, as these groups now receive generous annual budgets from the Ministry of Labor and Social Affairs.[88] Indeed, the
Environmental Research and Wildlife Development Agency provides
another excellent example given that it is chaired and funded by Shaikh
Hamdan al-Nuhayyan, the UAE's aforementioned minister of state for foreign affairs and the new second deputy prime minister.[89] Similarly, at the
individual-emirate level the picture is much the same (with the only notable
exception being the Abu Dhabi Natural History Group),[90] with obvious
examples of co-option including the Abu Dhabi–based Emirates Heritage
Club. Established by Emiri decree in 1997 and chaired by Shaikh Sultan al-
Nuhayyan, the UAE's other deputy prime minister and a key member of the
Abu Dhabian ruling family, the club effectively functions as an authority
belonging to the Abu Dhabi government. Moreover, the club also acts as an
umbrella organization for a number of other Abu Dhabi clubs and societies,
including the Amateur Astronomers Group, the Marine Races, and the
Emirates Sailing Academy.[91] Indeed, this "umbrella system" appears to
have been replicated throughout civil society in the UAE, with many smaller organizations falling under the direct or indirect control of larger organizations that are either government controlled or receiving patronage from
members of the various ruling families. Significantly, in recent years some
of these umbrella systems have even expanded to include formerly independent clubs and societies. Examples would include the many youth and
youth-related recreation clubs for UAE nationals, which although originally voluntary associations with autonomous budgeting are now all linked
under a federal umbrella organization represented by the Supreme Council
for Youth.[92]

Perhaps the strongest examples of the co-option of cultural and educational organizations, however, are to be found in the emirate of Sharjah,
which, given its long-term control of the federal education ministry and of
course its described history of close ties to the British residency (and consequently greater training opportunities for its population)[93] has always

prided itself on being the cultural and intellectual capital of the UAE.[94] Indeed, as the Press Affairs Directorate of the Sharjah Emiri Court describes, by the end of the 1980s there were twenty-six such organizations based in the emirate. These included eight cultural societies; six art associations such as the Sharjah Arts and Theater Association, the Sharjah National Theater Group, and the Marine Club for Arts and Tourism; and five significant "public interest" associations ranging from literary societies to folklore associations. Between the middle 1970s and the late 1980s these associations received more than 100 million dirhams in financial contributions from the Sharjah government and, as described by the directorate, also received significant "financial and/or moral support from the ruler, HH Shaykh Dr. Sultan bin Muhammad Al-Qasimi."[95] As this royal patronage and high level of government sponsorship appears to have continued unabated in Sharjah throughout the 1990s, ranging from financial backing for theatrical gatherings to organizational support for antismoking rallies,[96] it would seem that the smaller cultural and educational civil society organizations at the emirate level have lacked autonomous civic space in much the same way as their federal counterparts, even if this may have been unintentionally caused by their ruler's great benevolence and genuine patronage of the arts.

Finally, with further regard to educational associations, the role of academics must also be discussed. As described in the study of social growth, there has been a rapid increase in the number of academics and other university-related staff in the UAE given the massive expansion of the higher education sector in recent years,[97] and, as many civil society theorists claim, such intellectual social actors can play a major part in associational life. To a limited extent, this has taken place in the UAE, as following the Gulf War it was observed:

> In 1991, after Desert Storm, there was some informal discussion among a small group of educated nationals about the possibility of increased democratic participation in governance, and this was reported in the press at the time. Although it did not result in a significant movement in the UAE working for democratic reform, students and intellectuals still occasionally discuss the subject privately.[98]

However, for the most part there exists an unwritten but generally recognized ban on criticism of the government from such circles. In practice, this unwritten ban is normally enough to enforce self-censorship among academics, especially given that many are expatriates and are therefore cautious of jeopardizing their employment in a host country. On some occasions, however, as will be detailed later in this chapter, the ban can become very real. Furthermore, given that the government now tightly restricts the freedom of peaceful assembly and that all public gatherings require a permit, there would appear to be considerable disincentives for those academics attempting to organize seminars and conferences on sensitive subjects.[99]

*Recreational groups.* The recreational and sports clubs that exist in the UAE also paint a picture of government co-option and royal patronage. Although, unlike some of the cultural and educational organizations, their membership is not always restricted to UAE nationals, they nevertheless clearly cater to a divided heterogeneous society, with certain clubs aimed at Emiratis, with some targeting western expatriates, and with separate and specific ethnic-based groups existing for the various other expatriate communities. A number of the smaller recreational clubs, such as the Emirates Sailing Academy and Marine Races, are operated by emirate-level semi-governmental authorities such as the Emirates Heritage Club. In much the same way, many of the larger associations responsible for the more popular sports such as horse racing, golf, cricket, and football are controlled by federal umbrellas organized and chaired by government ministers, members of the ruling families, or other notables. The UAE Golf Association provides such an example given that its chairman is Muhammad al-Abbar, who, as described in the previous chapter, is not only a key associate of Shaikh Muhammad al-Maktum but also serves as the director-general of the Dubai Department of Economic Development and as the chairman of Emaar Properties.[100] Similarly, the Dubai Football Club also has very close links with the ruling family given that its president and main organizer is Shaikh Rashid bin Muhammad al-Maktum, one of Shaikh Muhammad's sons. Indeed, in a recent Ramadan football tournament organized by the club, it was clear just how far the club's royal patronage extended, with many of the participating teams being captained by young shaikhs and with the prize money and "inspiration" for the event having been provided by Shaikh Muhammad himself.[101]

*Welfare organizations.* Voluntary organizations and associations attempting to provide care for the handicapped and elderly also exhibit clear signs of government co-option. They are required to hold licenses from the Ministry of Labor and Social Affairs and most, like many of the UAE's cultural associations, restrict their membership to UAE nationals. The Handicapped Guardians Association is one such example. Established in 1996 in accordance with the directions of Shaikh Sultan al-Qasimi, the ruler of Sharjah, the organization is now also headed by Shaikh Sultan in addition to being funded by the government.[102] The Emirates Volunteers Association is broader in scope than many of the UAE's other welfare organizations given that it accepts both UAE national and expatriate members in its attempt to create a large body of volunteer workers in the fields of healthcare, helping the elderly, and protecting the environment. However, the association also displays clear signs of co-option and patronage, maintaining close links with the Sharjah ruling family and other local elites. Indeed, it receives generous awards and prizes from Shaikh Sultan and is chaired by Humaid al-Qutami, the general manager of a key government-funded institute[103] (the Emirates Institute for Banking and Financial Studies).[104] Also, given that subordinate branches of the association are now opening in Khor Fakkan and Ra's al-Khaimah, it would appear that the civil society umbrella system is again being reproduced, with the newer associations operating under the auspices of the original Sharjah-based authority.

*Women's groups.* Many of the national and Abu Dhabi–based women's organizations are government funded and are indirectly connected to the Abu Dhabi ruling family by either their chairperson or their president, often Shaikha Fatima al-Nuhayyan, Shaikh Zayed's favored wife and therefore the UAE's "first lady." A recent example of such co-option would be the establishment of the Women's Business Council in 2001 by a number of female entrepreneurs in Abu Dhabi. The council's main aim has been to provide a forum for female nationals to

> meet and discuss the issues of their common interest and exchange views on their expectations and aspirations in the world of business and finance . . . and to provide a connecting link between government and semi-government authorities on the one hand, and businesswomen on the other hand, to overcome obstacles and problems. These would include marriage and family responsibilities, and society's perception of a businesswoman and its doubts about her ability to succeed.[105]

Recent actions have included applying pressure on the government to grant greater maternity leave at full pay and to provide superior childcare facilities in the workplace.[106] However, while apparently a voluntary association organized by like-minded businesswomen, the council does not have true autonomy over its organization. In addition to requiring approval for its actions from the Federation of Chambers of Commerce and Industry, the association is also closely linked to Shaikha Fatima, who also serves as the chairperson of the UAE Women's Federation, the Abu Dhabi Women's Society, the Women's General Union, the Association of the Awakening of Abu Dhabian Women, and the Women's Committee of the Red Crescent Society.[107] As such, the genuine independence of the council's views and activities from those of the state and the al-Nuhayyan family would seem questionable.

Similarly, in Sharjah most women's groups are linked to the establishment through Shaikha Jawaher al-Qasimi, the wife of Shaikh Sultan. Specifically, the Sharjah Women's Club, which was set up in 1982 and financed by the ruler's office, is chaired by Shaikha Jawaher and has now branched out to include clubs in other parts of Sharjah and Khor Fakkan. Predictably, many of the other women's associations in the emirate, such as the Emirates Women Writers Association and the Young Ladies Club, fall under the club's administrative and financial umbrella. In other emirates, including 'Ajman, the pattern is much the same, with organizations such as the Umm al-Mominin Women's Association receiving "Rashid Award" funding from the 'Ajman ruling family and support from the local government.[108]

*Islamic/charity organizations.* As explained in Chapter 2, religious resources continue to play a key unifying role in the polity's legitimacy formula.[109] As such, almost all mosques, ulama', and Islamic-related organizations are carefully controlled by the government in its efforts to prevent any potentially harmful radicalism or religious-political opposition. Indeed, 95 percent of Sunni mosques in the UAE are now state-owned (many mosques were originally built by nearby families and named after a deceased family member, later to be operated and maintained by the government),[110] with the remaining 5 percent receiving large government subsidies—the only exceptions being the small number of privately funded Shi'a mosques, but even these, in Dubai at least, are now being brought under local government control. In addition to this financial co-option, the federal Ministry of Justice and Islamic Affairs (together with local emirate-specific departments) employs all Sunni Imams and distributes weekly guidance to Sunni clergymen regarding their religious sermons, thereby ensuring adherence to ministry-approved topics.[111] Indeed, the minister of justice and Islamic affairs, Muhammad al-Dhahiri, has been quite clear on this point, having admitted in a recent interview that his departments do exercise considerable "quality control" over religious preaching and the UAE's mosques:

> The Islamic world is teeming with people who claim knowledge about Islam, but experience has shown that many of the people who applied to the Awqaf department for the posts of Imams in the mosques were far below the required standards. . . . It was therefore necessary to set regulations and criteria for regulating religious teachings. . . . The ministry also provides written Friday sermons (Khutba) to be read out to the faithful. Those Imams who have proven themselves to be qualified and skilful are allowed to choose topics on their own free will provided that they inform the ministry about these topics.[112]

In much the same way as the mosques, most of the UAE's other Islamic associations and charities have also been co-opted by the government. Certainly, while some Islamic societies that aim to popularize Islam are permitted, these are either government funded or carefully screened. Examples include Al-Muntada al-Islami in Sharjah with its primarily Emirati membership[113] and the various expatriate Islamic societies serving the many Pakistani and Indian Muslims working in the UAE. With regard to Islamic charities, the most obvious example of co-option has of course been the UAE Red Crescent Society, which receives considerable financial and organizational support from the various ruling families and, predictably, serves as an umbrella organization for other smaller charities. The omnipresent Shaikh Hamdan al-Nuhayyan serves as the Red Crescent's president, with Khalifa al-Suwaidi (a member of another prominent Abu Dhabian family) chairing the organization. Moreover, many of the society's projects to promote activities for disabled citizens have been assisted and supervised by both the Ministry of Education and Youth and the Ministry of Labor and Social Affairs. A number of other recent activities, such as competitions for the disabled and first-aid training courses, have been organized under the patronage of Shaikha Fatima, who predictably serves as the president of the society's Women's Committee.[114] Significantly, the Red Crescent also distributes its considerable funds to other Islamic charity organizations in the UAE, a recent example being Shaikh Zayed's donation of 12 million dirhams via the society to the Shaikha Fatima Charity Award in order to improve the lives of orphans in the UAE.[115] Correspondingly, if the Red Crescent Society can be seen as an Abu Dhabi–dominated umbrella organization, then Shaikh Muhammad's Humanitarian and Charity Foundation in Dubai can be seen as a smaller, and more northern emirate-specific, counterpart. Presided over by Dubai's crown prince and chaired by Ibrahim bu Melha, Dubai's equivalent of an attorney general, the foundation effectively unifies the relief efforts of other Dubai-based Islamic charities within the framework of a controlled and co-opted organization. Indeed, most recently the foundation coordinated and supported the efforts of a number of charitable associations in the northern Emirates aiming to raise funds for the Iraqi people. These included the Fujairah Charity Association, the Sharjah Charity Association, Al-Islah wal-Tawjih, the Zakat Committee of Ra's al-Khaimah, and the Shaikha Latifa Charity for Children's Creativity (Shaikha Latifa being Shaikh Muhammad's daughter).[116]

*Media/press-related associations.* With regard to press and press-related organizations, the UAE's newspapers, like the UAE's other associations, have also become more limited, despite having their freedom guaranteed by Article 30 of the UAE's constitution.[117] Certainly, they do not yet constitute the "independent intellectual production" described by Carapico[118] and, although they may be tolerated, they are ultimately controlled. However, as Peck explains, this was not always the case. Many associations, especially workers' organizations, found much support from the UAE's press in the late 1970s and early 1980s, especially from the aforementioned Arabic newspaper *Al-Azmina al-Arabiyya*.[119] In particular, this newspaper played a key role in helping strikers, including many who worked in agencies of federal ministries, to gain their demands. Moreover, *Al-Azmina* addressed more general socioeconomic and political issues that other papers had previously shied away from, such as the human cost of the UAE's massive infrastructural development taking place at that time.[120] Another example, again from the early 1980s, is the role of the press in successfully opposing government education policy. When, in 1981, the undersecretary of education issued an edict permitting corporal punishment in schools, the press vehemently objected and subsequently the policy was revoked.[121] Nevertheless, by the mid-1980s the press was obliged to become more cautious over such matters following increasing government disapproval. After the forced closure of *Al-Azmina* due to its anticipated opposition to a further extension of the UAE's provisional constitution,[122] the UAE's press associations were seen to be as restricted and ineffectual as most of the UAE's other civil society organizations.

Indeed, the reality, as understood and practiced by both editors and journalists, became one of staying within the boundaries and respecting certain limits. After all, the majority of the UAE's journalists are Arab and South Asian expatriates and are therefore reluctant to step out of line in their wealthy host nation.[123] Furthermore, this control over the media was formalized in 1988 by a new federal law that clearly stipulated that all publications, including books and periodicals, had to be licensed for approval by the Ministry of Information and Culture.[124] Until then the only official restriction had been a rather vague federal law issued in 1973 that forbade any criticism of the president or members of the Supreme Council of Rulers.[125] Crucially of course, this new law governed the content of all of the licensed publications, thus effectively requiring journalists to exercise self-censorship when reporting on a range of potentially sensitive issues such as national security, political development, and oil policy.[126] In addition, the ministry also became empowered to review all imported publications and ban any materials deemed to be derogatory of Islam, supportive of Israel, or critical of the establishment.[127] In more recent years, this censorship has of course been extended to the Internet and all Emirati websites, given that, as explained in the previous chapter, the ministry cooperates with the UAE's telecommunications monopoly (Etisalat) by running a proxy server that aims to block undesirable Web content. Not only are sites relating to gambling, pornography, magic, and alcohol banned, as one might expect, but also restricted are links relating to civil society, democratization, and political development in general.

Interestingly, however, at a formal gathering to mark the launch of Dubai Media City in January 2001, Shaikh Muhammad al-Maktum proclaimed his formal agreement to allow freedom for the press and media in Dubai. Although clearly made in the context of the aforementioned transparency initiatives and the attempts to boost the attractiveness of the new free zones for foreign investors, the agreement was nevertheless seen by some, in Dubai at least, as the beginning of a new awakening for the UAE's press. Indeed, as was reported at the time:

> Having such freedom suddenly guaranteed was remarkable, as before this, open and uninhibited debate in the media on any issue was not sanctioned by any of the local governments making up the UAE. . . . This bold precedent heralded a new beginning in the Arabian Gulf. Following the announcement in Dubai, an oasis has appeared for the mass media.[128]

Of course, not all were convinced, and many continued to believe that the press would still need to avoid any direct criticism of the government and would therefore need to proceed with caution:[129]

> While Arabic-language publishers and media professionals are called here from far and near to quench their decades-long thirst for freedom, caution is still the order of the day, lest it turn out to be just another mirage on the edge of the blistering sands. . . . Although guaranteed in the Constitution, the UAE Criminal Code in its current form still does not allow the press to comment on certain issues. It remains to be seen whether or not, once media companies in the new free zone start to take off, the freedom promised to them by the Crown Prince will have any effect on the host country that nurtures them.[130]

Within only months of this announcement many of these suspicions were confirmed, as a number of press-related incidents indicated that little had changed, at least when it came to the need for self-censorship. In March 2001 the Ministry of Information and Culture filed a lawsuit against the Dubai-based newspaper *Gulf News* in response to a series of sharply satirical columns published by a Qatari journalist, Abdul-Wahid al-Mawlawi, that allegedly featured self-deprecatory humor regarding stereotypical Gulf Arabs. The government was not amused, and considered the articles to be offensive to Gulf citizens in general and to the country's citizens in particular. According to a U.S. government human rights report, in addition to the lawsuit, al-Mawlawi was also arrested shortly after the publication of the last of his columns. He was purportedly subjected to sleep deprivation and physical abuse during a two-week detention, before finally being expelled to Qatar.[131] Eventually the lawsuit against the offending newspaper was withdrawn, but only after the editor agreed to publish a front-page apology for the offensive material. Moreover, later that year a similar dispute arose between the ministry and the media, culminating in ten prominent writers, including four university professors, being banned from publishing opinion pieces in both the Arabic and English newspapers. Apparently the ban was imposed following the writers' support of over 100 employees who had been made redundant by the government-controlled Emirates Media Incorporated (EMI). As with the al-Mawlawi dispute, no official justification was given for the ban, although it was eventually lifted after the dust had settled.[132]

In addition to this self-censorship and often heavy-handed enforcement, another important characteristic of the UAE's press and press-related associations has been their increasing financial dependence on the governmental and semigovernmental organizations.[133] Indeed, three of the country's six Arabic-language newspapers are now state owned (including the Dubai government's *Al-Bayan*), with the other three receiving substantial government subsidies (including Sharjah's *Al-Khaleej*).[134] The case is much the same for the three English-language newspapers, which, although privately owned, all receive generous subsidies[135] (*Gulf News* and *Khaleej Times* are based in Dubai, while *Gulf Today* is based in Sharjah).[136] Similarly, most of the UAE's television stations and other broadcast media organizations are also very closely linked to the government and as such tend to present only government views,[137] and strictly conform to official reporting guidelines. The only exception had been 'Ajman's popular satellite television station, but in July 1999 even this was purchased by EMI.[138] Chaired by Shaikh Abdullah al-Nuhayyan, the minister of information,[139] EMI operates the national news agency Wikalat Anba' al-Imarat (WAM) in addition to owning Abu Dhabi's terrestrial and satellite television stations and two English and two Arabic radio stations, and publishing the Arabic *Al-Ittihad* newspaper. Tellingly, EMI has recently forbidden all of its employees, including its journalists, from speaking with unapproved foreigners and representatives.[140]

*Workers/professional bodies.* All employees in the UAE, both white- and blue-collar, have the right to lodge grievances with officials from the Ministry of Labor and Social Affairs, who are then obliged to investigate all complaints. Moreover, in theory, all workers are also able to appeal against the ministry's rulings and, if necessary, can take the matter to the courts. However, as has been reported, many workers choose not to protest for fear of reprisals or deportation; and for those who do protest, their complaints and compensation claims are often severely backlogged due to understaffing and underbudgeting in the ministry.[141] Indeed, the press often carries reports of employers punishing or abusing those employees, especially domestic servants, who lodge official complaints.[142] With regard to workers' groups and associations, although UAE law does not yet permit employees to engage in collective bargaining, many associations are granted some degree of freedom to collectively raise work-related issues, to lobby for redress, and (on occasion), to file protests with the government.[143] Thus, while these groups are essentially limited to making recommendations on behalf of their members and therefore possess few of the characteristics of fully functioning labor unions, they nevertheless offer the only real opportunity for employees to group together in order to voice their concerns.

In some cases these groups, especially the professional associations, have achieved relative autonomy in recent years and have been able to lobby the government successfully over certain work-related problems. A good example would be the Emirates Bankers Association. Established in 1982 as a nonprofit organization enabling employees of both local and national banks to subscribe to its membership, the association aimed to exchange opinions and knowledge between its members and to provide assistance and services to its members and all of those working in the banking profession.[144] In 1991, during a period of increasing automation in the banking sector, the association was capable of independently representing its members' concerns to the UAE Central Bank. As such, the association was able to provide something of a mouthpiece for the banking work force and was able to extract concessions and reassurance for those fearing unemployment and transitional problems.[145]

However, in much the same way as in the UAE's media sector, it would appear that, when more serious employment matters arise, the illusion of freedom and autonomy is swiftly dispelled as government ministries retain the right to supervise, inspect, and disband all such organizations.[146] The UAE Teachers Association, one of the largest of the UAE's professional bodies, provides such a case study given its repeated failures in confronting government ministries in recent years. One such example would be a teachers' dispute in 2002 that resulted in the Ministry of Education and Youth summarily suspending an instructor for his alleged beating of a pupil. Duly, the Teachers Association attempted to defend the teacher's rights and began to sue the ministry. Within days, however, the association found itself fighting a losing battle and unable to uphold the interests of its members, however misguided they may have been. Indeed, as a source from the ministry indicated with regard to the incident, such associations are effectively powerless in these disputes: "The Ministry has the right to take any legal action which it deems necessary against those violating rules, noting that beating students was prohibited in schools. The association does not have the legal power to sue the Ministry on behalf of its members. Its resolutions are just recommendations which do not have any legal value." Moreover, the source also inferred that the recent stand taken by the association may well result in it being dissolved, observing that "the association should have advised the teachers to settle the dispute in a peaceful manner without letting the issue reach the court."[147]

In addition, while some associations have found themselves unable to mount legal challenges against government ministries, others have of course been weakened by high levels of patronage from either the govern-ment or the ruling families. With formal and informal ties to the neopatri-monial network, they are thought unlikely to ever evolve into autonomous labor organizations and are therefore believed to be incapable of independ-ently representing their members' interests. While some of these associa-tions, such as the Emirates Medical Association and the Women's Business Council, chaired respectively by Shaikh Mansur al-Nuhayyan and Shaikha Fatima al-Nuhayyan, are visibly linked to the ruling families,[148] others, especially those in receipt of financial aid (either willingly or not), are often more indirectly linked. The most recent example (and in many ways the most painfully obvious) being the Crown Prince of Abu Dhabi's mas-sive 500,000 dirham donation to the UAE Journalists Association in March 2004, just three months after its establishment.[149] Finally, it is important to note that even those associations catering to expatriates would also seem to be indirectly tied into the patronage system. Indeed, even the American Business Council of Dubai and the Northern Emirates, which has elected officers and an exclusively American membership, is remarkably keen to maintain close and deferential ties with the various ruling families. In fact, in a form of reverse patronage, the recipients of the council's prestigious annual business award have included no less than four of the UAE's shaikhs since 1995: Shaikh Muhammad al-Maktum; al-Maktum's uncle Shaikh 'Ahmad; Shaikh Sultan al-Qasimi, the ruler of Sharjah; and Shaikh Hamad al-Sharqi, the ruler of Fujairah.[150] Similarly, other predominantly expatriate organizations, such as the Society of Petroleum Engineers and the many Indian and Filipino-specific workers' associations, also observe polite respect, with most tending to keep a low profile by focusing more on providing social and educational forums than seeking to protect their mem-bers' legal rights.[151]

*Expatriate community groups.* A survey of civil society organizations in the UAE would be incomplete without also considering the many expatriate welfare organizations and associations that exist in the major cities. Indeed, given the size of these foreign communities, many of which dwarf the local Emirati populations, it is little surprise that these are high in membership and probably constitute the bulk of civil society activity in the country. Among others, there are clubs for Europeans, North Americans, Indians, Filipinos, Africans, and indeed almost all of the diverse nationalities who make up the UAE's vast expatriate labor force. Many of these societies concentrate on social events and on building up a sense of community and familiarity for those far from their homelands, while others offer compatri-ots the opportunity to network with each other and learn how best to do business in the UAE and the Gulf. Some of these societies are even region-specific, with many offering social services and support to immigrants from particular areas of India, the Philippines, and the other main labor-providing nations. Examples include the Goan societies, which operate under the umbrella of the Indian Association,[152] the various Keralite and Malayalee associations for South Indians, the Bicol Anom organization for Bico-speaking Filipinos, and the Pangasinense Aligwas Club for expatriates from Luzon and the northern Philippines.[153]

As one might expect, given the cautious nature of expatriate workers and their presence in a comparatively conservative state, these organizations, like many of the UAE's other associations, are self-censoring and self-limiting. All are careful to emphasize their goals of providing solely welfare and cultural activities, with some even going so far as to state explicitly their nonpolitical agenda. One such example is the Kenya Friendship Society, which is a nonprofit and volunteer-based organization designed to help and support the large Kenyan community in the UAE. Among its aims are the provision of welfare services for members and their families, the encouragement of cultural and recreational activities, and the encouragement of "intellectual association" between like-minded Kenyans. On this last point, however, the society's chairman, Jalal Balala, felt it necessary to assert in a recent speech that "this society will involve strictly social, cultural, educational and humanitarian activities. Absolutely nonpolitical. All Kenyans will benefit."[154] Similarly keen to stress its apolitical nature has been the Goan Cultural Society. Established in 1988 to provide a social community for nonresident Indians in Dubai from the Catholic province of Goa, the society's mission statement has always maintained that it is "a social and cultural organisation without any political affiliations and its membership is open to all Goans residing in the United Arab Emirates."[155]

Of all the civil society organizations in the UAE, these expatriate welfare organizations appear to have been the least co-opted. Almost all have constitutions and committees elected from their membership, and, given their foreign and often non-Muslim constituencies, they have few if any ties to the ruling families or government-funded bodies. However, it is perhaps because of this relative autonomy that these are the organizations that are now facing the strictest regulations and overt government control. Indeed, another important aspect of the recent amendment to the Federal Social Welfare Societies Law is that the creation of any new social welfare societies, whether they be "religious, professional, cultural, humanitarian, theatre-related or concerning women," will be restricted to UAE nationals alone. As a senior official explained: "We do realise the importance of allowing communities of various nationalities to have a forum where they can get together and practise their cultural and social activities. But at the same time, we believe that the number of the community bodies should be restricted."[156] Presumably this will allow for greater control over future civil society associations while limiting the growth of expatriate forums that are less easily co-opted. Moreover, if any expatriate societies avoid or defy these restrictions, or indeed if they refuse to allow the ministries to inspect their books, records, and activities, Article 43 of the amendment provides the Ministry of Labor and Social Affairs with the right to immediately dissolve the association.[157]

### Globalizing Forces and External Motivation

Regardless of whether such civic corporatism and control is part of an uninstitutionalized strategy to reduce the potential constituencies of an emerging civil society, thereby consolidating the state's position, or in Michael Hudson's terms is merely the product of nonparticipatory patrimonial structures,[158] what is apparent is that under such conditions any significant indigenous growth of autonomous civil society in the UAE will remain a distant prospect. More optimistic, however, there is a growing recognition that such a deactivated and demobilized civil society can be significantly boosted by certain globalizing forces, in particular by the increasing number of international organizations now operating in the UAE that are believed to be capable of promoting more stable and democratic structures in domestic civil society organizations; by the increasing penetration of international communications, which not only may increase transparency and accountability in Emirati society, but also may provide indigenous associations with a "demonstration effect" of successful examples of civil society elsewhere; and by the civil society–related influences and requirements of those global organizations attempting to implement and uphold international standards.

Indeed, on one level it may be that domestic civil society organizations can become stronger and more internally democratic if they are operating alongside and cooperating with UAE-based branches of international nongovernmental organizations (NGOs). Certainly, as Carapico noted in her study of Yemen, an increasing number of international NGOs were seen to be fostering greater liberalism and civil society institution building from below, thereby significantly boosting domestic associational life.[159] Thus, as more of these NGOs and development assistance agencies establish themselves in the UAE, their influence may continue to grow as more of the local population become directly and indirectly involved with their activities. By employing local staff and providing training and greater expectations, these international NGOs may provide an insight into democratic practices and methods, and may supply blueprints for future local organizations. Examples of such UAE-based branches already include the United Nations Development Project in Abu Dhabi (employing several dozen UAE nationals), the World Health Organization, and the Médécin sans Frontièrs relief organization. Furthermore, when a critical mass of these democratically organized NGOs, employees, and volunteers exists, there may also develop an atmosphere of collective security in which indigenous civil society organizations can develop with greater confidence.[160] Thus, with greater internal democracy and moral support it is thought likely that the UAE's associations will better resist the weakening effects of corporatism and control.

Second, in addition to their profound sociocultural impact, mass communications may also provide a boost for the emergence of domestic civil society. Indeed, as Samuel Huntington noted in 1991 following the demise of the Soviet Union, such technological advances were already seen as providing a "demonstration effect" whereby people in one society were able to learn quickly how people in another society had either pressed for greater liberalization or even brought down an authoritarian government. Furthermore, the ability to exchange ideas and views also allowed people to learn how these objectives could be achieved.[161] As such, with increasing access to the Internet, satellite television, and many other global information sources capable of bypassing state-imposed restrictions, Emirati civil society organizations may be able to forge greater links with similar organizations in other countries, thereby providing mutual support and a greater opportunity to share experiences. Indeed, there are already a number of such examples, with some of the described associations, especially those providing recreational activities, having established Internet links with their overseas counterparts.[162] Although these are of course relatively apolitical, they nevertheless provide an early indication of the potential role of global communications for other existing and future Emirati associations.

Perhaps most significant, in much the same way that global organizations such as the WTO and the World Bank have recently begun to influence the UAE's economic structures, so too may international NGOs begin to shape domestic associational life, especially in the workplace. A strong example would be the recommendations drawn up at the 2002 "Declaration on Fundamental Rights and Principles at Work" symposium in Dubai, sponsored by the International Labour Organization (ILO). Essentially, the proposal's aims were to create new associations and enhance existing groups so as to "look after the interests of workers, including any private or government employee of any nationality, to defend their rights, to seek to improve their social and economic status, and to represent them in all matters of concern to them."[163] Furthermore, and most crucial, it was also hoped that the new legislation would redress the balance of power between employers and employees by allowing these organizations to file lawsuits against the government.[164] Thus, given the previously discussed case studies of ineffective workers' associations in the UAE, if the Ministry of Labor and Social Affairs approves such ILO-inspired legislation, as it is predicted, this will represent a significant departure from the past. Indeed, as Matar al-Tayir explains, the ILO's recent promotion of labor standards has certainly had a major impact on the UAE, requiring his ministry to "adapt to foreign influences and the tremendous development of the world economy" by better supporting professional and workers' groups:

> The economic situation in the country [the UAE] and the structure of its labour market will have to adapt to foreign influences and the tremendous development of world economy. International conventions and commitments require the development of legislation in the UAE in order to ensure continuation of economic development without neglecting the ILO's Declaration on Fundamental Principles and Rights of Workers. In the light of economic changes, a review of the country's laws has become a pressing issue. We have professional associations and we do not object to the formation of workers' bodies. In this context, the UAE has signed six ILO conventions despite being a young and developing country. These conventions are not binding, but being a member of the ILO, we feel that we should sign the conventions which benefit us and which reflect the civilised image of the UAE as a country committed to basic labour standards and rights which our constitution guarantees.[165]

Similarly, in the near future, motivation from international organizations may extend beyond reforms for labor associations to include support for other areas of civil society, including types of organizations that do not presently exist in the UAE. One such example would be human rights groups, which have thus far been unable to perform meaningful investigations in the UAE due to the described restrictions on the press and the freedom of public participation. Although a small section now exists within Dubai's police force to monitor allegations of human rights abuses, genuinely independent domestic groups have yet to emerge. However, with increasing criticism from foreign sources, including influential bodies such as the U.S. Bureau of Democracy and Human Rights,[166] this may change as the UAE government is pressured and embarrassed into implementing reforms more consistent with those of its global partners.[167]

## Conclusion

The seemingly inevitable acceleration of global integration, in part due to the liberalizing reforms of the "new rentiers" seeking to boost foreign investment and promote fresh sources of economic rent, certain new external forces, perceived as both benign and malignant, are now also beginning to shape and influence indigenous structures, and must therefore be included alongside domestic factors in a comprehensive assessment of Emirati development. First, with regard to the UAE's economic structures, it has been indicated how globalization has led to both increased international competition and greater marketing opportunities for Emirati firms. Second, and equally controversial, it has been suggested that increasing global economic integration may have led to a neglect of regional integration, widely believed to serve as an important safety net for most developing economies. Third, the impact of international organizations such as the WTO and the IMF on the domestic economy has been both far-reaching and ambiguous, with clear divisions having emerged over the UAE's acceptance of any international agreements thought likely to alter existing structures permanently. On the one hand certain groups have championed the prospects of the WTO-led removal of monopolies and the implementation of copyright controls, while on the other hand conservatives have cautioned against the opening up of key industries and the political complications that may result from the UAE's commitments.

The impact of sociocultural forces has been equally contentious, especially given globalization's perceived role in the erosion of Emirati culture and the rapid marginalization of the Arabic language, and (more positively) given its association with improved international communications and increasing accountability. Indeed, globalizing forces have been blamed for the increasing "cultural contamination" that appears to have all but destroyed the traditional Emirati way of life, and in turn this sociocultural attack has provided an additional impetus for the government's multipurpose cultural revival. Similarly, the increasing presence of non-Arabs, foreign media, and foreign-language education have all combined to marginalize the Arabic language, again prompting a reaction to what is widely believed to be the consequence of intrusive globalization. However, with regard to the improvements in global communications and their accessibility in the UAE, it is evident that such developments have been better received, with many agreeing that such supranational sources of information have already begun to increase the accountability and transparency of neighboring Gulf communication networks, a trend that may soon reach the UAE.

In addition to these significant influences on domestic socioeconomic development, some of which have helped to reinforce existing pathologies and others of which have helped to overcome such obstacles, globalizing forces may begin to play an important role in reshaping civil society and associational life in the UAE. Specifically, though the UAE's current civil society remains in a weakened state due to a combination of rentier-dependency-related structures (namely cultural heterogeneity resulting from the massive foreign labor force, increasing levels of government co-option, royal patronage, and in some circumstances greater control and repression), a fresh wave of external forces may nevertheless offer a means of reactivating and supporting demobilized associations in the near future. In particular, the transfer of ideas and methods from the increasing number of UAE-based branches of international organizations may lead to stronger internal structures for indigenous associations and a greater network of collective security and mutual support. Second, the improvements in global communications may also provide a demonstration effect for the UAE's civil society organizations as they become better connected and more able to share experiences with their counterparts in other parts of the world. Finally, and perhaps most significant, certain external bodies may be capable of motivating the UAE government to free up civic space from above, with domestic labor groups and human rights associations already likely to benefit from recommendations and proposals made to the relevant ministries by prominent global NGOs and major international partners.

## Notes

1. HIRST (1995), p. 3.
2. DICKEN (1992), p. 1.
3. See http://www.mydsf.com.
4. HIRST (2001).
5. EMIRATES CORPORATE COMMUNICATIONS (2002).
6. See "The Foreign Investment Debate," p. 235 in this volume.
7. See AMIN (1997) and AMIN (1982) for a discussion of antiglobalization theory.
8. As Herb states with reference to the Gulf monarchies, the fragmentary effects of globalizing forces are often readily blamed for many of the serious internal antagonisms in the more unstable developing states, resulting in hardship and suffering for much of the population. See HERB (1999).
9. Held, who although warning of the dangers of predatory globalization, concludes that globalization is not beyond regulation and can be harnessed as a civilizing and democratizing force. See HELD, MCGREW, GOLDBLATT, and PERRATON (1999), pp. 444–452.
10. PRATT (2001).
11. HEARD-BEY (1982), p. 11.
12. GCC DEVELOPMENT PLANS: UNITED ARAB EMIRATES (1982), pp. 10, 18–19.
13. Personal interview, Dubai Chamber of Commerce and Industry, Department of Research Studies, December 2001.
14. ABDULLAH (1978), pp. 106–107.
15. AL-SAYEGH (1998), p. 92.
16. ABDULLAH (1978), pp. 106–107.
17. AL-SAYEGH (1998), p. 92.
18. FENELON (1973), pp. 18–19.
19. Ibid.
20. PECK (1986), p. 76.
21. See "Ideological Resources," p. 80 in this volume.
22. BUSINESS IN DUBAI (2002b), pp. 18–19.

23. Ibid.

24. Personal interviews, Abu Dhabi, March 2002.

25. Personal interviews, Dubai, December 2001, March 2002, and September 2002.

26. DUBAI DEPARTMENT OF PORTS AND CUSTOMS (2001c), p. 131.

27. See "Readily Identifiable Development Problems," p. 163 in this volume.

28. JREISAT (1992), pp. 1–2.

29. HANAFI (2001). Sari Hanafi is director of the Palestinian Diaspora and Refugees Centre in Ramallah.

30. Ibid.

31. KAWACH (2001).

32. Personal interviews, Dubai Chamber of Commerce and Industry, Department of Research Studies, December 2001.

33. WORLD TRADE ORGANIZATION NEWS (2002).

34. AL-JABIL (2002).

35. Julphar is a Ra's al-Khaimah–based pharmaceutical company. Established in 1985 it now has three factories: one in the UAE, one in Ecuador, and one in Germany. See OXFORD BUSINESS GROUP (2000), p. 91.

36. See BUSINESS MONITOR INTERNATIONAL (2003b).

37. Personal interviews, Sharjah, October 2002.

38. Created in 1976 after the nationalization of its Cable & Wireless–owned predecessor Emirtel, Etisalat is now the UAE's largest company (according to research undertaken by the HSBC), second only to Saudi Arabian Basic Industries Corporation in the Gulf. See OXFORD BUSINESS GROUP (2000), pp. 85, 109.

39. ECONOMIST INTELLIGENCE UNIT (2000), p. 17. Also see HILOTIN (2003) for a discussion of the pros and cons of Etisalat's dominance.

40. OXFORD BUSINESS GROUP (2000), p. 109.

41. TAMIMI LAW UPDATE (2001).

42. ASHOUR (2001).

43. Ibid.

44. STAUFFER (2001).

45. HILOTIN (2003).

46. TAMIMI LAW UPDATE (2001). Shaikh Fahim al-Qasimi, the minister of economy and commerce, said the UAE would free up the textile and ready-made clothes industry through three stages, to end by 2006.

47. MERZA (2001), p. 16. Ali Merza represents the UNDP project in Libya.

48. BIBBO (2002), as explained by Khazraji, undersecretary of the Ministry of Labor and Social Affairs. For a discussion of U.S. pressure for the UAE to reform, see MALLETT (1999), p. 13, quoting Robert Mallett, deputy secretary of commerce, U.S. Department of Commerce, speaking at the 20 April 1999 conference convened by the Middle East Policy Council. Also see OXFORD BUSINESS GROUP (2000), p. 123.

49. See TAMIMI LAW UPDATE (2001).

50. Double taxation treaties are bilateral agreements ensuring the mutual reduction or elimination of import/export duties.

51. JIYAD (2001). Furthermore, with an increasing number of U.S. business partners, the UAE may have difficulty maintaining such a boycott as certain contract wording may be considered in breach of U.S. antiboycott laws. See OXFORD BUSINESS GROUP (2000), p. 123.

52. ROBERTSON (1992), cited in RANDALL and THEOBALD (1998), p. 248.

53. FINDLOW (2000), p. 36, citing the contrasting examples of ALESCO con-

ferences in 1977 and 1998.

54. Personal interviews, Abu Dhabi, March 2001; Dubai, December 2001; and Sharjah, October 2002.

55. KHALAF (2001).

56. KHALAF (1999), pp. 85–106. Also see KHALAF (2000), pp. 243–261.

57. See KHALAF (2001); and "Cultural and Religious Resources," p. 77 in this volume.

58. Personal interviews, Abu Dhabi, September 2002. There are plans to establish a major UAE-based English-language satellite television station; this is hoped to offer an alternative to Al-Jazeera and to provide Western journalists with a more accessible source of Arab opinion. Also see KAWACH (2003).

59. Interview with English-language library staff, Sharjah Public Library, September 2002.

60. ZEITUN (2002a).

61. Ibid.

62. At present, the Arabic-language component of courses at Zayed University counts for 10 percent of the student's overall grade.

63. YAMANI (2001).

64. NONNEMAN (2001), p. 150.

65. YAMANI (2001).

66. SHARABI (1988), pp. 150–152.

67. CARAPICO (1998), p. 2.

68. DE TOQUEVILLE (1981), cited in RANDALL and THEOBALD (1998), p. 202.

69. CARAPICO (1998), p. 2.

70. See CARAPICO (1998). With regard to tribal society, see, in this volume, "The Traditional Social Structure," p. 10, and "The Traditional Political Structure," p. 14.

71. KAMRAVA (2000), p. 192.

72. CARAPICO (1998), p. 12.

73. KAMRAVA (2000), pp. 202–203.

74. WEIGLE and BUTTERFIELD (1992), pp. 1–22, cited in RANDALL and THEOBALD (1998), pp. 203–204.

75. CARAPICO (1998), p. 15.

76. Ibid., p. 12.

77. See "Emiratization," p. 144 in this volume.

78. KAMRAVA (2000), p. 195.

79. RUGH (1997), p. 16, quoting William Rugh, U.S. ambassador to the UAE between 1992 and 1995.

80. Ibid.

81. Most middle-class nonresident Indians working in the Gulf will claim they are simply there to earn sufficient money so as to emigrate to Canada, Australia, New Zealand, and the like, within the next few years.

82. For a similar discussion see KAMRAVA (2000), pp. 202–203.

83. See "Maintaining the Polity and Resisting Reform," p. 69 in this volume.

84. AL-SAYEGH (1999), pp. 13–16, speaking at the 20 April 1999 conference convened by the Middle East Policy Council.

85. See UNDP-POGAR (2002).

86. MADAD (2001).

87. KHALEEJ TIMES (1987).

88. CALLAN and ROBISON (2000), p. 187, "Environmental Organisations."

89. GULF NEWS (2003).

90. A notable exception to co-option and patronage given that it was founded in 1975 by British enthusiasts and has remained largely autonomous. However, in recent years the group has been making an effort to attract more UAE national and Arab members. Personal interviews with Peter Hellyer, Abu Dhabi, September 2003; and Frauke Heard-Bey, Abu Dhabi, January 2004.

91. As the 2000 mission statement of the Emirates Heritage Club explains, "In June 1997 Emirates Heritage Club is considered as an independent authority belonging to Abu Dhabi Government headed by His Highness Shaykh Sultan bin Zayed Al-Nuhayyan, Deputy Prime Minister, chairman of the Emirates Heritage Club according to the Emiri Decree number 14/1997."

92. Personal interviews, Dubai, December 2001.

93. ANTHONY (2002), pp. 86–87. As Anthony describes, in 1971 Sharjah was able to bring to the negotiating table far more educated citizens than any of the other Trucial states.

94. Indeed, in 1998 UNESCO named Sharjah the "Cultural Capital of the Arab World."

95. PRESS AFFAIRS DIRECTORATE OF SHARJAH EMIRI COURT (1988), pp. 183–185.

96. Recent examples include Sharjah's hosting of "theatrical gatherings" sponsored by both the Sharjah Department of Culture and Information and the ruler, Shaikh Sultan al-Qasimi. See ZEITUN (2002b). Examples of rallies and public demonstrations include the recent antismoking campaign supported by Shaikh Muhammad bin Saqr al-Qasimi, director of the Sharjah Medical District; see KHALEEJ TIMES (2002b).

97. See "Social Growth," p. 139 in this volume.

98. RUGH (1997), p. 18.

99. U.S. DEPARTMENT OF STATE (2001), sec. 2(b).

100. See http://www.ugagolf.com. Also see "Elite Interest Groups: Old Rentiers Versus New Rentiers," p. 225 in this volume.

101. ALI (2002); and personal observations.

102. See http://ww.hga-uae.org.ae. Membership is restricted to UAE nationals, as per the first condition of the association's working membership requirements.

103. 'AHMAD (2002).

104. The Emirates Institute for Banking and Financial Studies is a government-funded institute for upgrading the knowledge and skills of UAE bankers. See http://www.eibfs.com.

105. ABU DHABI ECONOMY (2001), pp. 5–7.

106. See U.S. DEPARTMENT OF STATE (2001).

107. ABU DHABI ECONOMY (2001), pp. 5–7.

108. See http://www.moumineen.org.ae.

109. See "Cultural and Religious Resources," p. 77 in this volume.

110. This contrasts sharply with mosques elsewhere in the Arab world, where very often the proceeds from a local shop (often part of the mosque building) will pay for the upkeep of the mosque. Personal interviews with Frauke Heard-Bey, Abu Dhabi, January 2004.

111. U.S. DEPARTMENT OF STATE (2001), sec. 2.

112. KHALEEJ TIMES (2001).

113. See http://www.muntada.org.ae.

114. MUSSALLAM (2002).

115. See the 1999 "Monthly News" for K. I. Books as http://members.tripod.com/kibooks/news/jan99.htm.

116. MADAD (2003).

117. UAE MINISTRY OF INFORMATION AND CULTURE (2002). Free press is guaranteed in the UAE as per the constitution under Article 30, which states, "Freedom of opinion, expressing it verbally, in writing or by other means of expression, shall be guaranteed within the limits of the law."

118. CARAPICO (1998), p. 12.

119. See "Ideological Resources," p. 80 in this volume.

120. PECK (1986), pp. 78–80.

121. Ibid., p. 80.

122. Ibid.

123. See "The Drive for Greater Transparency," p. 222 in this volume.

124. UAE MINISTRY OF INFORMATION AND CULTURE (2002), regarding Federal Law no. 15 of 1988.

125. Federal Law no. 5 of 1973. For a full discussion, see ABDULLA (1985), p. 232.

126. U.S. DEPARTMENT OF STATE (2001), sec. 2(a).

127. Ibid.

128. SALDAMANDO (2001a).

129. U.S. DEPARTMENT OF STATE (2001), sec. 1.

130. SALDAMANDO (2001a).

131. U.S. DEPARTMENT OF STATE (2001), secs. 1(c)–1(d).

132. Ibid., sec. 2(a).

133. Ibid.

134. OXFORD BUSINESS GROUP (2000), p. 95.

135. SALDAMANDO (2001b).

136. OXFORD BUSINESS GROUP (2000), p. 95.

137. SALDAMANDO (2001b).

138. U.S. DEPARTMENT OF STATE (2001), sec. 2(a).

139. OXFORD BUSINESS GROUP (2000), p. 93.

140. U.S. DEPARTMENT OF STATE (2001), sec. 2(a).

141. U.S. DEPARTMENT OF STATE (2001), sec. 6(e).

142. Ibid. Workers are often reluctant to lodge complaints for fear of reprisal. "The press periodically carries reports of abuses suffered by domestic servants, particularly women, at the hands of some employers. Allegations have included excessive work hours, non-payment of wages, and verbal and physical abuse."

143. Ibid., sec. 6(b).

144. EMIRATES BANKERS ASSOCIATION (1997), pp. 4–6.

145. See UAE CENTRAL BANK (1991).

146. MADAD (2002).

147. MADAD and FLEIHAN (2002).

148. See EMIRATES MEDICAL ASSOCIATION (2002). Shaikh Mansur al-Nuhayyan is a son of Shaikh Zayed. Also see ABU DHABI ECONOMY (2001), pp. 5–7.

149. KHALEEJ TIMES (2004).

150. See http://www.abcdubai.com.

151. See http://www.spedubai.org.

152. See http://www.goanculturaldubai.com.

153. See http://www.pinoyuae.com/clubs_pang.htm.

154. See http://www.kfs-uae.org. This speech was made in Abu Dhabi in 1999 by Jalal Balala, the Kenya Friendship Society's chairman.

155. See http://www.goanculturaldubai.com.

156. MADAD (2001).

157. Ibid.

158. HUDSON (1977), pp. 85–88.

159. CARAPICO (1998), pp. 4–5.

160. KAMRAVA (2000), p. 195.

161. HUNTINGTON (1991), p. 242.

162. Personal interviews, Dubai, March 2002 and September 2002.

163. MADAD (2002).

164. Ibid.

165. KHALEEJ TIMES (2002e), citing the UAE minister of labor and social affairs speaking at the Dubai Chamber of Commerce and Industry.

166. U.S. DEPARTMENT OF STATE (2001), sec. 4.

167. Personal interviews, Dubai, December 2001.

# 6

# Conclusion

In the centuries preceding the oil era the economy of the lower Gulf had entered into a distinct period of international peripheralization due to its heavy reliance on both the export of primary products to distant markets and the steady influx of foreign labor from South Asia and East Africa. Crucially, however, this early period saw the emergence of a small but powerful merchant/entrepreneurial class. This class was capable of not only fostering a capitalist mode of production in the pearling industry and financing a wide range of local socioeconomic development projects, but also of operating within an extremely flexible and decentralized political system. This system combined surprisingly efficient nascent extractive institutions with open consultation and direct access to the coastal towns' relatively humble ruling shaikhs.

From the beginning of the nineteenth century the region's increasing contact with the core economy and imperial power of Britain had the effect of gradually removing many of these inherited structures and displacing indigenous economic networks while permanently, and in many ways unnaturally, reinforcing those select traditions that were deemed useful in transforming the native rulers into a British client elite. By the 1920s, this dependency of the elites on Britain deepened much further as the rulers began to receive an unprecedented level of personal economic benefits in exchange for facilitating British oil exploration and granting British air landing rights. Essentially, these incomes represented considerable non-earned economic rent many years before the first significant oil exports. Able to discontinue almost all extraction and switch to a distributive system, the rulers managed to placate large sections of their populations and thereby modify the historical ruler-merchant balance of power. Exploitation of the new wealth therefore provided the shaikhs with their first real political autonomy from nonruling elites. Although there were attempts to reinvigorate indigenous development and redirect the rentier wealth (most notably the reform movement of the Dubai merchants), these were easily contained by a campaign of indirect imperial coercion and misinformation.

British retrenchment in the late 1960s necessitated the withdrawal of almost all personnel from the region, but the empire's former clients and future oil partners were far from abandoned. Indeed, in close collaboration with the rulers, Britain's remaining administrators embarked on an extraordinarily rapid program of local institution building and federal negotiations in an effort to provide the lower Gulf with some degree of security from both external interference and the very real threat of internal fragmentation in a postimperial age. The resulting United Arab Emirates was proclaimed in 1971 and soon proved to be an extremely astute compromise agreement. By combining a carefully limited number of new central institutions alongside historically proven local systems, the newly independent state was able to avoid any significant break from the past. It was also able to provide just enough inter-emirate cooperation to ensure successful political union during a tumultuous period of fantastic wealth, regional power vacuums, military realignments, and competing ideologies.

The continuing survival of the UAE's traditional monarchies and the existence of a complex and dynamic "ruling bargain" has thus far allowed the shaikhs to carefully circumvent the old "shaikh's dilemma" of assimilating new groups alongside old. Specifically, personal and patrimonial-clientalist resources have remained key components of the legitimacy formula even during an era of unprecedented modernization and population explosion. Shoring up this network of privileges, loyalties, and vertical relations, the UAE's shrewd exploitation of cultural, religious, and ideological resources has engendered a greater sense of national identity, reduced the appeal of radical causes, and has helped to mobilize large sections of the population behind shared concerns and common ethnic memories. Adding a further layer of legitimacy, the polity's delicate constitutional engineering and selective institution building have provided much needed structural resources and some degree of public credibility without actually weakening the patrimonial or rather "neopatrimonial" linchpins of the monarchical system.

Augmenting these legitimacy components has of course been the UAE's massive oil wealth. Allowing for considerable expansion of the earlier distributive system, the rulers have been able to establish the world's purest example of a rentier state—a state in which the entire citizenship unwittingly enter into a tacit pact of receiving free housing, welfare, education, and a host of other economic benefits in exchange for their almost total political acquiescence. Unlike many other oil-rich states in the region, this pact has remained virtually intact as the local merchant elites were considerably weakened by the time of the UAE's rather late entry into the oil era. Whereas those merchants elsewhere in the Gulf were still operating from a position of strength when their rulers began to receive oil revenues much earlier in the century, the UAE possessed no real bargaining power. Further connected to the UAE's material resources has been the polity's favorable international relations with its superpower oil customers and behind-the-scenes oil investors. These valuable business alliances have been effectively translated into military treaties, providing a sense of real security for the militarily feeble monarchs in an increasingly dangerous neighborhood.

Alongside these components, I have demonstrated how the ruling families themselves are also providing the system with strength and resilience. By evolving into self-regulating institutions and behaving as surrogate large-scale political parties, the major dynasties have promoted their own longevity. Power-sharing strategies and consolation prizes in a more unitary rentier state combined with a reinforcement of the succession process and the frequent bandwagoning against potentially harmful factions have considerably reduced both the threat of internal division and any unwanted outside meddling in private business. Essentially, as the ruling families have politically matured, the need for collective action has become paramount as their internal dynamic now forces all members to act positively for the group as a whole and indeed for the wider neopatrimonial and rentier networks.

The UAE's socioeconomic development trajectory from the 1970s to the present day reveals the key strategies employed by the "modernizing monarchs" in their attempts to reduce some of the more serious weaknesses associated with the UAE's dependency situation, namely the country's reliance on overseas demand for oil exports, the supply of foreign technology for its industries, and the spiralling immigration of foreign workers. Specifically, in an effort to promote greater self-sufficiency and reinforce the material and welfare components of the ruling bargain, the rulers' development planners have sought to diversify the economy, facilitate technology transfers between foreign and domestic enterprises, build up a comprehensive social state to maintain a healthy and motivated labor force, and promote the nationalization or "emiratization" of positions in both the public and private sectors.

The industrial diversification strategy has enjoyed modest success in recent years with a variety of domestic nonoil-related concerns establishing themselves and in some cases even managing to substitute previously imported foreign technologies. Even more successful, though, has been the UAE's diversification through its commercial and tourist sectors. Although these sectors have not expressly reduced the country's reliance on foreign economies, they have nevertheless considerably reduced oil's relative contribution to the GDP. Furthermore, while the agricultural sector has grown at a much slower rate given the region's geographic restraints, its development still represents an important symbolic layer of diversification, especially as the UAE's food security has been able to improve. Finally, the oil-funded creation of a massive new infrastructure of transport, utility, and communication networks has ensured that the UAE can continue to physically accommodate such rapid and diverse nonoil developments, at least for the immediate future.

Also directly benefiting from massive oil investments has been the UAE's social development. The education sector has enjoyed considerable growth with dozens of new schools and several new universities now able to provide both national and expatriate youths with relatively high standards of tuition, small class sizes, and first-rate facilities. Equally noteworthy has been the expansion of the healthcare system, with many hospitals and clinics staffed by well qualified professionals now offering low doctor-to-patient ratios and comprehensive care for all but the most severe cases.

The emiratization strategy has enjoyed less noticeable success, with the UAE's dependence on expatriates remaining as great as ever. There have nonetheless been important recent indications that the nationalization of certain managerial and professional positions is beginning to gain momentum. Moreover, these accomplishments are particularly impressive given that emiratization, unlike diversification or social development, cannot be solved by large injections of oil wealth. Indeed, in many ways the strategy was initially derailed as early attempts to offer financial inducements to nationals effectively priced them out of the UAE's highly competitive labor market. Thus far, the best results appear to have been the product of a combined approach in which the planners have relied not only on restrictive practices such as quotas and visa limitations but also on the promotion of greater vocational education, internships, and other professional training programs for qualified young nationals.

Under these broad strategies there have also been significant emirate-level substrategies, which in many ways account for the slightly different development paths being pursued within the federation. Most notably at odds have, of course, been the trajectories of the two principal emirates of Abu Dhabi and Dubai. Abu Dhabi has been able to rely on considerable overseas investments financed by its vast oil wealth and heavy export industries courtesy of its comparative advantage of cheap energy. Dubai's much longer history of trading and accumulation of entrepreneurial expertise coupled with its far more modest oil reserves have promoted a much greater effort to fully diversify. In particular, Dubai has had to make a greater commitment to nonenergy-related import-substitution industries, and has sought to expand considerably its commercial and tourist sectors in a further effort to boost its non-oil-sector's contribution to the GDP. Although popularly viewed as a source of considerable tension, these different approaches have achieved some degree of success in their own right and should now be regarded as mutually supportive substrategies. Indeed, the federation's flexibility at the socioeconomic development level has allowed one area of the country to concentrate on the exploitation of its abundant natural resources and behave as something of a financial pillar for the poorer areas; while another area has begun to promote greater variation in the UAE's economy, has been able to integrate the country into the international marketplace, and is now increasingly able to provide the national population with genuine private sector employment opportunities.

Some of the more obvious development problems that have been encountered and thus far remain unsolved by the planners are important to note. The UAE's economy is still primarily consumption oriented, a long-term predicament that continues to cause a trade imbalance and a declining balance of payments. Even though Abu Dhabi and Dubai appear to be cooperating at a much greater level than ever before, there are nevertheless a considerable number of duplicated development projects across the UAE, especially in the smaller emirates where underutilization is an increasing concern. The relative wealth gap between the richest and poorest emirates has remained as great as it was thirty years ago. Such regional disequilibrium is preventing development and balanced growth and is likely to catalyse a host of fresh socioeconomic problems in the near future. In a similar fashion to the early wealth-related emiratization strategies, these ongoing development concerns are particularly problematic given that oil-financed investment is not a viable solution, and indeed in many cases may actually worsen the situation. Instead, it would seem that a number of internal pathologies must be addressed if circumstances are to improve, namely the predominantly allocative nature of the state, the rentier-induced consumer culture of the population, the lack of effective interemirate cooperation, the lack of proper transparency, and the frequent mismanagement of existing resources.

In an effort to explain more fully some of these persisting problems, one must look at the role of domestic structures and their associated weaknesses. By expanding on the all-pervading implications of rentierism and the kind of subsidy-based development that seemingly filters all the way down to the level of individual UAE nationals—and by underscoring the impact of reinvigorated neopatrimonial networks, bureaucratic self-interests, and differing client elite orientations on the UAE's policymaking and policy implementation processes—it is clear that many of the reinforced dependency structures that have allowed for the remarkable survival of the UAE's anachronistic monarchies are now so deeply rooted in the political economy that they actively shape and invariably undermine the planners' more rational socioeconomic development objectives. Certainly, in many ways these problems can be viewed as the hidden costs of the UAE's ruling bargain, its political stability, and the persistence of traditional forces, and therefore the price that must be paid in order to circumvent permanently the shaikh's dilemma and the inevitability of the early modernization theories.

An awkward hybrid form of neopatrimonial government of seemingly modern institutions astride much older traditional authorities allows the hereditary rulers and their closest relatives to dominate directly the highest levels of the federal decisionmaking process and, through the use of carefully selected representatives, to control tightly the UAE's token legislature. Moreover, operating in parallel to (and in some cases overlapping) these federal authorities exist a multitude of emirate-level government departments. Although there are now signs of their increasing subordination to centralized power, it is important to note that until very recently there have been major divisions over key issues of national interest such as oil policy, foreign relations, and even defense. Thus, while the federation has ostensibly matured over the years, especially with the greater incorporation of Dubai, it is nevertheless little more than a loose confederation holding together potentially uncoordinated and ultimately autonomous regional power bases.

Policy implementation takes place within a large number of ministries, parastatals, and other bureaucracies, and as such these institutions are also capable of influencing Emirati development. Managed almost exclusively by nonelected appointees with close ties to the traditional polity, the majority of the UAE's chambers of commerce, judicial bodies, and financial organizations are firmly fixed into the neopatrimonial network. In many cases, the rigidity of these institutions has been compounded by a number of other pathologies including bureaucratic self-interest, opaqueness, and of course a complete lack of impartiality.

Although not a pathology as such, another important internal factor has been the widening division emerging within the UAE's client elite. Essentially, the debate over the path of future development between the "old rentiers" seeking to perpetuate the steady flow of oil revenues and the increasingly powerful camp of "new rentiers" seeking fresh sources of economic rent from nonoil-related activities, such as the leasing of property and business parks to foreign investors, has highlighted the nonhomogeneous nature of the UAE's dominant rentier class. As such, there is a genuine struggle between conservatives and reformers, with the latter needing to attack the status quo on a number of levels in order to remove the many existing restrictive regulations that currently block or hinder their particular vision of Emirati development.

The rapidly increasing influence of new external forces on the UAE's socioeconomic development shows how various aspects of globalization, both benign and malignant, have already begun to reshape the UAE's domestic economic structures. On the one hand, global integration is leading to increased international competition for struggling infant industries, whereas on the other hand a number of Emirati enterprises have already proved themselves capable of harnessing the greater marketing opportunities afforded by the "new economy." Moreover, such accelerating globalization is believed to have led to a substantial decline in regional integration, a development feared by those who regard more localized economic links as providing a better safety net in times of crisis. Equally contentious has been the impact of international organizations on the UAE's economy, especially on its numerous monopolies. Whereas supporters of WTO and IMF membership have welcomed the requirements to free up such sectors, many conservatives have opposed external involvement in any of the UAE's key industries and remain wary of the political complications that may result from further commitments to international organizations.

Also ambiguous has been the impact of external sociocultural forces on the UAE. In particular, such forces have been held responsible for the increasing "cultural contamination" that has ostensibly eroded much of the traditional Emirati way of life and therefore provided an additional impetus for the government's multipurpose cultural revival. The considerable marginalization of the Arabic language has also been blamed on intrusive global influences, specifically the increasing presence of non-Arabs and foreign-language education. Developments in global communications and their accessibility in the UAE have, however, been far better received, perhaps given that such external sources of information are thought likely to engender or maybe even require much greater accountability and transparency from existing domestic services.

The role of globalization in reshaping the UAE's civil society and associational life demonstrates how a fresh wave of external forces may provide sufficient support for the revitalization of many of the UAE's currently weakened civil society organizations, especially those that have been demobilized by carefully controlled rentier and dependency-related structures (namely cultural heterogeneity resulting from the massive foreign labor force, increasing levels of government co-option, royal patronage, and, in a small number of cases, even repression). Of these new influences, the importance of transferable ideas from the numerous UAE-based branches of international organizations has been cited as providing a stronger foundation for future domestic associations in addition to fostering a better sense of collective security. Similarly, there would also seem to be something of a "demonstration effect" resulting from improved global communications, allowing associations in the UAE to benefit from shared global experiences and enjoy greater mutual support. Last and perhaps most significant have been the recommendations and proposals made to domestic ministries and other policymaking institutions by prominent NGOs and the UAE's other major international partners. Given time, these external bodies may be able to motivate the UAE government to free up civic space from above, perhaps even allowing for the operation of previously restricted organizations such as labor groups and human rights associations.

# Glossary

| | |
|---|---|
| *abaya* | a form of traditional dress |
| *Abu Musa* | strategic island in the lower Gulf, formerly belonging to Sharjah, but currently occupied by Iran |
| *'amil* | a person involved in an almost capitalist system of pearling in which boats would be outfitted by an entrepreneur, who would then claim a share of all profits |
| *'amir* | the ruler's local representative, especially on the Abu Dhabian island of Dalma |
| *Amoco* | a subsidiary of the Standard Oil Company of Indiana |
| *ardha* | a show or display (e.g., camel races in Bedu society) |
| *'arif* | an official responsible for the maintenance of falaj irrigation channels in agricultural towns such as Hatta and Al-'Ayn |
| *'ashira* | a narrowly defined familial organization or tribe |
| *'askars* | armed tribesmen paid a salary to enforce the ruler's authority in outlying regions |
| *Atheer* | a major Abu Dhabian gas company |
| *'azima* | a voluntary contribution paid by pearling merchants to provide for feasts in honor of visiting dignitaries, especially on the Abu Dhabian island of Dalma |
| *baggala* | a type of fishing/trading vessel commonly used in the Gulf |
| *Bani Yas* | a powerful Abu Dhabi–based tribal federation |
| *Banian* | a British Indian subject |
| *baraka* | charisma |
| *Bastakiyah* | an old quarter of Bur Dubai once donated by the ruler to Persian merchants; some of the Bastakiyah houses still have their original wind towers |

| | |
|---|---|
| *Batinah* | refers to both a tribe in Oman and the UAE's Indian Ocean coastline |
| *bay'a* | collective recognition of another person's authority |
| *Bedu* | nomadic people (the double plural *Bedouin* is not commonly used in the lower Gulf) |
| *Bridgeston* | U.S. oil company |
| *Buraimi* | a conurbation of Omani villages surrounding a large oasis close to Al-'Ayn and the UAE border |
| *Bushire* | an important Iranian harbor town |
| *Dalma* | a small Abu Dhabian island, formerly a thriving center of the pearling industry |
| *dar al-harb* | the non-Muslim world, referring to the Wahabbi attempts to conquer non-Wahabbi lands |
| *Das* | an Abu Dhabian island transformed into an offshore oil terminal |
| *Dibba al-Fujairah* | a small town on the UAE's Indian Ocean coastline, currently being redeveloped into a tourist resort |
| *dirah* | the elastic concept of an area in which a tribe exercised sway |
| *dirham* | the UAE's currency |
| *dishdasha* | a form of traditional dress |
| *diwan* | the ruler's court |
| *Dnata* | a Dubai government-owned supplier of cargo air services |
| *duris* | armed guards in the oasis towns and outlying regions responsible for protecting camels and other livestock from raiders |
| *Emirtel* | the predecessor to Etisalat |
| *Etisalat* | the UAE's telecommunications monopoly |
| *Exxon* | Standard Oil of New Jersey |
| *falaj* (pl. *aflaj*) | subterranean stone tunnels designed to bring water down from the mountains and provide irrigation in agricultural areas |
| *Al-Faqit* | a small town on the UAE's Indian Ocean coastline, currently being redeveloped into a tourist resort |
| *al-ghanima* | the booty collected by desert raiders, of which four-fifths would be divided among the tribesmen and one-fifth retained by the leader |
| *ghasa* | the "pearling proletariat" of crewmen that emerged as a result of the 'amil system |
| *al-ghaus al-kabir* | the pearling season (which began in June and ended in early October) |
| *Ghayathi* | an Abu Dhabian settlement close to the Saudi border |

| | |
|---|---|
| *ghazu* | desert raiding |
| *hadhr* | settled people |
| *Hajar mountains* | a range of mountains running down from the Musandam peninsula into the UAE's hinterland |
| *hakim* | a regime with no constitution |
| *Hamriyyah* | a coastal town near to Sharjah |
| *haras* | armed guards at the ruler's fort in the main town |
| *hasila* | a pearling tax requiring all pearling boats to contribute a share equal to the income of one crew member |
| *Hatta* | a town in the Hajar mountains, an enclave of Dubai emirate and an increasingly popular tourist destination |
| *Hispanoil* | Spanish oil company |
| *hukumah* | the traditional tribal administration |
| *ikhluwi* | a communal system of pearling in which the crew would jointly own a boat and share all profits |
| *imam* | a communal prayer leader |
| *Al-Ittihad al-Thuna'i* | the 1969 union between Abu Dhabi and Dubai |
| *Al-Ittihad al-Tusa'i* | the proposed nine-member federation including the seven Trucial states, Bahrain, and Qatar |
| *jalbut* | a type of fishing/trading vessel commonly used in the Gulf |
| *Jamyat al-Islah* | "Reformation Association"—an amorphous Islamic political party in the UAE |
| *Jumeirah* | a western district of Dubai, now dominated by beach hotels, leisure parks, and European expatriates |
| *kafil* | a sponsor—all foreign businesses operating in the UAE require at least one local partner |
| *Kalba* | a small town on the Indian Ocean coastline, briefly granted independence from Sharjah in order to facilitate British negotiations over air landing rights |
| *al-khawiya* | the period of oil exploration by foreign firms in the 1930s |
| *Khojah* | a Punjabi region of present-day Pakistan |
| *Khor Fakkan* | a container port on the UAE's Indian Ocean coastline, part of Sharjah emirate |
| *khutba* | Friday sermons |
| *lakh* | a very high denomination of British-Indian currency |
| *Lingah* | an important Iranian harbor town, formerly ruled by a branch of the Qawasim |
| *Liwa oases* | a string of oases deep inside the Abu Dhabian hinterland |
| *majlis* (pl. *majalis*) | a meeting place/council |
| *majlis al-tujjar* | the council convened by Shaikh Sa'id al-Maktum in |

|  |  |
|---|---|
|  | the 1940s to rejuvenate many of the projects originally proposed during the Dubai reform movement of 1938 |
| *Al-Majlis al-Watani lil-Ittihad* | the Federal National Council, comprising appointed representatives |
| *masha* | a tax collected by the 'arifs to help maintain the falaj irrigation channels in agricultural towns |
| *Al-Mashriq* | the eastern Arab world |
| *al-mithaq* | the pact between rulers and other groups; also the name of the Bahraini emir's new national charter |
| *Mitsu* | Japanese oil company |
| *Mobil* | U.S. oil company |
| *musaqqam* | pearling broker |
| *mutarizaya* | the ruler's armed retainers |
| *muzakki* | an official responsible for tax collection |
| *na'ib* | the ruler's local representative, especially in Al-'Ayn |
| *naub* | a pearling tax levied on all pearl merchants proportionate to the size of their business |
| *nisab* | the tax threshold quantity of dates |
| *Partex* | Gulbenkian Interests |
| *qadi* | a judge responsible for dispensing justice according to Islamic law |
| *qalta* | a pair of pearling crewmen, normally a diver and a hauler |
| *Qawasim* (adj. *Qasimi*) | a tribal federation that grew prosperous from maritime trade in the early nineteenth century and whose descendants continue to rule Sharjah and Ra's al-Khaimah |
| *Qishm* | a large island close to the Straits of Hormuz and the present-day Iranian port of Bandar 'Abbas |
| *ra'iyy/ra'aiyya* | a shepherd/his flock |
| *Rams* | a small coastal town north of Ra's al-Khaimah |
| *Rol Dibba* | a small town on the UAE's Indian Ocean coastline, currently being redeveloped into a tourist resort |
| *Royal Dutch Shell* | Dutch oil company |
| *Rub' al-Khali* | the "Empty Quarter," a desert that stretches across the Najd peninsula into Oman and the UAE |
| *Sadiyat* | an Abu Dhabian island currently being redeveloped as a real estate investment park |
| *saib* | a pearling boat crewman, normally a hauler or rope-puller for divers |
| *Saja* | Sharjah oil company |

| | |
|---|---|
| *Salalah* | an Omani deep-water container port |
| *salifa al-ghaus* | "pearling courts" used to settle disputes relating to pearling and the pearl trade |
| *shaikh* | the leader of a tribe; a title of respect |
| *shaikhdom* | a shaikh's area of influence |
| *shari'a* | Islamic law |
| *sharif* | the camel-herding tribes who achieved a higher socioeconomic status/noble status over their sheep-herding counterparts |
| *Shi'a* | the general name for a large group of Muslim sects, all of which contest the recognition of 'Ali as the legitimate caliph following the death of the Prophet Muhammad |
| *Shindagha* | a creekside district of Bur Dubai |
| *shura* | consultation |
| *souq* | a town's marketplace |
| *Straits of Hormuz* | the strategic straits between Iran and the Musandam peninsula through which all shipping must pass to enter the Gulf |
| *Sunni* | orthodox Muslims, accounting for the majority of the UAE's Arab population |
| *Sur* | an Omani port; its slaving merchants were offered French citizenship in the 1890s |
| *ta'addudiyya* | pluralism or multipartyism |
| *tamima* | a paramount shaikh; the "shaikh of shaikhs" |
| *taraz* | a tax collected to pay guards to protect the towns during the pearling season, when many of the men were out at sea |
| *Tunbs* | two small islands in the lower Gulf currently occupied by Iran, specifically the Greater Tunbs (Tunb al-Kubra) and the Lesser Tunbs (Tunb al-Sughra) |
| *turath* | cultural heritage |
| *ulama'* | Islamic clergymen |
| *Wadi* | a dry watercourse |
| *Wadi al-Mawt* | the "Valley of Death"—an area on the border between Abu Dhabi and Dubai, originally planned to be the site of the UAE's new capital city |
| *Wahda* | the "Union"—specifically the short-lived union between the republics of Egypt and Syria between 1958 and 1961 |
| *Wahhabi/*<br>  *Wahhabism* | followers of Muhammad bin Abdul-Wahhab's movement, many of whom preached a purified form of |

Islam and sought to renew the Prophet's golden era of
Islam

*Wikalat Anba'*
  *al-Imarat*       WAM—the UAE News Agency
*wali*              the ruler's local representative in an outlying region
*Ya'aribah*         the imams of East Africa, who were accused of attack-
                    ing Portuguese shipping in the Indian Ocean
*zakat*             an Islamic-mandated tax levied on livestock/
                    agricultural production and other movable property
*Zarara*            Abu Dhabian oil fields close to the Saudi border,
                    reportedly offered to Saudi Arabia in an effort to settle
                    the long-running Buraimi dispute
*Zaya*              a small coastal town close to Ra's al-Khaimah, a key
                    target for the British attacks in 1819

# Abbreviations and Acronyms

| | |
|---|---|
| ADCCI | Abu Dhabi Chamber of Commerce and Industry |
| ADCO | Abu Dhabi Company for Onshore Oil Investments |
| ADGAS | Abu Dhabi Gas |
| ADIA | Abu Dhabi Investments Authority |
| ADMA | Abu Dhabi Marine Areas |
| ADNOC | Abu Dhabi National Oil Company |
| ADPC | Abu Dhabi Petroleum Company |
| ALESCO | Arab League for Educational, Scientific, and Cultural Organization |
| ARAMCO | Arab-American Oil Company |
| BBME | British Bank of the Middle East |
| BCCE | Bank of Credit Commerce Emirates |
| BCCI | Bank of Credit Commerce International |
| BP | British Petroleum |
| CFP | Campagnie Française des Petroles |
| COM | Council of Ministers |
| CRR | cash reserve requirement |
| DIFC | Dubai International Financial Centre |
| DIPD | Dubai Investments Park Development Company |
| DSF | Dubai Shopping Festival |
| DUBAL | Dubai Aluminium |
| DUPETCO | Dubai Petroleum Company |
| ECSSR | Emirates Centre for Strategic Studies and Research |
| EIB | Emirates Industrial Bank |
| EIBFS | Emirates Institute for Banking and Financial Studies |

| | |
|---|---|
| EMI | Emirates Media Incorporated |
| EOI | export-oriented industrialization |
| EPZ | export-processing zone |
| FATF | Financial Action Task Force |
| FDI | foreign direct investment |
| FLOEA | Front for the Liberation of Occupied Eastern Arabia |
| FNC | Federal National Council (Al-Majlis al-Watani lil-Ittihad) |
| GCC | Gulf Cooperation Council |
| GDP | gross domestic product |
| GUPAC | Gulf Permanent Assistance Committee |
| HSBC | Hong Kong and Shanghai Banking Corporation |
| IDEX | International Defence Exhibition |
| ILO | International Labour Organization |
| IMF | International Monetary Fund |
| IPC | Iraqi Petroleum Company |
| ISI | import-substitution industrialization |
| JAFZ | Jebel Ali Free Zone |
| JODCO | Japan Oil Development Company |
| LOB | lease office building |
| NGO | nongovernmental organization |
| OECD | Organization for Economic Cooperation and Development |
| OPEC | Organization of Petroleum Exporting Countries |
| PDTC | Petroleum Development Trucial Coast Ltd. |
| POGAR | Programme on Governance in the Arab Region |
| SCR | Supreme Council of Rulers |
| TRIDEX | Triple International Defence Exhibition |
| TRIPS | Trade-Related Aspects of International Property Rights (a WTO agreement) |
| UAE | United Arab Emirates |
| UDF | Union Defence Force |
| UNDP | United Nations Development Programme |
| UNESCO | United Nations Educational, Scientific, and Cultural Organization |
| UNIDO | United Nations Industrial Development Organization |
| UNPAN | United Nations Online Network in Public Administration and Finance |
| WAM | Wikalat Anba' al-Imarat (the UAE News Agency) |
| WTO | World Trade Organization |
| ZADCO | Zakum Development Company |

# Bibliography

ABDEKARIM, Abbas (ed.) (1999), *Change and Development in the Gulf*, London, Macmillan.

ABDULGHANI, Abdulhamid Muhammad (1986), "Culture and Interest in Arab Foreign Aid: Kuwait and the United Arab Emirates as Case Studies," PhD thesis, University of California at Santa Barbara.

ABDULLA, Abdulkhaleq (1985), "Political Dependency: The Case of the United Arab Emirates," PhD thesis, University of Georgetown.

ABDULLAH, Muhammad Morsy (1969) (in Arabic), *Between Yesterday and Today*, Abu Dhabi.

—— (1978), *The United Arab Emirates: A Modern History*, London, Croom Helm.

AL-ABED, Ibrahim (2001), "The Historical Background and Constitutional Basis of the Federation," in AL-ABED, Ibrahim, and HELLYER, Peter (eds.), *The United Arab Emirates: A New Perspective*, London, Trident.

ABEIDOH, Rawhi (2000), "Arabs: A Shrinking Minority in the UAE," in *Dawn Magazine*, Karachi, 28 October 2000.

ABERCROMBIE, Nicholas, HILL, Stephen, and TURNER, Bryan S. (1994), *The Penguin Dictionary of Sociology*, London, Penguin.

AL-ABID, Saleh (1976) (in Arabic), *The Qawasim's Role in the Arabian Gulf, 1747–1820*, Baghdad.

ABIR, Mordechai (1974), *Oil, Power, and Politics: Conflict in Arabia, the Red Sea, and the Gulf*, London, Frank Cass.

ABU 'ATHIRA, Sa'id (1987), "Ship of the Desert Sails Back," in *Khaleej Times*, Dubai, 24 March 1987.

ABU BAKER, Albadr (1995), "Political Economy of State Formation: The United Arab Emirates in Comparative Perspective," PhD thesis, University of Michigan.

ABU DHABI ECONOMY, Abu Dhabi Chamber of Commerce and Industry, Department of Publications and Press Relations (1999), *Abu Dhabi Economy: Special Issue*, vol. 28, no. 322, March 1999.

—— (2001), "A Big Boost for Businesswomen," May 2001.

ABU DHABI PLANNING DEPARTMENT, ECONOMIC DIVISION (1976), "Directive Documents for the Preparation of the Economic and Social Development Plan of 1977–1979," Abu Dhabi, June 1976.

309

AGWANI, M. (1969), *Politics in the Gulf*, New Delhi, Vikas.

'AHMAD, Ashfaq (2002), "Volunteers Play Key Role in Society," in *Gulf News*, Dubai, 29 November 2002.

—— (2003), "Majority of Expats Suffer from Some Sort of Depression," in *Gulf News*, Dubai, 11 January 2003.

AL-AKIM, Hassan Hamdan (1989), *The Foreign Policy of the United Arab Emirates*, London, Saqi Books.

ALI, Sayed (2002), "Ramadan Tournament Gets Big Cash Boost," in *Gulf News*, Dubai, 3 December 2002.

AMIN, Abdul Amir (1965), *British Interests in the Persian Gulf*, Leiden.

AMIN, Samir (1978), *The Arab Nation: Nationalism and Class Struggles*, London.

—— (1982), *The Arab Economy Today*, New York.

—— (1997), *Capitalism in the Age of Globalisation: The Management of Contemporary Society*, London.

ANDERSON, Lisa (2000), "Dynasts and Nationalists: Why Monarchies Survive," in KOSTINER, Joseph (ed.), *Middle East Monarchies: The Challenge of Modernity*, Boulder, Lynne Rienner.

ANTHONY, John Duke (1975), *Arab States of the Lower Gulf: People, Politics, Petroleum*, Washington, D.C., Middle East Institute.

—— (1981), "Transformation Amidst Tradition: The UAE in Transition," in CHUBIN, Sharam (ed.), *Security in the Persian Gulf: Domestic Political Factors*, Montclair, N.J., Allenheld Osman.

—— (1999), "Succession in the Emirate of Abu Dhabi and the UAE: An Assessment of the Players and the Likely Possibilities," in *Gulfwire*, August 1999.

—— (2002), *The United Arab Emirates: Dynamics of State Formation*, Abu Dhabi, Emirates Centre for Strategic Studies and Research.

APS REVIEW (1998), "UAE Profile: Dr. Muhammad Khalifa bin Kharbash," in *APS Review: Gas Market Trends*, New York, June 1998.

APTER, David E. (1965), *The Politics of Modernisation*, Chicago, University of Chicago Press.

ARNDT, H. W. (1987), *Economic Development: The History of an Idea*, Chicago, University of Chicago Press.

ASHOUR, M. F. (2001), "The GCC and the WTO," in *Al-Tamimi*, January 2001.

AYALON, Ami (2000), "Post-Ottoman Arab Monarchies: Old Bottles, New Labels?" in KOSTINER, Joseph (ed.) (2000), *Middle East Monarchies: The Challenge of Modernity*, Boulder, Lynne Rienner.

AL-AYDERUS, Muhammad Hassan (1983) (in Arabic), *Political Developments in the UAE*, Kuwait, Zat al-Salasil.

—— (1989) (in Arabic), *The State of the United Arab Emirates*, Kuwait, Zat al-Salasil.

AYUBI, Nazih N. (1995), *Over-Stating the Arab State*, London, Tauris.

BADAWI, Jamal (1975) (in Arabic), *Supporting the Federal System*, Abu Dhabi, Al-Ittihad Press.

AL-BAHARNA, Hussain (1975), *The Arabian Gulf States: Their Legal and Political Status and Their International Problems*, Beirut.

—— (1985), "The Consequences of the Exclusive Treaties: A Gulf View," in PRIDHAM, B. (ed.), *The Arab Gulf and the West*, London, Croom Helm.

BANNOCK, G., BAXTER, R. E., and DAVIS, E. (1992), *The Penguin Dictionary of Economics*, London, Penguin.

BASHIR, Iskander (1982) (in Arabic), *The United Arab Emirates*, Beirut.

BATIKH, Ramadban Muhammad (1997) (in Arabic), *The Development of Political and Constitutional Thought in the UAE*, Al-'Ayn, UAE University.

BBC MONITORING (2002), "Change in Bahrain Welcomed," London, 15 February 2002.

BEBLAWI, Hazem (1987), "The Rentier State in the Arab World," in BEBLAWI, Hazem, and LUCIANI, Giacomo (eds.), *The Rentier State*, New York, Croom Helm.

BECK, Nelson R. (1978), "Britain's Withdrawal from the Persian Gulf and the Formation of the United Arab Emirates, 1968–1971," in *Towson State Journal of International Affairs*, vol. 12, no. 2.

BELGRAVE, Charles (1966), *The Pirate Coast*, London, G. Bell and Sons.

BHARGAVA, Pradeep (1989), *Political Economy of the Gulf States*, New Delhi, South Asian Publishers.

BHUTANI, Surendra (1980), *Contemporary Gulf*, New Delhi, Academic Press.

BIBBO, Barbara (2002), "New Contract Rule to Benefit Nationals," in *Gulf News*, Dubai, 14 December 2002.

BILAL, Muhammad (1990) (in Arabic), *Changes in Population and Power Among Immigrants and Citizens of the UAE, 1976–1980*, Sharjah Sociologist Society.

BLANCHE, E. (1997), "Offset Industry to Gain from UAE Programs," in *Jane's Defence Weekly*, 29 January 1997.

BOOT, Aernout (1995), "Tribes and Families of Abu Dhabi," unpublished study commissioned by the European Union.

BOWEN, Richard LeBaron (1951), "The Pearl Fisheries of the Persian Gulf," in *Middle East Journal*, vol. 5, Spring 1951.

BROWN, Gavin (1998), *OPEC and the World Energy Market*, London, Longman.

BULLOCH, John (1984), *The Gulf*, London, Century.

BUSCH, Briton (1967), *Britain and the Persian Gulf, 1894–1914*, Los Angeles, University of California Press.

BUSINESS IN DUBAI, Dubai Chamber of Commerce and Industry (2001a), vol. 1, no. 3, March 2001.

——— (2001b), vol. 1, no. 5, May 2001.

——— (2001c), "Foreign Investments: Total Blockade vis-à-vis Open Door Policy," vol. 1, no. 6, June 2001.

——— (2002a), "DIFC Puts Emirate on International Financial Map," vol. 2, no. 15, March 2002.

——— (2002b), "Family Companies the Day After: How Would Local Family Owned Businesses Survive in Globalisation?" vol. 2, no. 15, March 2002.

BUSINESS MONITOR INTERNATIONAL (1997), "The United Arab Emirates, 1995–1997."

——— (1998), "The United Arab Emirates."

——— (2000), "The United Arab Emirates," 3rd-quarter report.

——— (2001), "The United Arab Emirates," 2nd-quarter report.

——— (2003a), "The United Arab Emirates," 1st-quarter report.

——— (2003b), "The United Arab Emirates," 2nd-quarter report.

CALLAN, L., and G. ROBISON (2000), "Dubai," Auckland, Lonely Planet Publications.

CAMBRIDGE INTERNATIONAL DICTIONARY OF ENGLISH (2002). Cambridge, Cambridge University Press.

CARAPICO, Sheila (1998), *Civil Society in Yemen: The Political Economy of Activism in Modern Arabia*, Cambridge, Cambridge University Press.

CARDASO, F. H., and FALETTO, E. (1979), *Dependency and Development in*

*Latin America*, Berkeley, University of California Press.

CHATELUS, Michel (1987), "Policies for Development Attitudes Toward Industries and Services," in BEBLAWI, Hazem, and LUCIANI, Giacomo (eds.) (1987), *The Rentier State*, New York, Croom Helm.

CHAUDHRY, Kiren Aziz (1997), *The Price of Wealth: Economies and Institutions in the Middle East*, New York, Cornell University Press.

CHUBIN, Sharam (ed.) (1981), *Security in the Persian Gulf: Domestic Political Factors*, Montclair, N.J., Allenheld Osman.

CITIBANK UAE (2002), "Annual Report," Dubai.

CLEMENTS, Frank A. (1998), *United Arab Emirates*, World Bibliographical Series, vol. 43, Oxford, ABC-CLIO.

CODRAI, Ronald (1990), *The Seven Shaykhdoms: Life in the Trucial States Before the Federation of the United Arab Emirates*, London, Stacey International.

COLLARD, Elizabeth (1973), "Economic Prospects for the United Arab Emirates," in *Middle East International*, no. 21, March 1973.

CORDESMAN, A. H. (1997), *Bahrain, Oman, Qatar and the UAE: Challenges of Security*, Boulder, Westview.

COTRELL, Alvin (ed.) (1980), *The Persian Gulf States*, Baltimore, John Hopkins University Press.

CROWN PRINCE COURT, DEPARTMENT OF RESEARCH AND STUDIES (1996), "Development Indicators in the UAE: Achievements and Projections," Abu Dhabi.

CRYSTAL, Jill (1990, 1995), *Oil and Politics in the Gulf: Rulers and Merchants in Kuwait and Qatar*, New York, Cambridge University Press.

DAVIDSON, Christopher M. (2003), "The United Arab Emirates: A Study in Survival," PhD thesis, University of St. Andrews.

DAVIES, Charles E. (1997), *The Blood Red Arab Flag: An Investigation into Qasimi Piracy, 1797–1820*, Exeter, University of Exeter Press.

DAVIS, E. (1991), "Theorising Statecraft and Social Change in Arab Oil-Producing Countries," in DAVIS, E., and GAVRIELIDES, N. (eds.), *Statecraft in the Middle East: Oil, Historical Memory, and Popular Culture*, Miami, Florida International Press.

DE TOQUEVILLE, A. (1981), *Democracy in America*, New York, McGraw-Hill.

DEUTSCH, Karl W. (1961), "Social Mobilisation and Political Development," in *American Political Science Review*, vol. 55, no. 3, September 1961.

DICKEN, P. (1992), *Global Shift and the Internationalisation of Economic Activity*, London, Guildford.

EL-DIN, Amin Badr (1997), "The Offsets Program in the UAE," in *Middle East Policy*, vol. 5, no. 1, January 1997.

DUBAI CHAMBER OF COMMERCE AND INDUSTRY (2001), "Our Services," Dubai.

DUBAI DEPARTMENT OF ECONOMIC DEVELOPMENT (1999), *Development Statistics*, Government of Dubai.

——— (2001), *Development Statistics*, Government of Dubai

——— (2002), *Development Statistics*, Government of Dubai.

DUBAI DEPARTMENT OF PORTS AND CUSTOMS (2001a), "Dubai: Major (Non-Oil) Trade Partners—Exports," in DUBAI DEPARTMENT OF ECONOMIC DEVELOPMENT, *Development Statistics*, Government of Dubai.

——— (2001b), "Dubai: Major (Non-Oil) Trade Partners—Imports," in DUBAI DEPARTMENT OF ECONOMIC DEVELOPMENT, *Development Statistics*, Government of Dubai.

—— (2001c), "Dubai: Major (Non-Oil) Trade Partners—Re-exports," in DUBAI DEPARTMENT OF ECONOMIC DEVELOPMENT, *Development Statistics*, Government of Dubai.

—— (2001d), "Dubai: Non-Oil Foreign Trade—Total," in DUBAI DEPART-MENT OF ECONOMIC DEVELOPMENT, *Development Statistics*, Government of Dubai.

—— (2002), "Dubai: Non-Oil Foreign Trade—Total," in DUBAI DEPARTMENT OF ECONOMIC DEVELOPMENT, *Development Statistics*, Government of Dubai.

DUBAI GOVERNMENT (2000), "Dubai Technology, Electronic Commerce, and Media Free Zone Law No. 1."

DUBAI MUNICIPALITY (1999), "Results of Income and Expenditure Survey: Dubai City, 1997–1998," Administrative Affairs Department, Statistics Centre, May 1999.

EASTON, David (1965), *A Systems Analysis of Political Life*, New York, Wiley.

The ECONOMIST (1981), London, 25 April 1981.

ECONOMIST INTELLIGENCE UNIT (2000), "United Arab Emirates," London.

—— (2001), "United Arab Emirates," London.

ECSSR (Emirates Centre for Strategic Studies and Research) (2002), "UAE and the Red Crescent," Abu Dhabi.

EMIRATES BANKERS ASSOCIATION (1997), "Financial Position of Commercial Banks of the UAE, 1996–1997," Dubai.

EMIRATES CORPORATE COMMUNICATIONS (2002), "Countdown to Dubai 2003," press release issued by Emirates Airways Department of Media Relations, 23 October 2002.

EMIRATES INDUSTRIAL BANK (1983), "Annual Report," Abu Dhabi.

EMIRATES MEDICAL ASSOCIATION (2002), "Annual Report," Abu Dhabi.

EMIRATES TELEVISION (2003), "Emirates Stable and Secure, Says Muhammad," Abu Dhabi, 17 March 2003.

ENCYCLOPEDIA OF ISLAM, new edition (1960), H. A. R. Gibb (ed.), Leiden, Brill.

EVERETT-HEATH, Tom (2002), "Dubai's Financial Future," in *Middle East Economic Digest*, London, vol. 26, no. 8, 22 February 2002.

EVERETT-HEATH, Tom, and DUTTA, A. (2002), "Bridging the gap," in *Middle East Economic Digest*, London, vol. 46, no. 10, 8 March 2002.

AL-FAHIM, Muhammad (1995), *From Rags to Riches: A Story of Abu Dhabi*, London Centre of Arab Studies.

FALK, Richard A. (1999), *Predatory Globalisation: A Critique*, Cambridge, Polity Press.

FARAZMAND, A. (ed.) (1991), *Handbook of Comparative and Development Public Administration*, New York, Marcel.

FEDERAL RESEARCH DIVISION (2003), "United Arab Emirates: A Country Study," Blackmask.

FEDERATION OF UAE CHAMBERS OF COMMERCE AND INDUSTRY (1993), "The Establishment of Economic Enterprises in the UAE: In Light of the Provisions of the Law and Its Executive Regulations," Abu Dhabi.

—— (1994a), "The Components of Investment and the Methods of Promoting Investment Opportunities in the UAE," Abu Dhabi.

—— (1994b), "Goals and Achievements," Abu Dhabi.

FENELON, Kevin (1969), *The Trucial States: A Brief Economic Survey*, Beirut, Khayats.

—— (1973), *The United Arab Emirates: An Economic and Social Survey*, London, Longman.

FIELD, Michael (1984), *The Merchants: The Big Business Families of Arabia*, London, John Murray.

—— (1987), "Arabia Keeps the Faith," in *Financial Times*, London, 10 January.

FINDLOW, Sally (2000), "The UAE: Nationalism and Arab-Islamic Identity," Abu Dhabi, Emirates Centre for Strategic Studies and Research (ECSSR), ECSSR Occasional Paper no. 39.

FINKLE, J. L., and GABLE, R. W. (1971), *Political Development and Social Change*, New York, John Wiley.

FLEIHAN, Tarek (2002), "Informal Association to Raise Marriage Funds for Nationals," in *Khaleej Times*, Dubai, 19 October 2002.

FOLEY, Sean (1998), "The United Arab Emirates: Political Issues and Security Dilemmas," in *Middle East Review of International Affairs (MERIA)*, vol. 3, no. 1, March 1998.

FOREIGN OFFICE HISTORICAL SECTION (1920), "Persian Gulf," London, HMSO, no. 76.

FRANK, André Gunder (1971), *Capitalism and Underdevelopment in Latin America: Historical Studies of Chile and Brazil*, New York, Monthly Review Press.

FREEDOM HOUSE (2001), "Freedom in the World Country Ratings, 1972–1973 to 2000–2001," New York, Freedom House.

GALLAGHER, John, and ROBINSON, Ronald (1953), "The Imperialism of Free Trade," in *Economic History Review*, vol. 6, no. 1.

GAUSE, F. Gregory (1992), "Gulf Regional Politics: Revolution, War, and Rivalry," in WRIGGINS, Howard (ed.), *The Dynamics of Regional Politics: Four Systems on the Indian Ocean Rim*, New York, Columbia University Press.

—— (1994), "Oil Monarchies: Domestic and Security Challenges in the Arab Gulf States," New York, Council on Foreign Relations Press.

—— (2000), "The Persistence of Monarchy in the Arabian Peninsula: A Comparative Analysis," in KOSTINER, Joseph (ed.), *Middle East Monarchies: The Challenge of Modernity*, Boulder, Lynne Rienner.

GCC DEVELOPMENT PLANS: UNITED ARAB EMIRATES (1982), "Economic and Social Development Plans for the UAE, 1975–1980," Abu Dhabi.

GELLNER, E. (1981), *Muslim Society*, Cambridge, Cambridge University Press.

GHANEM, Shihab (1992), *Industrialisation in the United Arab Emirates*, London, Avebury.

GHUBASH, Moza (1996) (in Arabic), *Human Development in the UAE, 1971–1994*, Abu Dhabi Cultural Foundation.

GRAHAM, G. S. (1967), *Great Britain in the Indian Ocean, 1810–1850*, Oxford, Stevenson.

GREEN, Timothy (1968), *The World of Gold*, London, Michael Joseph.

GULF NEWS (1997), "Emaar to Set Up Dh700 Million Complex," Dubai, 25 November 1997.

—— (1998a), "Emaar Flies High with Mega Project," Dubai, 19 August 1998.

—— (1998b), "Emaar Ups Project Outlay," Dubai, 26 February 1998.

—— (2002), "Dubai Tops Nation in Urban Population," Dubai, 4 December 2002.

—— (2003), "Hamdan bin Zayed Is Deputy Premier," Dubai, 9 October 2003.

HALL, Marjorie J. (1987), *Business Laws of the UAE*, vol. 1, London, Jacobs.

HALLIDAY, Fred (2000), "Monarchies in the Middle East: A Concluding Appraisal," in KOSTINER, Joseph (ed.), *Middle East Monarchies: The*

*Challenge of Modernity*, Boulder, Lynne Rienner.

HALPERN, Manfred (1963, 1965), *The Politics of Social Change in the Middle East and North Africa*, Princeton, Princeton University Press.

AL-HAMID, Muhammad 'Ahmad (1997) (in Arabic), "Gulf Security and Its Impacts on the GCC," Abu Dhabi, Emirates Centre for Strategic Studies and Research, Emirates Lectures Series no. 16.

HANAFI, Sari (2001), "Globalisation Without Regionalisation: The Paradoxical Effects of the Political Economy of the United Arab Emirates," excerpt and statistics from a presentation given at the "Globalisation and the Gulf" conference at the University of Exeter, July 2001.

HARRIS, Nigel (1987), *The End of the Third World: Newly Industrializing Countries and the Decline of an Ideology*, New York, Meredith.

HAWLEY, Donald (1970), *The Trucial States*, London, George Allen and Unwin.

HAY, Rupert (1955), "The Impact of the Oil Industry on the Persian Gulf Shaykhdoms," in *Middle East Journal*, vol. 9, no. 4, Autumn 1955.

HEARD-BEY, Frauke (1972), "The Gulf States and Oman in Transition," in *Asian Affairs*, February 1972.

—— (1982, 1996), *From Trucial States to United Arab Emirates*, London, Longman.

—— (1999), "The UAE: A Quarter Century of Federation," in HUDSON, Michael C. (ed.), *Middle East Dilemma: The Politics and Economics of Arab Integration*, London, Tauris.

AL-HEGELAN, Abdelrahman, and PALMER, Monte (1985), "Bureaucracy and Development in Saudi Arabia," in *Middle East Journal*, vol. 39, no. 1, Winter 1985.

HELD, David, MCGREW, Anthony, GOLDBLATT, David, and PERRATON, Jonathan (1999), *Global Transformations: Politics, Economics, and Culture*, Oxford, Polity Press.

HELLYER, Peter (2001), "The Evolution of UAE Foreign Policy," in AL-ABED, Ibrahim, and HELLYER, Peter (eds.), *The United Arab Emirates: A New Perspective*, London, Trident.

HENDERSON, Edward (1988), *The Strange Eventful History: Memoirs of Earlier Days in the UAE and Oman*, London, Quartet.

HERB, Michael (1999), *All in the Family: Absolutism, Revolution, and Democracy in the Middle Eastern Monarchies*, New York, State University of New York Press.

HILOTIN, J. B. (2003), "Should Telecom Monopolies End, or Is One Provider Better?" in *Gulf News*, Dubai, 11 October 2003.

HINNEBUSCH, Raymond A. (1989), *Peasant and Bureaucracy in Ba'thist Syria: The Political Economy of Rural Development*, Boulder, Westview.

HIRO, Dilip (1987), *Iran Under the Ayatollahs*, London, Routledge.

HIRST, David (2001), "The Emirs in the Internet Era," in *Le Monde Diplomatique*, Paris, February 2001.

HIRST, P. (1995), "Globalisation in Question," Political Economy Research Centre, University of Sheffield, Occasional Paper no. 11.

HITTI, P. K. (1964), *History of the Arabs*, 8th ed., London, Macmillan.

HOAGLAND, Jim (1991), "Across the Cultural Chasm: BCCI Viewed from East and West," in *Washington Post*, 5 August 1991.

HOBBY, Gerard (2001), *The Development of the Dubai Internet City*, Dubai.

HOLDEN, David (1966), *Farewell to Arabia*, New York, Faber and Faber.

—— (1971), "The Persian Gulf After the British Raj," in *Foreign Affairs*, vol. 49, no. 4, July.

HSBC MIDDLE EAST (2001), "Foreign Investment Statistics for GCC States," Dubai, 2nd Quarter 2001.

HUDSON, Michael C. (1977), *Arab Politics: The Search for Legitimacy*, New Haven, Yale University Press.

—— (1999), *Middle East Dilemma: The Politics and Economics of Arab Integration*, London, Tauris.

HUNTINGTON, Samuel P. (1968), *Political Order in Changing Societies*, New Haven, Yale University Press.

—— (1991), *The Third Wave: Democratisation in the Late Twentieth Century*, Norman, University of Oklahoma Press.

HYAM, Ronald (1976), *Britain's Imperial Century, 1815–1914: A Study of Empire and Expansion*, London, Macmillan.

IBRAHIM, Abd Al-Aziz (1978) (in Arabic), *Britain and the Emirates of the Omani Coast*, Baghdad, Matba'at al-Irshad.

IBRAHIM, M. E. (2002), "Dalma Island to Emerge as Regional Tourist Spot," Dubai, in *Khaleej Times*, Dubai, 2 September 2002.

IBRAHIM, Muhammad (1975) (in Arabic), *Foundations of the Political and Constitutional Organisation of the UAE*, Abu Dhabi.

IRVING, Janis (1972), *Victims of Groupthink*, Boston, Houghton Mifflin.

—— (1982), *Groupthink: Psychological Studies of Policy Decisions and Fiascos*, Boston, Houghton Mifflin.

ISA, Shakir Musa (1981) (in Arabic), *The Experience of the UAE*, Beirut.

ISMAEL, Jacqueline S. (1982), *Kuwait: Social Change in Historical Perspective*, Syracuse, Syracuse University Press.

—— (1993), *Kuwait: Dependency and Class in a Rentier State*, Gainesville, University Press of Florida.

AL-JABIL, Muhammad (2002), "GCC: The Emerging Common Market," in *Africa Business Guide*, Cairo, December 2002.

JAML, Abu (1985), "Of Pearls and Pearl Kings," in *Gulf News*, Dubai, 5 April 1985.

AL-JANDALY, Bassma (2003), "Rail Project May Take Six Years," in *Gulf News*, Dubai, 14 January 2003.

JANE'S DEFENCE WEEKLY (1997), "Gulf States Told to Get Tough over Offsets," 10 December 1997.

JEBEL ALI FREEZONE AUTHORITY (2000), investment statistics, Jebel Ali, Dubai.

JIYAD, 'Ahmad (2001), "The Role of Foreign Direct Investment in the Globalisation of the Gulf," excerpt from a presentation given at the "Globalisation and the Gulf" conference at the University of Exeter, July 2001.

JOHNS, Richard (1973), "The Emergence of the United Arab Emirates," in *Middle East International*, vol. 21, March 1973.

JOHNSON, M. E. (1997), "The Lessons from Emaar Properties Issue," in *Gulf News*, Dubai, 17 May 1997.

JOHNSTON, Philip (2001), "Fingers Point at Iraqi Leader as Evidence Grows," in *Daily Telegraph*, London, 1 December 2001.

JOYCE, Miriam (1998), *Kuwait 1945–1996: An Anglo-American Perspective*, London, Frank Cass.

—— (1999), "On the Road Towards Unity: The Trucial States from a British Perspective, 1960–1966," in *Middle Eastern Studies*, vol. 35, no. 2, April 1999.

JREISAT, J. E. (1992), "Managing National Development in the Arab States," in

*Arab Studies Quarterly*, vol. 14, nos. 2–3, Spring–Summer 1992.

AL-JUM'A SUPPLEMENT (1981), "The Reason for the Iran Connection," in *Gulf News*, Dubai, 21 August 1981.

KAMRAVA, Mehran (2000), *Politics and Society in the Developing World*, London, Routledge.

—— (2002), "Civil Society and Political Democratisation in Comparative Perspective: Lessons from Latin America and the Middle East," presentation at the University of Warwick, February 2002.

KAWACH, Nadim (2001), "IMF Urges GCC to Levy Income Tax," in *Gulf News*, Dubai, 16 October 2001.

—— (2002a), "UAE Deficit Dh7.8b Lower than Projected," in *Gulf News*, Dubai, 4 December 2002.

—— (2002b), "UAE Refutes Report on Oil Sharing," in *Gulf News*, Dubai, 13 October 2002.

—— (2003), "Call for Arab TV in English," in *Gulf News*, Dubai, 20 January 2003.

AL-KAWARI, Ali Khalifa, and AL-SADUN, Jasim (1996) (in Arabic), "The GCC Countries: A Futuristic View," Development Forum Annual Meeting Documents, January 1995, Kuwait, Girttas Publishing House.

KAZIM, Aqil (2000), *The United Arab Emirates AD 600 to the Present: A Socio-Discursive Transformation in the Arabian Gulf*, Dubai, Gulf Book Centre.

KEDOURIE, Elie (1984), "The Kingdom of Iraq: A Retrospect," in KEDOURIE, Elie (ed.) (1984), *The Chatham House Version and Other Middle Eastern Studies*, New Haven, University Press of New England.

KEEGAN, John (2002), "Bush Faces Long Wait to Build Up Enough Forces Against Baghdad," in *Daily Telegraph*, London, 5 September 2002.

KELLY, John B. (1964), *Eastern Arabia Frontier*, New York, Praeger.

—— (1968), *Britain and the Persian Gulf*, Oxford, Oxford University Press.

—— (1986), "Arabia, the Gulf, and the West: A Critical View of the Arabs and Their Oil Policy," New York, Basic Books.

KEMP, Peter (1997), "MEED Special Report: France," in *Middle East Economic Digest*, 24 October 1997.

KERRY, John, and BROWN, Hank (1992), "The BCCI Affair: A Report to the Committee on Foreign Relations in the United States Senate by Senator John Kerry and Senator Hank Brown," Washington, D.C., 102nd Congress, 2nd Session, Senate Print, December 1992.

KHADDURI, Majid (1981), *Arab Personalities in Politics*, Washington, D.C., Middle East Institute.

KHALAF, Sulayman (1992), "Gulf Societies and the Image of Unlimited Good," in *Dialectical Anthropology*, vol. 17, no. 1, 1992.

—— (1999), "Camel Racing in the Gulf: Notes on the Evolution of a Traditional Cultural Sport," in *Anthropos*, 1999.

—— (2000), "Poetics and Politics of Newly Invented Traditions in the Gulf: Camel Racing in the United Arab Emirates," in *Ethnology*, vol. 39, no. 3, Summer 2000.

—— (2001), "Globalisation and Heritage Revival in the Gulf: An Anthropological Look at the Dubai Heritage Village," excerpt from a presentation given at the "Globalisation and the Gulf" conference at the University of Exeter, July 2001.

KHALDUN, 'Abd-ar-Rahman Abu Zayed ibn Muhammad (1377), *The Muqaddimah: An Introduction to History*, translated by ROSENTHAL, Franz [republished in 1967 by Routledge and Kegan Paul, London].

AL-KHALEEJ ARAB STUDIES (1991) (in Arabic), "Gulf and Arab Security," November 1991.

KHALEEJ TIMES (1987), "Folk Art Forum to Be Given Federal Status," 10 October 1987.

—— (1998a), "Dubai Investments Park Excites Investors," 25 October 1998.

—— (1998b), "Dubai Investments to Lift Returns, Assets," 13 May 1998.

—— (2001), "Country's Judiciary Is Independent: Dhahiri," 6 December 2001.

—— (2002a), "'Ajman Fantazia to Begin Tomorrow," 15 January 2002.

—— (2002b), "Anti-Smoking Rally in Sharjah," 10 October 2002.

—— (2002c), "National Panel Set Up for Palestinian Relief," 6 April 2002.

—— (2002d), "UAE Gets a Clean Chit," 6 February 2002.

—— (2002e), "UAE Seeks ILO Help on Labour Reforms," 16 January 2002.

—— (2004), "Khalifa Donates 500,000 Dirhams to Journalists' Association," 22 March 2004.

KHALIFA, Ali Muhammad (1979), *The United Arab Emirates: Unity in Fragmentation*, Boulder, Westview.

KHOURY, Enver M. (1980), *The United Arab Emirates: Its Political System and Politics*, Maryland, Institute of Middle Eastern and North African Affairs.

KOSTINER, Joseph (ed.) (2000), *Middle East Monarchies: The Challenge of Modernity*, Boulder, Lynne Rienner.

KUBURSI, Atif (1984), *Oil, Industrialisation, and Development in the Arab Gulf States*, London, Croom Helm.

AL-KUWARI, Ali Khalifa (1978), *Oil Revenues in the Gulf Emirates: Patterns of Allocation and Impact on Economic Development*, Essex, Bowker.

LANGLEY, Joanna (2000), "Mashreq Bank Joins Hand with NHR to Promote Emiratisation," in *Gulf News*, Dubai, 3 September 2000.

LEFTWICH (1993), "Governance, Democracy, and Development in the Third World," in *Third World Quarterly*, vol. 14, no. 3, 1993.

LERNER, Daniel (1958, 1964), *The Passing of Traditional Society: Modernising the Middle East*, Toronto, Free Press.

LIENHARDT, Peter (1975), "The Authority of Shaykhs in the Gulf: An Essay in Nineteenth Century History," in *Arabian Studies*, vol. 2, 1975.

LOCKWOOD, Christopher (1996), "Warring Nation Holds Key to Oil Riches of Central Asia," in *Daily Telegraph*, London, 11 October 1996.

LONG, David (1978), *The Persian Gulf*, Boulder, Westview.

LORIMER, J. G. (1915a), *Gazetteer of the Persian Gulf, Oman, and Central Arabia*, vol. 1, Historical Part 1A, Calcutta, Superintendent Government Printing [republished in 1970 by Gregg International Publishers].

—— (1915b), *Gazetteer of the Persian Gulf, Oman, and Central Arabia*, vol. 1, Historical Part 1B, Calcutta, Superintendent Government Printing [republished in 1970 by Gregg International Publishers].

—— (1915c), *Gazetteer of the Persian Gulf, Oman, and Central Arabia*, vol. 1, Historical Part 2, Calcutta, Superintendent Government Printing [republished in 1970 by Gregg International Publishers].

—— (1915d), *Gazetteer of the Persian Gulf, Oman, and Central Arabia*, vol. 2B, Geographical and Statistical, Calcutta, Superintendent Government Printing [republished in 1970 by Gregg International Publishers].

LUCIANI, Giacomo (1987), "Allocation Versus Production States: A Theoretical Framework," in BEBLAWI, Hazem, and LUCIANI, Giacomo (eds.), *The Rentier State*, New York, Croom Helm.

MADAD, Sana (2001), "Welfare Societies Will Need a Federal Licence," in

*Khaleej Times*, Dubai, 27 September 2001.

—— (2002), "Ministry Details Proposal for Workers' Associations," in *Khaleej Times*, Dubai, 15 January 2002.

—— (2003), "Dubai Charity Telethon to Support Iraqi People," in *Khaleej Times*, Dubai, 23 March 2003.

MADAD, Sana, and FLEIHAN, Tarek (2002), "Issue of Teacher Beating Student May Go to Court," in *Khaleej Times*, Dubai, 29 May 2002.

AL-MAJD, Kamal Abu (1978) (in Arabic), *The Constitutional System of the United Arab Emirates*, Cairo.

EL-MALLAKH, Ragi (1981), *Economic Development in the United Arab Emirates*, New York, St. Martin's.

MALLETT, Robert L. (1999), "Symposium on Shaykh Zayed," in *Middle East Policy*, vol. 6, no. 4, June.

MANN, Clarence (1969), *Abu Dhabi: Birth of an Oil Shaykhdom*, Beirut, Khayats.

MANNAN, M. A. (2001), "Dubai Stands High in List of Best Skylines," in *Khaleej Times*, Dubai, 12 May 2001.

McGRORY, Daniel (2002), "UAE Seizes Al-Qaeda's Gulf Leader," in *The Times*, London, 24 December 2002.

MELAMID, Alexander (1956), "The Buraimi Oasis Dispute," in *Middle Eastern Affairs*, vol. 7, no. 2, 1956.

MERZA, Ali (2001), "Economic Reforms in the Major Oil-Producing Countries," excerpt from a paper presented at the "Globalisation and the Gulf" conference at the University of Exeter, July 2001.

MIDDLE EAST ECONOMIC DIGEST (1968), London, 2 May 1968.

—— (1977), London, vol. 22, 7 July 1977.

—— (1978), London, 10 February 1978.

—— (1982), "MEED Special Report: UAE," London, November 1982.

—— (1984), "Foreign Firms Reject Investment Proposal," in "MEED Special Report: UAE," London.

—— (1994), "UAE Special Report," London, 1 December 1994.

—— (1997), London, December 1997.

MIDDLE EAST RESEARCH INSTITUTE OF JAPAN (2002), statistics relating to UAE cabinet compositions.

MOBLEY, Richard A. (2003), "The Tunbs and Abu Musa Islands: Britain's Perspective," in *Middle East Journal*, vol. 57, no. 4, Autumn 2003.

MOORE, Clement H. (1970), *Politics in North Africa*, Boston, Little, Brown.

MOYSE-BARTLETT, Hubert (1966), "*The Pirates of Trucial Oman*, London, Macdonald.

MUGSON, Steven (1991a), "British Judge Delays Plan to Dismantle BCCI," in *Washington Post*, 31 July 1991.

—— (1991b), "A Slam Heard 'Round the World: Closing of BCCI's Doors Leaves Unresolved Dilemmas," in *Washington Post*, 23 July 1991.

AL-MUSFIR, Muhammad Salih (1985), "The United Arab Emirates: An Assessment of Federalism in a Developing Polity," PhD thesis, State University of New York at Binghamton.

AL-MUSHARRAKH, Zaikya (2000), "University Students Take Al-Futtaim Trading Courses," in *Khaleej Times*, Dubai, 26 July 2000.

MUSSALLAM, N. S. (2002), "RCS Projects to Help Disabled," in *Khaleej Times*, Dubai, 1 December 2002.

MUTAWA', Muhammad A. (1991) (in Arabic), *Development and Social Change in the Emirates*, Beirut, Al-Farabi.

AL-NABEH, Najat Abdullah (1984), "The United Arab Emirates: Regional and Global Dimensions," PhD thesis, Claremont Graduate School.

AL-NAQIB, Khaldun H. (1991) (in Arabic), *The Authoritarian State in the Contemporary Arab Mashriq: A Comparative Structural Study*, Beirut.

NIBLOCK, Tim (ed.) (1980), *Social and Economic Development in the Arab Gulf*, London, Croom Helm.

NONNEMAN, Gerd (2001), "Rentiers and Autocrats, Monarchs and Democrats, State and Society: The Middle East Between Globalisation, Human 'Agency,' and Europe," in *International Affairs*, vol. 77, no. 1, January 2001.

NORTON, A. R. (1999), "Associational Life: Civil Society in Authoritarian Political Systems," in TESSLER, Mark (ed.) (1999), *Area Studies and Social Science: Strategies for Understanding Middle East Politics*, Bloomington, Indiana University Press.

AL-NUHAYYAN, Shaikha Shamma bint Muhammad bin Khalid (2000a), "Political and Social Security in the Arabian Gulf Region and United Arab Emirates After the Second Gulf War: External and Internal Challenges," Research Centre of Slovak Foreign Policy Association, Studies on International Issues, vol. B05.

—— (2000b), *Political and Social Security in the UAE*, Dubai.

NYROP, Richard (1977), *Area Handbook for the Persian Gulf States*, Washington, D.C., Foreign Areas Studies.

ONLEY, James (2003a), "Britain's Native Agents in Arabia and Persia, 1758–1958," in *Comparative Studies of South Asia, Africa, and the Middle East*, vol. 33, 2003.

—— (2003b), "The Politics of Protection in the Gulf: The Arab Rulers and the British Resident in the Nineteenth Century," in *New Arabian Studies*, vol. 6, 2003.

AL-OTAIBI, Manna Sa'id (1977) (in Arabic), *Petroleum and the Economy of the United Arab Emirates*, Kuwait, Al-Qabas Press.

—— (1982), *The Petroleum Concession Agreements of the United Arab Emirates*, vols. 1–2, London, Croom Helm.

OVERTON, J. L. (1983), "Stability and Change: Inter-Arab Politics in the Arabian Peninsula and Gulf," PhD thesis, University of Maryland.

OXFORD BUSINESS GROUP (2000), *Emerging Emirates 2000: The Annual Business, Economic, and Political Review*, London.

PAL, Dharm (1945), "British Policy Towards the Arabian Tribes on the Shores of the Persian Gulf, 1864–1868," in *Journal of Indian History*, vol. 24, 1945.

PECK, Malcolm C. (1986), *The United Arab Emirates: A Venture in Unity*, Boulder, Westview.

PETERSON, J. E. (1988a) "The Arab Gulf States: Steps Towards Political Participation," in *Washington Papers*, no. 131, New York, Praeger.

—— (1988b), "The Future of Federalism in the United Arab Emirates," in SINDE-LAR, Richard, and PETERSON, J. E. (eds.), *Crosscurrents in the Gulf*, London, Routledge.

PLATTS GLOBAL ENERGY (2002), http://www.platts.com/opec.

POGGI, G. (1978), *The Development of the Modern State*, London, Hutchinson.

POLSCI.COM (2001), *Political Reference Almanac: UAE Political System*, New York, Keynote Publishing.

POPE, M. T. G. (1996), *Businessman's Guide to the United Arab Emirates*, Sharjah, Dar al-Fatah.

PRADO, Alfred B. (1996), "Saudi Arabia: Post-War Issues and U.S. Relations," in

*CRS Issue Brief*, no. 93113, December 1996.

PRATT, N. (2001), "Conceptualising Globalisation: Some Political Implications for the Arab World," excerpt from a presentation given at the "Globalisation and the Gulf" conference at the University of Exeter, July 2001.

PRESS AFFAIRS DIRECTORATE OF SHARJAH EMIRI COURT (1988), "Sharjah in Fifteen Years Time: 1974–1988," Sharjah, Al-Bayan.

PRIDHAM, B. (ed.) (1985), *The Arab Gulf and the West*, London, Croom Helm.

AL-QADIR, Mustafa (1978) (in Arabic), *Contemporary Studies on the History of the Arabian Gulf*, Cairo.

QASIM, Jamal Zakariyya (1978) (in Arabic), *Old Emirates and New State*, Cairo.

AL-QASIMI, Shaikh Fahim bin Sultan (1999), "Symposium on Shaykh Zayed," in *Middle East Policy*, vol. 6, no. 4, June 1999.

AL-QASIMI, Shaikh Sultan bin Muhammad (1986), *The Myth of Arab Piracy in the Gulf*, London, Croom Helm.

RAFAT, Hassan, and RIZVI, Meraj (2002), "Schools Asked to Seek Licence for New Books," in *Khaleej Times*, Dubai, 15 January 2002.

AL-RAHMAN, Abdullah Abd (1990) (in Arabic), *The Emirates in the Memory of Its Children*, Dubai, Dubai Printing Press.

RAMAHI, Saif, and EL-WADY, A. (1973), *Economic and Political Evolution in the Arabian Gulf States*, New York, Carlton.

RANDA, Habib (2000), "Succession First for Arab 'Republican Monarchies' but Maybe Not Last," in *Jordan Times*, 13 June 2000.

RANDALL, V., and THEOBALD, R. (1998), *Political Change and Underdevelopment*, London, Macmillan.

RAO, Sunil (2002), "UAE Makes Progress in Achieving Food Security," in *Gulf News*, Dubai, 20 January 2002.

RASHID, Ali Muhammad (1989) (in Arabic), *Political and Economic Agreements Made Between the Oman Coast Emirates and Britain (1806–1971)*, UAE Writers Union Publications.

REUTERS (2003), "Tanks Back Succession Move in UAE's Ra's al-Khaimah," Abu Dhabi, 15 June 2003.

REYNOLDS, David (1991), *Britannia Overruled: British Policy and World Power in the 20th Century*, London, Longman.

RICHARDS, Alan (2001), "Symposium on Shaykh Zayed," in *Middle East Policy*, vol. 6, no. 4, June 1999.

RICHARDS, Alan, and WATERBURY, John (1996), *A Political Economy of the Middle East*, Boulder, Westview.

RIGGS, Fred (1991), "Bureaucratic Links Between Administration and Politics," in FARAZMAND, A. (ed.), *Handbook of Comparative and Development Public Administration*, New York, Marcel.

RIZVI, Meraj (2000), "Only Nationals to Be Captains of Fishing Vessels," in *Khaleej Times*, Dubai, 26 July 2000.

RIZVI, S. N. Asad (1993), "From Tents to High Rise: Economic Development of the UAE," in *Middle Eastern Studies*, vol. 29, no. 4, October 1993.

ROBERTS, David (1985), "The Consequences of the Exclusive Treaties: A British View," in PRIDHAM, B. (ed.), *The Arab Gulf and the West*, London, Croom Helm.

ROBERTSON, R. (1992), *Globalisation: Social Theory and Global Culture*, London, Sage.

RUESCHEMEYER, D. (1992), *Capitalist Development and Democracy*, Cambridge, Polity.

RUGH, William A. (1997), "The United Arab Emirates: What Are the Sources of Its Stability?" in *Middle East Policy*, vol. 5, no. 3, September 1997.

AL-RUMAITHI, Muhammad G. (1975) (in Arabic), *Petroleum and Social Change in the Arabian Gulf*, Cairo, Dar al-Sha'b.

—— (1977) (in Arabic), *The Impediments to Development in the Contemporary Arab Societies of the Gulf*, Kuwait, Matabi' Dar al-Siyasah.

—— (1980), "The Mode of Production in the Arab Gulf Before the Discovery of Oil," in NIBLOCK, Tim (ed.), *Social and Economic Development in the Arab Gulf*, London, Croom Helm.

EL-SABA, Soheir (2002), "The Impediments to Industrial Development in the UAE," Dubai Chamber of Commerce and Industry, Studies and Research Department.

SADIQ, Muhammad, and SNAVELY, William (1972), *Bahrain, Qatar, and the UAE: Colonial Past, Present Problems, and Future Prospects*, Lexington, Mass., Heath.

SALDAMANDO, Martin (2001a), "Big News for a Dogged Freedom," in *Star Magazine*, Onirban, Bangladesh, 11 November 2001.

—— (2001b), "Human Rights in the UAE," in *Star Magazine*, Onirban, Bangladesh, 23 September 2001.

AL-SAYEGH, Fatma (1997) (in Arabic), *The UAE: From Tribe to State*, Dubai, Al-Khaleej Books.

—— (1998), "Merchants' Role in a Changing Society: The Case of Dubai, 1900–1990," in *Middle Eastern Studies*, vol. 34, no. 1, January 1998.

—— (1999), "Symposium on Shaykh Zayed," taken from a conference convened by the Middle East Policy Council on 20 April 1999, in *Middle East Policy*, vol. 6, no. 4, June 1999.

AL-SHAMLAN, Saif Marzuq (1989) (in Arabic), *History of Pearl Diving in Kuwait and the Arabian Gulf*, Kuwait, Zat al-Salasil.

AL-SHAMSI, Fatima S. (1999), "Industrial Strategies and Change in the UAE During the 1980s," in ABDEKARIM, Abbas (ed.), *Change and Development in the Gulf*, London, Macmillan.

—— (1999a), "Symposium on Shaykh Zayed," in *Middle East Policy*, vol. 6, no. 4, June.

SHAMSI, Sa'id Muhammad (1986), "The Buraimi Dispute: A Case Study in Inter-Arab Politics," PhD thesis, Washington, D.C., American University.

SHARABAH, Naji Sadiq (1980) (in Arabic), "The Federal Experiment of the United Arab Emirates, 1971–1977," PhD thesis, University of Cairo.

SHARABI, Hisham B. (1966), *Nationalism and Revolution in the Arab World*, Princeton, Van Nostrand.

—— (1988), *Neopatriarchy: A Theory of Distorted Change in Arab Society*, New York, Oxford University Press.

SHARAF, Muhammad Yasir (1997) (in Arabic), *UAE Society*, Abu Dhabi, Al-Mutanabi Books.

SHARAH, Naji Sadiq (1995) (in Arabic), *The UAE: Politics and Rulership*, UAE, Al-Kitab al-Jamiy.

AL-SHARHAN INTERNATIONAL CONSULTANCY (2000), "UAE Country Report 2000," Dubai.

—— (2001), "UAE Country Report 2001," Dubai.

SHARJAH LAW (2001), Local Instructions no. 1 of 2001 and Executive Council Resolution no. 12 of 2001, supplied by AFRIDI and ANGELL, Dubai.

AL-SHINDAGAH (1998), "By Women for Women," Dubai, 20 January 1998.

SINDELAR, Richard, and PETERSON, J. E. (eds.) (1988), *Crosscurrents in the Gulf*, London, Routledge.

STAUFFER, Thomas (1987), "Income Measurement in the Arab States," in BEBLAWI, Hazem, and LUCIANI, Giacomo (eds.), *The Rentier State*, New York, Croom Helm.

—— (2001), "Global Oil Markets and Their Implications for Revenue Instability in the Gulf," excerpt from a presentation given at the "Globalisation and the Gulf" conference at the University of Exeter, July 2001.

TABATABAI, Adil (1978) (in Arabic), *Comparative Studies in the Emirates*, Cairo.

TAMIMI LAW UPDATE (2001), "Law Update: UAE Committed to Implementing WTO Agreements," Tamimi Consultants, Dubai, January 2001.

TARYAM, Abdullah (1987), *The Establishment of the United Arab Emirates, 1950–1985*, London, Croom Helm.

TESSLER, Mark (ed.) (1999), *Area Studies and Social Science: Strategies for Understanding Middle East Politics*, Bloomington, Indiana University Press.

THEODOULOU, M. (2002), "Biggest Man-Made Isles Rise from the Gulf," in *The Times*, London, 5 January 2002.

THESIGER, Wilfred (1991), *Arabian Sands*, London, Penguin.

AL-TIKRITI, Walid (2003) (in Arabic), *Aflaj*, Department of Antiquities and Tourism, Al-'Ayn.

TODARO, M. (1994), *Economic Development in the Third World*, London, Longman.

TOMKINSON, Michael (1975), *The United Arab Emirates*, London, Jarrold and Sons.

TOYE, J. (1987), *Dilemmas of Development*, Oxford, Blackwell.

TRIDENT GUIDE (1996), "United Arab Emirates," London, Trident.

TRUED, Peter, and GURWIN, Larry (1992), *False Profits*, New York, Houghton Mifflin.

UAE CENTRAL BANK (1991), "Annual Report 1991," Abu Dhabi.

—— (1994), "Annual Report 1994," Abu Dhabi.

—— (1996), "Annual Report 1996," Abu Dhabi.

—— (2002), "UAE and Dubai: Commercial Banks," in DUBAI DEPARTMENT OF ECONOMIC DEVELOPMENT, *Development Statistics*, Government of Dubai.

UAE MINISTRY OF AGRICULTURE AND FISHERIES (2001a), "Dubai: Agricultural Holdings," in DUBAI DEPARTMENT OF ECONOMIC DEVEL-OPMENT, *Development Statistics*, Government of Dubai.

—— (2001b), "Dubai: Cattle Farms—Milk Production," in DUBAI DEPART-MENT OF ECONOMIC DEVELOPMENT, *Development Statistics*, Government of Dubai.

—— (2001c), "Dubai: Fish Production," in DUBAI DEPARTMENT OF ECO-NOMIC DEVELOPMENT, *Development Statistics*, Government of Dubai.

—— (2001d), "Dubai: Fruit Production," in DUBAI DEPARTMENT OF ECO-NOMIC DEVELOPMENT, *Development Statistics*, Government of Dubai.

—— (2001e), "Dubai: Vegetables Production," in DUBAI DEPARTMENT OF ECONOMIC DEVELOPMENT, *Development Statistics*, Government of Dubai.

UAE MINISTRY OF EDUCATION AND YOUTH (2001a), "Dubai: Government Schools—Student/Teacher Ratio," in DUBAI DEPARTMENT OF ECONOM-IC DEVELOPMENT, *Development Statistics*, Government of Dubai.

—— (2001b), "Dubai: Private Schools—Enrollment by Sex," in DUBAI

DEPARTMENT OF ECONOMIC DEVELOPMENT, *Development Statistics*, Government of Dubai.

—— (2001c), "Dubai: Private Schools—Teachers by Sex," in DUBAI DEPARTMENT OF ECONOMIC DEVELOPMENT, *Development Statistics*, Government of Dubai.

—— (2001d), "UAE and Dubai: Secondary School Graduates," in DUBAI DEPARTMENT OF ECONOMIC DEVELOPMENT, *Development Statistics*, Government of Dubai.

UAE MINISTRY OF FINANCE AND INDUSTRY (2001), various statistics, Abu Dhabi.

UAE MINISTRY OF HEALTH and DUBAI DEPARTMENT OF MEDICAL SERVICES (2001a), "Dubai: Health Centres," in DUBAI DEPARTMENT OF ECONOMIC DEVELOPMENT, *Development Statistics*, Government of Dubai.

—— (2001b), "Dubai: Health Development Indicators," in DUBAI DEPARTMENT OF ECONOMIC DEVELOPMENT, *Development Statistics*, Government of Dubai.

—— (2001c), "Dubai: Hospital Beds," in DUBAI DEPARTMENT OF ECONOMIC DEVELOPMENT, *Development Statistics*, Government of Dubai.

—— (2001d), "Dubai: Hospitals," in DUBAI DEPARTMENT OF ECONOMIC DEVELOPMENT, *Development Statistics*, Government of Dubai.

—— (2001e), "Dubai: Medical Doctors," in DUBAI DEPARTMENT OF ECONOMIC DEVELOPMENT, *Development Statistics*, Government of Dubai.

—— (2001f), "Dubai: Medical Technical Assistants," in DUBAI DEPARTMENT OF ECONOMIC DEVELOPMENT, *Development Statistics*, Government of Dubai.

—— (2001g), "Dubai: Nursing Staff," in DUBAI DEPARTMENT OF ECONOMIC DEVELOPMENT, *Development Statistics*, Government of Dubai.

UAE MINISTRY OF INFORMATION AND CULTURE (1973a), Federal Law no. 6, Abu Dhabi.

—— (1973b), Federal Law no. 10, Abu Dhabi.

—— (1983), Federal Law no. 3, Abu Dhabi.

—— (1984, 1988), Article 3 of Updated Federal Law no. 8 of 1984 as amended by Federal Law no. 13 of 1988 regarding commercial companies, Abu Dhabi.

—— (1988), Federal Law no. 15, Abu Dhabi.

—— (1995), "UAE Yearbook: 1995," Abu Dhabi.

—— (2002), various statistics, Abu Dhabi.

UAE MINISTRY OF PLANNING (1995), "Annual Statistical Report on UAE Hotels," Abu Dhabi, Central Statistics Department.

—— (2001), "UAE and Dubai: GDP at Factor Cost and per Capita GDP, 2000," in DUBAI DEPARTMENT OF ECONOMIC DEVELOPMENT, *Development Statistics*, Government of Dubai.

—— (2002a), "Dubai: GDP—Real Growth Rates," in DUBAI DEPARTMENT OF ECONOMIC DEVELOPMENT, *Development Statistics*, Government of Dubai.

—— (2002b), "Dubai: GDP at Factor Cost," in DUBAI DEPARTMENT OF ECONOMIC DEVELOPMENT, *Development Statistics*, Government of Dubai.

—— (2002c), "UAE and Dubai: Employment by Economic Sectors," in DUBAI DEPARTMENT OF ECONOMIC DEVELOPMENT, *Development Statistics*, Government of Dubai.

—— (2002d), "UAE and Dubai: GDP at Factor Cost and per Capita GDP, 2001," in DUBAI DEPARTMENT OF ECONOMIC DEVELOPMENT, *Development Statistics*, Government of Dubai.

–––––– (2002e), "UAE and Dubai: Population," in DUBAI DEPARTMENT OF ECONOMIC DEVELOPMENT, *Development Statistics*, Government of Dubai.

UAE UNIVERSITY IN AL-'AYN (2001a), "UAE University Graduates," in DUBAI DEPARTMENT OF ECONOMIC DEVELOPMENT, *Development Statistics*, Government of Dubai.

–––––– (2001b), "UAE University Registered Students," in DUBAI DEPARTMENT OF ECONOMIC DEVELOPMENT, *Development Statistics*, Government of Dubai.

UNDP-POGAR (2002), "Programme on Governance in the Arab Region: UAE," various reports.

UNDP-UAE (2000a), "The Launch of Ra's al-Khaimah Vision," press release, Abu Dhabi, 28 March 2000.

–––––– (2000b), "National HRD Report," press release, Abu Dhabi, 8 July 2000.

–––––– (2000c), various reports, Abu Dhabi, 27 May 2000.

UNESCO (1998, 1999, 2000, 2001), primary, secondary, and tertiary enrollment ratios.

–––––– (2001), literacy rates.

UNITED NATIONS STATISTICS DIVISION (2002), various UAE-related statistics.

UNPAN (2002), various UAE-related statistics, http://unpan1.un.org/intradoc/groups/public/documents/un/unpan000199.pdf.

U.S. CENSUS BUREAU (2002), various UAE-related statistics, International Programs Center, international database.

U.S. CENTRAL INTELLIGENCE AGENCY (2001a), *Chiefs of Staff and Cabinet Members of Foreign Governments*, 1 August 2001.

–––––– (2001b), *World Fact Book: Morocco*, January 2001.

–––––– (2001c), *World Fact Book: United Arab Emirates*, January 2001.

U.S. DEPARTMENT OF STATE (1975), "U.S. Policy in the Area of the Persian Gulf," Bulletin no. 73, 14 July 1975.

–––––– (2001), "United Arab Emirates: Country Reports on Human Rights," Bureau of Democracy, Human Rights, and Labor, 23 February 2001.

U.S. EMBASSY TO SAUDI ARABIA (1999), "Economic Trends," Riyadh, October 1999.

U.S. ENERGY INFORMATION ADMINISTRATION (1997), "Energy and Petroleum Exports: Thousands of Barrels per Year."

U.S. LIBRARY OF CONGRESS (2001), "Country Study: Jordan."

VAN DER MEULEN, Hendrik (1997), "The Role of Tribal and Kinship Ties in the Politics of the United Arab Emirates," PhD thesis, Fletcher School of Law and Diplomacy.

WALLERSTEIN, Immanuel (1979), "The Rise and Future Demise of the World Capitalist System: Concepts for Comparative Analysis," in WALLERSTEIN, I. (ed.), *The Capitalist World Economy*, Cambridge, Cambridge University Press.

WAM (1977), Abu Dhabi, 16 November 1977.

–––––– (2001a), "New Avenues for UAE Women," Abu Dhabi, 17 May 2001.

–––––– (2001b), "UAE Paper Calls for an International Coalition Against Israeli Terror," Abu Dhabi, 21 October 2001.

–––––– (2002), "UAE to Rebuild Demolished Palestinian Houses," Abu Dhabi, 15 January 2002.

—— (2003), "Elected Councils for Dubai," Abu Dhabi, 2 April 2003.

—— (2004), "Sultan Grants 100 Million Dirhams for Nationals in Emirate," Abu Dhabi, 14 February 2004.

AL-WASAT (1994) (in Arabic), Riyadh, no. 147, 21 November 1994.

—— (1997) (in Arabic), "UAE: Youthful Trend in UAE Parliament," Riyadh, 22 January 1997.

WEIGLE, M. A., and BUTTERFIELD, Jim (1992), "Civil Society in Reforming Communist Regimes: The Logic of Emergence," in *Comparative Politics*, vol. 25, no. 1, October 1992.

WEITZMAN, Bruce Maddy (2000), "Why Did Arab Monarchies Fall? An Analysis of Old and New Explanations," in KOSTINER, Joseph (ed.), *Middle East Monarchies: The Challenge of Modernity*, Boulder, Lynne Rienner.

WORLD BANK (1985), "Research News 1985."

WORLD HEALTH ORGANIZATION (2002), various UAE-related statistics.

WORLD TRADE ORGANIZATION NEWS (2002), "Press Releases, Press/293," 3 May 2002.

WRIGGINS, Howard (ed.) (1992), *The Dynamics of Regional Politics: Four Systems on the Indian Ocean Rim*, New York, Columbia University Press.

YAMANI, Mai (2001), "Challenged by Example: Globalisation and the New Arab Awakening," excerpt from a presentation given at the "Globalisation and the Gulf" conference at the University of Exeter, July 2001.

YAPP, Malcolm (1980), "British Policy in the Persian Gulf," in COTRELL, Alvin (ed.), *The Persian Gulf States*, Baltimore, John Hopkins University Press.

—— (1996), *The Near East Since the First World War: A History to 1995*, London, Longman.

YORKE, Valerie (1980), *The Gulf in the 1980s*, London, Royal Institute of International Affairs.

ZABARAH, Muhammad 'Ahmad (1982), *Yemen: Traditionalism Versus Modernity*, New York, Praeger.

ZAHLAN, Rosemarie Said (1978), *The Origins of the United Arab Emirates*, New York, St. Martin's.

—— (1989), *The Making of the Modern Gulf States*, London, Unwin Hyman.

ZA'ZA, Bassman (2004), "New Law Gives Edge to Fight Against Money Laundering," in *Gulf News*, Dubai, 18 February 2004.

ZEITUN, Doa (2002a), "Direct Quote: Safeguarding Purity of Arabic," in *Gulf News*, Dubai, 22 December 2002.

—— (2002b), "Theatre Artists to Gather in Sharjah," in *Gulf News*, Dubai, 13 October 2002.

# Index

# About the Book

The United Arab Emirates has remained a mainstay of stability in an increasingly volatile Middle East, managing to maintain a traditional polity despite the impact of rapid modernization and globalization. This in-depth study explores the many contradictions that characterize the UAE and its position within the international system.

Davidson first provides a detailed historical background, tracing the recent history of the lower Gulf region, the British involvement in the area, and the establishment of the federation of emirates. He then turns his attention to the UAE's seemingly anachronistic political structure and its socio-economic development. His astute analysis highlights the UAE's achievements—as well as the problems that have persistently undermined its development objectives.

**Christopher M. Davidson** is assistant professor of political science and area studies at Shaikh Zayed University, Abu Dhabi.